LANGUAGE TYPOLOGY

NORTH-HOLLAND LINGUISTIC SERIES

46

Edited by S. C. DIK, J. G. KOOIJ *and* S. A. THOMPSON

LANGUAGE TYPOLOGY

Cross-linguistic Studies in Syntax

GRAHAM MALLINSON
BARRY J. BLAKE

Linguistics Department
Monash University
Clayton, Victoria 3168
Australia

1931 N·H 1981
P∿C

NORTH-HOLLAND PUBLISHING COMPANY
AMSTERDAM • NEW YORK • OXFORD

©North-Holland Publishing Company, 1981

ISBN: 0 444 86311 7

Published by:

NORTH-HOLLAND PUBLISHING COMPANY
AMSTERDAM • NEW YORK • OXFORD

Sole distributors for the U.S.A. and Canada:

ELSEVIER NORTH-HOLLAND, INC.
52, VANDERBILT AVENUE
NEW YORK, N.Y. 10017

Library of Congress Cataloging in Publication Data

Mallinson, Graham, 1947-
   Language typology.

   (North-Holland linguistic series ; 46)
   Bibliography: p.
   Includes indexes.
   1. Typology (Linguistics) 2. Grammar, Comparative
and general--Syntax. I. Blake, Barry J. II. Title.
III. Series.
P204.M3   415   81-16810
ISBN 0-444-86311-7 (Elsevier North-Holland)
               AACR2

Printed in The Netherlands

PREFACE

A few years ago the authors, independently of
each other, began to feel that students in linguistics
were concentrating on English to the exclusion of
other languages.   We felt there was a need to broaden
our students' perspectives and to introduce them to
the variety of morpho-syntactic devices to be found in
language in general.   For this reason in 1978 we
established a course for third year undergraduates in
which we survey morpho-syntactic variation across a
range of languages.   Our aim has been to make the
range of languages as wide as possible, going beyond
the languages of western Europe.   Many linguists
unfortunately still seem content to confine their
studies to these more familiar languages.   That is
like trying to base a science of botany on a study of
succulents.

For the purposes of administration the course
was given the title "Language Typology and Universals".
In practice, however, the course has evolved into a
course in typology, since universals, or at least
strict universals, usually prove to be fragile and
short-lived.   The course is divided into two parts,
with Blake taking the simple sentence and concentrating on case-marking and Greenberg's universals of
word order; Mallinson taking compound and complex
sentences and dealing with the ways in which languages construct their co-ordinate and subordinate
structures, including a review of the ways in which
repeated material is avoided.   In both parts of the
course we have endeavoured not only to illustrate the
variation to be found in morpho-syntactic phenomena
but also to stress the nonrandomness of the distribution of data and to attempt to account for it.   It
was also intended that the course should serve as
some sort of a model for the way in which a typological study of a particular area of language could be

carried out, as well as demonstrating some of the
pitfalls that beset anyone attempting to control data
from a large number of languages.   On finding that
no single book covered the range of material we were
interested in, we set about compiling this volume.
It represents a text for senior students and takes it
for granted that our readers will be familiar with
general linguistic terminology in phonology and
morpho-syntax, both synchronic and diachronic.   We
have, however, explained our use of terms such as
subject, *topic* and *clitic pronoun* as well as terms
that are not always encountered in elementary courses
- such as *ergative*, *accusative language* and *cross-
referencing*.

    The book represents not only a text for senior
students but also an integrated set of five research
papers plus an introduction.   Each of the main
chapters is aimed at a fairly exhaustive treatment of
the relevant data and a review of the relevant literature, but also throws some new light on the topics
selected for discussion and therefore can be read as
an original contribution to the field.   We hope,
therefore, that the book as a whole will be of interest to established linguists as well as to students
and relative beginners in language typology.

    Although we have worked closely together on the
production of this volume, each of us has his own
area of specialization.   Chapters one, four and five
are essentially the work of Mallinson, and chapters
two, three and six that of Blake.   We have, however,
provided material for each other and have worked
together more closely on the introductory and concluding chapters, in which we set the scene for the four
main chapters and draw together some of the threads
that appear throughout the book.

    A book of this kind would simply not have been
possible without the help of a large number of
people.   We are particularly grateful to the following people for reading and commenting on drafts of
chapters at various stages: Keith Allan, Gwen Awbery,
Des Derbyshire, Bob Dixon, Gerald Gazdar, Dick Hudson,
Geoff Pullum, Bob Robins, Graham Scott, Ian Smith,
Neil Smith, Tasaku Tsunoda and Anna Wierzbicka.   We
would also like to thank the following for helpful
comments, copies of papers and/or data on particular
problems: David and Maya Bradley, Peter Bruell,
Peter Carroll, Bernard Comrie, Claes Christian Elert,
Stephen Paterson, Peter Paul, Bruce Rigsby, Anna

Siewierska, Stan Starosta, Claude Tchekhoff, Alan
Thomas and Lynn Wales.   The following also acted as
native informants: Gwen Awbery (Welsh), Peter Bruell
(Polish), Chang Chintin (Mandarin), Henry and Sofia
Donenfeld (Romanian), Abul Hasnath (Hindi), Maria
Aurora Keon (Tagalog), Wies Lalamentik (Indonesian),
Thao Lê (Vietnamese), Sumie Miyake (Japanese),
Suwilai Premsrirat (Thai) and Thel Thong (Cambodian).
Finally we would like to express our gratitude for
the secretarial help we received: Daniela Antas,
Joan Juliff and, in particular, Ursula Kutschbach,
who typed most of the camera ready copy.

Clayton, July 1981   Graham Mallinson
                              Barry J. Blake

CONTENTS

LIST OF ABBREVIATIONS AND SYMBOLS

A	agent animate adjective	emph	emphasis/ emphatic marker
abl	ablative	erg	ergative
ABS	absolutive	ERG	ergative
abs	absolutive		
acc	accusative	f	feminine
act	active	fem	feminine
adj	adjective	fr	free
adn	adnominal marker	fut	future
		FWO	free word order
ag	agent		
agr	agreement		
agt	agent	G	genitive
antipass	antipassive	gen	genitive
a/p	antipassive	GEN	genitive
art	article		
aux	auxiliary (verb)	H	human
		HC	hierarchy constraint
ben	beneficiary	hsy	hearsay
C	consonant	I	inanimate
Cl	clause	imp	imperfect
coll	collective	incl	inclusive
comp	complementizer	indic	indicative
compl	completive	inf	infinitive
contin	continualis aspect	instr	instrument (al)
		interr	interrogative
dat	dative	inv	inverse
DEM	demonstrative	IO	indirect object
det	determiner		
DO	direct object		
		lig	ligative/ ligature

loc	locative	RG	relational grammar
m	masculine		
masc	masculine	S	sentence/ clause
mkr	marker		
mod	modifier	S	subject
monop	monopersonal	s	singular
M/W	morpheme/word (ratio)	sg	singular
		S_i	intransitive subject
N	noun		
neut	neuter	sing	singular
nom	nominative	S_m	matrix clause
nomzn	nominalization		
NP	noun phrase	sm	subject marker
		spec	specifier
O	object	stat	stative
obj	object	std	standard
OBL	oblique	SU	subject
O Comp	object of comparison	subj	subjunctive
		sup	superessive
P	preposition	T	topic
p	plural	TG	transforma-tional grammar
part	participle		
pass	passive		
pat	patient	top	topic
perf	perfect	trans	transitive (verb marker)
pl	plural		
polyp	polypersonal		
poss	possessive	TVP	transitive verb phrase
post	postposition		
PP	prepositional phrase		
pp	past participle	UG	universal grammar
pr	pronoun		
pred	predicate		
prep	preposition	V	verb vowel
pres	present		
pro	pronoun	V_i	intransitive verb
Q	quote/quotation qualifier	VP	verb phrase
		V1	verb first
		V2	verb second
RC	relative clause		
ref	referential		
refl	reflexive	1/1st	first person
rel	relative clause	2	second person
REL	relative marker		

3/3rd	third person	<	is acted upon
3'	third person obviative		comes from
1/2,3/4...	noun class	?	of doubtful grammaticality
I/II/III	noun class		
∅	zero (form)	*	ungrammatical unattested
⊃	implies	#	intonation boundary
>	acts on	∨	or
	takes precedence over		
	becomes		

CHAPTER 1

INTRODUCTION

1.0   General Aims

Linguistics in the 1960s, particularly in the United States, was dominated by the transformational-generative approach to language.   Transformationalists were primarily concerned with syntax and semantics and such an orientation demands a native or native-like command of the language under study. Since the theory emerged in the United States, most of the work carried out in the transformational model dealt exclusively with English.

The 1970s saw the emergence of more cross-language study both within theoretical linguistics and within the field of empirically-based theory-neutral approaches to language.   On the one hand we find Perlmutter and Postal developing the theory of Relational Grammar on the basis of data drawn from a large number of languages (see, for example, Perlmutter & Postal 1977 and Johnson & Postal 1980), and Dik testing his Functional Grammar against a wide variety of languages (Dik 1978).   On the other hand we have linguists like Comrie and those represented in the series of volumes edited by Charles Li (1975, 1976, 1977), whose commitment to a particular model is minimal but whose prime concern is to make significant generalizations about language on the basis of large-scale comparative studies.   Now that studies of cross-linguistic variation have gained an important place in linguistics it is likely that such a trend will continue into the 1980s and beyond, and hopefully this shift in emphasis will find its way into introductory textbooks so that beginning students will be introduced to linguistics through a comparative study of a sample of the world's languages.

Such a trend should lead to a welcome decline in

(particularly Anglo-Saxon) ethnocentricity, but at
the same time it may present problems.   The dangers
and pitfalls in examining any single language object-
ively are increased when the language is not one's
own, and so the study of a number of languages may be
even more perilous.   It is, therefore, our intention
to introduce students to some of the problems that
might be met in the study of cross-linguistic variation and generalization, and to present four case-
studies from the area of morpho-syntax to demonstrate
how such work might be carried out.

        In this respect, this and the following chapters
have a strong pedagogical aim, although the layout is
not that of a textbook.   We do not, for example,
provide exercises or directly ask the reader to consider particular contentious points, but we do aim to
present a rather full account of the type of variation to be found in language in the four syntactic
areas selected, as well as providing references to
published material that the reader can pursue if so
inclined.   At the same time, it is intended that each
of the four main chapters will include an original
contribution to the field of language typology, and so
have at least some appeal to researchers as well as to
students.

        The four areas we cover in chapters two to five
are:
   (a)   the marking of agent and patient

   (b)   word order

   (c)   co-ordination: conjunction reduction

   (d)   subordination: relative clauses

(a) and (b) are essentially concerned with the simple
sentence while (c) and (d) are concerned with compound and complex sentences respectively.   However,
all four topics are related.   The marking of agent
and patient and choice of word order are, to some
extent, alternative devices for distinguishing the
agent from the patient, and our discussion of co-ordination and subordination shows that the strategies
used to build up non-simple sentences are also partly
dependent on case marking and word order.   Essentially our aim is to point out the non-randomness of
morpho-syntax, both with respect to specific parameters (e.g. word order) and between different parameters
(e.g. word order and co-ordination), and also to try
to explain the distribution of the data in terms of
extra-systemic factors such as functional value,

short-term memory limitations, egocentricity, and so on.

The remainder of this chapter will be concerned with identifying some of the problems faced in cross-linguistic study, and also with justifying the pre-occupation with syntax that has arisen among typologists in recent years, a preoccupation that we also share.

1.1   The Aims and Uses of Typology

1.1.1.   Defining Typology

Typology is the classification of a domain.   In our understanding of the term it is synonymous with taxonomy.   Languages can be classified in terms of any of their structural characteristics, but the most successful typologies have been those that have attempted to establish broad classifications on the basis of a number of interrelated features.   Greenberg's famous study, 'Some universals of grammar with particular reference to the order of meaningful elements' (Greenberg 1963), has demonstrated that languages can be classified according to the basic order of *subject*, *object* and *verb* (S, O and V).   This is a particularly successful typology since a number of other features can be predicted from the order of these three elements.[1]

In theory one can attempt to find implicational universals of the form: p implies q.   In practice it is difficult to find many implicational universals that survive testing over a wide range of languages. It is possible, however, to find a number of high correlations between features, so that one can say: p *usually* implies q.   Classifying languages in terms of the order of subject, object and verb is useful precisely because the order of these elements tends to imply some dozen other features.   For example, the order VSO implies, according to Greenberg's data, that the language has prepositions, adjectives following nouns, relative clauses following nouns, and so on. Thus one can speak of the VSO *type*.   The type label is revealing in that it summarizes a range of characteristics.

To return to the term taxonomy, which we equated with typology, transformationalists have been consistently disparaging in their references to this linguistic approach, the implication being that taxonomy is non-explanatory and that the transformational-

generative approach can provide explanations. It is
true that taxonomy is non-explanatory, but we reject
the view that the transformational-generative approach,
or indeed any other model, can provide explanations.
It is scarcely possible to provide strong, watertight
explanations in linguistics, and as for explanations
in the everyday sense of the word (see section 6.5),
the most satisfying of these, in our opinion, have
come from those who have worked outside transformational and other theories.

Lehmann (1978a:4-5) claims that typology is more
revealing than taxonomy provided it is 'based on the
analysis of patterns and principles which have been
identified as central in language, such as the structure of the simple sentence and its constituents'.
He compares the ideal linguistic typology with the
taxonomy of plants produced by Linnaeus which he
claims is 'based on characteristic physical features
such as stamens' and implies that the botanical classification based on 'external characteristics' is
inferior. We feel that this comparison is unfair to
Linnaeus, whose classification and its later developments are based on characteristics that imply or tend
to imply others. If one knows that a specimen is of
the Mimosa family, one knows that it is a tree or
shrub with bipinnate leaves or leaves reduced to
phyllodes (with juvenile leaves bipinnate), small
yellow or white flowers, numerous stamens, four or
five sepals and petals, and so on.

The family label in botany could be compared to
the type label in linguistics, a label such as VSO
being roughly analogous to *Mimosaceae*. Unfortunately
it is more difficult in linguistics to provide a
system of hierarchical type labels than it is in
botany. There are reasons for this, as we shall see
in section 6.6.

Unlike Lehmann we do not distinguish between
typology and taxonomy, only between good typology/
taxonomy and not so good typology/taxonomy. Botanical
taxonomy provides a good model and we would be satisfied to see a linguistic typology that was as revealing.

While the typological study of language is basically concerned with categorizing languages according to their structure, it is by no means the only
type of classification that can be carried out.
Smith 1969, for example, distinguishes three bases
for language classification - genetic, typological and

areal.   But he claims that these are not comparable
approaches because:

> '... genetic classification is in reality no
> more than an hypothesis of historical rela-
> tionship, based on the evidence of the other
> two modes of classification, which alone can
> really claim to be rigorous.' (Smith 1969:486).

While we agree with Smith that typological classification of a language is 'according to the structural characteristics of the language', we feel justified in claiming that only typological classification
is basic.   Areal as well as genetic classification
might well be thought of as merely an application of
the results of typological analysis to attempt to
account for *why* certain features are shared by two or
more languages.   Thus, just as a genetic classification claims that historical relationship is responsible for shared characteristics, an areal classification accounts for common features by positing diffusion through language and other cultural contact.

However, as can be clearly demonstrated from the
field of Indo-European comparative linguistics, the
sort of characteristic used to distinguish languages
typologically is not necessarily the most suitable
for establishing genetic relationships.   The modern
Romance languages can be linked genetically to Latin,
and they still retain the widespread lexical correspondences on the basis of which such affiliation has
been claimed.   Nevertheless, they have all developed
typologically from a basic SOV order in Latin to the
present SVO order, and so would be considered typologically distinct within the Greenberg system.

Thus, although only some typological features will
be of use in the postulation of genetic relatedness
and cultural contact between languages, typology *per
se* involves the classification of languages in terms
of a much wider range of features, and often in terms
of features which cut across genetic and areal classifications.   Typologically, languages can be
analysed at all levels.   At the morphological level,
for example, they have commonly been categorized as
largely isolating, inflecting or agglutinating, while
at the phonological level they might be classified
according to the range of vowels they make use of, or
the shapes of the systems that the vowels form.
However, it is at the syntactic level that typology
has borne the most fruit, as we hope to demonstrate.

Whichever features are investigated they can be
investigated quite independently of any application
they might have to other forms of language classification, but a mere cataloguing of sameness and difference between languages is a rather sterile occupation
unless there is some useful application of the material collected. Apart from providing material for
areal and genetic studies, typological analysis also
produces data on the basis of which cross-language
generalizations can be made about the nature of language itself, the ultimate aim being either to list
those features or characteristics which languages
share, or to define the limits within which languages
can vary. Thus, although there will be a brief
mention later in this chapter of the application of
typological data to genetic and areal classification,
the main aim of this volume is to examine some aspects
of language structure for the light they may throw on
the nature of human language in general. This we
take to be the overriding aim of language typology.

1.1.2.   Typology and Universals

The search for cross-linguistic generalizations,
or in their extreme form *language universals*, is
widely recognized today as being the main rationale
behind large-scale typological research. By definition, the search for universals also requires typological studies to be carried out across as wide a
range of languages as possible. There had been particularly strong interest in Europe during the eight-
eenth century in universal features, especially among
philosophers.   As Robins points out, Rationalist
grammarians of the period attempted:

'... to reveal the unity of grammar underlying the separate grammars of different
languages in their role of communicating
thought, itself comprising perception,
judgement and reasoning.' (Robins 1967:123).

Unfortunately, this approach suffered from a restriction in the range of languages considered, as well as
a rather subjective belief in the inherent worth of
classical languages, that seemed to blinker a more
realistic approach to cross-language study.

During the nineteenth century there was great
interest in language typology but oddly enough this
does not appear to have been coupled with an interest
in universals, and it is only in the second half of

the twentieth century that there has been any serious
attempt to carry out typological and universals
research in tandem.   Even today, of course, it may
seem to the uninitiated something of a contradiction
in terms to handle these apparently quite distinct
areas of investigation together.   Since typology is
ostensibly concerned with classifying languages according to their differences, and universals with
determining which features are common to all languages, such a reaction would not seem unreasonable.
However, it is now clear that one important relationship between them is that of using the results of typological research to provide material for establishing language universals.   Even so, it is important
to realize that we are not simply making the obvious
and unoriginal claim that only by carrying out typological investigation on a wide scale can we thereby
eliminate those features which are not found in every
language and thus be left with the highest common
factor, which will be, by definition, the universal
features of human language.   Much of the recent work
on universals has, on the contrary, endeavoured to
justify the claim that the apparent brute distinctions between languages are very often precisely the
material from which universal statements can be made.

Such is the theme of a number of the universals
claimed in Greenberg 1963 ed., the proceedings of a
conference on language universals held at Dobbs Ferry,
New York in 1961.   Greenberg's universals are generally of the implicational variety:

If Language X has Feature A, then it will
also have (or conversely not have)
Feature B.

An example is his Universal No. 13:

If the nominal object always precedes the
verb, then verb forms subordinate to the
main verb also precede it.

The negative form of a universal - that languages of
a certain type cannot have a particular feature - is
illustrated by the second part of Universal No. 10:

Question particles or affixes, when specified in position by reference to a particular word in the sentence, almost always
follow that word. *Such particles do not
occur in languages with dominant order VSO.*

One characteristic of Greenberg's principles is

that they are sometimes qualified by terms such as:
'almost always', or 'with overwhelmingly more than
chance frequency'.   In other words, a feature may be
termed universal even though it is found in a very
large number of languages but by no means all languages.   For this reason it may be more realistic to
abandon the term *universal* and to retain instead a
term we used earlier: *cross-linguistic generalization*,
which in no way commits us to the concept of a watertight universal in the strictest sense of the word.

There are at least two good reasons why we should
adopt this more pragmatic approach.   First, since it
is clear that we have as yet no complete access to
full descriptions of all the world's extant languages
and never will have access to those which have died
without record, then universals of the type 'this
feature is found in all languages' are quite untestable;   furthermore, they can be all too readily dam-
aged by the facts of newly-discovered languages, and
an example of this is the discovery of a number of
languages which are object-initial and therefore of a
type, in terms of constituent-order in sentences,
earlier claimed to be unlikely to occur in language.
In any case, even a very widespread but not completely
universal feature of language has to be accounted for
in some way.   That a feature is so widespread may
well be the result of chance, but this is unlikely to
be the case with the large number of not-quite-water-
tight generalizations that have been put forward, and
these will require some explanation in the same way
that a strict universal does.

In fact, one could claim that the 'statistical
universals' or strong tendencies are more interesting
than the strict universals, since the best candidates
for universality tend to be obvious and uninteresting,
e.g. all languages have vowels and consonants.   Thus,
the second reason why we should be more pragmatic in
our search for generalizations in language is that,
given how few in number the strict universals are,
even among the languages available for investigation,
they may be of extremely limited interest to linguists.

Bolinger 1968 provides a short list of true
syntactic universals and these include the following:

(1)   All languages use nominal phrases and verbal
      phrases, corresponding to the two major classes
      of noun and verb, and in all of them the number
      of nouns far exceeds the number of verbs.   One

can be fairly sure that a noun in one language
translates a noun in another.

(2)   All languages have ways of turning sentences into
      interrogatives, negatives, and commands.

(3)   All languages show at least two forms of inter-
      action between verbal and nominal, typically
      'intransitive' (the verbal is involved with only
      one nominal, as in *Boys play*) and 'transitive'
      (the verbal is involved with two nominals, as in
      Boys like girls).[2]

Of these, the second would appear to be true, if one
interprets it to mean that all languages can express
questions, negation and commands.   The first is only
partially true.   Not all languages have nominal
equivalents for the English nouns *laughter*, *sorrow* and
joy.   Moreover, even obvious verbs such as *to jump*,
to spill, *to chase*, etc. do not have verbal equivalents in all languages if *verb* is defined formally;   if
verb is not defined formally the assertion is almost
vacuous.   The point here is that in some languages
only a small number of words have the grammatical properties that one could use to define verbs (e.g. hos-
ting marking for tense, aspect, mood, voice, etc.) and
most verbal concepts are expressed by words that are
nominal.   The third 'universal' is also dubious.
Claude Tchekhoff has pointed out to us that the Caucasian language, Avar, very nearly lacks the transi-
tive/intransitive distinction.   Almost all verbs in
the Avar lexicon require the expression of only one
participant but allow the optional addition of a second (see examples (2.28) and (2.29) in chapter two).
About ten verbs are restricted to a sole participant.
Even if one calls the majority class *transitive*
(though they do not require the expression of two participants) and the minority class *intransitive*, it is
obvious that the distinction between the two is only
rather tenuously maintained.   In the light of this it
is therefore not impossible that there is a language
in which all verbs require the expression of only one
participant.   Thus, it appears that even though universals in the strictest sense of the word may exist,
some of the most likely candidates for strict universality can turn out to be disappointing.

     Essentially, the aim of typological research is
to establish those features which are very widespread,
whether or not they are completely universal, and which

illuminate the nature of human language, and the
limits within which languages can vary as arbitrary
but conventionalized coding systems for human communication.   Some features may be shaped by perceptual
constraints and thus have something to say about the
cognitive capacities of humans.   Such constraints
would, for example, point to limitations on short term
memory (see chapters 3, 5 and 6 for further discussion), and account for the outlawing of complex sentence structures involving multiple self-embedding.
In (1.1), there are three relative clauses, each embedded into the preceding clause, and such examples
present no problems at all for processing.   But in
(1.2), again with three relative clauses, the first
relative clause has within it a second relative clause
and the second yet another relative clause.   That is,
only the third, most deeply-embedded relative clause
is presented as a continuous sequence, and the result
is clearly a problem for the hearer/reader, and also
for the person producing the example.

(1.1)   The child hit the man who chased the girl who
         stole the oranges

(1.2)   ?The girl that the man that the child hit
         chased stole the oranges

The claim that even partial universals are of
value is, however, open to some abuse.   Chomsky, in
his early and his later work, has demonstrated an interest in universals, as shown by the following
quotations:

        '... the main task of linguistic theory must
        be to develop an account of linguistic
        universals.'   (Chomsky 1965:27-8)

and:

        'To a large extent, the rules of the base
        may be universal, and thus not, strictly-
        speaking, part of particular grammars.'
                    (ibid.:141).

But Chomsky seems to be suggesting not that all languages make use of the same set of categories or rules,
merely that they *select* from a universal set:

        '... the category symbols appearing in base
        rules are selected from a fixed universal
        alphabet.'   (ibid.:141-2).

For example, not all languages have prepositions and
thus such a category will only be a part of the base
rules of those languages that do have them.   This
claim that languages merely select from a universal
inventory is, however, relatively trivial unless one
is prepared to predict in advance what the membership
of that inventory will be, or what the limits are on
its membership.   A much stricter notion of what the
universal set of categories might be is put forward by
Bach 1968 (a paper presented at a conference on language universals held in Austin, Texas in 1967).   As
he says:

> 'One frequent statement is that each lan-
> guage makes some undetermined selection
> from a stock of universal elements.   This
> is a completely empty claim, of course,
> without an exhaustive specification of what
> these elements are.   Otherwise, we can
> simply list all elements that have occurred
> in the descriptions of particular languages
> and say that this is a partial set of such
> universal elements awaiting completion as we
> describe more languages.   Obviously, there
> is no way to refute the statement that the
> universal set of elements comprises simply
> those which have been postulated for indi-
> vidual languages and which might be postu-
> lated in the future.'   (Bach 1968:113).

However, in a later paper, Chomsky also adopts what
appears to be a much tighter notion of what is meant
by a universal:

> 'By a "true universal" we mean a principle
> that holds as a matter of biological neces-
> sity and therefore belongs to UG [= Universal
> Grammar] as contrasted with a principle that
> holds generally as a matter of historical
> accident in attested languages.   The dis-
> tinction may be difficult to establish, but
> it is fundamental.' (Chomsky & Lasnik 1977:437
>   fn. 24).

This aim is also reflected in Pullum 1980, in which
the author claims that the goal of a syntactic theory:

> '... is to develop universal principles
> that preclude variation from language to
> language concerning the way in which gram-
> mar works, and to develop them in a way

that simultaneously explains what does
occur while excluding what does not.'
                    (Pullum 1980:9).

   While Chomsky and Bach are working within a
transformational framework, Pullum's approach to grammar is Relational.   Consequently, although the aims
they have might be shared, the results of their investigations might differ dramatically.   This is because
the assumptions made about language will differ from
model to model - for example Relational Grammar takes
the notion of subject to be a primitive of the theory
whereas the transformational approach of Chomsky regards the subject function as only a secondary feature
(for further discussion see section 3 of this chapter).
Inevitably the universals arrived at will be highly
dependent on the features assumed to occur in language,
and thus there will be variation in the type of generalization that can be culled from the data available
for interpretation.

   Of course, there are also limits on the amount of
data available for investigation and perhaps the most
important reason why we should, as we suggested above,
adopt a rather pragmatic approach to the formulation
of cross-linguistic generalizations is because of the
many problems associated with the collection and interpretation of data.

1.1.3.   Problems with Data

   Any linguist carrying out cross-linguistic investigation of any sort is clearly dependent on the avail-
ability and reliability of data.   His data is potentially available from three sources:

   (a)   primary sources, typically grammars

   (b)   secondary sources

   (c)   informants

All of these avenues of information can be unreliable.

(a)   *Grammars*

   If a grammar consists of only one volume, we can
presumably find it guilty of at least some sins of
omission before we open it.   A speaker of English
can readily appreciate that a description of English
with any pretensions at all to completeness would fill
twenty volumes without any attempt at a lexicon

(witness for example the size of the incomplete
English grammars of Jespersen (7 volumes), Poutsma
(5 volumes) and Curme (3 volumes)).   It would, then,
be rather ethnocentric to assume that other languages
could be condensed into a single volume.   Even given
that most grammars are simply outlines, it is common
to find that they pay unequal attention to various
aspects of grammar.   In particular, some have little
or no phonology and others have no syntax.   Most
grammars leave unanswered fundamental questions even
in the areas they purport to cover.   For example, one
grammar states that negatives come first in the clause
and, at another point, that interrogatives come first.
This leaves unanswered what happens in a negative
interrogative sentence.   One problem we have encountered frequently is the practice of presenting exclusively or almost exclusively sentences with a pronominal subject and/or object.   This practice derives
from a laudable desire to use only real, i.e. actually
recorded, sentences and of course pronouns abound in
real running text.   However, the reader is often
unable to check statements about case marking and word
order involving nouns proper, which are often different from those involving pronouns.   One might argue
that general statements should be sufficient, that we
should be able to predict instances from the general
statements.   In practice, it is unusual to find carefully worded generalizations that cover all possibilities and if one cannot check for oneself, one is
never sure that the writer of the grammar did consider
the case one is interested in.

     This last point about generalizations leads us to
another problem.   It is quite unreasonable to write
any form of generative grammar for a language that has
not already been exemplified in the literature.   A
generative grammar cannot be used for reference.   In
theory, if the rules were constructed correctly, and
if the reader interpreted them correctly, he would be
able to ascertain the grammatical characteristics of
the sentence types he was interested in.   In practice,
generative grammars, or generative 'fragments', usually contain errors and the user is likely to make errors
in applying the rules.   Without sentence examples,
the user would not know if there were mistakes in the
rules or in his application of them, and a generative
grammar *per se* does not contain any sentences at all.
And of course it is obvious that the time and effort
required to extract information from a generative
grammar would deter all but the most motivated
researcher.

Many grammars are unnecessarily tedious to read.
One variety of tagmemic grammar glosses grammatical
morphemes by number, so that a verb will be glossed
as perhaps: *hit* + 461 + 729 + 204 + 362, each number
referring to a marker for tense, aspect, number or
person of the subject, and so on.   We hope that a
just God sends the authors of such grammars to Purg-
atory and sets them the task of reading their own and
each other's works.

Dying languages present particular problems.
The linguist may be forced to make a lot of use of
sentences elicited via English or some other language.
This should not affect morphology, but one would have
to be wary of any syntactic conclusions based on elicited material in such cases.

What one needs to do is form an estimate of the
reliability of a grammar.   This can be done by looking for information on just how familiar the linguist
was with the language being described.   Was he a
native speaker or did he collect all his information
in one day from an informant he happened to meet
(this has been done, at least in the case of some published papers!)?   Is the grammar internally consistent?   Has the grammar been reviewed by linguists
with some familiarity with the language or related
languages?   Was the linguist likely to have been
influenced by a desire to prove particular theoretical
points arising from work on other languages?   One of
the most useful guides to the reliability of grammars
is the 'bush telegraph' or 'grapevine', and access to
this is almost as important as access to the published
material itself.

(b)   *Secondary Sources*

The secondary sources can only be as reliable as
the primary sources on which they are based.   Most
of the work that has been based on a large number of
languages has been vitiated in part by the use of poor
primary material.   Up till very recently anyone who
wanted to cover more than thirty or forty languages
from different language families and areas found themselves forced to use, perhaps unwittingly, poor grammars.

There is also a tendency for secondary sources to
use other secondary sources as primary material and
the most obvious danger here is the perpetuating of
errors.   A good example of this appears in Keenan

1978b:185. He cites data on Dalabon from Comrie
1978:386-7, who cites it from Silverstein 1976:129,
who cites it from the original source, Capell 1962.
Keenan repeats part of a point made by Silverstein
that the subject of a transitive verb is marked if it
is equal to or below the patient on a hierarchy that
runs: first person > second > third > human > animate > inanimate.   Silverstein's point is not supported by the data, contains an incorrect page reference
to the source (102-3 for 111), and omits some diacrit-
ics.   Ironically, Silverstein's incorrect reference
is to a page of Capell's grammar that contains a
counter-example to his hierarchical explanation for
the distribution of case-marking in Dalabon.

(c) *Informants*

    One of the most healthy developments in cross-
linguistic work in recent years has been the greater
use of live informants.   Linguists are finding that
increasing numbers of immigrants, guest workers, ref-
ugees and foreign exchange students are becoming
available and they are making use of the opportunity
this development affords.   Live informant work is
not without its pitfalls, but it does promise to overcome some of the shortcomings of reliance on poor
primary and secondary sources.

    In the last decade or so a number of speakers of
languages other than the much-studied western European
ones have been introduced to linguistics and we can
hope to see more descriptions in the future that have
been produced by linguists who have a native command
of their material.

    Nevertheless, even if data is accurate, there is
a danger that conclusions based on it will be unreliable because it is unrepresentative of the possible
human languages.   That is, there are serious *sampling*
problems in cross-linguistic investigation.

    The question of how representative of human lan-
guage data is is dealt with in Bell 1978, who discusses the reliability or otherwise of particular sampling techniques.   The sort of errors that can arise
are *errors of observation*, *errors of over-generaliza-
tion* and *errors of sampling*.   The first of these,
Bell claims the linguistic community is well aware of
and the second, too, but it seems that linguists are
less aware of the third kind of error.   The sample

may not be merely too small, it may be too narrow.
That is, merely by enlarging the corpus of material
from a fixed range of languages we cannot hope to
avoid sampling errors that are the result of too
great a restriction on the range of languages taken to
be representative of the phenomena being studied.
Given our greater access today to languages outside
the Old World, there is little excuse for selecting
too narrow a range of languages for our sample. What
is clear is that a sample which is presumably random
because it is based on the sources available in a
library may not be a satisfactory method of achieving
realistic generalizations since there are particular
biases which can only with difficulty be avoided.
And it is precisely what Bell terms the *bibliographic
bias* - a result of the uneven distribution of descriptive material on the world's languages - that is
at the basis of sampling errors.   But perhaps more
important than this is what he calls *areal and genetic
bias* - with some areas of the world demonstrating a
greater concentration of certain features because of
contact or common parentage.

This last point brings us to the problem of isolating those features of a language which can be used
to assign it to a particular linguistic type, and
those which are of more relevance in assigning its
genetic affiliation, or in plotting the languages
that it has come into contact with.   The solution
ought to be, in principle at least, a fairly simple
one.   In the case of language contact some features
are much more likely than others to be borrowed, lexical and phonological loans being more common than
those at the morphological or syntactic levels.

In determining whether contact or inheritance is
involved, it is possible to find clues of both a linguistic and non-linguistic kind.   In the case of
Mazateco (Fries & Pike 1949) there is a phonological
rule that voiceless plosives become voiced after
nasals.   The existence of several exceptions to this
rule, including the frequently used word *siento*
(= 100) can be accounted for by borrowing from Spanish
because (a) it is similar to the Spanish word for 100
and (b) it fails to follow the normal pattern for
nasal and stop clusters in the language.   Thus the
occurrence of 'co-existent phonemic systems' is a
linguistic clue that borrowing has taken place.   However, had the word *siento* become *siendo* in Mazateco
we would have had to rely on extra-linguistic knowledge that the language had been in contact with

Spanish.   The presence of an almost identical word in two unrelated languages with the same meaning could be a case of pure chance, but contact is more likely the reason when a number of such items are found.   The presence of cognate elements in large numbers may also be the result of genetic relationship, in which case evidence comes from sound correspondences - regular patterns of phonemic alternation between two languages or more that can be attributed to divergence from a common source.   However, the borrowing and assimilation of words between unrelated languages may be the reason for this set of alternations and other evidence must come from extra-linguistic knowledge (such as a history of the movements of the peoples speaking the languages) or from examination of other structural features (such as shared morphological oddities). Unfortunately it can never be ruled out that borrowing has taken place on a massive scale, as is the case when pidgins are formed by the amalgamation of features of two languages.

Of particular interest is the *linguistic area* or *Sprachbund*.   A linguistic area is an area in which languages share characteristics that set them off as a group from other languages.   The notion of the linguistic area depends on hypotheses about genetic affiliation, so that one can meaningfully speak of such an area only if one can rule out resemblances due to common genetic inheritance.   Since borrowing is presumably a process that no language is immune to, there must be a large number of such groupings in the world, but some have received more attention than others. India, in the sense of the subcontinent as a whole, is a linguistic area embracing languages from the Dravidian, Indo-European, Munda, Tibeto-Burman and other families (Masica 1976).   China and Indo-China form a linguistic area of monosyllabic, analytic languages (Henderson 1965), embracing Sinitic, Tai and Mon-Khmer languages.   The languages of the Balkan peninsula form an interesting Sprachbund, in that here we have a group of languages (including Romanian, Albanian, Bulgarian and Modern Greek) which show a number of cases of syntactic convergence but which, with the exception of Turkish (which is in any case only marginally a member of the group), are known to be genetically related anyway, as members of the Indo-European family.   One such feature is the marking of definiteness on nouns by suffix, which is found in Romanian, Albanian and Bulgarian/Macedonian, even though in the other Romance languages definiteness is marked by

preposed articles, and in most Slavic languages definiteness is not marked at all on nouns.   For further
Balkan features see Sandfeld 1930.

Much of the certainty with which we assign languages to the same areal or genetic grouping stems
from extra-linguistic knowledge.   Unfortunately, not
all groups of languages are as well documented in
their development as the Romance languages.   The
Bantu languages of southern Africa are a particularly
vexed problem and it is far from clear whether the
features shared by these languages point to genetic
relationship or widescale borrowing (see Guthrie 1967).

But whatever the truth of the matter in such
cases it is clear that the only reliable facts are
those resulting from a purely objective analysis of
each language, without any supposition as to the
reasons *why* two or more languages may share particular
features at any grammatical level (though, indeed,
the facts resulting from such 'objective' analysis
may be tainted by the methodology used by the linguist
conducting the analysis - see in particular our discussion in section 1.3 for comment on this problem).

What the foregoing comments demonstrate is that
linguists concerned with cross-linguistic variation
and generalization perhaps require some preconceptions
about the structure of particular languages and about
the nature of human language in general;   and since
preconceptions are generally based on experience, however limited that experience may be, it is to be expected that these will be influenced by at least three
factors:

(a)   the language background of the linguist
       carrying out the investigation

(b)   the theoretical approach he adopts towards
       language

(c)   extra-linguistic knowledge about the his-
       tory of the languages and peoples under
       consideration.

The more he can throw off ethnocentricity, avoid the
dangers in model-specific approaches to data, cross-
check wherever possible any secondary sources he uses,
and gather as wide a range of material from as wide a
range of languages as possible, then the more realistic the results may be.

1.2   Typology and Syntax

1.2.1.   The Syntactic Bias

In section 1.2.3. we will be briefly discussing
some of the recent work on language typology, and one
of the series of publications we mention - Lingua
Descriptive Studies - is based on a questionnaire
largely, though not exclusively, devoted to the investigation of syntactic properties of language.   This
imbalance reflects the great amount of work that has
been carried out at the syntactic level in recent
years, but does not mean that no other grammatical
level is worthy of investigation on a cross-linguistic
basis.   There is a great deal of material available
for such investigation at the phonological level, for
example, and the Prague School of linguistics in particular demonstrated great interest in language typing
at this level (see Trubetzkoy 1939, and Baltaxe 1969
for a translation into English).   See also the work
on phonological systems by Hockett 1955.[3]   In the
nineteenth century, on the other hand, typing of languages was carried out mainly at the morphological
level, a preoccupation which continued well into the
twentieth century.

The interest in syntactic typology today, however,
reflects the current interest in syntax within theoretical linguistics, which can be traced back to the
mid 1950s.   Indeed, it is quite natural to expect
typological work to reflect the contemporary interest
in particular aspects of language from a purely theoretical viewpoint.   Theoretical linguistics is, of
course, concerned with language at all grammatical
levels, irrespective of their value in typological
work.   On the other hand, the history of typological
investigation has been in large measure (whether this
was realized by investigators or not) the quest to
determine which aspects of language will bear the most
fruit on a cross-linguistic basis.

In order therefore to see the current preoccupation with syntax in some sort of perspective, it might
be useful to trace this historical development from
morphological to morpho-syntax-based typology;   for
the current preoccupation with syntax both in theoretical and typological studies is to a large degree a
result and expression of the inadequacy of morphological structure to provide a realistic basis for typological classification of languages, and in particular to accomplish the more important aim that we have

claimed for language typology - of discovering cross-
linguistic generalizations that have something to say
on the nature of human language and on the capacity of
humans for language.

1.2.2.   The Emergence of Syntax-based Typology

As we mentioned in section 1.1.2., language typology was a particularly important part of linguistics
in the nineteenth century, being characterized in that
period by a preoccupation with morphological structure.   Although a number of different classifications
were proposed (for details see Horne 1966), the esse-
nce of language classification into types was a four-
way division into *isolating, agglutinating, inflecting*
and *polysynthetic*.   These are illustrated below:

A.   <u>Isolating</u>:   words are made up of one morpheme
                        each.

Vietnamese

cơm   nấu   ngoài   trời   ăn   rất   nhạt

rice   cook   out   sky   eat   very   tasteless

'Rice which is cooked in the open air is very
    tasteless'

                              (Lê 1976)

B.   <u>Agglutinating</u>:   separable affixes on verbs and
                           other roots.

Hungarian

a ház   'the house'   a házak   'the houses'
a házban 'in the house' a házakban 'in the houses'
a házukban 'in their   a házaikban 'in their
         house'   houses'

                         (Bánhidi et al. 1965)

C.   <u>Inflecting</u>:   morphemes are represented by affixes
                        but it is usually impossible to de-
                        termine precisely which part of an
                        affix represents which morpheme.
                        Thus, in the following example, the
                        -am ending on *puellam* (and the ad-
                        jective *bellam* that agrees with it)
                        marks the noun as being a feminine
                        singular in the accusative case.
                        Similarly, it is impossible to seg-
                        ment the ending -o on the verb *amo*,

which represents first person singular, present active indicative.

Latin

puellam   bellam   amo

girl   beautiful   I:love

'I love the beautiful girl'

D.   <u>Polysynthetic</u>:   greater use of affixation, often
                   involving incorporation of nouns
                   and adverbs within the verb.

Greenlandic Eskimo

silar   -luk -ka   -u   -ssi   -qa

outside bad   strongly   be   become   have

 -lu   -ni   -lu

 inf   3sg   and

'and it becoming very apt to be bad weather'

(Woodbury 1977).

Apart from an unfortunate tendency to apply value
judgements to such categories (so that isolating languages were regarded as 'primitive' and inflecting
languages as 'most advanced'), one fault among linguists at this time was to regard such language types
as clearcut.   In fact, the reader will have difficulty seeing a clearcut distinction between the inflecting and polysynthetic types.   Furthermore, it is
perhaps unreasonable to talk about any language con-
forming to a particular type at the morphological
level.   English, for example, has structures of types
A, B and C, being relatively isolating, but also
having the remnants of an earlier inflectional system
together with a tendency towards compounding and multiple affixing in derivational morphology.   And even
the most isolating languages, such as Thai or Vietnamese, cannot be restricted entirely to a system of one
morpheme per word.   All languages, for example, have
compounds and these two languages are particularly
rich in them.

The inherent variation in the morphological structure of particular languages was more clearly recognized by later linguists.   With the exception of
Müller 1880, whose terms *radical*, *terminational* and
inflectional matched the classification used in the
earlier part of the century, linguists in the latter

half of the nineteenth century used a far more complex
system of categorization.   And perhaps no morphological typing system was more complex than that of Sapir
1921.   Sapir's was a three-parameter system with multiple values for each parameter (grammatical concepts,
grammatical processes and firmness of affixation),
giving rise to a large number of potential classifications - Horne computes as many as 2,870 language types
with Sapir's system.   Although more realistic than
his predecessors, in recognizing that languages do not
lend themselves to over-simple classification and in
refusing to associate the state of a language with a
particular level of civilization among its speakers,
Sapir does, by the very complexity of his system,
expose the inherent weakness of a morphology-based
approach to language typing.   Horne's comment (Horne
1966:32) that there is almost one type per language if
one uses such a system should be seen as an indictment
of Sapir's approach, not as a tribute to its versatil-
ity.

The most recent attempt to attach some respectability to a strictly morphological typology is Greenberg 1960, where the author's aim is to quantify
statistically the division of languages into the four
main types.   By taking typical passages of each language and counting the number of morphemes, words and
morpheme boundaries, languages can be plotted as to
their overall degree of analytic or synthetic morphology.   The isolating language *par excellence* would
have a ratio of precisely one morpheme to one word,
while synthetic languages would have a larger number
of morphemes per word, agglutinating types being more
readily segmented and thus having more morpheme boundaries than the fused type of inflecting language.

The clear advantage of a system such as this is
that typing is based on precise statistical results,
rather than on what Greenberg refers to as 'intuitive
estimates' in earlier approaches, including Sapir's.
But no matter how clinical a statistical analysis
might be, problems still remain and, in particular,
any morphological analysis begs the two questions:

(a)   How is the morpheme to be defined?

(b)   How is the word to be defined?

Linguists are still unable to agree on whether
the morpheme is basically an abstract grammatical or
semantic unit.   Thus, it depends on one's view of the
morpheme whether *receive, deceive, conceive, perceive*

are each to be regarded as monomorphemic or dimor-
phemic.   Nevertheless, the importance given to morphology today in syntactic description certainly suggests the usefulness of the morpheme as a grammatical
unit.   The *word* also defies stringent definition,
being more clearly discernible in some languages than
others.[4]   However, the danger is that orthographic
convention will lull some into believing that it can
be defined as a group of letters with a space at each
end, rather than in terms, say, of a 'minimal free
form' (as suggested by Bloomfield) or in terms of
internal stability.

Given these problems, any division between language types, whether on clinical or intuitive grounds,
must involve arbitrary definitions, depending on the
linguist's theoretical stance vis-à-vis language
structure, and this is true of morphology as much as
of any other linguistic level, a point we return to
later in our discussion of grammatical models.

An added complication induced by the clinical
approach of a statistical analysis is the question of
where to draw the line between the types.   Although
a perfect isolating language would present no problems
since there would be a constant ratio of one morpheme
per word, more synthetic languages would have to be
ranked in terms of some arbitrary cut-off figure.
Using the formula M/W to express the number of morphemes per word, Greenberg categorizes languages morphologically in the following way:

*Suggested quantification of synthetic/
analytic language distinction -
M/W index of synthesis*

1.00   -   1.99   analytic

2.00   -   2.99   synthetic

3.00+   polysynthetic

The question must, of course, be asked - why should
the line between analytic and synthetic languages be
drawn at 2.00 if at all?   Why not 1.83, or 1.92 or
2.28 as the threshold of synthesis?   In fact, an
examination of various styles of English shows that,
depending on one's theoretical view of the status of
the morpheme, it is possible to categorize English as
analytic in casual conversation, but synthetic in
heavy text-book prose.   Yet even the figures for the
latter would be sufficiently low to support the

general feeling that English is more analytic than
synthetic.   Yet this is precisely the intuitive conclusion reached by linguists not using Greenberg's
statistical analysis.   As so often happens, the formalized approach to a common problem will serve merely
to bear out the conclusion arrived at informally by
the investigator.   However, in this instance, there
is the added disadvantage that the formal approach may
give a semblance of respectability to a form of language typing that has long since been shown to be of
questionable usefulness.   Bazell 1958 recognized the
inherent weakness of attempting to set up discrete
types and suggested instead a categorization based on
the relative difficulties of segmentation experienced
by linguists in approaching different languages.
Bazell's attempt to make a virtue of a vice was, nevertheless, clearly an admission of the unsuitability of
morphology as a basis for linguistic classification.

     As we pointed out in section 1.2.1., approaches
to typology normally reflect contemporary interests in
purely theoretical linguistics.   The 1950s were witness to a change within theoretical linguistics from
an essentially morphology-based structuralism (as
typified by the work of Hockett, Nida and Harris) to
an increasing interest in syntax in the late 1950s
after the publication of Chomsky's 'Syntactic Structures'.   It is, then, no coincidence that the move
from morphology to syntax in typology should take
place almost at the same time.   In both theoretical
and typological linguistics it was quite clear that
grammar based almost entirely on morphological analysis was far from revealing, and Greenberg in particular had taken morphological typing as far as it could
go.

1.2.3.   Recent Work on Syntactic Typology

     The change in emphasis from morphology to syntax
in typological studies can be placed at the beginning
of the 1960s in as much as 1961 was the date of the
Dobbs Ferry conference on Language Universals.   As we
have stressed, the study of typology and universals
are not necessarily mutually exclusive, and the osten-
sible preoccupation of this conference with syntactic
universals tends to disguise the fact that a *sine qua
non* of establishing the implicational universals put
forward by Greenberg was a concern with the ways in
which languages vary syntactically.   Thus, Greenberg's
universal number 2:

> In languages with prepositions, the
> genitive almost always follows the
> governing noun, while in languages with
> postpositions it almost always precedes.
>   (Greenberg 1963:78)

and universal number 3:

> languages with dominant VSO order are
> always prepositional.   (ibid.)

both imply that the languages on which the universals
are based have been subjected to a syntactic typological analysis in terms of what Greenberg calls 'the
order of meaningful elements'.

The Dobbs Ferry conference showed that the joint
study of language typology and universals (that is of
the ways in which languages vary or conform to general
patterns) was a viable proposition - though as Ferguson 1978 points out in his useful review of universals
research in the 1960s and 1970s, not all the participants at the conference seem to have recognized the
validity of this dual approach to cross-linguistic
investigation.

Since the Dobbs Ferry conference a large amount
of work has been done by various groups of linguists.
In North America these include the Language Typology
and Syntactic Fieldwork project in California under
Stephen Anderson, and an extensive research programme
carried out by members of the Language Universals
Project at Stanford University, which as Ferguson
(1978:17) puts it:

> '... had no explicit theoretical orientation
> and the researchers associated with it
> represented a variety of theoretical
> approaches ... [but] ... much of its work
> was in the spirit and manner of Dobbs Ferry.'

The Project at Stanford also produced a series of
working papers over a long period (beginning in 1969
and finishing in 1976) which presented many of the
findings of members of the project and other interested scholars.   Greenberg et al. 1978 brings together a lot of the research carried out under the
Stanford Project.

In Europe there have also been research program-
mes on a cross-linguistic basis, including the Cologne
Project on Language Universals (see Seiler 1978 for a

discussion of the aims of this group and some examples
of the work done under their aegis), and the Research
Project on Language Universals and Language Typology
under Östen Dahl at the University of Göteborg.

Publications on typology have also increased in
number over the last few years.   First there have
been anthologies on specific linguistic topics -
including Li 1976 ('Subject and Topic'), Shibatani
1976 on causative structures, and more recently Plank
ed. 1979 on ergativity.   Secondly, there have been a
number of series of publications on particular languages or groups of languages.   Among these, the
Cambridge University Press series 'Cambridge Language
Surveys', beginning with Dixon 1980, will present
studies of particular language groups, while two
further series will involve grammars of individual
languages.   The Handbook of Australian Languages is a
series of volumes containing several grammars.   The
first volume appeared in 1979 and it is intended that
several other volumes will appear at intervals of a
year or so.   Each of the grammars is written according to a set of instructions drawn up by the editors,
Dixon and Blake.   This provides for a unified format,
style and terminology.   It is required that the
'grammars produced for the *Handbook* be empirical
studies written in as straightforward a style as
possible, with a minimum of esoteric terminology and
conventions' (Blake & Dixon 1979:5).

The other series of individual grammars is the
Lingua Descriptive Studies series.   Each volume (2
had appeared at the time this book went to press) is
a set of answers to a large range of structural
questions in a questionnaire published as a special
issue of the journal *Lingua* (Comrie & Smith 1977), and
the series as a whole promises to provide a rapidly-
growing corpus of language material from a large range
of lesser-known languages, to supplement the wide
material on better-known languages, and make it easier
for the armchair linguist to fulfill the important
role of formulating language universals, or cross-
linguistic generalizations.   Until a wide range of
languages has been covered in depth by such publications as these, serious work on cross-language variation and generalization will be severely handicapped.

What is certainly clear is that the next decade
and beyond promises to be a very exciting period in
the history of linguistics, with an increasing number
of linguists carrying out research on a wide range of

typological topics and languages.   With so much work
being done there cannot fail to be at least some progress towards ascertaining the limits within which
human language operates, provided that we keep a
fairly open mind about our conclusions.   Above all
we should be wary of imposing on the data we discover
a preconceived notion of the most suitable theoretical framework.   Rather we should allow the data itself to in some measure dictate what type of model is
appropriate.

Unfortunately, this advice has not always been
heeded and some linguists have attempted to fit the
data to the theory rather than the other way round.
However, the type of publication that has been appearing in the late 1970s shows that not all linguists
have been bitten by the desire to make the model more
important than the data, and the current trend
appears to be towards a relatively model-neutral form
of cross-linguistic investigation.   Nevertheless, a
number of theoretical approaches have been used in
typological research and two of these at least de-
serve some mention.

1.3   Cross-linguistic Investigation and the Selec-
tion of a Grammatical Model

1.3.0.   At the beginning of this chapter we referred to the division within cross-linguistic study
between on the one hand proponents of particular
theories and on the other hand those whose concern is
with 'empirically-based theory-neutral approaches to
language'.   Although it is inconceivable that any
investigation of language can be carried out without
at least some theoretical assumptions, if only that
there exist grammatical categories such as noun and
verb, our own prejudice is towards a greater independence from particular schools of linguistic theory.
Of course we have to consider the possibility that
some theoretical approaches may have more to offer
than others in the field of language typology and
universals.   Two possible candidates are Transformational Grammar (TG) and Relational Grammar (RG).

1.3.1.   Transformational Grammar

One characteristic of grammatical theory since
the mid 1950s has been the trend towards positing
structures and categories not open to empirical observation, but instead hypothesized as an attempt to

account for *surface structures* in language.   With
this approach it may be possible to type languages
and establish cross-linguistic generalizations in
terms not only of observable features but also of the
deep structures underlying surface form and of the
rules (in the shape of syntactic *transformations*)
required to relate deep and surface structure.

One variant of TG in particular has concerned
itself with establishing underlying similarities between languages.   *Generative Semantics* (also known as
semantic syntax or *semantax*) posits underlying structures in the form of semantic representations - as
opposed to the much less abstract, strictly syntactic
nature of underlying structures envisaged by Chomsky
and other supporters of *Autonomous Syntax* (for a critical comparison of the two schools of thought see
Newmeyer 1980 in particular, but also Seuren 1974:102-
122).   The major result of this development was an
increase in the depth and complexity of transformational derivations, leading in turn to a reduction in
the number of underlying structures and grammatical
categories across languages.   In its strongest form,
semantic syntax involved a reduction in differences
between languages at some deeper level, culminating
in the Universal Base Hypothesis.   As the name
suggests, this was a claim that languages share underlying structure, their obvious surface differences
being the result of distinct transformational derivations.

This type of approach was adopted in the work of
a number of linguists, including Ross, Lakoff and
Bach, who proposed a reduction in the number of syntactic categories available to languages at deep
structure level.   Prompted perhaps by the apparently
closer relationship between verbs and adjectives in
languages such as Japanese and Mohawk than is the
case in English, Lakoff 1970 presents a number of
arguments for collapsing these two categories in the
deep structure of English.   The idea was extended to
other categories; Ross proposing a single category to
cover verbs and auxiliaries, and Bach a single category to cover these and also noun phrases (for a very
full criticism of this approach to grammatical categories on both theoretical and empirical grounds see
Schachter 1973a).

In similar vein, McCawley 1974 claimed that English word order is VSO at deep structure level, as
opposed to its basic SVO surface order.   If one

accepts McCawley's contention that all languages will
have either underlying verb-initial or verb-final
order, this is certainly a simplification in the
possible shape of underlying structure in the languages of the world.   However, while SOV languages such
as Japanese and VSO languages such as Welsh will
require little machinery to account for their surface
order, the difference between deep and surface order
in a language like English, with its verb-medial order,
will require the use of extra transformational machinery.   The implication that English word order is
less natural than that of Welsh simply because of a
decision by some linguist about underlying structure
seems to us to be quite unwarranted.

Bach 1965 is also concerned with the relationship
between underlying and surface order across languages.
Though restricting his discussion to the rules required to account for a range of NP-modifying structures, including relative clauses, his general aim is
expressed as follows:

> 'Far from trying to describe each language
> "in terms of its own structure alone", we
> must try to describe each language in terms
> of the structure of all other languages.'
> (Bach 1965:10).

Whereas in English relative clauses follow their head
noun, in Japanese they precede their head noun.
Bach claims that both languages have the underlying
order *Head Noun - Relative Clause* and that there is
therefore a closer relationship between them.   However, the simplification in deep structures achieved
in this way is cancelled out by the need to attribute
to Japanese a transformation that moves relative
clauses from post- to pre-nominal position, a rule not
otherwise required.

In terms of elegance or simplicity there is
little if any value in Bach's approach.   In any case,
a claim that languages are more closely related at
some underlying level is quite uninteresting while we
have no means of observing or otherwise testing the
existence of the transformations thereby required.

Of course, this is only one of the developments
that have taken place within TG since its genesis and
it is perhaps invidious to condemn the whole theory
just because of the excesses of one particular branch
that has few if any remaining adherents.   Today, many
transformationalists have a shallower conception of

underlying structure with a reduction in the number
and power of transformational rules (see, for example,
Bresnan 1978).

   Furthermore, the claim is still made - whether
implicitly or explicitly - that the model used for
English will have universal application, differences
between languages being matters of detail.   While
any proponent of a particular grammatical approach
will want to use that approach in examining all the
languages available, much more work needs to be done
within chomskyan theory before the assumption can be
made that it is ideal for a much wider range of languages than English.   For example, one feature of
mainstream TG has been the segmentation of sentences
into *subject* and *predicate* (or NP and VP, in categorial terms).   Whilst such a binary division is not
unreasonable for an SVO language like English, and
may also be warranted for other word order types in
which the V and O constituents are adjacent (VOS, OVS,
SOV), it presents serious problems for VSO and OSV
languages, in which V and O are separated by S (we
return to a discussion of the notion VP in section
4.5.1.).

   The problem is essentially one of choosing
primitives, the units in terms of which languages are
to be described.   The selection of a primitive such
as VP is unfortunate if the model which includes that
primitive is to be successfully used to examine a
wide range of language types.   It is perhaps for
this reason that RG has enjoyed some success as a
basis for cross-linguistic investigation.

1.3.2.   Relational Grammar

   RG is one of the more popular offshoots of transformational theory, involving a continued concern with
sentence relatedness.   Although the primitives of RG
are different from those of standard TG, in many instances its rules can be seen as rewritten versions
of transformations.   Both approaches recognize a
syntactic and semantic relationship between examples
such as (1.3) and (1.4) - active and passive respectively.

(1.3)   The goalie kicked the referee

(1.4)   The referee was kicked by the goalie

RG is in a state of flux and no doubt will continue

to develop (as has standard TG over the last quarter-
century) but can still be seen as a system for relating sentence types in a language.   It is this primary concern with sentence relatedness which leads
Comrie to minimize the difference between RG and TG.
Thus, whilst they can be distinguished in the following way:

> '...representation of syntactic structure [in
> RG] utilizes a single diagram (an arc-pair dia-
> gram) incorporating simultaneous representa-
> tions of all strata, rather than a derivation
> [in TG] that maps one representation onto
> another.'

Comrie is happy to:

> '...abstract away from the differences in the
> role of derivations between Transformational
> Grammar and Relational Grammar by referring
> to them collectively as theories with multi-
> stratal syntax, i.e. having at least two syn-
> tactic strata, however these are related to
> one another.'
>
>   (Comrie 1979a:269).

Whereas TG minimizes the role of grammatical relations (such as *subject of*, *direct object of*) in the
formulation of syntactic rules, for RG such relations
are central.   The claim is made, furthermore, that
linguists have been finding it increasingly difficult
to avoid the statement of rules without reference to
such relations and particularly in the formulation of
cross-linguistic generalizations (see Johnson 1974:
1-2 for examples of such a trend among linguists).
One such generalization is that for handling the
active-passive relationship, as exemplified by (1.3)
and (1.4).   To relate such examples, RG envisages
the *promotion* of the direct object *the referee* to
subject status, and the *demotion* to *chômeur* status of
the goalie.[5]   On the other hand, standard TG (see for
example, Chomsky 1973:233-4) envisaged the movement
of the NP *the referee* from a position after the verb
into pre-verbal position.

A further primitive of RG is the *indirect object*.
Again, a promotional rule would promote the indirect
object in (1.5) to subject in (1.7) via direct object
in (1.6).

(1.5)   The girl gave the present to the boy

(1.6)   The girl gave the boy the present

(1.7)   The boy was given the present by the girl

On the other hand, in TG terms (1.5) might be seen as *feeding* the passive rule by undergoing a permutation and deletion rule (permutation of *the present* and *to the boy* and deletion of *to*).[6]

    We have no wish to take a strong stand either way here but it does appear that many languages are sensitive to the relational status of the NPs in sentences as much as to their linear position, which appears to be the case in English. Thus, in Swahili, the verb in (1.8) cross-references the direct object and in (1.9) cross-references the *derived* direct object. Furthermore (1.10) shows that the derived direct object can be promoted to subject.

(1.8)   Msichana   ali⌐Ufungua   mlango   kwaajiliya

          girl   opened   door   for

            mwalimu

            teacher

        'The girl opened the door for teacher'

(1.9)   Msichana   aliMfungulia   mwalimu   mlango

          girl   opened   teacher   door

        'The girl opened teacher the door'

(1.10)   Mwalimu   alifunguliwa   mlango   na   msichana

          teacher   was opened   door   by   girl

        'Teacher was opened the door by the girl'

On the other hand, *the boy* in (1.6) may undergo passivization (or promotion to subject) in English but for many speakers it cannot submit to other rules normally applicable to *initial* direct objects. Thus 'derived' DOs cannot be subjected to Complex NP Shift, Tough-movement, or Wh-Question formation. The a. examples involve initial, the b. examples derived, DOs.[7]

(1.11) a. (i)   The child gave a present she had bought

               with her own money to the man

       (ii)   The child gave to the man a present
                she had bought with her own money

   b. (i)   The child gave a present to the man
              who had been kind to her

      (ii)   The child gave the man who had been
              kind to her a present

    (iii) ?The child gave a present the man who
              had been kind to her

(1.12) a. (i)   To lend money to poor people is
              difficult

      (ii)   Poor people are difficult to lend
              money to

   b. (i)   To lend money to poor people is
              difficult

      (ii)   To lend poor people money is difficult

    (iii) ?Poor people are difficult to lend
              money

(1.13) a. (i)   You lent the money to someone
      (ii)   Who did you lend the money to?

   b. (i)   You lent the money to someone
      (ii)   You lent someone the money
    (iii) ?Who did you lend the money?

    Of course, in transformational terms there has to be some statement as to *why* the NP to the right of the verb cannot undergo these other rules, so that such examples cannot be seen as being strong evidence for TG and against RG. Nevertheless, proponents of RG largely promote their model on the basis of its ability to cope with languages of quite different types, whereas TG, with its stress on constituent structure, is less successful in making universal statements because of the wide differences between languages in the order of elements and morphological marking of relationships between sentence constituents.

    Since RG takes as basic the *promotion* of direct object to subject, this relational rule transcends

the wide structural differences between languages in
their methods for marking the distinction between
actives and passives.   Thus, as Newmeyer points out,
languages like English, Chinese and Japanese have
quite different word order strategies for capturing
the active-passive distinction and any constituent
structure model of grammar is forced to write the word
order change into the passivization rule - with a
language-specific passivization rule in each case
(see for example Perlmutter & Postal 1977).   Whatever
the developments within RG that may take place in the
future, it is clear that a central theme is the non-
linearity principle, the final word order of particular languages being the result of rather late rules
that apply after the final grammatical relations in a
sentence have been established by the relational
rules.

However, RG may well fail to deliver the goods
in spite of its appeal as a model for cross-linguistic study.   This is because the laws established by
its proponents have been found not to hold water in
all languages.   Comrie, for example, demonstrates
quite convincingly that the Motivated Chômage Law does
not apply in a number of languages with impersonal
passives.[8]   This law is the claim that central relations such as subject can only be displaced to peripheral status if another relation, such as direct
object, dethrones them.   In Latin, Welsh, Polish and
Finnish (see Comrie 1977 for other languages and further references) subject demotion can be shown to
take place independently of object promotion.   In
the Welsh example (1.14) it can be demonstrated that
the clitic form *'i* in *fe'i* is a direct object and
thus has not been promoted to subject status, while
the subject has been demoted.

(1.14)   Fe'i lladdwyd   gan ddraig

          him   was-killed by   dragon

          'He was killed by a dragon'

While the failure of merely a single relational
law may not mean the death of the theory as a whole,
it can be expected that an increasing number of such
laws will be shown to be no longer viable in the light
of new data.   Furthermore, in the case of RG, a major
assumption is a trust in the universality of grammatical relations and their hierarchical ranking with
respect to each other (thus subject outranks direct

object and direct object outranks indirect object).
Yet it is by no means certain that even the subject
allows a universal definition.[9]

For these reasons, we feel there is a strong case
to be made for not approaching cross-linguistic study
from within the straitjacket of a particular grammatical model.   As we have said, any approach to language *does* involve some theoretical assumptions but
it is clear that the fewer these assumptions are, the
less danger there will be of imposing an inappropriate
model on a particular language with recalcitrant data.
It seems to us that what is required is a much more
open-minded approach to typology, allowing the data
to determine the theory, rather than the other way
round.

1.3.3.   Model-Neutral Typology

In his review of grammatical theory in the 1970s,
Newmeyer speaks rather disparagingly of model-neutral
approaches to syntax.   His view is summed up as
follows:

'An essentially atheoretical approach to syntax
has emerged at several linguistics departments
in California, where the sentiment that "we
must be prepared to devote much more time to
empirical investigation" (Li 1977:xix) is
regarded as counterposed to theory construction,
rather than complementary to it.   Many of the
papers in the three volumes of conference proceedings edited by Charles Li (Li 1975, 1976,
1977) illustrate this regression to descrip-
tivism'.   (Newmeyer 1980:249fn.).

It seems to us that, far from being a 'regression', such a trend is a very welcome recognition of
the realities of cross-linguistic work, in view of
the failure of TG and RG to apply theory successfully
to data and also in view of the great problems associated with the collection and interpretation of data
that we discussed in section 1.1.3.

Ideally we require an approach that avoids imposing theoretical preconceptions on data which may not
be amenable to them, but does not slide into the
opposite extreme of merely cataloguing data.   A compromise approach would distinguish between features
of a model that were a product of that model, and
features which all or most linguists would want to
incorporate into a grammar and which thus can be seen

as merely terminological variants on theoretical
notions about which there is some kind of consensus.
To illustrate this point, we return to Bach's discussion of relative clauses in English and Japanese.
Bach's claim that Japanese has an underlying order
Head Noun-Relative Structure imposes on a description
of Japanese a rule moving the relative clause into
pre-nominal position. Model-neutrally there would
be merely a recognition that Japanese shared with all
languages the use of structures equivalent to relative
clauses in English, whatever these structures are
called and whether they occur in pre- or post-nominal
position in a particular language. Of course, this
is a claim that all languages have relative clauses -
or have structures with the same function as the relative clause in English - and this assumption is
clearly open to empirical disconfirmation at any time,
but it seems not an unreasonable claim to make in the
light of the communicative needs of human language-
users.[10]

We might however discuss some structures in
model-specific terms *provided* it is recognized that we
are doing so only as a matter of convenience. Thus,
even some non-transformationalists may be guilty of
talking in terms of 'deriving passives from actives',
but this can be taken as merely a recognition of the
consistent syntactic and semantic relationships between the sentence types, not as an acknowledgement
that one type does derive from the other (or, to be
more accurate, shares an underlying structure).
What is important is whether it can be regarded as a
universal that languages have the active-passive
option and whether there are any similarities between
languages in the distribution and syntactic structure
of passive sentences.

In examining active and passive sentence pairs
on a cross-linguistic basis one need not be attempting to prove the validity of a particular model but
merely be attempting to characterize the circumstances under which an active sentence in a language can
have a passive equivalent.

Thus, in English, (1.15) can have a passive form,
whereas (1.16) cannot.

(1.15)   a.   The police arrested the demonstrators

         b.   The demonstrators were arrested by the
              police

(1.16) a. The first chapter contains the definition
        b. *The definition is contained by the first
            chapter

    In TG the verb *contain* in (1.16) (but not *contain*
in *The reinforced section of the dam contained the
water satisfactorily*) could be marked as a lexical
exception to the passive rule.   In RG *contain* is considered to have a subject that has been promoted from
locative and thus cannot be demoted by the passive
rule.   Characterizing *contain* as having a locative
subject is a move in the right direction, since it
involves seeking a semantic basis for this exception
to the passive rule.   However, RG has to admit that
locative promotion in English (but not in certain
other languages) is a sporadic lexical phenomenon.

    Pragmatically, then, we need to aim at a form of
description that falls between two extremes: (a) a
model-specific description that imposes on languages
constructs that are a product of the linguist's inge-
nuity, and (b) a bland listing or cataloguing of
those features which appear to occur in languages.

    In the four chapters which follow the primary
aim will be to show how languages can vary and how
generalizations can be made to capture seemingly irre-
gular cross-linguistic facts.   In doing so we will
be aiming, no matter how unattainable the ideal, at
an approach which falls somewhere between the two
extremes just described.

NOTES

[1]Our material is drawn from the second edition
of Greenberg's paper, published in 1966.   However,
we refer in the text to Greenberg 1963 as this is the
date of the first edition and the one by which the
paper is generally known.

[2]Bolinger extracts his informal universals from
Martin's 1964 review of Greenberg 1963 ed.   For
further details see Bolinger 1968:18.

[3]For a more recent study of phonological typology and universals see the collection of papers in the
second volume of Greenberg et al. 1978.

[4]Some languages have regular word stress -
Polish, for example, on the penultimate syllable and
Hungarian on initial syllables.   For a discussion of
further criteria see Robins 1971:184-192.

[5]The term 'chômeur' (a French word meaning 'unemployed') is used of a nominal which at a particular
level (or *stratum*) no longer holds the relational
status it did hold at an earlier level.   In English
passives, for example, the agent *by*-phrase contains a
nominal that is an unemployed subject.

[6]Some approaches to TG take (1.6) to be more
basic than (1.5), so that the transformation relating
them will be the mirror-image of the one assumed here.

[7]For further discussion of examples of this type
see Culicover & Wexler 1977 and Mallinson 1979.

[8]For a reply to Comrie's attack on this law see
Perlmutter 1978.

[9]For a discussion of criteria for defining
subject see the papers in Li 1976, in particular
Keenan (pp.303-333) and Schachter (pp.491-518).
RG takes the agent of a transitive verb to be the
initial (underlying) subject.   In ergative languages
the patient of a transitive verb seems to be at the
top of a grammatical hierarchy, not the agent.   For
problems with the application of RG to ergative languages see Dixon 1979:122-4.   See chapter two for a
discussion of ergative languages.   See section
2.1.1. in particular for the problem of defining
subject.

[10]See, however, chapter five (section 5.1) for
discussion of *adjoined* relatives, which can only with
some difficulty be regarded as functioning in the
same way as other relative structures.

CHAPTER 2

AGENT AND PATIENT MARKING

2.0   Introduction

     One sometimes hears it said that English has a
fixed word order while Latin had a comparatively free
one.   This freedom, it is said, was made possible by
the inflectional system of Latin, which provided a
means of distinguishing the subject from the object.
This view, which we have heard expressed from time to
time in philological circles, seems not unreasonable.
It represents an attempt to make sense of morpho-
syntactic systems.   It implies that the function of
subject and object marking is to distinguish between
subject and object; it implies that word order is an
alternative means of distinguishing subject and object;
and it implies an implicational universal, viz.: if
there is free word order, then there is some form of
marking to distinguish between subject and object.
However, this view leaves a number of questions
unanswered.   It says nothing about the possibility of
a language having marking for subject and object *and*
fixed word order; it fails to ask why a language
chooses one order rather than another; and it fails to
consider why a language employs one particular system
of marking the subject/object distinction rather than
another.

     We are interested in pursuing these questions.
In this chapter we review the various systems languages employ to mark subject and object, or at least
agent and patient, since it appears that not all languages are organized in terms of the grammatical relations, subject and object.   In sections 2.8 and 2.9
we review attempts to explain the distribution of
agent and patient marking.   In chapter three we describe the various word orders found in languages, discuss the motivation for these orders, and attempt to

relate word order and agent/patient marking.

2.1   Preliminaries

2.1.1.   Descriptive Framework

If we compare English and Latin on the basis of
how they treat subject and object and then try to
extend our enquiry to other languages, we soon find
that our basis for comparison breaks down.   In European languages, with the exception of Basque, the
agent of a transitive verb in the active voice and
the obligatory participant found with typical intransitive verbs receive the same morpho-syntactic treatment.[1] For example,

   (a)   they receive the same formal treatment,
          usually the same case marking.   In English
          they are distinguished by sharing pronoun
          forms suppletively distinct from other
          forms, e.g. *She goes, She hit her.*

   (b)   they share the same position in the clause,
          usually before the verb.

   (c)   they control verb agreement (see section
          2.1.2.), e.g. *The girl goes, The girls go,
          The girl sees him, The girls see him.*

   (d)   they remain covert or unexpressed in infi-
          nitive complements, e.g. *He wants to go,
          He wants to see the show.*

It is on the basis of this common treatment that we
are justified in establishing the grammatical relation of subject.

The difficulty with using the term *subject* in
language comparison is that in some languages the
grammatical criteria that link the agent of a transitive verb with the intransitive subject may be lacking,
or criteria of the same type may link the patient of
a transitive verb with the intransitive subject.   In
some languages the criteria may be conflicting, e.g.
case marking may identify the patient of a transitive
verb with the intransitive subject while agreement
may identify the agent of a transitive verb with the
intransitive subject.   Nor do the problems end there.
In a few languages the intransitive subject receives
different treatment according to whether it is agent
or patient, while in another group of languages the
agent, patient, locative, instrument and beneficiary
of a transitive verb all have equal access to the

marking associated with an intransitive subject (see
section 2.3.5.).

An obvious way around the difficulty is to make
comparisons on the basis of agent and patient.
Theoretically this seems sound, but in practice it is
unwieldy.   Languages do not normally mark agent and
patient consistently.   Although agent and patient
are usually distinguished with transitive verbs, this
distinction is normally neutralized with intransitive
verbs.   Even with transitive verbs there is usually
no marking reserved just for agent and just for
patient.   In Latin, for example, the nominative case
marks not only the agent of a verb like *caedere* 'to
kill', but also the experiencer of *amare* 'to love'.

Recently it has become popular to compare the
relevant case marking in terms of three entities: S_i
(intransitive subject), A (transitive subject) and
O (object).   This system, which originated with
Dixon 1972, involves three syntactic primes, though
the system is semantically based to the extent that A
must cover the agent of a transitive verb and O the
patient, irrespective of morpho-syntactic considerations.   This system facilitates comparison between
languages irrespective of whether there is identification of the agent with the intransitive subject,
the patient with the intransitive subject, conflicting identification or lack of identification.   It
does, however, break down for those few languages
that mark the intransitive subject according to
whether it is semantically agent or patient (see sections 2.3.4., 2.4.3. and 2.4.4.).

We have adopted the Dixon system here (albeit
with slight notational variation).   Where we use the
term subject (S) it refers to a conjunction of S_i and
A.   We use the term only in a grammatical sense.
We do not use it in a semantic sense i.e. we do not
use it for a conjunction of S_i and A as deep or underlying subject, at least not without qualification.
Where a grammatical relation embraces S_i and O, we
shall refer to that relation as the *absolutive* relation.

2.1.2.   Direct and Indirect Marking

The marking for S_i, A and O may be *direct* or
indirect.   By *direct marking* we mean marking for the
function of a noun phrase on the noun phrase itself.
This marking may be in the form of affixes (prefixes,

infixes or suffixes) or adpositions (prepositions or postpositions).   By *indirect marking* we mean forms appearing not on the noun phrases whose relationship they signal but in some other position in the clause. These forms are usually clitics or affixes and in most instances they appear on the verb.   In some languages they appear in second position in the clause, following the first constituent (see section 3.3.3.).   Although the term *indirect marking* is appropriate for these forms inasmuch as they may function like affixes and adpositions on noun phrases to mark the relationship of a noun phrase, it is per- haps a little misleading in that these indirect forms usually have their own reference.   Historically these forms are reduced stems, with or without affixes, and in many languages they function synchronically like unstressed NPs and have their own reference. Where this is true they may be said to cross-reference the NPs with which they stand in apposition.   To make this clearer, we present the following examples.

In Swahili (Hinnebusch 1979) typical intransi- tive and transitive simple sentences look like (2.1) and (2.2).

(2.1)   Ali   a-na-kimbia

         Ali   he-pres-run

         'Ali runs'

(2.2)   Ali   a-na-m-penda   m-wanamke   m-rembo

         Ali   he-pres-her-love   m-woman   m-beautiful

         'Ali loves a beautiful woman'

In both these examples *a*, the first element in the verb, cross-references *Ali*.   In (2.2) *m*, the third element in the verb, cross-references *wanamke rembo*. This *m* also appears as a prefix to *wanamke* and, by concord within the NP, with *rembo*.   Since word order in Swahili is characteristically SVO, i.e. subject- verb-object (the use of the terms subject and object is not controversial in Swahili), it can thus serve to mark S and O and hence agent and patient.   How- ever, the cross-referencing forms can also serve to mark agent and patient since there are distinct positions within the verb for the S forms and O forms. Providing the cross-referencing forms can be matched up unambiguously with NPs, the grammatical relations S and O can be identified.   By and large Swahili

does not have distinct cross-referencing forms for S
and for O, but nouns fall into 18 classes and each
class has its own class-marker (prefixed to the
constituents of an NP) and verb-prefix.   These
classes are formed mainly on the basis of semantic
category (humans, plants, etc.) or number (singular,
plural).   This means that in many instances S and O
will be in different classes and so there will be
unambiguous matching between the relevant verb prefixes and the NPs.   With nouns of the human singular
class and with most pronouns there are in fact separate forms for S and O.   In (2.2) *a-* is the S form
for the human singular class, and *m-* the O form for
the same class.   However, one cannot match the S and
O prefixes unambiguously with the noun phrases in
this instance, and identification of S and O thus
depends on word order.

The main point we want to illustrate is that in
Swahili the verb can stand on its own to form a
sentence, the pronominal prefixes on the verb functioning like unstressed pronouns.   In fact, the S
and O NPs are optional in terms of sentence structure.
The S prefix is obligatory and the O prefix obligatory for first and second person and for nouns of the
human class.   Prefixes are also used for other Os
when they are topicalized (Allan 1980).   In (2.1)
Ali could be omitted to produce a sentence meaning
'He runs', while in (2.2) both NPs could be omitted
to yield a sentence meaning 'He loves her'.   In the
following example (after Hinnebusch 1979:219), the
free first person pronoun is used in addition to the
prefixed forms.   The use of free forms indicates
emphasis.

(2.3)   Mimi, ni-na-ku-penda

         I   I-pres-you-love

         '*I* love you'

In Germanic languages there is some agreement
between the verb and the person and number of the
subject, but the verb cannot stand alone.   The
agreeing elements are not pronominal.   Consider for
example the following Old English sentences.

(2.4)   God lufað menn

         'God loves men'

(2.5)   God lufiað menn

          'Men love God'

In (2.4) the form of the verb indicates that there is
a third person singular subject.   In (2.5) the form
of the verb indicates that there is a plural subject.
However, one cannot omit the subject.

    Note that this agreement can serve to distin-
guish agent and patient.   In Old English the subject/
object distinction is made only in some nominal paradigms and word order in independent clauses can be
fairly free (a characteristic we have exploited in
contriving this 'minimal pair').   In (2.4) and (2.5)
we have nouns from paradigms where the nominative and
accusative are not distinct and, since word order is
not an absolutely reliable indicator of subject and
object, we must rely on matching the number marking
of the subject on the verb with the number marking of
the NPs to determine the subject.

    In this text we will use *agreement* as the super-
ordinate term covering the Germanic type of verb
agreement and the Swahili type. We will use the term
cross-referencing agreement or simply *cross-referencing* for the Swahili type.

    Cross-referencing agreement and non-cross-
referencing agreement are not mutually exclusive.
French exhibits both types.

    In French the verb exhibits agreement with the
subject, but the system is defective in that it fails
for the most part to distinguish first, second and
third person in the singular.   This non-cross-
referencing agreement system is complemented by a
series of subject pronouns.   Here is a typical paradigm, the present indicative of *arriver* 'to arrive'.
We give the paradigm in phonetic notation as well as
in written form since the written form, which makes
five distinctions in this paradigm, is not a good
guide to the spoken form.

1.   j'arrive   [ʒaʀiv]   I arrive

2.   tu arrives   [tyaʀiv]   you arrive

3.   il arrive   [ilaʀiv]   he arrives

1.   nous arrivons   [nuzaʀivõ]   we arrive

2.   vous arrivez   [vuzaʀive]   you arrive

3.   ils arrivent   [ilaʀiv]   they arrive

The subject pronouns, although normally written as
free forms, in fact have a status intermediate between
free and bound.   Unlike free forms they cannot be
stressed nor can they be co-ordinated with free forms.
They can, however, take part in inversion: *Arrivez-
vous à cinq heures?*   'Do you arrive at five?'   The
subject pronouns are sometimes referred to as *clitic*
pronouns, the term *clitic* indicating a status between
free and bound (or *proclitic* pronouns, *pro-* indicating
they stand before the verb).   The term *clitic* is also
used for the unstressed object pronouns in French,
but it is not clear that these are not completely
bound forms.   They do not seem to have any characteristics of free forms.   Combinations of them are
possible, but the forms can be considered first-order,
second-order, etc. affixes.

(2.6)   Jean me la montre

         John me it shows

         'John shows me it'

Some writers also use the term *clitic* to refer to unstressed pronouns in English as in *He hit her*
[(h)i(h)ítə], but this is an entirely inappropriate
use of the term.   The English pronouns *can* be
stressed and *can* be co-ordinated with nouns.   The
only bound pronouns in English are *'em* (assuming it
is not synchronically a reduced form of *them* but an
unstressed alternant) and the colloquial [əs] of
Give us a book, which refers to a first person indirect object singular or plural and which must be replaced by *me* (in the singular) if stress is required:
Give me a book.

     French has a set of stressable pronouns, some-
times referred to as disjunctive pronouns.[2]   To
stress a first person subject, for instance, one
places the form *moi* either before the clitic *je* or
following the clause.   In either case, it is set off
from the clause proper by an intonation break, at
least in slow speech.

(2.7)   Moi, je lis Le Monde

         Me, I read Le Monde

         '*I* read Le Monde'

One could say there is cross-reference between *moi*
and *je*, so that French has both an agreement system,
albeit a defective one, and a cross-referencing
system, albeit between subject proclitics and noun
phrases standing outside the clause proper.[3]

2.2   Plan of Attack

     Up to this point we have suggested that our in-
vestigation of the ways in which languages distinguish agent and patient be carried out in terms of S_i,
A and O and that the investigation involve direct and
indirect forms of marking.   The body of data to be
dealt with is daunting and therefore potentially confusing.   We propose to break it down as follows.
We will describe direct marking first (section 2.3),
then indirect marking (section 2.4).   Many languages
do not have one simple, overall system for marking
agents and patients.   These complications will be
omitted from section 2.3 and 2.4 and dealt with separately in section 2.5.   In section 2.6 we will consider the various types of direct marking and indirect marking together.

     By and large our method is to present the data
first and then to discuss attempts at explaining its
distribution later.   However, some remarks may be
appropriate at this point to serve as an orientation.

     The dominant view is that the function of case
marking in the agent-patient area is to discriminate.
Under this hypothesis a language is not likely to mark
an agent/patient distinction in the subject of intransitive verbs because no such distinction is
necessary.   Furthermore, it is not likely to mark S_i,
A and O by three separate forms since such a system
would be extravagant.   It is likely on the other hand
to mark either A differently from O (and S_i) or O
differently from A (and S_i) since there is obvious
utility in such a system.

     We will describe the systems of marking that are
to be found in terms of:

     (a)   accusative: O treated differently from
                           S_i/A

(b)   ergative: A treated differently from
                       S_i/O

(c)   3-way: S_i, A, O each treated separate-
                       ly.

(d)   active: agent and patient distinguished
                       irrespective of transitivity,
                       i.e. S_i split into agent and
                       patient.

Unfortunately, not all systems can be fitted
into this framework.   The language type found in the
Philippines (and extending to Formosa and Madagascar)
requires a separate classification (section 2.3.5.)
as does the type found among the Algonquian languages
(section 2.4.5.).

We recognize the following types of direct and
indirect system:

	direct (on NPs)		indirect (usually on V)
1.	accusative	1.	accusative agreement
2.	ergative	2.	ergative cross-refe-rencing
3.	3-way	3.	3-way cross-referencing
4.	active	4.	active cross-referen-cing
5.	Philippines-type	5.	inverse cross-referen-cing

2.3   Direct Marking - Affixes and Adpositions

2.3.1.   Accusative Marking

An accusative pattern of marking usually involves positive marking for O and zero marking for S,
but the traditional European type, exemplified by
Latin (see (2.26) (2.27)), involves marking for both S
and O.   A few languages have positive marking for S
but zero for O.   These include Houailou (Lichtenberk
1978), Malak-Malak (Birk 1976) and Mojave (see
comments in Dixon 1979:77).   In these languages the

unmarked accusative is the citation form. In some
Cushitic and Nilotic languages too the accusative
rather than the nominative is the citation form.   In
most of these languages both S and O are positively
marked, though in some Cushitic languages S is positively marked only in some noun classes while in a
few S is not marked at all.   Nevertheless the positively marked accusative is the citation form (Tucker
& Bryan 1966, Bender 1976).

It is difficult to find a pure example of accusative marking in which the system applies to all
nominals.   Many languages restrict accusative marking to definite participants or to animate or human
participants (see section 2.5.2.).   In the 'older'
European languages no nominative/accusative distinction is marked in neuter nouns (the label *neuter* is
misleading - membership in the class is determined
arbitrarily, though most neuter nouns are inanimate).

Japanese and Korean are good examples of the
type.   Both mark O by a postposition.   S is marked
either by a subject postposition or a topic postposition, the latter not being exclusive to S.   Our
example is from Korean (Hwang 1975:75, 80).   We have
glossed the subject postposition as nominative.

(2.8)   ønni   ka   ʉyja   e   anja   itta
         sister nom chair loc   sit   is
         'Sister is sitting on the chair'

(2.9)   ønni   ka   jungkuk yoli lʉl   hanta
         sister nom China   dish acc   do
         'Sister cooks a Chinese dish'

In a number of languages the patient and the
recipient share the same marking.   If there is a
recipient in the clause, then it takes the marker.
If there is no recipient, the patient may take the
marker.   The following example is from Khasi (Rabel
1961:159, 124).

(2.10)   ʔuu   la   kña   ya   ʔuu   sʔiar
         he   past sacrifice acc   the   cock
         'He sacrificed the cock'

(2.11)   ʔuu hiikay   ya ŋa ka   ktien   phareŋ

        he   teaches to me the language English

        'He teaches me English'

These shared markers are normally used only for definite or human patients or for pronominal patients.
A recipient of course is characteristically definite
and human and it may be that the 'sharing' of the
marking is on this basis, i.e. it is marking the
human/definite participant. Where the history of
such marking is known, it is the case that the marker
originally meant 'to' or 'for' and spread from this
local function to being a marker for some or all
patients. This is the situation in Spanish where a
'to' has come to be used also for specific human
patients in clauses where there is no recipient (see
section 2.8.3.). This sharing of patient/recipient
marking is found also in Sahaptin (Jacobs 1931, Rigsby
1974), Gidabal (Geytenbeek & Geytenbeek 1971),
Tigrinya and Amharic (Bender et al. eds. 1976), Sora
(Starosta, pers.comm.) and Tarascan (Foster 1969).

In theory an accusative marker can be any kind
of affix or adposition but in practice suffixes and
postpositions predominate. This is related to the
fact that suffixes and postpositions are characteristic of SOV languages and these languages mark the
agent/patient distinction, whereas prefixes and prepositions are characteristic of SVO languages, but
these tend not to mark the agent/patient distinction
(see section 3.4).

2.3.2.   Ergative Marking

Ergative patterns usually involve positive
marking for A and no marking for S and O. As with
accusative languages, it is difficult to find a pure
example, but the Pama-Nyungan language, Yalarnnga
(Blake, Breen field notes) is such a one.

(2.12)   kupi waya kunu-ŋka

        fish that water-locative

        'That fish is in the water'

(2.13)   kupi-ŋku milŋa ṭaca-mu

        fish-erg fly   bite-past

        'The fish bit the fly'

(2.14)   ŋa-t̪u   kupi   wal̪a-mu

          I-erg   fish   kill-past

          'I killed the fish'

The marking for ergative is rarely exclusive to
A function.   It is normally homophonous with the
marking for another function.   In Tibetan the ergative form also expresses instrumental, in Pitjantjatjara it expresses locative and in Eskimo genitive.

In Chukchee personal pronouns have a special
ergative case, distinct from all other cases, but
proper names and certain common nouns in A function
appear in the locative and other nouns express A via
the instrumental (Comrie 1979b:223).

In some languages ergative marking is optional,
being used only when it is necessary for disambiguation.   This is the case in Muriny Pata (Walsh 1976)
and in Hua (Haiman 1979).

A distinction is sometimes made between languages
that are syntactically ergative and languages that are
syntactically accusative.   It has been claimed that
some but not all languages that exhibit some ergative
case marking or cross-referencing (see section 2.4.2.)
are syntactically ergative.   A syntactically ergative
language is one in which S_i and O are treated alike
in the syntax as opposed to A.   It could be that S_i
or O are obligatory in a clause, but A optional.
It could be that the head of a relative clause has to
be S_i or O.   Languages can be syntactically ergative
according to one criterion and not according to another.   Syntactic ergativity is a matter of degree.
The distinction between syntactically ergative languages (treating S_i and O alike) and syntactically
accusative languages (treating S_i and A alike as
opposed to O) goes back to Dixon[1] 1972 who showed that
the Australian language Dyirbal was not only ergative
in its morphology but also in its syntax.

2.3.3.   3-way Marking

There is only one language known to us which
makes a 3-way distinction in case marking for all
instances of S_i, A and O and that is the Pama-Nyungan
language, Wangkumara (Breen 1976 and pers.comm.).
Two other Pama-Nyungan languages, Duungidjawu (Wurm
1976) and Dhalandji (Dixon 1980:331, 501 quoting P.
Austin), approximate to the type.   Dhalandji lacks A

marking only on first person, and O marking occurs on all nouns.   Sahaptin, a Penutian language, exhibits both A and O marking with some added complications (see section 2.5.3.).   Motu has been cited as having 3-way marking, but Dixon (1979:69) points out that this is doubtful.   As we noted earlier in section 2.2, the rarity of this type can probably be related to the fact that case marking on both A and O is unnecessary.   See also section 2.8.2.   It makes no sense to say that we can 'explain' the occurrence of the 3-way distinction, but we can make it seem less mysterious by pointing out that Pama-Nyungan langua- ges generally have ergative case marking for nouns and accusative case marking for pronouns.   Some of these languages have an overlap of ergative and accu- sative marking on some or all pronouns (see section 2.5.2. below) and the case marking in Wangkumara con- sists of what are transparently case-marked pronouns suffixed to nouns.   There is a masculine/feminine natural gender distinction in the third person singu- lar pronoun (more precisely non-feminine/feminine).

	non-feminine	feminine
S_i	ṉia	ṉani
A	ṉulu	ṉanrru
O	ṉiṉa	ṉaṉa

These 'pronouns', affixed to nouns, act as class mar- kers (compare the Swahili examples in 2.1.2.) albeit on a slightly different semantic basis, viz. mascu- line singular versus everything else.

	masculine singular	other
S_i	-ia	-((ṉ)a)ni
A	-(u)lu	-(a)nrru
O	-(i)ṉa	-(ṉ)aṉa

(2.15)   kaṇa-ulu kaĺka-ŋa ṯiṯi-ṉaṉa

   man-erg   hit-past   dog-fem:acc

   'The man hit the bitch'

(2.16)   kaṇa-ia   palu-ŋa

   man-nom   die-past

   'The man died'

2.3.4.   Active Marking

Some recent works on morpho-syntactic typology mention a case marking schema of the type Klimov has called *active*.   In this system an agent/patient distinction is made with intransitive verbs so that the subject of a verb like *run* will be marked the same way as the A of a verb like *kill* and the subject of a verb like *be stuck* will be marked like the O of *kill*. Most of the examples of this system are to be found among American Indian languages, and almost all of these examples exhibit the system only in the bound pronouns (see section 2.4.4.).   In Eastern Pomo, however, the active system occurs with free forms, although apparently only with pronouns, kinship nouns and proper names (McLendon 1978).   As far as we know there is no pure example of the type.   We will include examples of Eastern Pomo here, but strictly it should be treated in section 2.5 as an example of a type of mixed system.

In Eastern Pomo A-type marking is found with the subject of *go away* and *sit* etc., but O-type marking with the subject of verbs for *bleed, sneeze, be tired* and *be frightened* etc.   With some intransitive verbs it is possible to have A or O marking according to whether the activity is conceived of as under the control of an agent or not.

(2.17)   há· mí·pal šá·k'a

          I   him   killed

          'I killed him'

(2.18)   wí   če·xelką

          'I'm slipping' (accidentally)

(2.19)   há·   če·xelką

          'I'm sliding' (deliberately)

The language exhibits a mixture of ergative marking for common nouns and accusative marking for pronouns, kinship nouns and proper nouns.   The active phenomenon occurs only with pronouns, kinship nouns and proper nouns and the alternation involved is between an unmarked form for agent and an accusative -al for patient, with first and second singular pronouns showing suppletive alternation.

The northeast Caucasian language, Bats, is often listed as being an active language - see S. Anderson

(1976:5), Comrie 1978, Dixon 1979 and Dešeriev 1953.

2.3.5.   Philippines-type Marking

In the languages of the Philippines a set of prepositions is used to mark the semantic role of a participant.   In any clause, other than existentials, one participant is marked as topic by a preposition that replaces the role-marking preposition.   If the agent is topicalized, a prefix occurs on the verb marking agent as topic;   if a beneficiary is topicalized, a prefix occurs on the verb marking beneficiary as topic, and so on.   Our example is from Tagalog (Schachter 1976, see also Schachter & Otanes 1972). The topic marker is ang while ng marks agent and patient, sa marks locative and para sa beneficiary.

(2.20)   Mag-salis   ang babae   ng bigas   sa sako
         A-will:take   woman   rice   sack
         topic

              para sa bata

                   child

         'The woman will take rice out of a/the sack
           for a/the child'

(2.21)   Aalisin   ng babae   ang bigas   sa sako
         O:will:take   woman   rice   sack
         topic

              para sa bata

                   child

         'A/The woman will take the rice out of a/the
           sack for a/the child'

(2.22)   Aalisan   ng babae   ng bigas   ang
         Loc:will:take   woman   rice   sack
         topic

              sako   para   sa bata

              sack   child

         'A/The woman will take some rice out of the
           sack for a/the child'

(2.23)   Ipag-salis   ng babae ng bigas sa sako
          Ben-will:take   woman   rice   sack
          topic

              ang bata
                  child

              'A/The woman will take some rice out of a/
              the sack for the child'

As can perhaps be gathered from the translations, the
topicalized participant must be definite.   In an intransitive sentence the sole obligatory participant
is topicalized and the verb prefix indicates its role.

(2.24)   Magtatrabaho   ang lalaki
          A:will:work   man
          topic

          'The man will work'

(2.25)   Papawisan   ang lalaki
          O/Loc:will:sweat   man
          topic

          'The man will sweat'

     It should be noted that agent, patient, locative,
instrumental and beneficiary have equal opportunity to
be marked by ang.   One can take the constituents
marked by ang to be subject, but this subject does not
embrace S. and A to the exclusion of other possibilities.   The pattern with agent marked by ang is not
unmarked, neither from the formal point of view nor
from the point of view of frequency.   We shall refer
to the ang-marked constituent as the *topic-subject*
and we shall use this term for the analogous phenomenon in other languages of this type (cf. J. Anderson
1977, 1979).

     Not all the semantic roles that can occur with
the verb in Tagalog can be topicalized.   Schachter
& Otanes (1972:383) make a distinction between
complements (which can be topicalized) and *adjuncts*
(which cannot).   They define a transitive verb as one
that takes a topic and one or more complements, and
an intransitive verb as one that takes a topic but no
complement.   Both types may appear with adjuncts.

2.4   Indirect Marking - (Cross-referencing)

Agreement

Cross-referencing pronouns operate in an ergative, accusative, 3-way or active system like free forms. However, it often happens that the cross-referencing pronouns are partially unanalysable and one often has to recognize portmanteau forms.   It is not uncommon to find one particular portmanteau to indicate second person plural acting on first singular and another portmanteau for third plural acting on second singular, and so on.   The Algonquian languages exhibit an inverse system of cross-referencing.   This is explained in section 2.4.5.

2.4.1.   Accusative (Cross-referencing) Agreement

The examples given earlier from Swahili ((2.1), (2.2) and (2.3)) illustrate an accusative system of cross-referencing.   In Swahili one cross-referencing series is used for S and another for O, the difference being one of order class (position in the verbal complex: S-tense-O-stem) and partly of form class (a- for human S, m- for human O).

In some languages S is cross-referenced but not O.   This is common in Indo-European languages.   Consider the following examples from Latin.

(2.26)   Rex   agricola-m   lauda-t

           king   farmer-acc   praise-3s

           'The king praises the farmer'

(2.27)   Reges   agricola-m   lauda-nt

           kings   farmer-acc   praise-3pl

           'The kings praise the farmer'

Compare the Old English examples of non-cross-referencing agreement given in (2.4) and (2.5).   These also involve S only.

2.4.2.   Ergative Cross-referencing

Ergative cross-referencing is not too common but does occur in the northeast Caucasian language, Avar. In this language, S_i and O are not marked for case but are cross-referenced, while A is marked for case

but not cross-referenced.   The cross-referencing
consists of a prefix that marks the class to which
the noun belongs: v- for masculine rational, y- for
female rational, and b- for everything else.

(2.28)   či   v-ač?-ula

          man   he-come-pres

          'The man comes'

(2.29)   ebél-alda   či   v-aṭ-ula

          mother-sup   man   he-discover-pres

          'Mother discovers the man'

Ebél 'mother' in (2.29) is marked by the sup(eressive)
case marker (Tchekhoff 1979:71).

     This system of cross-referencing also occurs in
some other Caucasian languages, e.g. Archi (Kibrik
1979) and Abkhaz (Hewitt 1979).   In the latter there
is no case marking for agent and patient, but one set
of forms cross-references A and another set cross-
references S_i/O.   A similar situation prevails in
the Mayan languages (Larsen & Norman 1979).

2.4.3.   3-way Cross-referencing

     In 'The Case for Case' Fillmore quotes Takelma
as having separate pronouns for S_i, A and O (1968:54).
In fact Takelma has only one free form to cover S_i, A
and O, but does distinguish these functions within the
system of bound pronouns that are suffixed to the verb
stem (Sapir 1922).   These cross-referencing bound
forms are fairly readily analyzable (if one allows
for a number of morphophonemic rules that seem to be
of a general phonetic character) and they can be seen
to occur in transitive clauses in the sequence O-A.
Actually the system is more complicated than Fillmore's
brief mention suggests.   As can be seen from the
table below, there are distinctions between S_i, A and
O but there are also distinctions within S_i of the
type found in active languages (see section 2.4.4.),
and on top of all this a number of syncretisms of
various semantic functions in different person/number
combinations.   Column I gives the S_i forms used for
action verbs and column II gives the S_i forms used
for verbs expressing states.   The column I forms are
predominantly agent-like (used with *come*, *go*, *run*,
dance) and the column II forms are predominantly
patient-like.   However, there are exceptions in both

directions.   Column I forms are used with *be, die* and *sleep*, while column II forms are used with *whoop, go about, rest.*

The bracketed kwa form in the following table is not strictly part of the system.   It may be used for a human O (see also section 3.4).

TAKELMA BOUND PRONOUNS

		I $(V_i \text{action})$	II $(V_i \text{state})$	A	O
			Aorist		
sing.	1	t e'	t e'	a ' n	i
	2	t	t am	t	b i
	3	'	t		(kwa)
pl.	1	i k	i k	na k	am
	2	t p	t ap	t p	a np
			Future		
sing.	1	t e'	t e'	n	i
	2	t a '	t a '	t a '	b i
	3	' t	t $\bar{\text{a}}$	n k	(kwa)
pl.	1	i kam	i kam	na kam	am
	2	t pa '	t apa '	t pa '	a np

Takelma does not in fact fit into any of our pigeon holes and it would be pointless to dream up pigeon holes for Takelma and numerous other languages that have mixed systems (see 2.5).   We have included it here simply because a widely read source lists it as exemplifying 3-way cross-referencing.

2.4.4.   Active Cross-referencing

A number of American Indian languages exhibit this pattern.   In Dakota there is no distinction made between agent and patient with free forms but such a distinction is made with bound forms irrespective of transitivity.   Here are the forms for first and second person; there are no third person pronouns (Boas & Deloria 1939).

	Free (emphatic)	*Bound* agent	patient
1.	miye'	wa	ma
2.	niye'	ya	ni

(2.30)   (miye') wa-i'

          I   I-arrive

          'I arrived'

(2.31)   (miye') ma-si'ca

          I   I-bad

          'I am bad'

(2.32)   ma-ya-kte

          me-thou-kill

          'You kill me'

We hasten to add that in most active languages there
seems to be some arbitrariness about which verbs take
the agent pronominal forms and which the patient
forms (compare the remarks about Takelma in the preceding section).   In Dakota the system seems to be
pretty much semantically based.   Verbs that describe
activities or conditions that could be under the control of an agent, in Dixon's terms (Dixon 1979:80),
take the agent pronouns, e.g. *wear, shoot, lose, fart,
eat, dance, moan, blame, jump, sneeze, walk, dwell,
crawl, weep, desire, fly, kill* and *snore*.   However,
in most active languages there are some unexpected
assignments of 'agent' and 'patient' pronouns with
intransitive verbs.[4]

2.4.5.   Inverse Cross-referencing

     As mentioned in section 2.4 the Algonquian lan-
guages have an inverse system of cross-referencing
pronouns.   There are forms for first person (1),
second person (2), third person-proximate (3) (roughly
the 'former') and third person-obviative (3') (roughly
the 'latter').   The compound pronominal forms used
in a transitive clause operate with respect to a
hierarchy: 1 > 2 > 3 > 3' (where > means 'takes precedence over').   If a higher person acts on a lower
person, one series of compound forms is used.   If a
lower person acts on a higher, another series is used.
Our example is from Cree (Gleason 1961:116-122).   An

inspection and comparison of the two columns reveals
that direct combinations (higher acting on lower)
begin with a- and inverse (lower acting on higher)
with ik- (<*ekw).[5] The forms are not completely analyzable, but this is not apparent from our sample.

(1-3 is to be read 'first person acts on third'
or '1 is A and 3 is O').

	direct		*inverse*	
1-3	aw	3-1	ik
1-3p	awak	3p-1	ikwak
1p-3	anan	3-1p	ikonan
1p-3p	ananak	3p-1p	ikonanak
3-3'	ew	3'-3	ik

2.5   Mixed Systems

Up to this point we have provided a five-way
classification for direct marking (accusative, ergative, 3-way, active and Philippines) and a five-way
classification for indirect marking (accusative, ergative, 3-way, active and inverse).   However, few languages fit neatly into just one of these ten pigeon
holes.   Many languages have both direct and indirect
marking.   Latin, for example, has an accusative system of direct marking (case marking) and an accusative
system of indirect marking (cross-referencing agreement).   In some languages there is a discrepancy between the direct and indirect systems.   In some Australian languages there is an ergative system of case
marking and an accusative system of cross-referencing.
It is fairly common for accusative marking to be used
only for some subclasses of nominals, for instance,
only for human nouns; it is not uncommon to find that
agreement systems are only partially analyzable, and
in a few languages there are different systems used
in different tenses.   All these factors taken together mean that many languages can only be classified as some kind of mixed system.

We review these mixed systems in the following
subsections.

2.5.1.   Tense and Aspect

A few languages have an ergative system of case
marking in the past, perfect or non-future and an
accusative pattern in the present, imperfect or future.   Georgian, for instance, has an accusative

system in the non-past tenses and an ergative system
in the past (Vogt 1971).   Hindi has, and a number of
other Indo-Iranian languages have or have had at some
stage, an ergative system in the perfect.   Our
example of this kind of mixed marking comes from
Pitta-Pitta, a Pama-Nyungan language sharing genetic
and possibly areal features with Wangkumara (see
section 2.3.3.).   In the non-future Pitta-Pitta
exhibits a 3-way distinction, A being marked by -lu,
O by -n̠a, and S$_i$ remaining unmarked.   In the future
both S$_i$ and A are marked by -ŋu while O is marked by
-ku. ^{i}-ku is the marker for the complement of a few
'non-impingement' verbs such as t̠iwa 'be jealous of',
yat̠a 'to like', want̠ili 'to wait for' and wapa 'to
look for'.   There is also a construction in which
the agent becomes S$_i$ and the patient appears marked
by -ku (see(2.38)below).   This construction has the
meaning 'NP would like to VERB NP'.   Historically
this construction, or at least a variety of it with
an ergative agent and dative patient (-ŋu as in (2.36)
reflects an earlier ergative allomorph), may have become the regular one in the future (see Roth 1897,
Blake 1979a, 1979b).

(2.33)   kan̠a   n̠u-wa-ka   panʸtʸi-ya
          man   he-nom-here   ail-pres
          'The man is ill'

(2.34)   kan̠a-lu   n̠u-lu-ka   piyawal̠i-n̠a   pit̠i-ka
          man-erg   he-erg-here   dog-acc   hit-past
              mar̠a-lu
              hand-instr
          'The man hit the dog with his hand'

(2.35)   kan̠a-ŋu   n̠u-ŋu-ka   panʸtʸi-∅
          man-nom   he-nom-here   ail-fut
          'The man will become ill'

(2.36)   kan̠a-ŋu   n̠u-ŋu-ka   piyawal̠i-ku   pit̠i-∅
          man-nom   he-nom-here   dog-fut:acc   hit-fut
              mara-ŋu
              hand-instr
          'The man will hit the dog with his hand'

(2.37) kaṇa piyawaḷi-ku yaṯa-ya

man dog-dat like-pres

'The man likes the dog'

(2.38) kaṇa piṯi-li-ya piyawaḷi-ku

man hit-a/p-pres dog-dat

'The man feels like hitting the dog'

In the last example -li is glossed as antipassive.
The term 'antipassive' (originating in Silverstein's
1976 paper, *Hierarchy of features and ergativity*),
is used to describe a detransitivized construction
and for the marker on the verb signalling such a construction (see sections 2.7.2. and 2.8 for further
discussion).

Note the instrumental case marking in the above
examples. In Pitta-Pitta, as in very many Australian languages, the case marking for A and instrumental is identical. In Pitta-Pitta this identity
extends to the future, though the homophony is then
between nominative and instrumental rather than ergative and instrumental. Historically, -ŋu is an
allomorph of the ergative, having once alternated
with -lu (see Blake 1979a) either in Pitta-Pitta or
in some more remote ancestral language.

In Yugulda, another Australian language, anti-
passive-type marking rather than the ergative construction is used for *irrealis* (I would like to ...)
and negative (Keen 1972).[6]

In some languages of eastern Europe, O is marked
by the genitive rather than the accusative in negative
clauses. This kind of marking can be found in
Lithuanian, Polish and Russian for instance. Our
example is from Polish (Moravcsik 1978b:264).

(2.39) Mam czas

Have-I time-acc

'I have time'

(2.40) Nie mam czasu

not have-I time-gen

'I have no time'

2.5.2.   Limited Accusative Marking

Many languages mark O only when it is specific
or only when it is definite.   Many mark O only when
it is animate or human or pronominal or more particularly first or second person.   The distribution of
this marking across languages lends itself to treatment in terms of an implicational hierarchy as noted
by Silverstein 1976.   For example, if a language has
accusative marking for animate O, it can be expected
to have accusative marking for human and pronominal O.
We can specify a hierarchy running from left to right
as follows -

1 > 2 > 3 > proper > human > animate > inanimate

and say that O marking for any item to the right implies O marking for items to the left (we return to
this point in section 2.8.1.1.).

Some languages mark O only when it is specific
or definite *and* at a certain level on the hierarchy.
For example, in Spanish O is marked only when it is
specific and human (see examples(2.100) and (2.101)).
In Catalan O is marked only when it is pronominal but
of course the pronouns are inherently definite (Yates
1975).

Restriction of O marking to nominals that are
human, definite, etc. is so widespread that it is
difficult to find a language in which every instance
of O bears an accusative marker.

In Mongolian a definite O is marked by -iig but
an indefinite O remains unmarked.   The accusative
marker is also used for an O that is separated from
the verb by other words (Poppe 1970).

(2.41)   Dorǰi   bagši   baesəŋ

          Dorji   teacher   was

          'Dorji was a teacher'

(2.42)   bagši   dorǰ(i)-iig   uʒəbə

          teacher   Dorji-acc   saw

          'The teacher saw Dorji'

(2.43)   Dorⱨi ʐurəg   ʐurəbə

          Dorji picture painted

          'Dorji painted a picture'

In Baluchi (Barker & Mengal 1969) O marking is
obligatory with pronouns, normal with rational beings,
common with animals, possible with inanimate concrete
referents and impossible with abstract referents.

In a number of ergative languages, first and
second person pronouns often operate in a nominative-
accusative paradigm.   Our example is from Guugu-
Yimidhirr (Haviland 1979).   In this language all
personal pronouns operate in a nominative-accusative
system.   Compare the marking of gangurru and biiba
on the one hand with the first person on the other.

(2.44)   Gangurru dhada-a

          kangaroo go-nonpast

          'The kangaroo goes'

(2.45)   Biiba-ngun gangurru gunda-y

          father-erg kangaroo kill-past

          'Father killed the kangaroo'

(2.46)   Ngayu dhada-a

          I   go-nonpast

          'I go'

(2.47)   Ngayu gangurru gunda-y

          I   kangaroo kill-past

          'I killed the kangaroo'

(2.48)   Biiba-ngun nganhi gunda-y

          father-erg me:acc hit-past

          'Father hit me'

In Washo (W. Jacobsen 1979) there is no marking
for S_i, A and O with nouns and free 1 and 2 pronouns.
The 3^i pronouns show a nominative/accusative distinction.   With the bound forms, 1 and 2 show a nomina-
tive/accusative distinction.

		S_i	A	O
Free	Noun	-ø	-ø	-ø
	1	lé·	lé·	lé·
	2	mí·	mí·	mí·
	3	gí·	gí·	gé·
Bound	1	l^e-	l^e-	?l-
	2	m-	m-	?m

The language is syntactically ergative in that A is freely omissible and this ergativity is reflected in the bound forms that indicate 3. If the noun phrase preceding the verb is absolutive, i.e. S_i or O, then the verb is prefixed by ?-. If O is not expressed, the verb is prefixed by k'-.

(2.49)   t'é·liwhu   gáŋala   ?ípama?

        man   his:own:house:loc 3-arrived

        'The man reached his (own) house'

(2.50)   t'é·liwhu   t'á·daš   ?í?wi

        man   meat   3-eat

        'The man is eating meat'

(2.51)   t'é·liwhu   k'i?wi

        man   3 unexpressed-eat

        'The man is eating it'

(2.52)   t'á·daš   ?í?wi

        meat   3-eat

        'He's eating meat'

There are a number of points to be made here. First of all it is not uncommon to find that accusative marking occurs with 1 and 2 only (see section 2.8.1.1.), but free forms in Washo are unusual in exhibiting accusative with 3 rather than with 1 and 2 (and thus run counter to the implicational hierarchy mentioned above). The bound pronouns do conform to expectation. Secondly, the form k'- is not a cross-referencing form. It marks a third person O directly. Thirdly, k'- being opposed to ?-, can serve to

disambiguate a sequence NP V as in (2.51) and (2.52).
Compare the Takelma form kwa in section 3.4.

In some languages a distinction is made in case
marking according to whether the patient is wholly or
partly affected. The marking for the partly affected patient is either a special partitive case or the
genitive. The marking for the wholly affected
patient is usually the accusative, if only by definition. This kind of alternation is found in eastern
and northeastern Europe. Moravcsik (1978b:263), who
points out that it is an areal feature found in Latvian, Lithuanian, Polish, Russian, Finnish, Estonian
and Hungarian, gives the following example from
Russian.

(2.53)   Peredajte   mne   xleb

          pass   me   bread-nom

          'Pass me the bread'

(2.54)   Peredajte   mne   xleba

          pass   me   bread-gen

          'Pass me some bread'

2.5.3.   Relative Hierarchical Marking

In the previous section we pointed out that the
distribution of accusative marking across languages
could be described in terms of an implicational hierarchy. In Baluchi there is evidence for a hierarchy
within the one language, as we have seen, but typically the situation is as in Spanish. There, the
presence of 0 marking is simply based on the properties of the nominal in question. No hierarchy is
evident in the language itself. A hierarchy emerges
only from a comparison of languages. However, in
some languages the use of accusative and/or ergative
marking is determined by the relative positions of A
and 0 on an internal hierarchy of the general form of
the one given in the previous chapter. 1 is usually
at the top of the hierarchy, or sometimes 1 and 2
share the first position, and 3 is lower. Where
other categories of nominal are involved the hierarchy runs from subclasses of human (personal proper
names, kinship terms), through human in general, to
animate, to inanimate. Not all points on the hierarchy are recognized in every language that displays
relative hierarchical principles.

We have already presented one example of the
relative hierarchical principle.   As we noted in
section 2.4.5., Cree and Algonquian languages generally have markers on the verb to distinguish direct
combinations from inverse ones, a direct combination
of A and O being one where A is higher than O, an inverse combination being one where A is lower than O.
The Algonquian languages differ, however, from the
ones to be described here in that they exhibit markers
for the direction of the hierarchical distinction between A and O whereas the languages described below
have ergative or accusative marking determined by the
relative positions of A and O on the hierarchy.

In Rembarnga, a northern Australian language
(McKay 1975), a hierarchy of the form 1 > 2 > 3 plural > 3 singular is reflected in the distribution of
the accusative marker within the cross-referencing
system and in the neutralization of number marking
within the same system (there is also an ergative
case marking system for all NPs).

If A is lower on the hierarchy than O, then the
O bound pronoun is suffixed by the accusative -n, but
if A is higher than O, no accusative is used.

(2.55)   ŋa-n-pa-na

          me-acc-they-saw

          'They saw me'

(2.56)   pa-ŋa-na

          they-me-saw

          'I saw them'

The singular/plural distinction is neutralized
for the lower participant in a transitive clause but
not for the higher.   Compare the following where -ra
marks na- 'second person' as plural in (2.57) but not
in (2.58).

(2.57)   na-ra-n-pa-na

          you-pl-acc-they-saw

          'They saw you (plural)'

(2.58)   na-ŋa-na

          you-me-saw

          'I saw you (plural)'

The form pa- is inherently plural inasmuch as it is
opposed to -φ for third singular, but it does exhibit
the plural marker -ra, subject to the hierarchy.
Thus -ra occurs for example in the combination of 3
plural > 3 singular.

(2.59)   φ-pa-r(a)-na

            he-they-pl-saw

            'They saw him'

     In the northeast Caucasian language, Dargwa, the
verb agrees with 1 or 2 as opposed to 3, irrespective
of which is A and which O.   Where both 1 and 2 occur
as A and O, the verb agrees with O (Meščaninov 1936;
our example is via Wierzbicka, 1981).

(2.60)   ɣu   nu-ni   wäkilli

            you   I-erg   made

            'I made you'

(2.61)   nu   ɣu-ni   wäkilla

            I   you-erg made

            'You made me'

(2.62)   hit   nu-ni   wäkilla

            he   I-erg   made

            'I made him'

(2.63)   hit   ɣu-ni   wäkilli

            he   you-erg made

            'You made him'

     Fore (Scott 1978) has an interesting system of
case marking for A and O.   Neither need be marked if
A is equal to or higher than O on the following hierarchy: pronoun, personal proper name, kinship term >
human > animate > inanimate.   Examples (2.64) and
(2.65) are interpreted on the basis of an unmarked
SOV word order.   The first NP is taken to be A and
the second O.

(2.64)   wa   mási   ágaye [a-ka-y-e]

            man   boy   him-see-he-indicative

            'The man sees the boy'

(2.65)   mási wá   ágaye

         boy   man   him-see-he-indicative

         'The boy sees the man'

Where A is higher than O on the hierarchy, OSV order
may be used.   Example (2.66) is interpreted on the
basis of the hierarchy rather than on the basis of
the word order.

(2.66)   yaga: wá   aegúye [a-egu-y-e]

         pig   man   him-hit-he-indicative

         'The man kills the pig'

If A is lower on the hierarchy than O, it is marked
by -ma (if human) or -wama (if non-human).

(2.67)   yaga:-wama wá   aegúye

         pig-agent   man   him-hit-he-indicative

         'The pig attacks the man'

The positions of A and O in (2.67) may be reversed
without the meaning being altered, since the sentence
will be interpreted according to the presence of
-wama rather than on the basis of word order.   The
marker -(wa)ma may be used optionally in sentences
such as (2.64) and (2.65) and if it is used then OSV
order is possible.

     From (2.67) one would gain the impression that
-wama is an optional ergative marker.   Further investigation reveals that it can occur on an agent S_i
(Scott, pers.comm.).   This makes it seem like an
optional agent marker acting irrespective of transitivity as in an active language.   However, it can
occur marking the patient of a transitive verb, albeit
rarely.   Consider (2.68).

(2.68)   yaga:-wama   nk-agaye

         pig-agent   acc-him-see-he-indicative

         'He sees the pig'

This sentence must be interpreted with yaga: as O
since there is an accusative marker on the verb induced by and referring to yaga:wama.   Scott recon-
ciles the apparent anomaly of an agent marker co-
occurring with an accusative marker by interpreting

(2.68) as 'He sees the pig (doing something)'.

The accusative marking in Fore is in the form of a morphophonemic change induced at the beginning of whatever follows the O.   In (2.68) nk- appears since the verb which follows begins with a vowel.   This accusative marking is used for pronouns, personal proper names and kinship terms (i.e. position 1 on the hierarchy) and for any other noun bearing the agent marker as in (2.68).

The Penutian language, Sahaptin, reveals a 1, 2 > 3 hierarchy in a clitic system, verb prefixes and A marking.   The word order is fairly free, but 1 and 2 are represented by clitics attached to the first word in the clause as well as by free pronouns.   1 and 2 exhibit precedence over 3 in that they are represented by clitics but 3 is not.   There is marking on the verb to signal 1, 2 > 3 as opposed to 3 > 1, 2. There are two markers for a third person A: one for 3 > 1, 2, the other for 3 > 3.   There is also marking for O.   The following table shows the various combinations of clitic, verb prefix and case marking. Some details have been omitted in the interests of simplification.   The data is drawn from Rigsby 1974. See also Jacobs 1931.

	Clitics	Verb Prefix	A	O
1, 2 > 1, 2	√	-	-	-nay
1, 2 > 3	√	(á)	-	(-na)
3 > 1, 2	√	i	-nɨm	-nay
3 > 3	-	pá	-in	-na
		i		(-na)

Something of the way this elaborate system works can be seen from the following example.   Note that the recipient takes precedence over the patient in that it takes the accusative marking rather than the patient (see also section 2.3.1.).

(2.69)   x̱ʷɨ́saat-nɨm=naš   i-nɨ́ya   ináy   k'úsi

old:man-erg=me   inv-gave   me:acc   horse

'The old man gave me a horse'

2.6   Combinations of Direct and Indirect Marking

Up to this point we have considered direct and
indirect systems of marking in isolation from one
another.   Obviously a language can employ one or the
other, both or neither.   Below we list the various
combinations of direct and indirect marking we have
encountered.   'Indirect marking' covers any form of
agreement on the verb or elsewhere in the clause or
any system of unstressed as opposed to stressed pronouns.   Under 'direct marking' we have included any
accusative, including those that are restricted to a
sub-class of nominals.

Type 1.   direct: nil
             indirect: nil

Languages lacking case marking for A and O
and not having any agreement system are not too
common.   An area of such languages occurs in
east/south-east Asia: Shan, Thai, Lao (Tai),
Chinese (Sinitic), Khmu, Sre, Cambodian and Vietnamese (Mon-Khmer), Malay and Indonesian (Indo-
nesian-Austronesian).   Scattered examples include Bari (Nilotic) and Ponapean (Micronesian-
Austronesian).

English approximates to this type in that it
has an accusative system of pronouns but otherwise no marking.   There are some vestiges of
agreement (-s, am/are/was/were etc.) but we discount these and analogous vestiges in other languages.

Type 2.   direct: nil
             indirect: accusative

Italian is of this type since the agreement
of the verb cross-references S and there is no
case marking.   The unstressed O pronouns are
potentially cross-referencing and would be
classified as an indirect accusative system.
French fits in here too, the verb agreement and
the unstressed pronouns constituting indirect
accusative systems.

The Bantu languages are of this type (e.g.
Swahili) as are many other African languages
classified by J. Greenberg[7] as Niger-Kongo (e.g.
Yoruba (Kwa group) and Fulani (West Atlantic))

and Nilo-Saharan (e.g. Bagirmi (Central Sudanic)).
Other examples include Ulithian (Micronesian-
Austronesian), Iai, and Lenakel (Melanesian-
Austronesian), Nahuatl (Otomanguean), Tiwi and
several other northern Australian languages.

We could recognize a sub-type in which the
free pronouns operate in an accusative paradigm.
This sub-type would include the Celtic languages
and some Chadic languages such as Hausa.

Type 3.   direct: accusative
                indirect: nil

There are a number of scattered examples:
Japanese, Korean; Mongolian (Mongol-Altaic),
Ngarluma, Lardil (Pama-Nyungan), Yaqui (Uto-
Aztecan), Wikchamni (Yokuts-Penutian) and Easter
Island (Polynesian-Austronesian).

Type 4.   direct: accusative
                indirect: accusative

This is the common Indo-European type and
is represented by most Indo-European languages.
English, Italian, French, Catalan and Portuguese
are exceptions since they have no agent/patient
marking with nouns.   Spanish and Romanian are
classified here since they have prepositions for
specific human nouns in O function.   Most Ural-
Altaic languages are of this type as are Dravidian, Semitic (though modern Arabic has lost its
accusative marking with free forms) and Cushitic
languages.   Other examples include Nubian
(Sudanic-Nilo-Saharan), Maasai (Nilotic-Nilo-
Saharan), Houailou (Oceanic-Austronesian) and
Guaraní (Tupian).

Type 5.   direct: nil
                indirect: ergative

The Mayan languages are of this type as are
the northwest Caucasian languages Abkhaz and
Abaza.

Type 6.   direct: ergative
                indirect: nil

Examples where all nominals including pronouns operate in an ergative system are rare.

Yalarnnga (Pama-Nyungan) and Gurung (Tibeto-Burman) are of this type.

Languages in which nouns operate in an ergative paradigm and first, second (and in some instances third) person pronouns operate in an accusative system are much more common.   A number of eastern Pama-Nyungan languages are of this type (e.g. Dyirbal, Guugu-Yimidhirr) as is Tongan (Polynesian-Austronesian).

Type 7.   direct: ergative
          indirect: ergative

Languages of this type are quite uncommon. The northeast Caucasian languages Avar and Archi are of this type.

Type 8.   direct: ergative
          indirect: accusative

A number of Pama-Nyungan languages are of this type e.g. Walbiri, Djaru, Kalkatungu.

We could recognize a sub-type in which the free first and second person (and in some instances third person) pronouns operate in an accusative paradigm.   A number of Pama-Nyungan languages approximate to this type e.g. Western Desert.

Type 9.   direct: accusative
          indirect: ergative

As far as is known there are no exponents of this type.

Minority Types.

The inverse cross-referencing type is found in the Algonquian family.   The active type is characteristically northern Amerindian, e.g. Dakota, Crow, Takelma, Arikara, Choctaw.   Some Caucasian languages also exhibit the active pattern, e.g. Bats (northeast Caucasian).

The Philippines type is confined to a group of genetically related languages found in the Philippines, Formosa and Madagascar.

The languages that employ neither direct nor
indirect marking (but which exhibit SVO word order
for the most part - see section 3.4) and the nil/acc.,
acc./nil and acc./acc. varieties together account for
something like seventy per cent of the world's languages.   The ergative varieties probably account for
no more than fifteen per cent of the world's languages but they are widely distributed (see table in
section 3.2).   One possible combination of ergative
and accusative seems not to occur.   No language has
been found to combine accusative marking on free
forms with an ergative agreement system (see section
2.9.4.2. for further discussion).

2.7   Marked Constructions

Up to this point we have described agent and
patient marking almost entirely with reference to the
most basic intransitive and transitive sentence
patterns.   However, most languages employ some alternative constructions for the same or similar propositional content.   Languages whose syntax is oriented
on an accusative basis, i.e. languages that treat S_i
and A alike in terms of sentence structure, usually
have a passive construction.   Languages whose syntax
is oriented on an ergative basis, i.e. languages that
treat S_i and O alike in terms of sentence structure,
usually have an antipassive construction.

2.7.1.   Passive

Accusative languages typically have a passive
construction in which the subject corresponds to the
patient of a transitive verb, and the agent is
expressed in an oblique phrase (e.g. marked by a preposition or postposition).   The passive is normally
thought of as a marked construction, but it is the
preferred construction for certain combinations of
participants.   For example, if an inanimate indefinite entity acts on a first person patient, the
passive is the unmarked alternative with respect to
this combination.   *I was crushed by falling debris*
is probably more likely than *Falling debris crushed
me* in a variety of discourse contexts.   In the Waka-
shan languages there is no active counterpart for
clauses in which the agent is 3 and the patient 1.
The passive is obligatory (Klokeid 1976:311).

The passive typically involves some form of marking on the verb and the construction is typically

intransitive inasmuch as the agent (and certain other roles, depending on the language) need not be expressed.   Latin exhibits the most typical form of the passive.

(2.70)   Danai   equuum   aedificant

          Danai   horse:acc   build:3pl

          'The Greeks build a (wooden) horse'

(2.71)   Equus   aedificat-ur   (a Danais)

          horse   build:3sing-pass   by Danai

          'A horse is built (by the Greeks)'

(2.70) is a typical transitive construction with an A and an O and the verb showing agreement with A. (2.71) is an intransitive construction with the verb exhibiting agreement with S_i.

Although the most common form of passive has an optional agent, some languages do not allow the agent to be expressed at all (e.g. Latvian, Urdu, Amharic and Sre) and a few require obligatory inclusion of the agent e.g. Achenese (Lawler 1977).   Further references can be found in Siewierska 1980.

2.7.2.   Antipassive

If a language is ergatively oriented, then it usually has an antipassive construction.   By 'ergatively oriented' we mean not simply that the direct and/or indirect marking operates in an ergative/absolutive paradigm, but that the syntax of the clause is organized on an ergative basis.   Perhaps the most widely applicable criterion is omissibility of a referentially nonspecific A.[8]

In an antipassive construction the agent appears in the same form as S_i (almost always the unmarked or zero case) and the patient is either omitted (this is probably possible with all antipassives - it is obligatory in Avar), demoted to an oblique case, or left with whatever marking or lack of marking is normally found on O, as in Bandjalang, and Archi (see below).[9] Schematically the difference between the ergative and typical antipassive may be shown thus,

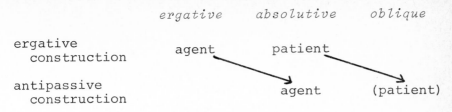

The antipassive construction seems to be intransitive, as evidenced by the case marking, the omissibility of O, and the fact that in languages where O is cross-referenced an O demoted to an oblique case is not cross-referenced.[10] The patient in the antipassive construction appears in the comitative in Eskimo, the dative in Kalkatungu, the instrumental or dative in Yidin^y.

The function of the antipassive may be syntactic (see section 2.9.4.2.) or semantic. In independent clauses it normally has a semantic function, indicating uncompleted or habitual activity or a nonspecific patient (see (2.38), sections 2.8.3., 2.9.4.2. and 2.9.4.3.) Yalarnnga provides a typical example. The normal ergative construction is shown in (2.72) and the antipassive in (2.73).

(2.72)   mat^{y}umpa-yu   kukapi   ṭaca-mu

          kangaroo-erg   grass   eat-past

          'The kangaroo ate the grass'

(2.73)   mat^{y}umpa   kukapi-u   ṭaca-li-ma

          kangaroo   grass-dat   eat-antipass-pres

          'The kangaroo eats grass'

Archi is interesting in that the antipassive is revealed through the agreement pattern as well as through the case marking. In (2.74) the grammatical verb (glossed as aux(iliary)) agrees with O.[11] In (2.75) the grammatical verb agrees with S_i.

(2.74)   buwa-mu   x̄$_o$alli   b-ar-ŝi   b-i

          mother-erg   bread   lll-bake-gerund   lll-aux

          'Mother is baking the bread'
                      (lll = neuter class)

(2.75)   buwa   x̄₀alli   b-ar-mat   d-i

          mother   bread   lll-bake-contin ll-aux

          'Mother goes on baking the bread'
                              (ll = feminine class)

(2.74) differs from (2.75) semantically in that it
expresses what Kibrik 1979 calls the 'continualis'
tense/aspect.

2.7.3.   Incorporation

     In many languages a noun may be incorporated in
the verb.   In the most common case O is incorporated,
with the result that instead of a transitive verb
plus O an intransitive verb is formed consisting of
the transitive verb stem and the O.   In Gunwinggu,
for example, O is regularly incorporated in the verb
(Oates 1964).   In some languages only a nonspecific
O can be incorporated, but in Gunwinggu a definite O
can be incorporated providing it is in one of classes
3 and 4.   There are four noun classes in Gunwinggu.
Class 1 contains masculine nouns and names of birds,
animals, insects, some artifacts and some other mis-
cellaneous referents.   Class 2 contains feminine
nouns.   Class 3 is entirely inanimate although it
does contain body parts.   Class 4 is the flora/food
class.   Thus incorporation seems to be confined, at
least approximately, to inanimates.   Compare (2.76),
where *boy* is unincorporated, with (2.77), where it is
incorporated (Oates 1964:105).

(2.76)   wam   gun-boy   maŋi?maŋi

          he-went   class3-antheap   he-was-getting

          'He went and got antheaps'

(2.77)   ŋaɽe   dangi   ŋa-boy-maŋ

          I-go   close   I-antheap-gather

          'I am going to get antheaps close by'

     Incorporation may be restricted to absolutives.
The following examples of incorporation of S_i and O
are from Nass-Gitksan, which can be shown to be oriented on an ergative/absolutive basis on other grounds
(e.g. A pronouns are suffixed to the verb; S_i and O
pronouns are suffixed to a host particle ḥi-)[1].
However, it has been suggested that O is the best

candidate for incorporation in any language and that
S. is also a candidate for incorporation, while A is
not normally incorporable (McKay 1976:503, Comrie
1978:336-37).   The Nass-Gitksan examples are from
Rigsby 1975.

(2.78)   Guwi-ỷ-hl   smax   (hl is a connective)

          shot-I   bear

          'I shot the bear'

(2.79)   Guxw-smax   hiỷ

          shot-bear   I

          'I shot a bear' or 'I shoot bears'

(2.80)   Is-xw-hl   hon

          stink-?   fish

          'The fish stinks'

(2.81)   Is-hon

          stink-fish

          'Fish stinks' or 'It stinks like fish'

(2.82)   Is-hon-hl   an'oni'ỷ

          stink-fish   hand:me

          'My hand stinks like fish'

     The incorporation illustrated here is a regular
syntactic process.   A very large number of languages
sporadically incorporate nouns and adverbs in verbs
as in English: *The chicken is deep-fried, Our safes
are time-locked.*

2.7.4.   Promotion or Advancement

     It is not uncommon for languages to provide
means whereby a participant that is a recipient, beneficiary, location or instrument can appear in the
position normally occupied by O and with the same
direct or indirect marking as O.

     In Indonesian, for instance, one can add the
suffix -i to an intransitive verb with a locative
complement to derive a transitive verb with an object
corresponding to the locative.   In (2.84) the men-
prefix simply marks the verb as transitive.

(2.83)   Ali   duduk   di-kursi   itu
           Ali   sit   on-chair   the
           'Ali sits on the chair'

(2.84)   Ali   menduduki   kursi   itu
           Ali   sit:on   chair   the
           'Ali occupies the chair'

In this particular instance, and in many other analogous instances in other languages, the peripheral
constituent seems to have been semantically reinterpreted as a patient and we have tried to capture this
with our translation.

    Where the derived verb allows a recipient or
beneficiary to be expressed as O, there does not
appear to be any semantic reinterpretation.   In
(2.86) a beneficiary is expressed as O, the verb
being suffixed with -kan.   Note that the beneficiary
contrasts syntagmatically with a patient (pintu).

(2.85)   Ali   membuka   pintu   untuk   guru
           Ali   open   door   for   teacher
           'Ali opens the door for the teacher'

(2.86)   Ali   membukakan   guru   pintu
           Ali   open   teacher   door
           'Ali opens the door for the teacher'

    In accusative languages with a passive, the
advancement or promotion of a peripheral participant
to be O or to be expressed like O may feed the
passive, which is itself an advancement or promotion
mechanism allowing O to become subject and topic.
For instance (2.84) above may be passivized.

(2.87)   Kursi   itu   di-duduki   (oleh)   Ali
           chair   the   pass-sit:on (by)   Ali
           'The chair is occupied by Ali'

    In an ergative language advancements of this
type involve a promotion to the absolutive. See
Dixon 1972 for Dyirbal, Dixon 1977 for Yidiny.   In
Philippines-type languages these advancements involve
direct promotion to 'topic-subject' (see section

2.3.5. for examples from Tagalog).

The following schematic representations are meant to capture the general pattern of advancements in accusative, ergative and Philippines-type languages.   Capital letters indicate syntactic relations, lower case letters represent semantic roles. In our view no role is an unmarked occupant for the Topic-S relation in Tagalog.

(a)   *accusative languages*

	S	O
	agt.	pat.

advancement to O: ←— loc. ben.
                                          instr.

passive: ←——

(b)   *ergative languages*

	A	Abs
	agt.	pat.

advancement to Abs.:   ←— loc. ben.
                                          instr.

antipassive: ——→

(c)   *Philippines-type languages*

Topic-S

advancement to Topic-S: ←—— agt. pat.
                                          loc. ben.
                                          instr.

2.8   Theories of Marking

When dealing with the locative, the instrumental or the ablative, one naturally takes the case marking to signify that a particular oblique phrase is expressing location, expressing instrument or expressing source.   In the area of marking for A and O, however, there is the view that case marking is used to *distinguish* A from O rather than characterize an NP as being A or being O.   The view that the function of case marking is to discriminate between A and O has been put forward by Comrie 1978 and Dixon 1979, for instance.   More recently a partly contrary view has emerged.   Hopper & Thompson 1980 point out that the marking of an NP as object is to 'index'

that the NP is an object, not just to distinguish it
from a subject.   Wierzbicka emphasizes the fact that
all cases, 'including the so-called "syntactic" ones,
like the nominative and the accusative, have meanings.
They are not mere distinguishers, they carry positive
semantic values' (1981:58).

In this section we shall examine these views of
the distribution of marking for agent and patient.

2.8.1.   Silverstein

2.8.1.1.   An Agency Hierarchy

Silverstein 1976 was perhaps the first to draw
attention to regularities among languages that mixed
ergative and accusative marking.

> 'In this paper, I want to bring out the fact
> that "split" of case-marking is not random.
> At its most dramatic, it defines a hierarchy
> of what might be called "inherent lexical
> content" of noun phrases, first and second
> person as well as third person.   This hier-
> archy expresses the semantic naturalness for
> a lexically-specified noun phrase to function
> as agent of a true transitive verb, and
> inversely the naturalness of functioning as
> patient of such.   The noun phrases at the
> top of the hierarchy manifest nominative-
> accusative case-marking, while those at the
> bottom manifest ergative-absolutive case-
> marking.   Sometimes there is a middle ground
> which is a three-way system of O-A-S [S = our
> S_i] case-markings.   We can define the hier-
> archy independent of the facts of split erga-
> tivity by our usual notions of surface-
> category markedness.'   (1976:113).

The hierarchy Silverstein refers to is as follows:

   1   2   3   proper   human   animate   inanimate

The left is the top of the hierarchy, the right the
bottom.   Silverstein claims that if there is a mixture of ergative and accusative marking, then accusative will be found over a continuous segment of the
hierarchy starting at the left and ergative over a
continuous segment starting from the right, with the
possibility of an overlap in the middle.

We have presented the hierarchy in the form in
which it is usually quoted, but we should point out
that Silverstein allows for the possibility of 2 out-
ranking 1 (1976:118).[12] We should also point out that
3 may be subdivided in some languages into human and
non-human or animate and inanimate, etc. and the sub-
divisions may exhibit different case marking according
to their semantic content, but usually a 3, whether
subdivided or not, behaves according to its position
on the hierarchy, irrespective of its reference.

Australia provides numerous examples of languages
with case marking distributed according to the hierarchy in the way Silverstein predicted.   Guugu-
Yimidhirr (Haviland 1979), the language illustrated in
section 2.5.2., has the following distribution of
ergative and accusative.

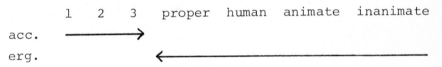

Commenting on a similar system, viz. that of
Dyirbal where 1 and 2 have accusative marking and
everything else ergative (Dixon 1972),   Silverstein
writes:

> 'So the case-marking system here seems to
> express a notion of the "naturalness" or un-
> marked character of the various noun phrases
> in different adjunct functions, particularly
> the transitive ones.   It is most "natural"
> in transitive constructions for first or
> second person to act on third, least "natural"
> for third to act on first or second.   Decom-
> posed into constituent hierarchies, it is
> natural for third person to function as pat-
> ient (O) and for first and second persons to
> function as agent (A), but not vice versa.
> The marked cases, ergative and accusative,
> formally express the violations of these prin-
> ciples.'   (1976:152).

Silverstein points out that the case marking of
A and O may be assigned on an absolute (or local)
basis, i.e. considering only the lexical content of
A or of O and marking it accordingly (see section
2.5.2.), or it may be assigned on a relative (or glo-
bal) basis, i.e. considering the relative positions
of A and O and marking accordingly.   The latter

principle has been illustrated in 2.5.3., where it
was shown, for instance, that bound pronouns in Rembarnga were marked for accusative when a lower A
acted on a higher O.

Silverstein's views, advanced at a time when
others were drawing attention to hierarchies of person and of animacy (Givón 1976, Kuno 1976a) and when
increasing attention was being paid to hierarchical
phenomena generally (Keenan 1976a, Keenan & Comrie
1977), have become widely accepted and are frequently
quoted. This should seem surprising to anyone who
stops to think about them. Although it is obvious
that inanimates (except for the forces of nature:
fire, lightning, flood, etc.) are good patients and
bad agents, it is by no means obvious that first and
second persons are unusual or unlikely patients
(Blake 1976b:492). Perhaps the reason that Silverstein's views are widely accepted is that numerous
languages obey the hierarchy.[13] However, the fact
that numerous languages exhibit case marking distributed according to the hierarchy does not necessarily
support the hierarchy as an *agency* hierarchy. Indeed the hierarchy also manifests itself in rules of
ordering, agreement, number marking and advancement.
We take up this point in the following section.

Dixon 1979 elaborates and extends Silverstein's
ideas and seems to see *ego* as the best candidate for
agent.

> 'In the speaker's view of the world, as it
> impinges on him and as he describes it in
> his language, he will be the quintessential
> agent. Radiating out from this egocentric
> focus, the next most likely agent will sure-
> ly be the addressee...' (1979:85)

This is a strong statement and so it is curious to
find in a footnote on the same page: 'Whether 1st
person should precede 2nd person on the hierarchy, or
vice versa, is a controversial question; there is
evidence for either ordering.' Certainly in the
original Silverstein paper there is no clear statement that 1 is always higher than 2 on an *agency*
scale.

The Silverstein thesis, or more particularly the
Dixon version of it, has been challenged in a recent
paper by Wierżbicka (1981). She counted instances
of 1, 2 and 3 as A and O in transitive action clauses
in six European plays. Taking her six counts

together we obtain the following figures. A is shown at the left, O at the top. Thus the cell containing 145 is to be read as 'first person agent acted on second person patient 145 times'.

European Plays

O

		1	2	3
	1	-	145	82
A	2	175	-	60
	3	109	53	?

Wierzbicka also made similar counts on samples from three European novels written in the first person.

First Person Novels

O

		1	2	3
	1	-	26	71
A	2	23	-	25
	3	156	9	?

Wierzbicka's tables show rather high figures for third person as agent but this results from her having restricted herself to clauses in which both A and O are human. Commenting on these figures (including some percentages showing agent-to-patient ratio for each person which we have not included), Wierzbicka writes:

'Nothing in the data supports the theory of the speaker as the quintessential agent. There is no reason whatsoever to think that "the speaker will think in terms of his doing things to other people to a much greater extent than of having things done to him". On the contrary, the opposite would seem to be true: the speaker is more interested in what

other people are doing to him than in what
he is doing to other people; he is more
sensitive to the ways in which people's
actions affect him than to the ways in which
his actions affect other people. The speaker regards himself as the quintessential
"victim", or, the quintessential experiencer'.
(1981:46).

Feeling that it is unsatisfactory to restrict
the sample to clauses involving human participants,
we made the following counts for three genres: (a)
plays, (b) first-person autobiography and (c) Australian Aboriginal texts.[14] We counted only finite clauses with explicit A and O (except that we admitted Ø
for third person in the Aboriginal samples).

Plays

O

		1	2	H	A	I
	1	-	38	27	2	124
	2	7	-	11	0	48
A	Human	13	6	9	0	61
	Animate	0	0	0	0	1
	Inanimate	12	3	2	0	4

Autobiography

O

		1	2	H	A	I
	1	-	11	68	10	200
	2	1	-	2	0	5
A	Human	85	2	17	3	92
	Animate	0	0	2	0	1
	Inanimate	48	0	12	2	29

Australian Aboriginal Texts

O

		1	2	H	A	I
	1	-	13	35	42	130
	2	3	-	5	1	5
A	Human	16	5	42	46	63
	Animate	7	2	4	2	7
	Inanimate	4	0	3	0	0

Combined Totals

O

		1	2	H	A	I
	1	-	62	130	54	454
	2	11	-	18	1	61
A	Human	114	13	68	49	216
	Animate	7	2	6	2	9
	Inanimate	64	3	17	2	33

Some of the differences between the tables
merely reflect differences of genre. Obviously
instances of second person are common only in the
plays and animal participants only in the Australian
Aboriginal texts (although we counted anthropomor-
phized animals as human).

As expected, inanimates and animals are good
patients and not such good agents. Our figures for
1 acting on 3 human and vice versa differ from Wierzbicka's figures. We do not find any 'significant'
difference between 1 > 3 human and human 3 > 1, whereas Wierzbicka's figures show 3 > 1 higher than 1 > 3.
'Significant' here must mean something like overwhelmingly skewed so as to be obvious to speakers of language. Our figures for 1 > 2 and 2 > 1 are based on
too small a sample. If we look at our figures and
the Wierzbicka figures together, it suggests that

there is no overwhelming proportion of 1 agents or 2 agents. The figures for 2 > 3 and 3 > 2 are all too small for us to be able to pick a favoured agent, but there does not seem to be an overwhelming proportion in favour of either candidate. In sum, we suggest that the only reflections of propensity for being agent or for being patient that could be discerned by language users are the differences between humans and non-humans. We would say that these figures support neither Dixon's notion of *ego* as the quintessential agent nor Wierzbicka's claim that *ego* is the quintessential victim or experiencer.

2.8.1.2.   A Topic Hierarchy

In the previous section we cast some doubt on the claim that the 'pronoun-animacy' hierarchy was an agency hierarchy. We also mentioned that the hierarchy manifests itself not only in the distribution of agent and patient marking but in other areas as well. In this section we mention some of these other manifestations of the hierarchy and suggest that they indicate that the hierarchy reflects a relative centre of interest. Events tend to be seen from the point of view of participants high on the hierarchy. First and second person are the best candidates for topic, inanimates the worst.

The hierarchy manifests itself in a number of areas. Here we deal with the following:

(a)   order of words or bound elements

(b)   agreement

(c)   number marking

(d)   advancement or promotion

(a)   *ordering*

In some languages where bound pronouns for A and O occur in juxtaposition, the order in which A and O appear is determined not by syntactic relation but by a hierarchy of the form 1 > 2 > 3 or 1, 2 > 3, the higher ranking participant preceding the lower. In the northern Australian language, Gunwinggu (Oates 1964), the latter form of the hierarchy prevails. Note that ŋa- 'I/me' comes first in both the following combinations:

(2.88)   ŋa-be-n-bun

          I-they-acc-will:hit[15]

          'I'll hit them'

(2.89)   ŋa-n-di-bun

          I-acc-they-will:hit

          'They'll hit me'

Hierarchically determined order is also found with direct and indirect objects. For example, in French the object bound pronoun precedes the indirect object bound pronoun (2.90), but if the indirect object is 1 or 2 then the order is: indirect object before direct object (2.91).

(2.90)   Marie   la   lui   donne

          Marie   it   to-him   gives

          'Mary gives it to him'

(2.91)   Marie   me   la   donne

          Marie   to-me   it   gives

          'Mary gives it to me'

Perhaps the best example of hierarchical order can be found in colloquial English where co-ordination involving pronouns follows a 1 > 2 > 3 hierarchy, e.g. *Me and you can go to the flicks*.   What makes this interesting is that it manages to live on despite a prescriptive tradition demanding a hierarchy that is the reverse, namely *3 > 2 > 1*, e.g. *You and I can go to the pictures*.   Prescriptivists of course have a genius for favouring the unnatural.

For other examples see section 3.3.2.

(b)   *agreement*

Agreement is determined by two hierarchies, a syntactic hierarchy and a person/number hierarchy. If there is agreement with one syntactic relation in an accusative language, it will normally be with S. If there is agreement with two relations, there will also be agreement with O.   In an ergative language these same possibilities are found, but there is also the possibility of only the absolutive controlling agreement or of A controlling agreement as well.   In

a number of languages a person hierarchy is also involved in the control of agreement.   For example, in
Dargwa, as we saw in examples (2.60) to (2.63), agreement in a transitive clause is controlled by 1 or 2
as opposed to 3.   In Sora (Starosta, pers.comm.), if
O is 1 or 2 it is marked on the verb, but not if it
is 3.   In many languages there are no separate bound
pronouns or agreement markers for indirect object,
but in a di-transitive clause the O forms mark the
indirect object not the direct object.   The indirect
object normally outranks the direct object on the
hierarchy.   In some western Pama-Nyungan languages,
not only S$_i$, A and O, but all local cases as well are
cross-referenced providing the exponent is animate.
See, for instance, J. Hudson 1978 for Walmatjari.

Ultimately there is only one principle underlying
agreement and that is topicalization.   Any syntactic
hierarchy that determines agreement seems to reflect
a topicalization hierarchy (see section 2.9.3.).

(c)   *number marking*

In many languages number is marked on pronouns
but not on nouns.   In a few it is marked for nouns
high on the hierarchy as well as on pronouns, e.g. in
Kalkatungu, it is marked on kinship nouns (Blake
1979c:80).   In the multiple-classifying languages of
northern Australia, number distinctions are usually
made only in human nouns (see also examples (2.57)
and (2.58) in Rembarnga).

(d)   *advancement or promotion*

Advancement seems at first blush to be based on
semantic relations.   A cursory inspection of languages reveals, for instance, that beneficiaries are
often advanced and treated like Os whereas the goal
of motion (as in *He went to the city*) hardly ever is.
However, the best candidate for advancement is the
recipient of verbs of giving and this is typically
human.   In fact one could consider that recipients
are animate locatives and that the advancement of
locatives is determined by animacy.[16] Beneficiaries,
the second best candidate for advancement across languages, are also typically high on the hierarchy.
In some languages only pronoun recipients are treated
like O.   For example, in Spanish recipients are
marked by a preposition but pronominal recipients
unless stressed are marked by bound pronouns preposed

to the verb.   See examples (3.51) and (3.52) in the
next chapter.

With passives one finds that though most languages with a passive alternative do not place hierarchical restrictions on its use, it is generally
true that the infelicity of a passive is roughly proportional to how far the passive agent is to the left
on the hierarchy, i.e. 1 and 2 make very poor passive
agents.   As we noted in section 2.7.1., in the Waka-
shan languages the passive is obligatory in clauses
where the patient is 1 and the agent 3.   In the
Aztec-Tanoan language, Tiwa (Allen & Frantz 1978),
only a third person can appear as the agent of a
passive and the passive is obligatory for 3 > 1 and
3 > 2.

In Indonesian, there is one passive construction
in which the agent appears optionally marked by a
preposition *oleh* and this passive is restricted to
third person agents.   There is another passive for
first and second person agents and it involves
placing the agent immediately before the verb.

(2.92)   Ali   mem-baca   buku   itu

          Ali   trans-read   book   the

          'Ali reads the book'

(2.93)   Buku   itu di-baca   (oleh)   Ali

          book   the pass-read   by   Ali

          'The book was read by Ali'

(2.94)   Saya   mem-baca   buku   itu

          I   trans-read   book   the

          'I read the book'

(2.95)   Buku   itu {saya baca}
                      {ku-baca }

          book   the   I read

          'The book was read by me'

The distinctive behaviour of 1 and 2 in the Indonesian passive lies in their appearing to the left
relative to where 3 appears in the analogous construction and in their not appearing in a peripheral
prepositional phrase.   1 and 2 show a consistent
tendency across languages to gravitate towards the

front of the clause.

If one takes the hierarchy to reflect how close
an entity is to the centre of attention, then the
various manifestations of it make sense.   The most
obvious example is the passive.   In a passive construction the patient is the grammatical subject and
usually the topic, whereas the agent is represented by
an oblique phrase.   We tend not to construct sentences with 1 and 2 in this non-topic position (e.g. *This
book has been read by me*).   1 and 2 are good candidates for topic and poor candidates for a non-topic
position.   In chapter three we demonstrate that most
languages tend to put topics to the left.   Rules of
ordering that place 1 and 2 before 3, etc., can be
seen as reflecting this tendency.   Advancement is
partly a matter of topicalization; the advancement of
recipients (or human locatives) to 0 position is certainly a topicalization strategy (see further discussion in section 3.3.2.).   The distribution of number
marking along hierarchical lines can plausibly be
taken as a reflection of the elaboration of morphological distinctions in those categories that are of
greater importance to language users.

We doubt if there is likely to be any real dispute over the fact that the hierarchy manifests itself
in rules of ordering, agreement and advancement and
we feel that it will be generally agreed that topicalization is involved in these rules.   We suggest that
the distribution of case marking is also likely to
reflect topicalization tendencies.

Consider for instance the following:

(a)   the implausibility of the notion of the hierarchy being an agency hierarchy.   What evidence is
there that first person is seen to act on second person more often than the other way around?   Are 1, 2
and 3 really unlikely patients?

(b)   accusative case marking is determined by definiteness in some languages and definite participants
are more topic-worthy than indefinite ones.   If we
claim that the distribution of accusative marking
according to the hierarchy reflects the topic-worthiness of participants, we can find a unified principle
for accusative marking, not that this constitutes any
proof of course.   It is interesting to note that in
the languages using an inverse system of marking (see
section 2.4.5.), the hierarchy includes two third

persons, proximate and obviative, and these can hardly
be said to differ in their propensity to be agent.
In fact proximate and obviative persons are distinguished entirely by the discourse context, by discourse topicality.   It is difficult to see inverse
systems as combining two different principles, an
agent-worthiness one and a topic-worthiness one.

(c)   ergative marking tends not to be found on 1 and
2.   Wierzbicka (1980, 1981) suggests that in an ergative language the zero or absolutive case represents
the unmarked choice for topic and the ergative a non-
topic.   1 and 2, in her view, tend to avoid the ergative because of their inherent propensity to be topic.
This is similar to their behaviour in accusative languages where they tend not to occur as agents of the
passive.

2.8.2.   Discriminatory Theories

     The notion that the function of case marking in
the agent/patient area is to discriminate between
agent and patient is strong in the works of both Dixon
and Comrie.   'The ultimate basis for any system of
case assignment, etc., writes Dixon, 'is the need to
distinguish which NP is which: i.e., which has A and
which O function'. (1979:69).   Comrie 1978 notes
that the discriminatory approach will explain the
existence of:

(a)   accusative and ergative systems,

(b)   the rarity of systems with a 3-way distinction
between S_i, A and O, since marking for both A *and* O
is functionally redundant,

(c)   the non-occurrence of languages in which S_i is
opposed to A/O.   This would involve maintaining a
non-functional distinction (between S_i and A/O) and
not making a potentially functional distinction (between A and O).

     Comrie 1975 also finds support for the dis-
criminatory approach in languages that use case marking for O only in the presence of an overt A.   He
presents an apparently persuasive example from
Finnish where O is marked when a nominative subject is
present, but remains unmarked (if a singular noun)
when no nominative subject is present.

(2.96)   Maija   söi   kala-n

          Maija   ate   fish-acc

          'Maija ate the fish'

(2.97)   Syö   kala-∅

          eat   fish-acc

          'Eat the fish!'

(2.98)   Syötiin   kala-∅

          eaten   fish-acc

          'Fish is eaten'   (impersonal passive)

In (2.97) and (2.98) *kala* can be shown to be accusative by substitution (pronouns would take an accusative -t in (2.97) and (2.98) as well as in (2.96)).
Comrie interprets the distribution of ∅ and -n as
reflecting the functional principle of using case marking only where it is necessary to distinguish the
agent and the patient. However, he has to admit that
the principle does not hold for plurals or for pronouns, nor does it account for the fact that -n is
used to mark the singular noun O of participles with
genitive A. In such cases -n is unnecessary by the
functional principle.

(2.99)   Poikien   avattua   ove-n,   mies   tuli

          boys:gen having:opened   door-acc   man   come

                 huoneeseen

                 room:into

          'The boys having opened the door, the man

          came into the room'

     In a number of papers (1978, to appear), Comrie
draws attention to the fact that accusative marking,
if not used for all instances of O, tends to be restricted to definite Os or to specific Os, and/or to
animate or human or pronominal Os as pointed out by
Silverstein (see section 2.5.2. for examples).   In
trying to account for this distribution of accusative
marking, Comrie states,

     '...certain grammatical relations tend to be
     characterized by certain features, in particular:
     that subjects tend to be definite, animate, and
     topic (thematic); while direct objects tend to

be indefinite, inanimate, and rhematic ... the
essential function of case-marking of subjects
and direct objects is not so much to have an
overt marking of subjects and to have an overt
marking of direct objects, but rather to have an
overt marking of the *difference* between subjects
and direct objects ... case marking of a direct
object with a form distinct from that of a subject would be particularly likely where there is
a greater likelihood of confusion between subject
and direct object. Since subjects are typically
animate and definite, one kind of direct object
that is particularly likely to get a special marker will be animate and/or definite direct
objects'.

(to appear:10).[17]

2.8.3.   Characterizing Theories

Recently there have appeared two challenges to
the view that the function of case marking in the
subject/object area is to distinguish the agent and
the patient - Hopper & Thompson 1980 and Wierzbicka
1980, 1981.

(a)   *Hopper & Thompson*

Hopper & Thompson (1980:291) point out that discriminatory theories of case marking seem to be insufficient when one considers the fact that 'many languages quite readily tolerate confusability at the
sentence level between subject and O' (see section
3.4).   They feel that the discriminatory function has
been overemphasized.   They point out that the in-
dexing or characterizing function of case marking
(and related phenomena) is just as important.

Under the Hopper/Thompson view, the fact that a
language marks specific patients but not non-specific
ones, definite patients but not indefinite ones, or
human or animate ones rather than non-human or inanimate ones reflects the fact that some participants are
more patient-like than others.   They point out that
the presence of O marking, whether it be signalled by
cross-referencing, position or case marking, is correlated with the semantic transitivity of the clause,
i.e. with the effective carrying over of an activity
from an agent to a patient.   Thus where there are
two or more different ways of describing an activity
involving an agent and a patient, the construction

that is formally more intransitive-like will be used
for a non-specific patient or for imperfective aspect
and so on.   By 'intransitive-like' we mean a construction with the patient in an oblique case or incorporated in the verb or lacking cross-referencing
(as opposed to a patient with cross-referencing).
Under this approach most of the variation listed in
section 2.5 can be accounted for, or at least given a
unified rationale (one exception being the tendency
for 1 and 2 not to take ergative marking).   Moreover,
this variation according to the properties of the
patient or according to aspect can be linked with
variation according to the inherent semantics of
verbs.   Not all two-place predicators are marked
alike.   If we take activity verbs involving impingement on a patient as a reference point (i.e. verbs
like *hit*, *break*, *grab*, *scrape*, etc.), then we find
that languages vary in the number of other two-place
predicates they treat like the impingement verbs.
Usually predicates expressing perception (*see*, *hear*,
etc.) are expressed like *hit*, *break*, etc. with the
perceiver being matched with the agent and the unaffected patient being matched with the affected
patient.   With predicates expressing *like*, *fear*,
hate, *remember*, etc. languages vary a good deal in
how they treat them.   English assimilates all of them
to the impingement type with the experiencer being
matched with the agent.   Many languages, however,
mark the unaffected patient with oblique marking, e.g.
dative.   Consider the Pitta-Pitta examples in section 2.5.1.   In the non-future, activity verbs
appear in frame (a), while verbs expressing emotions
appear in frame (b).

    (a)   ergative   accusative

            agent   patient

    (b)   nominative   dative

            experiencer   goal

However, when an activity verb is antipassivized it
takes frame (b).   Thus the permanent frame for emotion verbs is the frame for all two-place verbs in
the 'would like to' aspect.   In both cases there is
no effect on the patient, either because of the inherent properties of the verb or because of the 'aspect'
properties.

    Some of the variation encompassed by the Hopper

& Thompson transitivity hypothesis seems to involve differences of marking, and some differences of case. In Spanish a specific human O is marked by the preposition a (the same marking is used to express 'to'). Compare (2.100) and (2.101) (Hopper & Thompson 1980: 256).

(2.100)   Celia quiere mirar   un bailarín
           Celia wants   to-watch a   ballet:dancer
           'Celia wants to watch a ballet dancer (any
              ballet dancer)'

(2.101)   Celia quiere mirar   a un bailarín
           Celia wants   to-watch   a ballet:dancer
           'Celia wants to watch a (certain) ballet
              dancer'

We presume that in this instance no one would see a syntactic difference between the two sentences. We presume also that no one would entertain the view that *a un bailarín* is comparable to prepositional phrases expressing 'to' - *a Madrid* and so on. This could be shown to be false. There are passive equivalents for patients marked by *a* but not for intransitive verbs with allative adjuncts.

On the other hand the Polish and Russian examples quoted in section 2.5.2., and the antipassive examples from Pitta-Pitta (2.36) and Archi (2.75), involve the use of a different case.

(b)   *Wierzbicka*

Wierzbicka (1980, 1981) claims that all cases, including syntactic ones like nominative and accusative, have meanings. Cases, according to her, are not distinguishers, they carry positive semantic values. However, she notes that the forms of the cases (i.e. the case marking) not the cases themselves have a distinguishing function.

This is our view too, but it is worth commenting on some apparent exceptions. It sometimes happens that there is a discrepancy between the morphology and syntax of a language. In late Middle English, for example, some verbs took an oblique apparent subject rather than a nominative subject. Consider, for instance, the following sentence from Chaucer (Canterbury Tales, Prologue 785-6).

(2.102) Us thoughte it was noght worth to make it wys,
        And granted him withouten moore avys

The author can only omit the first person plural subject of *granted* in the co-ordinated clause on the
assumption that the co-ordinate verb of the first
clause is provided with such a subject.[18] On these
grounds we are justified in taking *us* in the first
clause to be subject despite its non-nominative form.
In our view *us* is functioning as an allomorph of the
nominative and is not a representative of the oblique.
These examples might appear at first glance to be
counterexamples to the proposition that cases are
meaningful.   However, (2.102) would only be a counterexample if *us* is taken to be oblique.   If it is
taken to be part of the nominative, then it is not
required to exhibit the meaning of any case or cases
signalled by the oblique.

     Analogous arguments can be put forward concerning
the ergative marker in some languages.   Hale 1968,
for instance, argued that Walbiri, a language with
ergative case marking, has an accusative syntactic
system.   It appears to have a subject relation and
the ergative marker could be described as a marker of
transitive subject.   The ergative marker does not
appear to reflect any relation recognized by the syntax, and the cross-referencing pronouns operate in a
nominative-accusative paradigm.   One could take the
ergative marker to be a kind of allomorph of the nominative.   Under this view one could see the ergative marker as having a distinguishing function without requiring that it have a meaning.[19]

2.9   The Theories Applied

     Before continuing with our discussion of the
distribution of the morphology involved in expressing
S_i, A and O, we would like to draw attention to the
possible functions such morphology might have.   Even
if we want to say that the prime function of the
morpho-syntactic devices listed in this chapter is to
characterize rather than to discriminate, we are not
committed to saying that they represent semantic
roles such as agent and patient.   We must consider
whether the relations that are marked are syntactic
rather than semantic, i.e. formally identified enti-

ties consisting of disparate semantic roles.   We
must also consider whether the marking is based on
discourse, i.e. whether it marks focus or topic (see
section 3.3 for further discussion).   For example,
the postposition ga in Japanese marks the grammatical
relation of subject whereas wa marks topic.   The
postposition wa can thus be found on an extraposed
topic or on the subject, where it replaces ga.[20] With
these possibilities in mind we now review the systems
of marking listed in section 2.2 to 2.6.

2.9.1.   Active System

    In some ways active systems are the easiest to
interpret.   They could be described as systems which
simply mark agent and patient, i.e. as systems sensitive to semantic roles only.   This interpretation
would require some qualification in most active languages since there appear to be some discrepancies
between the case marking and the role.   One could say
that the marking in an active language clearly cha-
racterizes rather than discriminates, but proponents
of the discriminatory view could say that the rarity
of the active type reflects the general tendency of
language to mark according to the need to distinguish.

2.9.2.   Philippines System

    The Philippines system is also easy to interpret
in that the marking of semantic role is for the most
part clearly separate from the marking for what we
referred to in section 2.3.5. as 'topic-subject'.

    In Tagalog, the constituent marked by ang, the
topic-subject, must be referential, and is usually
definite.   In a relative clause the co-referent participant must be encoded as topic-subject.   This requirement is not surprising when one considers that
the co-referent participant is definite by virtue of
its co-reference.   The co-referent participant is
suppressed in the relative clause, but the presence
of a role-marking prefix on the verb corresponding to
the role of this participant reveals that it is
covertly present in the construction.   In (2.103)
there are two clauses; the main clause is interesante
ang diyaryong and the relative clause is binasa ng
lalaki, which lacks an overt topic-subject (Schachter
1976:500).

(2.103)   Interesante ang diyaryong binasa   ng

          interesting the paper   O topic:read A

          lalaki

          man

          'The newspaper the man is reading is inter-
            esting'

In independent clauses there is in grammatical
terms a free choice between making an agent, patient,
location, beneficiary or instrument the topic-subject.
What determines the choice beyond the fact that the
chosen participant must be referential is not clear.

Consider the following sentence quoted by Hopper
& Thompson (1980:289) from one of Bloomfield's texts.
Note that topic third person pronouns are *sya* (modern
spelling *siya*) and non-topic *nya* (modern spelling
niya) and topic proper names are marked by the preposition *siy (si)*.

(2.104)   Siy Andres ay nagalit,   nagtindig at

          Top Andres   got:angry stood:up   and

          hinanap nya sa manga   sulok-sulok

          sought agt in plural corners

          nang   bahay ang unggo'

          of:the house top monkey

          'Andres got angry, stood up, and searched
            in all the corners of the house for the
            monkey'

In the last clause the monkey is topic-subject, though
Andres the topic (-subject) of the immediately preceding intransitive verbs seems to us the natural choice
of topic.   It appears from this example that the
choice of topic is not made on the same basis as it is
in English.

Schachter (1976:497) states that 'When a sentence
contains more than one noun phrase whose referentia-
lity is presupposed, it is not always clear why one of
these noun phrases, rather than another, is chosen as
topic'.   Hopper & Thompson 1980, however, point out
that Tagalog and other Philippines-type languages tend
to favour the patient as the choice for topic.   In
Tagalog the patient, if it is referential, must be

chosen as topic.   They note that, in languages generally, clauses that are highly transitive in semantic
terms tend to occur in foregrounded material (clauses
supplying the main points of discourse) while clauses
low in transitivity tend to occur as background.
High transitivity involves properties such as perfective rather than imperfective, a wholly-affected
patient rather than a partly-affected one and, what is
relevant here, a referential patient rather than a
non-referential one.   Thus they claim that there is
a correlation between definite O's and foregrounding
and that in Tagalog the O-topic construction has become a signal for foregrounding.

> 'Tagalog, then, represents an extreme case of a
> language where the statistical correlation bet-
> ween definite O's and foregrounding has resulted
> in a specialization of the "passive" to denote
> foregrounding.   This situation started out as a
> natural result of the tendency for O's to be
> known entities in foreground, that is, for new
> O's to be introduced in background through a
> "stagesetting" construction, and from that point
> on to be referred to as definite.   Eventually
> the correlation between definite O and fore-
> grounding becomes so strong that the grammatical
> construction once specialized for encoding defi-
> nite O's begins to take over as a signal of dis-
> course foregrounding, even being extended to use
> with indefinite O's ..., and to where it may not
> be used in backgrounding if the verb is realis/
> perfective'.   (Hopper & Thompson 1980:
>   290).

The favouring of the patient as a choice for topic is
reminiscent of ergative languages, as we shall see in
sections 2.9.4.2. and 2.9.4.3.

2.9.3.   Accusative System

Accusative systems of one kind or another account
for most of the world's languages.   Since the system
essentially involves S_i and A being treated alike and
since S_i and A cover a disparate semantic range we
are forced to see the common treatment of S_i and A as
syntactic.   The conjunction of S_i and A, i.e. the
subject, is typically topic, but it is easy to find
examples where the subject is not the topic and the
two should not be confused.   On the other hand the
features that unite S_i and A are of a kind that

suggests the subject is a grammaticalized topic.
Leftmost position, control of agreement and absence of
case marking (as opposed to positive marking for O)
are common characteristics of subjects, and all of
these are independently associated with topicalization
strategies.   Let us take each of these points in
turn:

(a)   *leftmost position*

   A word or phrase may be topicalized by placing it
outside a construction, usually by preposing it to a
construction: *Harry, he was into heavy rock when I
knew him in London*.   Subjects typically occur at or
near the beginning of the clause.

(b)   *control of agreement*

   There is often cross-reference between an extraposed topic and a pronoun in the adjacent construction (as in the example just given).   The cross-
reference is commonly with S_i and/or A and/or O; and
of course agreement within a clause is usually with
these, subject agreement (S_i and A) being one of the
possibilities.   Diachronically, it is likely that
the integration of extraposed topics into adjacent
clauses gives rise to agreement (with subject, object
or absolutive) as explained by Givón 1976.

   Harry, he was into rock → Harry he-was into rock
   Harry, he shot the tiger → Harry he-shot the tiger

(c)   *lack of case marking*

   Extraposed topics tend to lack case marking and
adpositions even if the form that cross-references
them bears a locative, instrumental, etc. relation in
the clause.   Consider the following: *Your freshly
painted mural, they rubbed their grubby hands all
over it*.   *Mural* bears no preposition, though *it* is
the object of a local preposition.   One does not
normally include markers with semantic content in
extraposed topic phrases since one usually wants to
talk about a participant not a relation, i.e. one
wants to talk about *X* not *in X*, *on X*, *over X*, etc.
Similarly, subjects lack marking that has clear semantic content.

   The accusative marking is usually positive (if
the difference between subject and O is made on the

basis of case marking).   It is possible to see the
accusative as being semantically motivated in many
languages providing one takes patient to embrace
affected, effected and neutral or unaffected varieties.
Patient emerges as a rather broad and negative concept, but it is possible to see the complements of
hit, *build* and *see* as sharing a common meaning.
This would not be possible with subjects where the S_i
of verbs like *ooze*, *trickle* and *die* is diametrically
opposed in meaning to the A of verbs like *bash*, *smash*
and *press*.   In some languages the accusative is used
not only for patients but for recipients that contrast syntagmatically with patients, e.g. in Malagasy
(Keenan 1976b).   In other languages beneficiaries and
other participants may be expressed by the accusative,
usually with a derived verb (as illustrated for Indonesian in (2.86)).   In these circumstances the accusative marks a syntactic relation of object.

   The high incidence of accusative systems, which
seem not to be semantically based, suggests that the
topicalization of A is natural.   Bearing this in
mind we turn to ergative languages which do not
afford a common treatment to S_i and A.

2.9.4.   Ergative System

2.9.4.1.   Semantic View of the Ergative System

   Some writers have seen ergative languages, or at
least some ergative languages, as having a system of
marking that is sensitive to semantic roles only and
as languages lacking grammatical relations and as
lacking any formal means of marking topic.   This is
essentially the view of John Anderson (1977, 1979)
and of Kibrik (1979), for instance.

   It may seem strange to many that anyone could
see S_i and O as being semantically alike and set off
from A, particularly in the light of the apparent
discrepancy between the agent-like nature of the S_i
of verbs like *swim* and the patient-like nature of
the S_i of verbs like *ooze*.   In fact one could consider that it would be as difficult to claim that S_i
and O formed a semantic unity as it would be to claim
that S_i and A were united on the basis of meaning.
It is interesting to note in this connection that
Gruber 1965, in establishing a set of what he called
'thematic relations', allotted the relation of theme
to S_i and O.   Gruber's thematic relations are semantic roles and his 'theme' is what other have called

patient (and other names).   Gruber does not make it
clear exactly what a 'theme' is and in fact he seems
to have confused a discourse function with a semantic
role, a confusion reflected in his choice of name.
The 'theme' emerges as a fairly negative concept, the
complement of more positively identifiable roles such
as agent and locative.   All clauses have a theme, so
S_i is always the theme of its clause.   Jackendoff
(1972:32) takes up Gruber's theme, but distinguishes
between intransitive subjects that are also agent as
well as theme, and intransitive subjects that are
simply theme.   In *John rolled down the hill*, *John*
can be held to be both agent and theme because he initiates and suffers the action.   In *The ball rolled
down the hill*, *ball* is simply theme.   John Anderson
requires that all clauses have an 'absolutive', absolutive corresponding to the Gruber/Jackendoff theme.
O is absolutive and so is S_i but Anderson allows absolutive to co-occur with other roles and some instances
of S_i are [+absolutive, -ergative] while others are
[+absolutive, +ergative], ergative being agent.
Starosta 1978 considers patient to be the fundamental
case relation (every clause must have one) and each
participant bears one case relation or role only.
This means that all instances of S_i are [+patient],
pure and simple and, since O is also [+patient], the
system of roles is ergatively oriented.

Starosta (1978:472) defines patient in the
following way (cf. Fillmore 1968:25):

> 'I will define Patient as the fundamental case
> relation.   Depending on the verb class with
> which it co-occurs, this in turn can mean
> (a) the entity which is viewed as affected by
> the action of the verb, (b) the entity which
> is viewed as moving or as being located in
> (abstract or concrete) space, or (c) the entity
> which is viewed as existing, in a state, or
> whose state is changing'.

This definition seems to embrace a rather hete-
rogeneous mixture and Starosta's Patient is more like
a syntactic entity than a semantic role.   However,
we feel that such a definition can be justified if
patient is considered the complement of the other
positively defined roles.

It is interesting to note that a number of linguists pursuing very different theories have seen a
semantic link between S_i and O.   Their views contrast
with the views of informal observers who tend to make

semantic distinctions of agent and patient within S_i.[21]

In comparing languages as we are doing here, it
is necessary to make an agent/patient distinction within S_i because such a distinction is forced on us by
the existence of active languages and by languages
like Tagalog that make an agent/patient distinction
in the verb (cf. Kibrik 1979:64). This does not pre-
clude the possibility of our describing different
languages as making an agent/patient distinction
along different lines. One could say that in an
active language an agent is an instigator of an activity but not necessarily of an activity that impinges
on an entity considered distinct from the instigator,
whereas in other languages, or at least in ergative
languages, an agent might be seen as an instigator
who initiates an activity that impinges on an external patient.

To explore this conception of agent and patient
would take us too far from our topic. The question
of whether S_i is a semantic unity is in fact controversial (see for instance Blake, to appear, Starosta
1978 and the references contained there). All we
want to do here is to point out that, under one particular conception of agent and of patient, ergative/
absolutive case marking could be held to reflect
semantic roles.

2.9.4.2.   Topic-based View of the Ergative System

A number of linguists over a long period of time
have noted that ergative languages are patient-orien-
ted and that the agent is peripheral relative to the
patient. Wierzbicka 1981 claims that in an absolu-
tive/ergative system the ergative signals an agent
acting on a patient while the absolutive signals an
entity that is not acting on anything else. In what
we are calling here a syntactically ergative language,
Wierzbicka claims the absolutive/ergative distinction
also signals topicality or prominence, the absolutive
indicating the central entity, the ergative the peripheral entity. She sees the absolutive as a
grammaticalized topic just as the subject is a
grammaticalized topic in an accusative language.
This view, like the common view of accusative languages but unlike the semantic view of the ergative,
does not require that one interpret S_i as homogeneous-
ly patient.

There is one particularly compelling reason to

support the topic-based view of the ergative/absolu-
tive system.   As we noted in section 2.8.1.2., Wierzbicka draws attention to the fact that first and
second persons regularly opt out of the ergative system.   This is true of languages such as Tongan
(Tchekhoff 1979) and Udi (Kibrik 1979) where 1 and 2
operate in an accusative system, and of languages like
Eskimo where 1 and 2 simply remain unmarked for S_i, A
and O (see, for instance, Reed et al. 1977).   Now if
the ergative/absolutive system is semantically motivated, there is no reason for 1 and 2 to operate outside this system, yet 1 and 2 (and sometimes 3) do
operate outside this system in a majority of ergative
languages.   On the other hand there are reasons to
accept that 1 and 2 are highly topic-worthy and to
relate their distinctive behaviour to their propensity
for being topic.   As we noted in section 2.8.1.2., 1
and 2 behave distinctively with reference to rules of
order, agreement and passivization and all their distinctive behaviour can be related to their affinity
for being topic.   There is a clear analogy between
the fact that they make bad passive agents and the
fact that they abhor the ergative (in the sense that
'Nature abhors a vacuum').   Moreover, it is clear
that in most but not all languages topics tend to
come early in the clause (see section 3.3) and it is
easy to relate the tendency of 1 and 2 to precede 3
to the 'topic-early' principle.   After all there is
one good reason to expect 1, and to a lesser extent 2,
to be the best candidates for topic.   Egocentricity
and 'us versus them' are well documented facets of
human behaviour.

Incidentally, the fact that 1 and 2 (and sometimes 3) operate in an accusative paradigm while
nouns operate in an ergative paradigm is related to
the fact that accusative cross-referencing agreement
sometimes occurs within an ergative language.   An
accusative bound pronoun system is presumably based
on an earlier free pronoun system.   There is no analogous motivation for an ergative cross-referencing
system to co-occur with accusative case marking and
it is significant that such a system has not been
reported.

If 1 and 2 avoid the ergative, one might also
expect them to resist being demoted to an oblique
case by the operation of the antipassive.   In some
languages the antipassive is used *only* for nonspecific
instances of O, so 1 and 2 resist demotion by virtue

of their inherent definiteness.   In some languages
the antipassive is used for imperfective aspect and,
since this is less likely with a first or second person patient, there will be a tendency for 1 and 2 not
to get demoted.   However, it must be admitted that
some ergative languages do allow 1 and 2 to be demoted.
In Kalkatungu, for instance, 1 and 2 may be demoted to
the dative in clauses that are progressive in aspect
if not imperfective.   On the other hand 1 and 2 do
resist demotion in Kalkatungu in certain circumstances.   In Kalkatungu, as in some other ergative languages, the antipassive does not have any semantic
significance when used in subordinate clauses, rather
it is syntactically motivated.   In this language
(Blake 1979c) two types of subordinate clauses involve
the use of bound pronouns and in both of these 1 and
2 resist the operation of the antipassive.   In
(2.105), for instance, the antipassive is used in the
purpose complement to signal that -i, the bound third
person pronoun, coreferences the absolute (S$_i$) of
the governing clause.   Note that the patient of the
subordinate clause is in the dative.

(2.105)   ṭuku   iŋka-ṇa   ṭuar-ku   a-i

            dog   come-past   snake-dat   comp-it

               ica-yi

               bite-antipassive

            'The dog came to bite the snake'

Now if we substitute the first person for *snake*, we
find that the antipassive is not used even though the
coreference conditions for its use prevail (use antipassive when A coreferences the absolute of the
governing clause).

(2.106)   ṭuku   iŋka-ṇa   a-ŋi   ica

            dog   come-past   comp-me   bite

            'The dog came to bite me'

In (2.106) -ŋi is an accusative form, the bound pronouns (which have cross-referencing and coreferencing
functions) operating in a nominative-accusative system.   Apparently the speaker resists the ignominy of
demotion to a peripheral position.   Of course this
view implies that the accusative is not peripheral
and this appears to be so (compare section 2.9.4.3.).

The accusative in Kalkatungu marks the absolutive
relation when there is a bound pronoun participant
with a transitive verb.   There is no syntactic accusative as in English.   In fact it is worth noting
that the Kalkatungu phenomenon is significantly
different from the common phenomenon of first and
second persons operating in a nominative/accusative
system while other participants operate in an erga-
tive/absolutive system, since the latter merely involves case marking - not the cases themselves. Kalkatungu does have a nominative/accusative system for
first and second (and third) bound pronouns, but
(2.106) illustrates the fact that, syntactically, 1
and 2 behave differently from 3.   1 and 2 do not just
exhibit different marking, they block the use of a
different syntactic construction.

Wierzbicka (1980:135, 139) following Regamey 1954
notes that if one adopts the view that the ergative
construction presents the action from the point of
view of the patient, one can make sense of those languages that exhibit an ergative construction only in
the past tense or perfect aspect.   Only a past or
perfect action has actually affected the patient.   A
future action and an uncompleted or ongoing action is
in a sense intransitive - it relates to the agent,
but not to the patient.   Similarly, Dixon (1979:40)
writes, 'Something that has not yet happened is best
thought of as a propensity of the potential agent'.
We could add that it is not surprising that in some
ergative languages verbs for *like*, *fear*, *hate*, etc.
take the liker etc. in the absolutive and the target
of the emotion in an oblique case.   These verbs take
the experiencer to be the centre of interest.

There is further support for the absolutive-as-
topic system in the fact that nonspecific patients
normally cannot appear in the absolutive, rather they
must be demoted to a peripheral marked case via the
antipassive construction (see (2.73)) with the agent
appearing in the absolutive.   One can see an analogy
here with accusative languages.   In English, nonspecific patients are not often expressed as subjects,
and in some languages only a definite NP can fill the
subject position.

2.9.4.3.   A Note on Topic

The notion that the absolutive is the basic topic
position in an ergative language seems strange to
English speakers, and presumably to speakers of

numerous other accusative languages.
fairly obvious.   In English, it is onl
of the passive that the patient of a tr
can be put in the basic topic position,
The ergative construction looks like a
struction because the patient is unmark
agent marked by a form that signals eit
or location or some other oblique case, and is reminiscent of the use of 'by' in passive constructions.
This leads us to equate the ergative with the passive
and to think of ergative languages as being quite
amazing in that they use passives as often as we use
actives.

In this section we briefly review the expression
of topic in accusative languages and then turn to a
discussion of topic marking in ergative languages.

(a)   *the topic in accusative languages*

One can ask with respect to a clause, 'Which
entity in the clause is the clause about?'   If this
question can be answered, we would say that the
clause has a topic, and that the entity that the sentence is about is the topic.   Not every clause has a
clear topic in this sense.

The topic in English, and in accusative languages
generally, is normally the subject.   As we pointed
out in section 2.9.3., a grammatical subject seems to
be a grammaticalized topic and seems to derive diachronically from an extraposed topic in some languages.   The topic and subject do not coincide in
every sentence.   If one asks: *Who took my knife?*
someone might reply: *John took it.*   In the reply
the topic is the knife or the taking of the knife.
John is certainly not the topic but rather the *focus*,
yet *John* is expressed as the subject.   Note, however,
that in a sentence like this, the subject, being the
focus, takes the main stress.

If the passive is used, then roles that would
have been expressed as O in the active are expressed
as subject.   The passive is used for a variety of
reasons, principally where the speaker does not want
to specify an agent.   As we noted in section 2.7.1.,
the passive is favoured where the entity that would
be subject in the active is a poor candidate for
topic, e.g. where it is indefinite and inanimate: *My
dog got run over by a car.*

Examples such as: *Who took my knife?* *John took*
it, give the impression that the topic is determined
by the discourse context. However, the topic is not
always determined by the context. The language can
impose a topic. Consider a situation in which
Bolivia attacks Equador and how such an event would
be reported in a British newspaper. A likely formulation would be: *Bolivia attacked Equador* (or, in
'headlinese', *Bolivia attacks Equador*). Now if one
is asked which entity this sentence is about, one is
likely to say *Bolivia*. Note that no discourse context leads to the choice of Bolivia as topic nor any
considerations of empathy (assuming both these
countries are equally remote from British interests).
It is just that, all other things being equal, one
tends to use the active, which involves making the
agent of a transitive verb the subject, and the resulting sentence is then interpreted as being about its
subject.

We look on 'topic-ness' as being to some extent
a relative matter. The object position is also a
topic position but not the primary topic position.
Consider a narrative about a lost ring. At one point
we have the sequence: *Mary decided to go for a walk*
around the tip. *She began rummaging through some*
paper waste. *Suddenly she saw the ring.* *She picked*
it up. If one is asked which entity the last clause
is about, we suppose *she* would be the favourite answer because it is grammatical subject, but *it* has
claims to being topic. It is the topic of the larger discourse and it has been introduced in the previous clause.

Topics can appear as S or O but cannot be 'semantically embedded'; by this we mean they cannot occur
within a phrase marked by a preposition that has
semantic content. A whole prepositional phrase can
be made topic, usually by fronting – *In the garden*
there are conifers and deciduous trees – but not the
NP within a prepositional phrase. This of course
applies to the *by* phrase of a passive. The NP within the *by* phrase cannot be a topic and for this
reason we find it strange that ergative languages can
exist if we think of ergative-marked constituents as
being like passive agents. As we noted earlier (see,
for instance, the end of section 2.8.1.2.), 1 and 2,
and to a lesser extent third person pronouns, tend
not to be found in the *by* phrase of a passive, though
these topic-worthy participants can appear quite

happily in the S or O position.

(b)   *the topic in ergative languages*

As we pointed out in section 2.9.4.2., there is
good reason to believe that in an ergative construction the absolutive represents a grammaticalized
topic just as the nominative marks a grammaticalized
topic in an accusative language.   We feel that while
the absolutive represents a grammaticalized topic, an
ergative participant can be a topic as much as an
accusative one can in an accusative language.   We
could look on the absolutive as representing the
prime topic position and the ergative as marking the
secondary topic position.

A rough analogy with the ergative construction
can be found in Latin, where the dative was used to
express the agent with the perfect participle, gerund
or gerundive.   These were all passive forms but the
construction with the dative of agent seems not to
have involved *semantic* marking on the agent, at least
there was no preposition used.   Whatever may be said
on this score, it is noteworthy that 1 and 2 regularly appeared as dative of agent as in the following.

(2.107)   Omnia   mihi   perspecta   sunt

          all   me:to   examined   are

          'I've examined everything'

(2.108)   Mihi   dormiendum   est

          me:to   sleep:gerund   is

          'I have to sleep'

(2.109)   Tibi   haec   res   facienda   fuit

          you:to this   matter   do:gerundive   was

          'You ought to have done this'

The 1 and 2 forms in these sentences seem to be topical though not occupying the prime topical position,
the S position.   (2.108) involves an intransitive
verb; *mihi* is competing only with a meaningless
grammatical third person subject.   If anything is
topic in (2.108), it is *mihi*.[23]

Latin also had a 'normal' passive with the agent
marked by the preposition *a(b)* 'by' and appearing in
the ablative case (see (2.71)).   This passive was

normal in the sense that it could be used for various
tenses, aspects and moods and it was analogous to the
English passive in that the agent was marked by a preposition with semantic content. We have had difficulty in finding Latin informants, but our impression
is that the Latin passive was used in much the same
circumstances as the English passive is used.   In
particular, it seems that 1 and 2 tended not to be
found in the agent phrase of the passive. The
passive, whether in Latin or in English, is a poor
analogue for the ergative, however, in that the
passive agent is not at all topical; whereas, in our
opinion, the ergatively marked constituent of an ergative construction can be a topic as much as the accusative can in an accusative construction.   The ergative is not the prime topic position, it is the
secondary topic position.   The fact that 1 and 2 opt
out of the ergative system in some languages reflects
the fact that the ergative is not the prime topic
position but it does not mean that the ergative is
analogous to the agent of the passive.

Our feeling is that a participant can be a topic
whatever its relation in the clause provided there is
no clear semantic marker attached to the participant.
Participants marked by the nominative, ergative,
accusative or dative can be topical, but not participants bearing local or instrumental marking.

The matter of topicalization in ergative languages is not dealt with extensively in the literature.
We present a few references from recent works.[24]

Kibrik 1979 touches on the question briefly.
He presents the following examples from Archi.   Example (2.110) represents an ergative construction and
(2.111) the corresponding antipassive.   In (2.110)
the prefix b- marks the agreement of the gerund and
the 'auxiliary' (actually the grammatical verb) with
O.   In (2.111) the gerund agrees with O but the
auxiliary agrees with the derived S_i (d-).

(2.110)   buwa-mu   x̄₀alli b-ar-ši   b-i[25]

           mother-erg   bread   III-bake-gerund   III-aux

           'Mother is baking the bread'

(2.111)   buwa   x̄₀alli b-ar-ši   d-i

           mother   bread   III-bake-gerund II-aux

           'Mother is baking the bread'

Kibrik (1979:69) notes that (2.110) answers the
question 'What is mother baking?', while (2.111) answers the question 'What is mother doing?'.   This
would mean that in the context of these questions
x̄₀alli in (2.110) would be new information (the
comment) whereas in (2.111) x̄₀alli ar would be new.
In (2.111) buwa is S. and topic and would be topic in
English.   In (2.110) x̄₀alli is O and the prime topic,
though buwa-mu has claims to being topic too.   It is
not surprising that x̄₀alli represents new information
in (2.110) yet appears in the prime topic position.
Compare English: *Who took the knife?   John took it*,
where new information appears in the prime topic
position, admittedly with stress.

     Kalmár 1979 argues that in Eskimo (Baffin Island
Eskimo/Inuktitut) the ergative construction is used
when the patient is 'given' and the antipassive when
the patient is 'new'.   He presents, among others,
the following examples:

(2.112)   Joosi   quqiq-si-y-uq   tuttu-mik

           Joosi   shoot-?-monop-he   caribou-oblique

           'Joosi shot a Caribou'

(2.113)   Joosi-up   quqi-kkaniq-t-a-ŋa

           Joosi-erg   shoot-again-part-polyp-he:it

               tuttu

               caribou

           'Joosi shot the same caribou again'

Klokeid & Arima 1977 argue against an earlier version
of Kalmár's argument, pointing out that one can say
(2.114) using the ergative construction where the
patient is 'new'.

(2.114)   Inna   tuktu   ṭaku-gunna-piuk?

           that   caribou   see-can-it:you

           'Do you see that caribou?'

They envisage a scenario in which someone sees a caribou and asks his companion if he has seen it.   They
claim that the caribou is 'new', having just been
sighted.   However, in our view the caribou is
'given', that is given by the context of situation.
Other points raised by Klokeid & Arima suggest some

qualification of Kalmár's position may be required,
but what Kalmár says of Eskimo seems to be approximately true of some other ergative languages as well.
Properties of the patient determine the choice between the ergative and antipassive constructions.   In
particular an indefinite patient tends not to be
expressed in the absolutive, just as indefinite
agents tend to be unfavoured as subject in some accusative languages or prohibited altogether from
appearing in that position.

    Creider (1979:15) claims that in Eskimo there is
a strong association between absolutive and topicality
and between ergative and focus.   He gives the following questions and answers (Rankin Inlet dialect):

(2.115)   Inuk   suna-mik   tautuk-pa?

          man   what-obl   look:at-interr:he

          'What is the man looking at?'

(2.116)   Inuk   tuktu-mik   tautuk-puq

          man   caribou-obl look:at-indic:he

          'The man is looking at a caribou'

(2.117)   Kia   tuktu   tautuk-pauk?

          who:erg   caribou   look:at-interr:he:it

          'Who is looking at the caribou?'

(2.118)   Inu-up   tuktu   tautuk-paa

          man-erg   caribou   look:at-indic:he:it

          'A man is looking at the caribou'

These examples support the contention that the absolutive is a topic position inasmuch as the indefinite
patient, a poor contender for topic, is put in an
oblique case (as in Kalmár's example above).   They
are misleading, however, in that they suggest the
choice of construction might be determined by whether
the agent is given, as in (2.116), or new, as in
(2.118).   On the basis of other Eskimo sources, we
feel the ergative construction would have been used
in (2.116) if the patient had been definite.   This
would mean that a topic would appear in the ergative,
but this is no more strange than a topic appearing in
the accusative in English (as in: *Who took the baby?
John took her*).

In Dyirbal the antipassive is used to maintain a discourse topic as a surface absolutive in complex sentences and in compound sentences or in a 'paragraph' of related sentences (the difference between the two not always being clear).[26] Consider, for instance, the first text in Dixon 1972. It begins like this:

> Ngagangunu came from somewhere on the other side of the sea, from the east; and *followed* the fresh water; he went uphill right up here to the forest country; to settle there up river at Dunganbara. He built a camp (i.e. a mia-mia) there.

The antipassive is used for the italicized transitive verb *followed*, which means the topic is in the absolutive down to *Dunganbara*. However, the following sentence in the text is not in the antipassive. What we would consider to be the first choice for topic is in the ergative.

(2.119)   balay   baŋgul   midᶌa   gadan

            there   that-erg   camp   build

            'He built a camp there'

This might seem surprising. After all 'he' is the discourse topic and midᶌa 'camp' is indefinite. However, this is no more strange than the appearance of an indefinite agent as S in English even when the discourse topic is present. Consider the last sentence of the following sequence: *I opened the door. I stood for a moment listening. Then I went up the stairs slowly. I reached the first landing. Suddenly a man grabbed me and tried to throw me over the balustrade.*

In almost all accusative languages S precedes O. On this basis one might expect O to precede A in ergative languages. This assumes that S precedes O in accusative languages *because* S is the prime topic (see discussion in section 3.3). Interestingly enough, A usually precedes O in ergative languages, which perhaps could be taken as support for the position that A is a topical position even if not the prime topical position.[27] However, in Dyirbal O does tend to precede A. Moreover, 1 and 2 operate in an accusative system and if A is 1 or 2 it tends to precede O (Dixon 1972:291 and remarks quoted in Pullum 1977:261).

We have included these notes on topicalization in ergative languages because we feel that there has been a tendency to see ergative constructions as passive-like.   We also feel there has been a tendency to think that the topic is determined solely by the discourse context.   We want to point out that accusative languages take the agent of a transitive verb to be the normal filler of the topic position but that this is not universal, however natural it might seem to English speakers.   Ergative languages take the patient to be the normal filler of the topic position.   If the fact that Bolivia has attacked Equador is reported in the Dyirbal Times or the Aleut Advertiser, then Bolivia will bear an ergative marker. And if a speaker of one of these ergative languages is then asked which entity a sentence of the form *Bolivia-erg Equador attacked* is about, we presume he would be likely to say Equador.

Finally we wish to point out again that languages of the Philippines type and indeed some other Austronesian languages are reported as favouring the patient for the topic position.[28] Note that in Tagalog whichever of A or O is not marked for topic is marked by the same form, viz. *ng*, which does not appear to have specific semantic content and presumably can mark a secondary topic position.

2.10   Summary

In this chapter we set out to examine agent/patient case marking as a prelude to comparing the use of case marking and word order as alternative strategies in chapter three.   *A priori* we might have expected to find A or O marking across the board in any language that relied on case marking to distinguish agent and patient.   In fact we found that A marking sometimes did not cover 1 and 2 (and sometimes third person pronouns) while O marking usually did not cover the whole spectrum of participants either, but tended to be used for pronouns only, or pronouns and human and/or definite nouns.

We reviewed various attempts at explaining the incomplete spread of A and O marking across the spectrum.   Silverstein saw the distribution as reflecting the propensity of a participant to be agent or patient, 'good' agents tended to lack A marking, 'good' patients tended to lack O marking.   In section 2.8.1.1., we suggested that the distribution of

A and O marking seemed to be related to topic-worthiness.   In sections 2.9.2., 2.9.3. and 2.9.4., we
suggested that the gross distribution of marking in
this area also reflected topicality.   In accusative
languages the nominative, typically unmarked, is the
prime topic position.   In ergative languages the
absolutive, almost always unmarked, is the prime
topic position.   The accusative and ergative mark
secondary topic positions.   In sections 2.8.2. and
2.8.3., we discribed two views of the distribution of
A and O marking.   Under the *discriminatory* view,
case marking is distributed according to the need to
distinguish A from O.   According to the *characterizing* view, case marking reflects the characteristics
of participants.   A definite O is more O-like than
an indefinite one, and if O marking is restricted it
will appear on the definite O not the indefinite O.
These two views are not diametrically opposed.   In
some languages case marking is optional, being used
only where confusion would arise if it were omitted.
This is true of Hua, for instance (Haiman 1979),
where the ergative marker is used only to avoid confusion.   Such instances clearly support the *discriminatory* view.   On the other hand the failure of an
indefinite O to take O marking seems to be more
satisfactorily explained in terms of its being less
O-like than a definite O.   Suppose the comparison is
between *John washes the dishes* and *John washes dishes*.
It makes no sense to say that accusative marking is
used in language X for *the dishes* but not for *dishes*
because there is greater chance of confusion between
the dishes and A than between *dishes* and A.   On the
other hand *John washes dishes* is clearly intransitive-
like from a semantic point of view, expressing a
characteristic of *John* rather than an activity initi-
ated by *John* and impinging on some *dishes*.   In fact
an indefinite O like this can be incorporated in the
verb: *John dish-washes*.   Such instances seem to
support the *characterizing view*.

NOTES

[1]Under 'obligatory participant' we include those represented in the verb.   For example, the Latin verb form *eo* means 'I go', *I* being represented by the verb inflection.

[2]Stressable pronouns are referred to in the literature by various terms: free pronouns, free-standing pronouns, self-standing pronouns, cardinal pronouns.

[3]French does exhibit cross-reference within the clause in questions with inversion, though these patterns are rather bookish.

A quelle heure le train arrive-t-il?

When does the train arrive?

[4]In the Muskogean language, Choctaw (Heath 1977), the bound pronouns exhibit a three-way distinction. There is an agent form and a patient form and a bene-ficiary/indirect object form.   Agent and patient are marked consistently with transitive and intransitive verbs as in active languages but some stative intran-sitive verbs take the beneficiary or experiencer form, e.g. 'feel good' (the same verb with the pat-ient bound pronoun means 'be good'), 'be lazy', 'be clever or capable'.   Free nominals show a nominative/ oblique distinction.   Details aside, S_i and A are in the nominative and other syntactic or semantic rela-tions are marked by the oblique.

[5]We have given the hierarchy in the form found in Gleason but it is not certain that 1 should pre-cede 2.   Combinations involving 1 and 2 are distin-guished by it- (for 1-2) and ϕ (for 2-1), but it is not clear that it- should be linked with a- and ϕ with ik-.

1-2	it in	2-1	in
1p-2	it inan	2-1p	inan

[6]See also Milner 1973 on Samoan.

[7]As in Gregerson 1977, appendix.

[8]The presence of ergative marking does not necessarily tell us anything about the syntax of a language. An ergative marker could be borrowed into a language like English. The Australian language Ngandi appears to have borrowed an ergative marker from its neighbour Ritharngu though it may have been an ergative language in its own right at an earlier stage of its history (Heath 1978a). See also section 3.3.1.

[9]For Bandjalang see Crowley 1978, for Archi see Kibrik 1979.

[10]Postal 1977 uses the term *antipassive* to cover detransitivized constructions in any language including accusative languages.

[11]By 'grammatical verb' we mean the verb that shows marking for tense, aspect, etc. We avoid the term *auxiliary* as there is sometimes disagreement about whether verbs of a small class showing marking for tense, etc. are main verbs (with an open class of dependent verbs) or auxiliaries to an open class of main verbs.

[12]In languages that have bound form pronouns for A and O occurring adjacent to one another, the forms for 1 > 2 and 2 > 1 are normally not made up of a 1 form and a 2 form, but more often than not are portmanteaus consisting either of a form of unknown provenience or of a form for 1 only or for 2 only. For example, in Hixkaryana (Derbyshire 1979) the 1 form is kɨ- and the 2 form mɨ-. The form for 1 > 2 is kɨ- and the form for 2 > 1 is mɨ-. In some languages, particularly the Algonquian languages, the 2 form takes precedence over 1 for representation (and both 2 and 1 take precedence over 3). See for example Bloomfield 1946, Wolfart 1973. The cases known to us of 2 appearing to take precedence over 1 are of this type. See Zwicky 1977 for examples and references.

[13]In fact we have found at least 100 languages that conform to it against only a handful that exhibit minor exceptions. This is a high percentage of success indeed. One exception occurs in Washo, as we noted in section 2.5.2., where accusative marking occurs on the free form for 3 singular but not on 1 and 2. Another occurs in Georgian where the accusa-

tive-genitive marker occurs with nouns but not with
free pronouns in the non-past tenses.   Georgian has
bound pronoun forms as well since the free forms are
used only for emphasis, co-ordination with nouns, and
so on.   It could be they stand outside the sentence
proper like the disjunctive pronouns in French, when
representing S$_i$, A and O, though this is not made
clear in the sources (e.g. Vogt 1971:38-9).

[14]The corpus consisted of the following:

Plays

Paddy Chayefsky: Printer's Measure

Tyrone Guthrie: Squirrel's Cage (both plays in
                      On the Air ed. P. Smith. Angus
                      and Robertson. 1959)

David Carr and David Stringer: Touch Wood (in
                      Plays for Radio and Television,
                      ed. by N. Samuel. Longmans 1959)

Autobiography/First Person Narrative

Daniel Defoe: Robinson Crusoe (first three
                      chapters)

Douglas Hyde: I believed (first five chapters)
                      (Heinemann 1950)

Australian Aboriginal Texts

Pitjantjatjara   (first four texts in Glass &
                      Hackett 1970)

Gunwinggu   (first two texts in Oates 1964)

Tiwi   (first two texts in Osborne
                      1974)

Malak-Malak   (first two texts in Birk 1976)

Ngandi   (first two texts in Heath 1978b)

Ritharngu   (first sixteen texts in Heath
                      1980a)

Djaru   (all texts in Tsunoda 1978)

Yidin[y]   (all texts in Dixon 1977)

Kalkatungu   (all texts in Blake 1979c)

[15]As Peter Carroll has reminded us, these glosses
are dubious from the synchronic point of view, though
doubtless accurate etymologically.   See also Carroll

1976b and Blake 1977:32-4.

[16]If we compare *He sent the book to Mary* and *He sent the book to London*, we find that *Mary* can be expressed as O but not *London* (unless it is thought of as people in London). We could see the different treatment as evidence for two separate semantic roles, say *recipient* and *locative* (or more specifically *allative* or *goal of motion*). On the other hand we could see *Mary* and *London* as having the same role but treated differently because one is animate and the other not. See examples (3.41) to (3.44).

[17]The quotation is from p.10 of the precirculated version, dated February 1976.

[18]Some may find this example unconvincing because of the distance between *us* and the position of the expected subject in the second clause. The point can be maintained, however, on the basis of examples such as *the kynge lyked and loued this lady wel* (Malory, quoted in Lightfoot 1979:235) where *lyked* takes an oblique marked subject yet is conjoined with *loued* which would take an unmarked subject. *Lyke* was in Old English an impersonal verb. In Middle English it was reinterpreted as a personal verb but for some time retained an oblique-marked subject.

[19]Although we endorse Wierzbicka's general views, we are not suggesting that she necessarily subscribes to this view of ergative marking in a syntactically accusative language.

[20]We use *extraposed* here as a cover term for *preposed* and *postposed* and the reference is to elements that are literally placed outside a sentence, set off by an intonation break as in,

(a)   John, he's a winner

(b)   In Africa, people live in huts

In transformational terminology, the term *dislocation* (left and right dislocation) is used for the phenomenon illustrated in (a) where *John* is represented within the clause proper by a pronoun, here a *resumptive* pronoun. In transformational circles the term *extraposition* is used to refer to elements that have been moved from positions they held in deep or intermediate structure as with the *that*-clause in *It sur-*

prised me that Troy won, where, under one analysis, the *that*-clause is held to be extraposed from the subject position with a dummy *it* left in its place. The term *dislocation* is an unfortunate one.   It seems to imply an adverse value judgement or at least a deviation from some more normal pattern.   However, the 'dislocated' pattern is the normal pattern in numerous languages.

[21] See also Perlmutter 1978.

[22] At least this is the only general rule. There is a lexical rule that allows the derivation of intransitive verbs as in *The book reads well*, but it is severely circumscribed.   New derivations are possible as in *Jones voted well* meaning not 'Jones cast his vote with skill' but that he 'polled well'.

[23] Example (2.108) occurs at least twice in Cicero.   (2.107) and (2.109) are modelled on examples found in the classical authors.

[24] We would consider the oblique pronouns to be topical in expressions such as Le piace Roma? (Italian: Do you like Rome? Lit. You: to it: pleases Rome) and Le gusta Madrid?   (analogous expression in Spanish).

[25] This example appeared previously as (2.74). III is the neuter class marker and II the feminine class marker.

[26] See (2.105) for an example of the same kind of thing in a subordinate clause in Kalkatungu.

[27] All discussion of ergative languages is complicated by the fact that a language with ergative case marking and/or cross-referencing may be syntactically ergative or only superficially ergative. The majority view is that most ergative languages are only superficially ergative and there is little reason to expect them to have O regularly before A. And there is the further complication that a topic does not necessarily precede its comment.   See sections 3.3 and 3.4 of the following chapter for further discussion.

[28] See Hopper 1979 for an interesting discussion of classical Malay.

CHAPTER 3

WORD   ORDER

3.0   Introduction

Ever since the publication of Greenberg's paper
'Some universals of grammar with particular reference
to the order of meaningful elements' there has been a
strong interest in classifying languages according to
the relative order of the subject, object and verb.
Greenberg demonstrated that this was a significant
parameter to use since not all the possible orders
were equally favoured and more importantly other properties of morpho-syntax correlated with the order of
S, O and V.   In particular he showed that there was a
relationship between case marking and word order
(universal 41).

In this chapter we are concerned with the methodological problems associated with establishing the
basic word order used for, subject, object and verb
(and to a lesser extent, indirect object), the relative frequency of the possible basic word orders, factors determining word order, and the relationship between case marking, agreement and word order.

The notion of the word order type and changes in
basic word order are discussed in chapter six.

3.1   Methodological Problems

3.1.1.   Subject

Most of the work done on basic word order typology deals in the grammatical relations subject and
object.   As we pointed out in section 2.1 the subject in European languages embraces S$_i$ and A and is
manifested by such features as case marking, agreement and word order as well as by the part it plays in
some syntactic relationships.   As we also pointed out,

121

in some languages S_i and O are similarly identified,
while in others there is scant evidence for the identification of either A or O exclusively with S_i.

Greenberg does not state explicitly how he determined the subject in various languages. He does
state (1963:74) that he assumes all languages have
'subject-predicate constructions' and he indicates
that if formal criteria equate certain phenomena
across languages, one accepts the equation only between entities that are semantically comparable. We
assume from this that Greenberg would not accept a
formally defined subject that embraced S_i and A in an
accusative language and S_i and O in an ergative language. We assume he takes S_i/A to be the subject
since he lists Loritja as SOV. 'Loritja' is a term
used by the Aranda of central Australia for the
Kukatja who speak an ergative language in which the
predominant word order is agent-patient-verb.

Pullum 1977 discusses word order universals in
terms of S, O and V and for him S is S_i/A. He
adopts a Relational Grammar framework in which S_i/A
is initial or underlying subject in all languages.

Ultan 1978 classifies 79 languages in terms of
the order of S, O and V. He does not discuss the
criteria used to establish S but from his classification of ergative languages like Tongan and Western
Desert (Australian) we can see that S is equated with
S_i/A.

Steele (1978:590) classifies 63 languages in
terms of SVO, SOV, etc. She states that for languages with which she was familiar, she took subject
and object to 'correspond roughly to English'. With
unfamiliar languages she took the decision of the
linguist responsible for the description she used.
She claims that 'Keenan's work has made clear that,
although *subject* is a term linguists use regularly
and with confidence, a precise characterization of
the notion eludes us'. The fact that linguists use
the term regularly and with confidence seems to us to
reflect two facts. One is that S_i and A are identified exclusively in the vast majority of languages.
The other is that many linguists simply base their
notion of subject on translation equivalence. If
they assign the notion of subject with confidence, it
is often only because they have not thought of using
formal criteria.

One could in theory compare word order across

languages in terms of a formally defined subject.
The properties that identify subjects seem to be topic-based and one might see word order in terms of
topic/comment.   This would seem satisfactory if the
formally defined subject behaved consistently (e.g.
always occurred first in the clause) irrespective of
whether subject embraced S_i/A, S_i/O or made no exclusive identification of any participant in a transitive
clause with S_i, as is the case in Philippines languages.   If semantically different subjects behaved differently according to their semantic type, then one
could simply treat various types of subject separately.
In practice no one seems to have compared word orders
in terms of a formally defined subject.

     If one compares basic word orders in terms of a
semantically determined subject (S_i/A), as is usually
the case, then one could justify the procedure if S_i/
A behaves consistently irrespective of formal criteria.   If S_i/A tends to behave differently in ergative
languages from the way it does in accusative languages, then one could treat the ergative A separately.
In other words whether one starts out with a formally
defined subject or a semantically defined one, one
will finish up with the same result providing one
checks variation in the 'formal survey' against semantics and variation in the 'semantic survey' against
'formal differences'.

     Ergative languages and other types in which S_i/A
are not formally identified make up only a small proportion of the world's languages, so no matter how
they are treated they will not affect generalizations
about word order to any great degree.   One can of
course take these minority types and investigate word
order in them.   Interestingly enough it turns out
that in practically every ergative language A precedes
O.   All the surveys of word order have shown that the
semantically defined subject precedes the object in
almost all languages (see section 3.2).   This means
that ergative languages will not disturb a sample based on a semantically determined (S_i/A) subject and
will appear to justify the use of an S_i/A subject.
However, it could be that ergative languages in fact
support the generalization that A precedes O, rather
than supporting the notion that S regularly precedes O.

3.1.2.   Object

     Most linguists seem to assume without question
that all languages have objects (but see Dik 1978:177,

Blake, to appear).   The issue involved here is
simply this.   If the entity that looks like an object
is always semantically patient, then it should be
treated as a semantic entity along with instrument,
location, etc.   If one defines patient very broadly
as the entity affected, effected, moved etc., it
might be possible to obviate the need for object in a
large number of languages (see Starosta's definition
of patient quoted in section 2.9.4.1.).

Dik (1978:177) raises the possibility of explaining away apparent exceptions to the generalization
that S always precedes O by reinterpreting O in some
languages as patient.   Although we believe that all
claims about the existence of grammatical relations
should be re-examined to see if in fact there are only
semantic relations involved, we do not see that a distinction between a semantic patient and a syntactic O
is of any importance in studies of word order.

3.1.3.   Indirect Object

English has the following two constructions to
express the same propositional content.

(3.1)   John gave a bottle of Benedictine to the
         Alderman

(3.2)   John gave the Alderman a bottle of Benedictine

If only the first construction existed, the label
'indirect object' would not be needed; *to the Alderman* is simply a prepositional phrase like any other.
In the second construction, however, the phrase *the
Alderman* exhibits two object properties but contrasts
syntagmatically with the patient *a bottle of Benedictine*.   The two properties are: (a) a position following the verb without any preposition preceding,
and (b) correspondence with the subject of a passive
equivalent, as in (3.3).   *The Alderman* rightly deserves a special label to distinguish it from the
normal type of direct object, and 'indirect object' is
an accepted label.   However, many linguists use the
term semantically and apply it to the translational
equivalents of *the Alderman* in (3.2) irrespective of
whether the phrase in question is grammatically parallel to *the Alderman* in (3.2) or whether it parallels
to the Alderman in (3.1).   Curiously enough they do
not apply the label of indirect object to the grammatical equivalents of *the Alderman* in (3.3).

(3.3)   The Alderman was given a bottle of Benedictine
         by John

This semantic use of the term 'indirect object' is
misleading and obscures generalizations that can be
made about the position of the (true) indirect object
relative to O.

3.1.4.   Variant Word Orders

    Where there is variation in word order, we can
attempt to determine whether one order is basic.
English exhibits a variety of word orders but no one
doubts that SVO is the basic or unmarked one.   A
pattern such as the following is highly marked:

(3.4)   The proposals contained in section one of the
         bill we support; those in sections two
         and three and those in the appendix to
         section four we cannot support in any
         shape or form whatsoever

This OSV pattern can be used to topicalize the object
or to focus it (see also section 3.3.1.).

    When we use the term 'basic word order' we mean
the order that obtains in stylistically-neutral,
independent, indicative clauses with full noun phrase
participants for S_i or for A and O. We have sought
to determine the basic word order from sentences with
definite nuclear participants since some languages do
not allow an indefinite S and others treat an indefinite O as part of the verb (see for example the
Kusaiean examples in section 3.3.2.).

    English is of course easy to classify as SVO.
However, a problem arises when the principle of ar-
ranging the words in a sentence is allowed to be more
responsive to the demands of topicalization and focus
than is the case in modern English.   In Old English
there appears to have been much more freedom in word
order.   In independent clauses two orders predominate, SVO and to a lesser extent VSO, as illustrated
in (3.5) and (3.6) respectively:

(3.5)   Se cyning   besæt   hie   on   ðære ceastre

         the king   beset   them   in   the   camp

         'The king besieged them in the camp'

(3.6)   Þa   metton hie micelne sciphere
         then met   they great   ship:army
         wicenga
         vikings:gen plur
         'Then met they a great viking navy'

The order OVS is also found:

(3.7)   Þa   æfter feawum dagum eall his þing
         then after few   days   all   his thing
         gegaderode se   gingra   sunu   ond
         gathered   the younger son   and
         ferde   wræclice on   feorlen
         travelled abroad   into distant
         rice
         kingdom
         'Then after a few days the younger son
         gathered together all he had and went
         off to a distant land'

The example is a translation of the Vulgate (Luke XV,
13) but the pattern is not one confined to translated
texts nor is it an imitation of the original in this
instance: *Et non post multos dies, congregatis omni-
bus, adolescentior filius peregre profectus est in
regionem longinquam* (lit. And not after many days,
having been gathered everything, younger son abroad
set out into a region distant).   Following a suggestion of Dik's (1978) we considered the possibility
that if the basic order were taken to be VSO then the
SVO and OVS orders could be interpreted as patterns
that involve placing a constituent that is topic or
focus to the left.   In (3.5) we could say that *se
cyning* is placed before the verb since it is topic.
In (3.6) we could say that the connective þa is in
focus, so the basic VSO pattern remains unaffected.
This pattern still survives in certain styles at least
with intransitive verbs (mostly verbs of motion) with
stressed subjects, e.g. *Away ran the rabbit.*   This
main clause þa contrasts with the subordinating þa
which not being focused does not impede the placing
of S before V.   Consider the following:

(3.8)   þa   ic geseah þa   halgan Godes
        then   I saw   the   holy   God's

           gerynu   þa   wearp ic me sylfe
        mysteries   then threw   I me self

           forð   on   þa   flor
        forth   on   the   floor

        'When I saw the holy mysteries of God, then
         I threw myself down on the floor'

In (3.7) we would have to assume that O is focused at
least relative to 'the younger son'.   This is to be
expected as the younger son is the topic and 'given'
relative to the new 'eall his þing'.   The reason the
topic is spelled out is simply that the preceding
sentence was 'He gave him his share of the inheritance' where the subject 'he' refers to the father.
If 'se gingra sunu' had not been spelled out in the
verse we have quoted, it might have been thought the
father was the subject.

     Dik claims that the first position in the clause
proper is one that can be used for topic or focus.
He is able to explain the word order patterns of independent clauses in Dutch and German quite neatly in
terms of this special position and a basic VSO order.
In these languages only one item can normally precede
the verb of an independent clause.   In the following
German examples we have an adverb preceding the verb
in (3.9) and the subject preceding the verb in (3.10).

(3.9)   Heute trinke ich einen leichten frischen
        today drink   I   a   light   fresh

           Wein
        wine

        'Today I'm drinking a light, fresh wine'

(3.10) Ich möchte gerne einen Weisswein
         I   want   gladly a   white:wine

        'I'd like a white wine'

Heute can be interpreted as an adverb in focus and
ich in (3.10) is the topic filling the first position.
Verb-first patterns occur in imperatives and interrogatives and these can be interpreted as having a

focused verb in the first position,

(3.11)   Haben   Sie   ein   Einzelzimmer

         have   you   a   single:room

         'Do you have a single room?'

Old English cannot be handled quite so neatly
since a number of sentences have more than one constituent in front of the verb, as in (3.7).   In fact
the order shown in (3.6) is not obligatory.   It is
very common with þa, but an adverb may be followed by
S or by V, or indeed by O as in (3.7).

(3.12)   Her   cuom   se   here   to   Readingum (VS)

         here   came   the   army   to   Reading

         'In this year the (Danish) army came to
             Reading'

(3.13)   Her   hæþne   men   ærest   on   Sceapige

         here   heathen   men   first   in   Sheppey

         ofer   winter   sætun (SXV)

         over   winter   sat

         'In this year the heathen wintered in
             Sheppey for the first time'

Dik does not make it clear whether some patterns
could be explained by ascribing some initial adverbs
to a preposed position.   This would be possible in
(3.7).   Presumably þa and æfter feawum dagum are set
off from the construction proper by intonation
breaks.   However, it is not worth pursuing this line.
There would be no principled way of distinguishing
between, say, her in (3.12) and her in (3.13), and
many features of word order, such as the position of
the verb in (3.13) relative to the adverbial phrases,
would remain unexplained.

Old English is a language that exhibits a good
deal of freedom of word order and a tendency for
AdvVS patterns.   The order used for a stylistically
unmarked sentence such as John saw Mary is almost
certainly SVO.   We would classify Old English as
SVO/Free.[1]

The order used for a stylistically unmarked version of John saw Mary in German would be SVO too, but
to simply call German an SVO language would disguise

the verb-second nature of its word order.   In Table 1
we list German as V2/Free and in the statistics in
section 3.2 we classify it under 'other'.[2]

Old English, Dutch and German have an SOV order
in subordinate clauses. We simply accept that the
word order rules for subordinate clauses are different
from those operating in main clauses. We do not see
any reason why a language must have one basic order
for all types of clause. Transformationalists are
led to look for a single underlying word order by the
nature of their theory. It requires an order in base
structures. This is an artifact of the theory. To
establish a single underlying word order for a language like German would demand transformations largely
unmotivated beyond the requirements of the theory.

In some Australian languages there is a good deal
of freedom of order in main clauses but subordinate
clauses are verb-final, probably SOV, but it is often
hard to find subordinate clauses with full NPs for
both S and O. In a situation like this there is no
conflict between the order found in main clauses and
that found in subordinate clauses. It is just that
topicalization and focusing affect main clauses but
hardly affect subordinate ones. In such languages we
would expect the basic order in main clauses to be SOV.
This seems to be the situation in Walbiri (Hale 1967)
and Kalkatungu (Blake 1979c).

3.1.5.   Absence of Evidence for Order

One particular problem that is largely ignored in
the literature is the difficulty of determining the
word order in languages in which S_i, A and O are all
represented in the verb or by clitics elsewhere in the
clause (but see Pullum 1977:267).   In languages like
this it is often difficult to find sentences with full
NPs for both A and O. The problem is particularly
acute if the language tends to incorporate a noun O in
the verb, since this further reduces the possibility
of finding a transitive clause with a full NP for both
A and O.

One would assume that the relevant sentence
patterns can occur in such languages, albeit not so
frequently as in other languages, but many linguists
seem to have managed to write grammars of these languages without including even one example of a clause
with NPs for A and O. Some grammars of these languages contain texts, and often a perusal of the text

material reveals few of the required sentence patterns
or none at all.   The texts presumably reflect performance.   We assume the full NP sentences can occur,
but we do not assume they necessarily occur with any
particular order.

     A good example of the problem occurs with Oates'
grammar of Gunwinggu.   Gunwinggu is a northern Australian language in which cross-referencing bound pronouns are prefixed to the verb and inanimate noun
objects incorporated into the verb (see also section
2.7.3.).   The following extended example is fairly
typical of Gunwinggu narrative (Oates 1964:94).   The
tense is indicated by the allomorphs of the S/O prefixes (in the third person) and also by suffixes, and
third person singular O is zero.   These factors are
not taken account of in the glosses, however.

(3.14)   Galug malaywi   biri-wam biri-gug-naŋ
           then   next:day   they-go   they-body-see
           'Then next day they went and saw (his) body

                dja namaṇde nuŋan   gu-ṛurg
                and devil   himself   loc:neuter-cave
                and the devil himself in (his) cave

                geyo?geyoyi wayyi?wayyini. Galug
                sleeping   playing   then
                sleeping (and) playing (sic).   Then

                biri-ṛurg-gendabeŋ   biri-yameŋ
                they-cave-surround   they-spear
                the men surrounded him in the cave and

                biri-weyn bininj.   Galug
                they-lot   man   then
                speared him.   Then

                biri-gug-gi:nyen gu-nag   galug
                they-body-burn   loc:neuter-fire   then
                they burnt (his) body in a fire;   then

                namegbe bininj biri-gug-mey
                that   man   they-body-take
                the body of that man they took and

biri-gug-dudji

they-body-bury

buried'

The sentences in this extract seem to be neutral in the sense that there is no special emphasis except for *namegbe bininj* in the final sentence, which is in focus, being contrasted with the devil.

Steele includes this language in her survey, and classifies it as SOV (1978:590, 607), though she spells it 'Gunwingju' (a revised phonemic spelling appears in Carroll 1976a - Gunwinjgu /gunwiŋgu/).[3] Oates (1964:75-6) gives the basic word order as 'usually SOV', but Steele was unable to find a single SOV sentence in the 23 pages of text material (we found one (p.96) but that is neither here nor there). There are few sentences in the texts with both free form S and a free form O. We found the following patterns occurred in the texts with the following frequencies (Q = direct speech quotation). We did not count sentences with incorporated objects.

S_iV	25
VS_i	1
SVO	5
VO	30
SOV	1
OV	32
SV	12
SVQ	12
VQ	9

Under these circumstances it is obviously difficult to ascertain what the basic word order is. Peter Carroll, who worked on the language for several years, has informed us that the basic order is SVO.[4]

3.2   Statistics on Basic Word Order

A number of linguists have taken samples of the world's languages and classified them in terms of the relative order of S, O and V. Recent examples include Greenberg, who produced statistics on 30 languages and data on many more, Ultan who sampled 79

languages (1969, 1978), Steele who took 63 languages
(1978), and Ruhlen who covered hundreds of languages
in his useful booklet 'A guide to the languages of
the world' (1975).   We considered taking the work of
these scholars as given and proceeding from there but
we found we were unable to do so for several reasons.
In the first place we were unable to determine how
Ultan and Ruhlen determined S and hesitant to accept
Steele's method of determining S (see comments above
in section 3.1.1.).   Secondly, we were alarmed by the
fact that these sources could not agree on the basic
word order in several languages.   Consider for
example the following discrepancies.

	Ruhlen	Ultan	Steele	Greenberg
Hungarian	SVO	SOV	-	SOV
Tagalog	VSO	VOS	VOS	VSO[5]
Diola-Fogny	-	VSO	SVO	-
Tongan	-	VSO	VOS	VSO

Thirdly, we were interested to investigate any possible correlation between word order, agreement and
case marking and these sources did not provide the
relevant information (Steele 1978 being a partial
exception).

We have prepared a sample of 100 languages
(Table 1) spread fairly evenly across genetic and typological groupings.   For each language we have given
some indication of the family to which it belongs and
in many cases some indication of the branch or sub-
group to which it belongs.   The headings in block
capitals refer to groupings larger than well established families.   These group labels are included for
bibliographic convenience and we have not concerned
ourselves with the problems of genetic and typological
classification involved in establishing these groupings.

The four columns to the right of each entry indicate the following categories:

1.   Basic word order (Order)

2.   Case marking system for nouns (N)

3.   Case marking for stressed pronouns (Pr)

4.   System of agreement (Agr)

Where our source or sources indicated that there was a basic or unmarked pattern of word order, we have accepted that.   If the source also indicated that there was a good deal of freedom in word order, we have given designations such as SOV/Fr.   We see freedom as a matter of degree and we were uncertain in many cases whether to add the designation 'Fr'. Some sources are rather ready to state a basic word order pattern and play down the variation, while other sources highlight variation.   A few sources simply declared that there was no basic order and we were happy to accept this.   In general we preferred to ascribe the label 'free' rather than assign a dubious label.

We have taken S to be S_i/A for the purposes of the table and the statistics[1] that follow.   Where A is not the unmarked choice for grammatical subject, this is indicated in the notes, or can be gleaned from the fact that erg(ative) appears in the N(oun) column.

Case marking on nouns is listed as acc(usative) or erg(ative) with footnotes on systems that could not be classified as either without some qualification.   We have allotted the labels acc. and erg. for optional marking and we have allotted acc. to a language that employs accusative marking only for some subclass or subclasses of noun.   The '?' in the stressed pronoun column indicates that our source did not make it clear whether the free pronouns took accusative marking.   It can be assumed with a fair degree of confidence that, if some nouns exhibit accusative marking *and* if the free pronouns are integrated into the clause, they will take accusative marking (see section 2.8.1.).

The agreement column (Agr) refers to any system of person or person/number/class agreement with any of S_i, A and O.   Included here are any unstressable pronouns since these are always potentially cross-referencing if only with preposed or postposed stressable forms (see section 2.2 for clarification and exemplification of the terminology).

Table 1

Word Order and Case Marking

Indo-European

		Order	N	Pr	Agr
1. Germanic:	English	SVO	–	acc	–
2.	German	V2[a]	acc	acc	acc
3. Romance:	French	SVO	–	–	acc
4. Celtic:	Irish	VSO	–	acc	acc
5. Baltic:	Lithuanian	SVO	acc	acc	acc
6. Slavonic:	Polish	SVO	acc	acc	acc
7. Hellenic:	Greek (classical)	SOV/SVO[b]	acc	acc	acc
8. Iranian:	Baluchi	SOV	acc	acc	acc
9. Indic:	Punjabi	SOV/Fr	acc[c]	acc	acc
10. Anatolian:	Hittite	SOV	acc	acc	acc

	Order	N	Pr	Agr
AFRO-ASIATIC (11-16)				
Semitic				
11. Northern: Hebrew (modern)	SVO^d	acc	acc	acc
12. Southern: Amharic	SOV	acc	acc	acc
13. Arabic (Iraqi)	SVO	–	–	acc
Cushitic				
14. Eastern: Galla	SOV	acc	acc	acc
15. Western: Welamo	SOV	acc	acc	acc
Chadic				
16. Hausa	SVO	–	acc	acc
NILO-SAHARAN (17-25)				
Saharan				
17. Kanuri	SOV	acc	acc	acc
Maban				
18. Maba	SOV	acc	?	acc

	Order	N	Pr	Agr
Fur				
19. Fur	SOV	acc	acc	acc
Chari-Nile				
20. Central Sudanic: Bagirmi	SVO	-	-	acc
21. Eastern Sudanic: Nubian	SOV	acc	acc	acc
22. Western Nilotic: Nuer	VSO	acc	?	acc
23. Maasai	VSO	acc	acc	acc
24. Eastern Nilotic: Bari	SVO	-	-	-
Koman				
25. Koma	SVO	-	-	acc
(isolate)				
26. Ibibio-Efik (Nigeria)	SVO	-	-	acc
CONGO-KORDOFANIAN (27-32)				
Niger-Congo				
27. West Atlantic: Fulani	SVO	-	-	acc
28. Kwa: Yoruba	SVO	-	-	acc

		Order	N	Pr	Agr
29.	Bantu: Swahili	SVO	–	–	acc
30.	Adamawa-Eastern: Nzakara	SVO	–	–	acc
	Kordofanian				
31.	Tumtum: Katcha	SVO	–	–	–
32.	Tagali: Tagoi	SOV	–	–	acc
	URAL-ALTAIC (33-37)				
	Uralic				
33.	Balto-Finnic: Finnish	SVO	acc	acc	acc
34.	Ugric: Hungarian	SVO/Fr	acc	acc	acc
	Altaic				
35.	Turkic: Uzbek	SOV	acc	acc	acc
36.	Turkish	SOV	acc	acc	acc
37.	Mongolian: Mongolian	SOV	acc	acc	–
	Korean				
38.	Korean	SOV	acc	acc	–

	Order	N	Pr	Agr
Japanese				
39. Japanese	SOV	acc	acc	-
CAUCASIAN (40-42)				
Southern				
40. Georgian	SVO	acc^e	$-^e$	acc
Northern				
41. Avar (northeast)	SOV	erg	erg	erg
42. Abkhaz (northwest)	SOV/FR	-	-	erg
(isolate)				
43. Basque	SOV/Fr	erg	erg	erg
SINO-TIBETAN (44-51)				
Sinitic				
44. Mandarin	SVO^f	-	-	-
Tibeto-Burman				
45. Tibetan: Tibetan	SOV	erg	erg	-

		Order	N	Pr	Agr
46.	Gurung	SOV	erg	erg	–
47. Burmese:	Burmese	SOV	acc	acc	–
Miao-Yao					
48.	Yao	SVO	–	–	–
Tai					
49.	Thai	SVO	–	–	–
50.	Shan	SVO	–	–	–
51.	Khamti	SOV	acc	acc	–
Austro-Asiatic					
52. Mon-Khmer:	Cambodian	SVO	–	–	–
53.	Khmu	SVO	–	–	–
54.	Khasi	SVO	acc	acc	acc
55.	Vietnamese	SVO	–	–	–
56. Munda:	Sora	SOV	acc	acc	acc
Austronesian					
57. Western:	Malagasy	VOS^g	acc	acc	–

		Order	N	Pr	Agr
58.	Indonesian	SVO	—	—	—
59.	Tagalog	V1/Fr[h]	*[h]	*[h]	—
60. Eastern:	Tongan (Polynesian)	VSO	erg	acc	—
61.	Ulithian (Micronesian)	SVO	—	—	acc
62.	Iai (Melanesian)	SVO	—	acc	acc
63.	Lenakel (Melanesian)	SVO	—	—	acc
64.	Houailou (Melanesian)	VOS	acc	acc	acc
Papuan					
65.	Fore	SOV/Fr	acc[i]	acc[i]	acc
66.	Enga	SOV	erg	erg	acc
67.	Siroi	SOV	acc[j]	acc[j]	acc
68.	Yessan-Mayo	SOV	—	—	—
Australian					
69. Pama-Nyungan:	Guugu-Yimidhirr	Free	erg	acc	—

		Order	N	Pr	Agr
70.	Dyirbal	Fr/OSV[k]	erg	1.2acc[k]	–
71.	Kalkatungu	SOV/Fr	erg	erg	acc
72.	Non-Pama-Nyungan:				
73.	Gunwinggu	SVO/Fr	–	–	acc
	Malak-Malak	SOV	acc[l]	–	acc
74.	Tiwi	SVO/Fr	–	–	acc
75.	Alawa	Free	erg	acc[m]	acc
Dravidian					
76.	Tamil	SOV	acc	acc	acc
77.	Telugu	SOV	acc	acc	acc
78.	Kannada	SOV	acc	acc	acc
Paleo-Siberian					
79.	Chukchee	SOV/SVO	erg	erg	acc/erg
Algonquian					
80.	Menomini	?[n]	–	–	inverse
81.	Wiyot (outlier)	free	–	–	acc

	Order	N	Pr	Agr
Siouan				
82. Dakota	SOV	–	–	active[o]
Caddoan				
83. Wichita	(S)OV(S)[p]	–	–	active[p]
Athapaskan				
84. Navajo	SOV/Fr	–	–	acc
Eskimo-Aleut				
85. Eskimo	SOV	erg	3erg[q]	erg
HOKAN (86–87)				
86. Washo	SOV	–	3acc	acc[r]
Yuman				
87. Mojave	SOV	acc[s]	acc	acc

PENUTIAN (88-91)

	Order	N	Pr	Agr
Sahaptin-Nez Perce				
88. Sahaptin	Free	3way[t] inverse	acc	acc
89. Nass-Gitksan	VSO[u]	–	–	–
Mayan				
90. Jacaltec (Kanjobalan)	VSO	–	–	erg
91. Quiche (Quichean)	VSO	–	–	erg
Uto-Aztecan				
92. Taracahitic: Yaqui	SOV	acc	acc	–
93. Takic: Luiseño	SVO/Fr	acc	acc	acc[v]
Oto-Manguean				
94. Zapotec	VSO	–	–	acc
(isolate)				
95. Tarascan	SVO/VSO	acc	acc	acc

	Order	N	Pr	Agr
Salishan				
96. Squamish	VSO	–	–	acc/erg^w
Carib				
97. Hixkaryana	OVS	–	–	acc^x
Tupian				
98. Guaraní	SVO/Fr	acc	acc	active
Quechua-Aymara				
99. Quechua	SOV/Fr	acc	acc	acc
Arawakan				
100. Piro	SOV	–	–	acc

Notes to the table

a. In German the verb comes second in independent clauses. SV(O) and Adverbial VS(O) are common patterns. OVS is possible. Dependent clauses are SOV).

b. Ancient Greek could be described as having free word order. SOV and SVO patterns predominate.

c. In the perfect there is an ergative pattern of case marking and agreement. This pattern of agreement is also found in some dialects of Baluchi, but not in the Rakshani dialect that we sampled.

d. Hebrew is classified as VSO in Greenberg 1963 and in Ruhlen and Ultan. Biblical Hebrew was VSO, modern Hebrew is SVO.

e. Georgian has an accusative pattern in the present and future and an ergative pattern in the past. There is no $S_i/A/O$ distinction in the stressed pronoun.

f. Mandarin Chinese is basically SVO with variations largely determined by definiteness. See section 3.3.2.

g. Malagasy has a morpho-syntactic system of the type described for Tagalog in section 2.3.5. but with fixed word order. The topic-subject is clause-final but the language is only VOS (in the sense of VOA) if we take the agent focus to be unmarked. We are not sure that this is correct. See Keenan 1976b, who argues that the agent focus is unmarked.

h. Tagalog has free word order with the verb regularly in clause-initial position. The patient is the favoured choice for focus or topic-subject and the favoured position of the topic-subject is clause-final.

i. Accusative marking is indirect in that it consists of a phonemic change induced at the beginning of the word following O.

j. The marking consists of an optional specific marker that can be used on S. It may be used on A to disambiguate.

k. Dyirbal has free word order but there is a 'preference' for nominative NPs to precede ergative (and dative) NPs. Dixon (1972:291). Since 1,2 pronouns operate in an accusative paradigm, this means SOV tends to occur with pronominal agents and OSV with noun agents.

l. The accusative system of marking consists of optional S marking. There is an accusative system of bound pronouns, S and O being suppletively distinct, and an uninflected free stressable pronoun. Malak-Malak is not an exception to the Silverstein hierarchy since that hierarchy refers to marking, not to a system of oppositions.

m. Free pronouns operate in a nominative-oblique paradigm, but the unmarked form is used as a stressed form for both S and other functions.

n. Since Menomini cross-references S_i, A and O and incorporates some O's, sentences with an NP for A and one for O are not common. Bloomfield (1962:442) notes the following tendencies: VS_i; an obviate actor usually precedes a transitive animate verb; objects usually precede the verb but often follow it; if an obviate actor precedes the verb, the object usually follows the verb. Bloomfield explains obviative as follows: 'Only one animate third person is proximate; all others are in obviate form. The proximate third person represents the topic of discourse, the person nearest the speaker's point of view, or person earlier spoken of and already known'.

o. Active pattern with 1,2. There are no 3 pronouns.

p. Active pattern with 1,2. 3 shows a distinction of definite or 'in-focus'

q. S versus indefinite or 'out-of-focus' S (Rood 1971). Rood is quoted by Dixon (1979:84) as stating 'word order in Wichita shows considerable fluidity'. Our entry is based on Rood 1971. We could have put simply 'free'.

r. No S_i/A/O distinction with 1,2 pronouns. 3 is ergative like nouns.

s. See section 2.5.2.

t. Positive marking for A; O unmarked.

u. S_i unmarked, O marked for accusative, A marked for $3 > 1,2$, and for $3^i > 3$. See section 2.5.3.

v. Nass-Gitksan is an analytic ergative language. Agent pronouns are incorporated in the verb; S_i, O pronouns are suffixed to a host particle (Rigsby 1975).

w. The agreement system consists of clitics suffixed to the first word in the clause.

x. 3 is ergative; 1,2 accusative.

   Accusative is a loose description. The transitive agreement system consists partly of portmanteau forms and partly of forms representing A *or* O, these being in a sense portmanteaus for the A/O combinations.

Our sample yields the following frequencies for basic word order:

VOS	2
VSO	9
SVO	35
SOV	41
OVS	1
OSV	1
Free	4
Other	7
	$\overline{100}$

These figures agree in the main with those that can be obtained from the samples of Greenberg, Steele, etc.   Our figure for VSO is a little lower than one would have obtained from other samples.   This is partly because we included modern Hebrew, which is SVO, rather than biblical Hebrew, which is VSO, partly because we were unwilling to classify Tagalog as VSO, and partly due to chance.   Other investigators have been more willing to ascribe orders than we have. There are 11 languages in the sample that we have not assigned to any of the six possible orders of V, S and O.

The orders in which S precedes O, namely VSO, SVO and SOV, together account for 85% of the sample. Moreover S precedes O in most of those listed under 'other'.

Only four languages in the sample have O before S: Hixkaryana (OVS), Dyirbal (OSV), Houailou (VOS) and Malagasy (VOS).

Until very recently the current orthodoxy was that there were no OVS languages; at least none had been noted in the mainstream literature.   However, Derbyshire and Pullum have discovered several examples of OVS in and around Brazil.   Hixkaryana, the OVS language in our sample, is one of these and has been the subject of extensive study by Derbyshire (see Derbyshire 1977 and especially Derbyshire 1979). Derbyshire & Pullum 1979 review the evidence (mostly in obscure sources) for OVS as the basic word order in several other languages of the Amazon basin and they conclude that Hianacoto-Umaua, Panare and

Asurinî are OVS and that Apalaí, Makúsi, Arekuna-
Taulipang and Bacairí may be OVS but it is uncertain.
All of these languages are of the Carib family except
for Asurinî, which belongs to the Tupian family (see
also Pullum 1980).

There have been a number of references in the
literature to languages having OSV as their basic
order. Pullum 1977 reviews claims that Dyirbal,
Hurrian, Aleut and West Greenlandic Eskimo are basically OSV and rejects all of them. We have accepted
Dyirbal as OSV. Dyirbal has very free word order,
but Dixon (1972:291) does give OSV as a preferred
order (which Pullum notes (1977:260)). We feel that
Aleut, Eskimo and Hurrian, a dead Anatolian language
known only from a small amount of text material, may
be OSV, but that the evidence is not clearly in
support of such an order.

Derbyshire and Pullum (1979:18-20) review further
references to OSV languages and dismiss them fairly
convincingly, though they consider that Haida, an
unaffiliated language spoken in the Queen Charlotte
Islands off western Canada and in the southernmost
extension of Alaska, may be OSV. Interestingly
enough they turn up some clear cases of OSV in the
Brazilian area, which means that the Amazon basin is
the home of the two rare word orders OVS and OSV.
They consider that Apurinã (Arawakan) and Urubú
(Tupian) are OSV, that Xavante (Gê) is very probably
OSV, and that Nadëb (Puinavean) may be OSV.[6] Our
example is from Apurinã.[7] In this language there is
considerable freedom of word order but if S and O are
on the same side of the verb the order must be OS.

(3.15)   anana   nota apa

           pineapple I   fetch

           'I fetch pineapple'

If either S or O follows the verb, then a cross-
referencing pronoun must be used on the verb.

(3.16) a. anana   n-apa   nota

           'I fetch pineapple'

       b. nota   apa-ry   anana

           'I fetch pineapple'

(3.16) c.   n-apa-ry anana nota
          'I fetch pineapple'

Pullum (1980:29) takes (3.15) to be basic, the pattern
that allows the verb to appear in its 'unmarked, in-
flectionless state' as does his source, Pickering
1973a.

    Keenan 1978a lists Malagasy, Fijian, Toba Batak,
Gilbertese, Tzeltal, Otomi, Ineseño Chumash and Baure
as VOS (see also Pullum 1977).   Our sample includes
Malagasy and Houailou, a language not listed by
Keenan.

    In Houailou the verb is preceded by a subject
clitic.   If a full noun phrase subject occurs, there
will be cross-reference between the clitic and the
full NP (Lichtenberk 1978).

(3.17)   na   aʔraʔ na   kamɔʔ
          3sg eat   sm   man
          'The man eats'

(3.18)   na   bɔri   aʔye bwɛʔ   beãrĩ ɣi-ə
          3sg sequence call woman old   poss-3sg
             na   kaɲa   ɣi-ə
             sm   uncle poss-3sg
          'Then his maternal uncle called his wife'

Under these circumstances one could claim that S precedes O.   However, in comparing word orders we have
followed the usual convention of considering the
position of full noun phrases.   If one considers the
position of clitics and of bound cross-referencing
pronouns, one finds a great number of deviations from
the orders we have listed.   It is tempting to explain
away Houailou as an exception to the general rule that
S precedes O, but if one considers the position of the
S clitic, then, to be consistent, one has to reconsider many of the orders we have listed.

    Malagasy is interesting in that it has a rigid
order: VOS.   As we pointed out in note (g) to table
1, it can only be counted VOA if we take the agent
focus to be unmarked, i.e. if we take as unmarked the
construction in which the agent is topic-subject.
One could explain away Malagasy as an exception to
the 'S before O' rule by claiming that in Malagasy

the agent-focus is not the unmarked construction.
This would mean that Malagasy would not be a VOA lan-
guage though it could be a topic-to-the-right language.
See (3.62) for an example.

3.3   Factors Determining Word Order

3.3.1.   The Basic Principles

    Word order can be accounted for in terms of three
general principles:

   (a)   more topical material tends to come nearer
          to the beginning of the clause (to the left)
          than non-topical material.

   (b)   heavy material tends to come nearer to the
          end of the clause (to the right) than light
          material (see also section 5.2.4.).

   (c)   constituents tend to assume a fixed position
          in the clause according to their grammatical
          or semantic relation or category status
          (noun, verb, prepositional phrase, etc.).

    Our account of word order tendencies is largely
based on the insightful discussion contained in chapters eight and nine of Dik's *Functional Grammar*.   We
use *topic* in the sense of what is being talked about
and *comment* in the sense of what is being said about
the topic.   Typically one thinks in terms of there
being only one topic, if any, in a clause, but we feel
that the constituents of a clause can exhibit degrees
of 'topic-ness' (see also the discussion in section
2.9.4.3.).   This is illustrated below in connection
with the discussion of indirect object (section
3.3.2.).   By *heavy material* we mean internally complex material.   A noun phrase that consists of two
co-ordinated noun phrases (*the boy and the girl*) is
heavier than a simple noun phrase (*the children*).
A noun phrase with a phrasal complement (*the girl on
the magazine cover*) or a clausal complement (*the girl
who was featured in the centrefold of the Financial
Review*) is heavier than a simple noun phrase (*the
girl*).

    Principles (a) and (b) are not unrelated.   A
topic is normally given, either by the preceding linguistic context or the wider context of situation.
It is typically a pronoun or a simple noun phrase.
Complements to heads of noun phrases typically occur
with material that is part of the comment, part of
what is being presented as new.

We use the term *focus* for any part of an utterance that is emphasized.   As with topic it seems
common to think in terms of a clause having a single
focus, but there can be more than one point of focus
or degree of focus.

A point of focus can be marked by stress and presumably this is true in any language; it can be indicated by an affix or adposition, and it can be marked
by placing the focused word or phrase at the beginning
of a clause.   This last possibility may be universal.
We do not know of a language that does not allow an
item to be fronted, though the most usual function
for fronting is topicalization.   The practice of
putting focused material to the left might seem to run
counter to the topic-to-the-left principle.   The
focus is normally part of the comment and could be
expected to come late in the clause.   There is in
fact some conflict here and it is the operation of
these partly conflicting tendencies that lies behind
a lot of the apparent freedom of free word order languages.   The conflict is only partial, however, since
a constituent may be both topic and a point of focus.
This will be true, for instance, where two topics are
contrasted as in the following exchange.

(3.19) A.   How're the kids today?

       B.   Well, Tommy's o.k. but Susie's got the flu.

Presumably *Tommy* and *Susie* are topics since the answer to A's question is about *Tommy* and *Susie*, but
Tommy and *Susie* are contrasted foci.   The phrases
o.k. and *the flu* are also foci.

Languages differ in the extent to which they use
word order variation in preference to, or as well as,
stress to signal focus.   In English, if we answer
the door and encounter an unexpected guest, Mary, we
are likely to announce her arrival to the other members of the household by saying *Máry's here*.   In
fact, we would retain the stress on *Mary* even if she
were an expected guest providing there were no special
circumstances leading to the presupposition that she
was elsewhere.   In Italian, however, Mary's arrival
would be likely to be announced in the form *È arrivata
Maria* with the stronger stress on *Maria*.   Although
Italian is clearly an SVO language it tends to place
S in sentence final position for emphasis.   For a
transitive example, see (3.20).

Not all parts of an utterance are part of a syntactic construction.   Phrases may stand before or
after a constructed sentence, or indeed they may
interrupt it.   There may, however, be language-specific constraints preventing the placing of such material in certain positions.   Japanese, for example, is
a strict-verb final language; however, this seems to
be true only of written Japanese and speakers regularly tag phrases on to the end of constructed sentences (for further discussion of the Japanese case
see section 5.2.4., Miyake in prep. and Miyake & Mallinson in prep.).

Phrases that present the setting (*In Sweden, all
the farmhouses are painted maroon*), and are set off
from the following construction by an intonation break,
have only a tenuous connection with the construction
they precede.   They tend to be immune from some of
the selection restrictions and subcategorization
rules that elements within the sentence proper must
follow - for example, they lie outside the case frame
of the verb, and are not able to be promoted to O
status by promotion or advancement mechanisms (see
section 2.7.4.).   The position at the head of an
utterance set off by an intonation break, the preposed position, is commonly used for such things as
topics, vocatives, focused constituents, certain linking words (*However, they could still hear*), speaker-
oriented adverbs (*Personally, I've got nothing against
women*) and adverbial expressions giving the setting
(as with *In Sweden* in the example given above).

In some languages, a constituent set off at the
beginning of an utterance is 'picked up' by a *resumptive* pronoun within the following construction.
This is common in colloquial Italian.

(3.20)   La   fanciulla, l'ha   assalita un

          the   girl   her-has   assailed   a

                 pappagallo

                 pappagallo

          'The girl was assailed by a pappagallo'

Sentences such as (3.20) present some difficulty in
typological work since grammars do not always make it
clear whether cross-reference between a noun phrase
and a pronoun is of the type illustrated here or of
the 'genuine' type where the cross-reference is with-

in the clause proper.   Some linguists would not use
the term 'cross-referencing for the phenomenon illustrated in (3.20).   The terminology is unimportant but
there is a big difference between cross-reference
within a construction and the apposition between a
constituent outside a construction and an element
within one as in (3.20).

It is common for utterances to contain phrases
that follow the sentence proper.   Typically these
postposed elements represent afterthoughts and often
they are in apposition to pronouns or generic nouns
within the preceding construction.

(3.21)   He's a good worker, that Harry.

The following example was spoken by a woman being
interviewed about her ideal man.

(3.22)   L'uomo ideale per me è l'uomo inglese ...

          ... non   lo   conosco questo uomo   inglese

              not   him   know:I   this   man   English

          'The ideal man for me is the Englishman ...

          ... I do not know him, this Englishman'

It is taken from an interview in the B.B.C. booklet of
interviews *Punti di Vista* (1974:41).   The tape
reveals that the sentence is spoken rapidly and without a break between *non lo conosco* and *questo uomo
inglese*.   Nevertheless, we feel on the basis of other
examples that this sentence does contain a postposed
phrase, but that the postposing is obscured in rapid
speech.   This example provides a good illustration of
the problem referred to above, viz. that of distinguishing preposed or postposed elements from integrated ones.

The topic-to-the-left principle can be used to
explain, at least in a weak sense, the preponderance
of SO orders in language.   As we pointed out in
section 3.2, SO orders (VSO, SVO and SOV) account for
85% of the languages in the sample and S usually precedes O in the languages we classified under 'other'.
For the purposes of our survey, we took S to be S_i/A
but, since most languages have an accusative morpho-
syntactic system in which A is the unmarked choice
for grammatical subject with a transitive verb, our
figures effectively show that the grammatical subject
tends to precede O.   In accusative languages the

grammatical subject is typically topic and indeed, as
we pointed out in section 2.9.3., the grammatical
properties that link S_i and A in an accusative language seem to be topic-based.   Subjects are like preposed topics in that they appear to the left and in
that they do not carry any semantic marking, usually
in fact appearing in the citation form.   Subject
agreement too seems to be topic-based.   Givón (1976:
155) gives the following schematic presentation to
demonstrate how subject agreement is likely to have
developed diachronically from a sequence of preposed
topic and resumptive pronoun.

(3.23)   The man, he came → The man   he-came

           TOPIC   PRO   SUBJECT   AG

     Ergative languages are interesting with regard
to the topic-to-the-left principle.   In an ergative
language S_i and O share the same grammatical properties that unite S_i and A in an accusative language.
As we saw in section 2.9.4.2., S_i/O, the absolutive,
seems to represent a grammaticalized topic in an
ergative language.   According to the topic-to-the-
left principle we should expect to find the absolutive
in a topic position, i.e. we should expect to find
VOA, OAV and OVA among ergative languages.   In practice we find that in most ergative languages A precedes O.   This is true of the following for instance:
Avar, Abkhaz, Basque, Tibetan, Gurung, Enga, Kalkatungu, Eskimo, Nass-Gitksan, Jacaltec, Quiche and
Squamish.   Dyirbal does have a preference for OAV as
we noted in the previous section and it is interesting that ergative marking occurs among the OVS Carib
languages.   Makúsi has ergative marking and an ergative pattern of bound pronouns, Arekuna-Taulipang has
ergative marking, Apalaí has restricted ergative marking and there are traces of ergative marking in subordinate clauses in Hixkaryana (Derbyshire & Pullum
1979).

     Some ergative languages are only superficially
ergative in the sense that there is no reflection of
an opposition between A and S_i/O in the syntax.   One
could perhaps dismiss some of these as having ergative marking only as a relic from a 'true' ergative
period or perhaps one could show that one or two of
them have borrowed their ergative marker (as Heath
(1978a:76) indicates is the case in Ngandi).   And of
course some ergative languages have an accusative
system of cross-referencing as is the case in Kalka-

tungu (Blake 1979c), which obscures the notion of a
grammaticalized topic.   However, this will still
leave a number of languages that have the grammaticalized topic following A.   This suggests that we
were wrong in saying that the topic-to-the-left principle accounts for the predominance of SO orders.
It suggests we establish an agent-to-the-left principle.   The difficulty with this is that it still
leaves all the OS languages unaccounted for.   Moreover, there is independent support for the topic-to-
the-left principle in the ordering of bound pronouns
and in the ordering of direct and indirect objects.[8]

Of course it is not impossible for a topic to
appear to the right of the comment.   This happens
some of the time in any language and it is not altogether surprising that a few languages regularly put
the subject to the right, e.g. Malagasy, Tzotzil and
Houailou.   See Keenan 1978a for a discussion of
subject-final languages.

The notion that S precedes O because S is normally topic is a satisfactory explanation (to the
extent that it is an explanation) only if we can explain independently why a topic should precede a
comment.   Topics do precede comments in mediums of
communication other than language.   In mime and dance
this is true, and it is true of at least some types of
visual display.   Can one imagine, for instance, a
television commercial for supermarket specials in
which a price was presented before the product to which
the price referred?   Normally comments do not make
sense without topics.

Principle (b), the heavy-to-the-right principle,
can be explained in terms of the demands that are
placed on our short-term memory by its violation.
Consider the following sentence.

(3.24)   I gave the school, who said they were having

difficulty finding suitable material for the

fourth formers, particularly those who were

slow readers, a copy of *The Secret Life*.

When the reader hears *NP give NP* (animate or quasi-
animate), he is expecting another NP (probably non-
human) to complete the construction.   If, as in
(3.24), the first NP is overly long, the listener
(and indeed the speaker) must retain the expectation

of the patient NP while processing the elaboration of
the recipient NP.   This causes some strain on the
short-term memory and a speaker is likely to use the
alternative construction - NP (agent) give NP (patient)
to NP (recipient) - in order to avoid the difficulty.
In general, centre-embedding, i.e. any form of embedding that involves returning to complete a construction started before the embedding, causes a strain,
often a conscious strain, on the short-term memory
and is avoided.   The heavy-to-the-right principle is
largely motivated by an apparent desire to reduce the
strain on the short-term memory.   However, as we
have already pointed out, formal Japanese tends to
resist the positioning of heavy constituents after
the (main) verb of the sentence (we discuss short-
term or, transient, memory-load in more detail in
Chapter 5).[9]

The principles of topic-to-the-left and heavy-to-
the-right are in harmony as we noted above.   It is
sometimes observed that pronouns often occupy different positions in the clause from noun phrases with
the same grammatical or semantic function.   It is
almost always the case that the pronoun occurs earlier in the clause than the corresponding noun.[10] For
instance, in the Romance languages an unstressed O
pronoun occurs before the verb, and a noun O in the
unmarked construction follows the verb.   Our examples are from Italian.

(3.25)   Lei   ha   visto   'Bicycle Thieves'?

          you   have   seen   Bicycle Thieves

          'Have you seen 'Bicycle Thieves'?'

(3.26)   Si,   l'ho   visto

          yes   it have:I   seen

          'Yes, I've seen it'

The principle at work here seems to be topic-to-the-
left (principle (a)), the tendency for more topical
material to be placed early in the clause.   The
heavy-to-the-right principle (principle (b)) is really
only applicable to cases involving quite heavy constituents, i.e. constituents involving chains of co-
ordinated constituents, relative clauses and the like.
(See also section 5.2.4. for examples of extraposition).

Principle (c) says that constituents tend to
assume a fixed position according to whether they are
subject, locative, dative (or whatever) or according
to whether they are noun phrases, prepositional phrases, etc.   Principle (c) is in conflict with (a) and
(b).   Strict adherence to (c) would mean strict word
order and no variation according to the demands of
topicalization, focusing and heaviness.

In one sense the admission of (c) as a principle
of word order robs (a) and (b) of any explanatory
value they might have.   If a language exhibits fixed
word order, we say it follows principle (c).   If it
shows some kinds of variation, we say it follows (a)
and/or (b).   There is not much that can be done about
this.   We are not able to establish precedence between principles (a), (b) and (c).   We can characterize some languages as following (c) almost entirely.
Cambodian seems to be such a language.   We can characterize other languages as being particularly responsive to the demands of (a), the topic-to-the-left
principle.   Latin is a good example of this.   There
is a discernible correlation between case marking,
agreement and relative freedom of word order, so to
some extent we can make predictions about the precedence of (a) vis-à-vis (c).   This is dealt with in
section 3.4.

3.3.2.   Topicalization Hierarchies

Which constituent of a sentence is to be topic is
largely determined by the context, linguistic or
situational, but over and above this there is a tendency for a topic to be chosen according to a variant
of the hierarchy given in section 2.8.1., namely
1, 2 > 3 > human > animate > inanimate.   Topics also
tend to be specific rather than nonspecific and definite rather than indefinite.

It is not surprising that the speaker is at the
top of the topicalization hierarchy.   Language use
presupposes the speaker.   I speak, therefore I am
topic, as Descartes might have said.   Similarly we
can argue that language use typically involves
communication with a hearer.   *You* are presupposed by
communication, second only after *me*.

In Kalkatungu (Blake 1979c:114) word order is
fairly free though AOV and AVO are the common patterns.
However, O can appear first if it is topic or focus
and in the following sentence O has been chosen as

topic since it is first person and the other participant is inanimate.   The event is seen from the point
of view of ego, not from the point of view of the
rain.

(3.27)   ŋaika uṉṯayi   kuu-ŋku

          me   soak   rain-erg

          'I got caught in the rain'

     In English, of course, we would also tend to
topicalize ego, as in the translation of (3.27), but
where Kalkatungu changes the word order from the unmarked pattern without changing the construction, we
use the passive as opposed to the active to place the
patient in topic position.

     There is a marked tendency to choose definite
referents as topics over indefinite ones.   Of course
a referent will often be definite only because it has
been introduced in the immediately preceding context
and such a referent will naturally be a good candidate for topic because it is given as opposed to new.
Some referents are given as part of the shared knowledge of the speech participants.   A wife reporting
to her husband the misfortune that has befallen their
beloved pet is more likely to use (3.28) than (3.29),
empathizing with the cat (see Kuno 1976a).

(3.28)   The cat was attacked by a bloody great

               Alsatian

(3.29)   A bloody great Alsatian attacked the cat

     In some languages only a definite noun phrase
can appear as topic or subject.   In Tagalog, for
instance, only a definite NP can be marked by *ang*
(see examples in section 2.3.5.).

     Givón (1979:81) reports that in Kinya Rwanda O is
definitized by placing it before the verb (note the
cross-referencing in (3.31)).

(3.30)   ya-bonye   u-mu-gabo

          he-saw   ref-mu-man   (ref = referential)

          'He saw a̱ man'

(3.31)   u-mu-gabo   ya-mu-bonye

      ref-mu-man   he-him-saw

      'He saw the man'

      'The man, he saw him'

In Mandarin (Li & Thompson 1978:228) a noun phrase not marked for definiteness is interpreted as definite if it appears before the verb and indefinite if it follows.   Examples (3.32) and (3.33) involve S_i, the rest O.

(3.32)   Zéi   păo   le

      thief   run   perfect aspect

      'The thief has run away'

(3.33)   Păo   le   zéi

      run   perf   thief

      'A thief has run away'

(3.34)   Wŏ   măi   shū   le

      I   buy   book   perfect

      'I bought a book'

(3.35)   Shū   wŏ   măi   le

      book   I   buy   perfect

      'The book, I bought it'

(3.36)   Wŏ   shū   măi   le

      I   book   buy   perfect

      'I bought *the book*' (contrastive)

Definiteness is not unrelated to the pronoun-animacy hierarchy in that noun phrases high on the hierarchy are definite: pronouns, personal names, and in their most common usage, kinship terms.

In some languages a nonspecific O is incorporated in the verb. In others the sequence indefinite object-verb or verb-indefinite object is treated as a unit.   In Kusaiean (Sugita 1973 quoted by Hopper & Thompson 1980) the completive aspect marker -læ follows the verb.   If O is indefinite -læ follows the sequence VO.   The forms ɔl and owo are suppletive stems for 'wash'.

(3.37)   nga   ɔl   læ   nuknuk   ɛ
          I   wash   compl clothes   the
          'I finished washing the clothes'

(3.38)   nga   owo   nuknuk   læ
          I   wash   clothes   completive
          'I finished washing clothes'

As Hopper & Thompson point out, V and O in (3.38)
'are regarded as a morphological unit' (1980:259).

In some African languages aspect is relevant to
the word order, the perfective taking the unmarked
order and the imperfective a marked order.   In the
following examples from Lendu (Tucker 1940:402) it
appears that the SOV order of the imperfective may be
an example of the same phenomenon illustrated in the
Kusaiean examples given above.

          SVO *order: perfective*
(3.39)   má   'a   oú
          I   eat   chicken
          'I've eaten a chicken'

          SOV *order: imperfective*
(3.40)   má   'ou   'á
          I   chicken   eat
          'I am eating a chicken'

This phenomenon occurs also in Moru, Mangbetu
and some other central Sudanic languages.

The topicalization hierarchy also manifests itself in the behaviour of indirect objects.   An indirect object is typically high on the hierarchy and
the patient in a sentence with an indirect object is
typically low, usually being inanimate in fact.   It
is not surprising then to find that in most languages
the indirect object precedes the direct object.   Of
course, the existence of an indirect object is hierarchically determined in the first place.   Many languages are like English in allowing human locative
(more specifically allatives in the case of English)
to be expressed as indirect objects but not non-human

ones.

(3.41)   I sent my old greatcoat to the Salvation
          Army.

(3.42)   I sent the Salvation Army my old greatcoat.[11]

(3.43)   I sent my old jeans to the tip.

(3.44)   *I sent the tip my old jeans.

It is probably true that all other things being
equal a definite recipient will tend to be expressed
as an indirect object especially if the patient is
indefinite.   It is difficult to demonstrate this
since it involves finding examples with both patient
and recipient on the same level of the pronoun-
animacy hierarchy.   Consider, however, the following
examples.

(3.45)   The committee allotted the couple a baby.

(3.46)   The committee allotted a baby to the couple.

(3.45) seems more natural.   (3.46) is natural enough
if the main stress is placed on *baby*, but it suggests
an odd situation in which a baby is allotted as
opposed to something else.

In some languages the recipient (or a human participant with the role of goal of motion) is simply
represented in the same way as any (other) phrase expressing 'to' or 'towards'.   This 'marked recipient'
follows the patient in some languages, occupying the
same position as other local phrases.   This is true
of Lenakel, for instance, and also of French and
Spanish, if we ignore pronouns in these two cases.
In other languages the marked recipient regularly
precedes the patient.   This is true of Hausa, Swahili, Portuguese and German (but see (3.50) below).

In Ulithian (Sohn & Bender 1973) the verbs for
'give', 'deprive' and 'ask/borrow' take an unmarked
'recipient' that precedes the patient, while the
verbs for 'feed' and 'teach' take a prepositionally
marked 'recipient' and this also precedes the patient.
At this point it becomes obvious that one should not
generalize over 'notional indirect objects' or
loosely defined recipients.   In theory one has to
make distinctions according to roles or according to

particular verbs. In this brief survey we will overlook this problem.

In a large majority of languages the relative
order of the patient and recipient is hierarchically
determined, a participant higher on the animacy hierarchy appearing first and a definite participant preceding an indefinite one.

This kind of hierarchically determined variation
occurs in Turkish, Japanese and Kanuri, where the
recipient is marked, and also in English, Dutch, Swe-
dish, Indonesian, Mundari, Djaru, Acooli, Dehu, Nengone, Syrian Arabic and Avatime, in all of which the
recipient is either marked or unmarked, the marked
recipient following the patient and the unmarked preceding it.

In Kikuyu (Blansitt 1973:11) this latter type of
variation occurs, the indirect object being used when
the patient is non-human, but prepositional marking
being used for the recipient when the patient is
human.

(3.47)   Mūthuri   ūriā   mukūrū   nⸯanengerire

       man   old   gave

          mūtumⸯa   ihūa

          woman   flower

       'The old man gave the woman the flower'

(3.48)   Mūtumⸯa   nⸯanengerire   mwarⸯ   wake   gwi

       woman   gave   daughter   her   to

          kahⸯⸯ

          boy

       'The woman gave her daughter to the boy'

It is tempting to see the use of the preposition *gwi*
as a distinguishing marker, but the patient and recipient could have been distinguished by order. What
seems to be happening here is that a recipient
appears to the left of the patient when it is higher
than the patient on the topicalization hierarchy.
In (3.48) the recipient and patient are level on the
hierarchy, since both are human, so the recipient
appears to the right in the normal position for prepositional phrases.

In a number of languages the order of patient

and recipient is sensitive to the pronominal status
of the participants.   In Bimoba (Sedlak 1975:133)
the recipient precedes the patient unless the patient
is a pronoun.

In German a recipient is expressed in the dative
and, if it is represented by a noun, it precedes O
just as the indirect object does in English.

(3.49)   Hans   gab   dem   Mann   das   Buch
          Hans   gave   the:dat man   the   book
          'Hans gave the man the book'

However, a dative recipient, whether noun or pronoun,
cannot precede a pronominal O.   Thus, (3.50) can
occur but the order of pronoun and full noun phrase
cannot be reversed.

(3.50)   Hans   gab   es   dem   Mann
          Hans   gave   it   to:dat   man
          'Hans gave it to the man'

In English, of course, we would not say *Hans gave the
man it*, but if the indirect object is pronominal it
precedes any O: *I gave him it*, though some varieties
of English allow *I gave it him*.   It is worth pointing out that detailed study of the expression of
recipients usually reveals complications not revealed
in the average grammar.   See, for example, Zimmermann 1972 on German and English.

Some languages allow recipients to be represented by bound pronouns and these pronouns appear earlier in the clause than the corresponding full noun
phrase.   In Spanish there is no indirect object phenomenon except with bound pronouns.

(3.51)   Carlos   da   boletos   a   sus   amigos
          'Carlos   gives   tickets   to   his   friends'

(3.52)   Carlos   les   da   boletos
          'Carlos gives them tickets'

It is possible in Spanish to use the bound pronoun *and* the prepositional phrase in cross-reference.

(3.53)   Carlos   les   da   boletos   a   sus   amigos
          'Carlos gives tickets to his friends'

Catalan, French and Italian also have bound form pronouns for recipients, but they have pro-forms for all allatives.   In Italian, for example, *ci* (or *vi*) is a bound form meaning 'to there'.

(3.54)   Va   a   Roma?   Si, ci vado

        'You're going to Rome? Yes, I'm going there'

In Italian, as in Portuguese, Romanian and Spanish, the recipient bound pronoun regularly precedes the patient pronoun.

(3.55)   Maria   me   lo   dà

        Maria   me   it   gives

        'Maria gives it to me'

(3.56)   Maria   gli-e-lo   dà

        Maria   him:lig:it gives

        'Maria gives it to him' (or 'to her' or in
                the colloquial language 'to them')

In the Romance languages, with the exception of Romanian,[12] there are no separate forms for direct and indirect object in the first and second person. In Italian, for instance, 'Maria sees me' is *Maria mi vede*, where *mi* represents first person.   It may appear that there are two forms *mi* and *me* (as in (3.55)), but these are allomorphs, the vowel being conditioned by the presence of a succeeding *n* or *l* in the same unstressed sequence (cf. *di* 'of', *della* 'of the').

In Italian, French and Spanish a first or second person bound pronoun will not permit the co-occurrence of a bound pronoun representing a recipient.   The recipient must be expressed in a prepositional phrase.

In French, for instance, one can have a third person patient with a third person recipient (in the order: patient-recipient) or a third person patient with a first or second person recipient (in the order: recipient-patient).   This has been illustrated in (2.90) and (2.91).   If, however, one wants to say 'I'll introduce you to him', one must say the following:

(3.57)   Je   vous   présenterai   à   lui   (not *vous
         I   you   present:fut:1s   to   him   lui nor
                                                     *lui
         'I'll introduce you to him'   vous)

Similarly, if one wants to use a first or second person recipient with a first or second person bound pronoun patient:

(3.58)   Il   te   présentera   à   moi   (not *Il
         He   you introduce:fut   to   me   te me...
                                                   nor *Il
         'He will introduce you to me'   me te...)

(3.59)   Il   me   présentera   à   toi   (not *Il
         He   me   introduce:fut   to   you   te me...
                                                  nor *Il
         'He will introduce me to you'   me te...)

It is clear from these examples in English, German, Spanish, Italian and French that a recipient tends to be given preferential treatment over a patient or over a referent that represents the goal of motion ('to the tip') without being a sentient recipient ('to the Salvation Army'). The preferential treatment consists of precedence in word order or bound pronoun marking. The patient and the recipient are rivals and one can succeed in displacing the other depending on their relative status in terms of the topicalization hierarchy.

In English a more topic-worthy recipient precedes a patient but a noun recipient cannot precede a pronoun patient. In German a pronoun patient takes precedence over all recipients including pronominal ones. In the Romance languages only a pronominal recipient is any kind of rival for the patient, but no recipient can rival a first or second person patient.

In languages where the patient and recipient share positive marking, the marking is usually regular for the recipient and either optional for the patient or regular with human or definite patients. We could say that only those patients that exhibit the properties typically associated with recipients take the recipient marker. This may be the basis on which an allative form such as Spanish a spreads to human specific patients (see also sections 2.3.1. and 2.5.2.).

If one distinguishes a marked oblique recipient
from one that is unmarked or marked by the accusative,
one finds that there are very few languages in which
the unmarked or accusative recipient follows the
patient, but Thai is such a language.   In Thai the
verb hây 'give' can occur in the construction illustrated in (3.60) and (3.61).   We understand the
latter is the more widely used, informal construction.

(3.60)   phǒm   hây   khâaw   kàp   khun

          I   give rice   with   you

          'I give rice to you'

(3.61)   phǒm   hây   khâaw   khun

          I   give rice   you

          'I give you rice'

The construction illustrated in (3.61) is impervious
to any hierarchical topicalization tendencies.   See
also Jacob (1968:78) for the analogous phenomenon in
Cambodian.

     In the VOS language, Malagasy (Keenan 1976b:251),
the recipient, whether marked by a preposition or
simply by the accusative, regularly follows the
patient.

(3.62)   Nanome vola   azy   aho

          gave   money him(acc) I

          'I gave him the money'

However, Malagasy seems to topicalize from the right
contrary to the language-general tendency, so the placing of the recipient to the right of the patient is
consistent with the topicalization procedure in this
language.   In fact it is to be expected that the
order patient-recipient occurs in VOS languages and
there is some evidence that this is so.   Cowan (1969:
9) provides an example of this from the VOS language,
Tzotzil.

(3.63)   láx   y-ak'-be   ʔíšim ti   vínike ti
         past he-gave-her   corn   the man   the
             xpétule
         Peter

      'Peter gave the man corn'

See also Keenan (1978a:281).

3.3.3.   Position of Clitic Pronouns

     Clitic pronouns typically occur affixed to the
verb.   In some languages they are suffixed to the
first word or first constituent of the clause and in
others they are affixed to some kind of grammatical
particle.   In a few languages a pair of bound forms
in a transitive clause combine to form a free form.

     If one considers where free pronouns occur in
clauses, the position of bound pronouns makes sense.
In real spoken discourse, as opposed to written text
or the artificial examples of grammars, pronouns
rather than nouns abound.   This has already been
alluded to in connection with the problem of determining the word order of cross-referencing languages
(section 3.1.5.).   Typical sentences of real speech
consist of a verb and one or two pronouns and often
not much else.   Adverbial expressions are often
separated from the verb and its pronouns.   It is not
surprising then to discover that the most common
place to find bound pronouns is on the verb.   One
can also presume that the position of the bound pronouns reflects the earlier position of the free unstressed pronouns, though one cannot deduce the earlier position of stressed noun phrases.

     Real life sentences, besides containing a verb
and one or two pronouns, are likely to contain a
patient noun phrase, an oblique noun phrase or an adverbial.   Any of these could occur at the head of
the clause if they are focused, and oblique phrases
or adverbials indicating the setting for the clause
are particularly likely to appear at the beginning of
the clause.   Of course if the language is verb final
these words and phrases will not normally have the
verb as an opponent seeking first place in the clause.
It is not altogether surprising then to find that a
number of languages, especially in the Pama-Nyungan
family and the Uto-Aztecan family, have clitic pronouns that suffix themselves to the first word or

first constituent of the clause.   The pronouns are
likely to have found themselves sandwiched between
the focus and the verb and they could attach themselves as satellites to the preceding or succeeding
stressed word.   The following example is from
Luiseño (Steele 1977).

(3.64)   hunwuti-pum   ǵeʔiwum

          bear:obj-they   are:shooting

          'They are shooting a bear'

     Smith & Johnson (pers.comm.) inform us that in
the Australian language, Nganhcara, enclitic pronouns
attach to the last word before the verb, or to the
verb if no other words occur.   Nganhcara seems to be
unique in this respect, but the phenomenon is not unexpected if we consider the typical form of a real
life sentence in a verb-final language.

     Clitic pronouns are not the only constituents
that show some affinity for the second position in
the clause.   Linking words naturally tend to come at
or near the beginning of the clause.   They tend to
compete for the first position in the clause with a
topic or a focus, in some cases with an extraposed
topic or focus.   In English, the linking adverb
'however' tends to come either at the beginning of
the clause, often set off by an intonation break, or
following the first constituent, where it usually
receives parenthetical intonation (though it may
appear later in the clause).

(3.65)   However, the women were not prepared for this

(3.66)   The women, however, were not prepared for
          this

Some linking words must occur at the head of the
clause (*and*, *but*, *or* in English), but others become
obligatory 'second position' words.   In Latin, *enim*
'for', 'indeed', *vero* 'truly' and *autem* 'however'
could not be first in the clause and generally came
in second position.   In classical Greek the conjunc-
tive particles μέν and δή occur as second word in
their clauses.

3.4   Marking, Agreement and Word Order

We now turn to the question of the relationship
between marking or agreement on the one hand and word
order on the other.   In particular we discuss the
notion raised at the beginning of chapter two that
free word order is possible only when there is some
form of case marking to distinguish A from O.

Steele (1978:608-9) discusses this notion.   She
writes:

> 'hypotheses about what allows freedom of word
> order have concentrated on the presence of
> case marking.   For example, it has been sug-
> gested that ENGLISH word order became rigid
> as case inflections were lost (see, e.g.
> Vennemann 1974a).   The first part of this
> section examines that claim - and explodes it.
> The second part of this section suggests that
> freedom of word order ..... correlates rather
> with a certain type of agreement'.

Steele does not deal directly with Vennemann's claim
about English.   She presumably thinks his claim is
untenable on the grounds that lack of case marking
for A and O does not necessarily mean rigid word
order.   She establishes this by pointing out that
Classical Aztec, Karok, Achi, Wiyot, Tuscarora,
Garadjari and Maleceet-Passamoquoddy have free word
order but no case marking.   In fact Garadjari has
case marking and this is clearly indicated in her
source, Capell 1962.   However, leaving Garadjari
aside, we can accept that there are languages that
lack both case marking and fixed word order.

Steele uses 'free word order' in a rather special
sense.   A language is said to have free word order
if it breaks certain constraints that she lays down.
For example, a language with a basic SOV word order
is allowed to have SVO as a variant without being declared a 'free word order language'.   However, an
SVO language will be declared a free word order language if it allows SOV and certain other variations.
Steele, of course, can define 'free word order language' in any way she likes, but her sense is not
relevant to the question of whether only languages
with case marking allow free word order.   What lies
behind this question is the functional notion that
case marking and word order are alternative means of
distinguishing A from O and that a language must have

one or the other or possibly both.   The sense of
'free word order' relevant here is a freedom that
would cause confusion in the absence of some other
means of distinguishing A from O.   A variation of
OSV in a language that is basically SOV will not be
considered evidence of free word order in Steele's
sense, but it is a variation that could cause confusion, since the sequence NP NP V could be either OSV
or SOV in the absence of contextual clues or marking.
In fact a language with absolutely rigid word order
and no marking could have this problem if the order
was on the basis of topic-comment.   Something like
this appears to be true of Lisu (see discussion below).

　　Steele claims that all languages with free word
order have the person of the subject marked somewhere
in the clause (usually on the verb but not always -
see section 3.3.3.), though not all languages with
subject agreement have free word order.   In fact she
claims that free word order languages tend to have
'copy agreement' (where the pronominal element -
usually cross-referencing - has a transparent relationship with the free pronoun) or 'semi-copy agreement' (where the pronominal agreement forms show some
resemblance to the free forms) as opposed to 'inflectional agreement' (where the agreement forms bear no
resemblance to the free pronouns).

　　She finds that in a sample of 63 languages 49
have person agreement.   Within the 49 she finds that
12 languages exhibit free word order.   These are the
following:

　　Czech   (inflectional person agreement)

　　Luiseño, Walbiri, Classical Aztec, Maleceet-
　　Passamoquoddy, Chinook, Garadjari   (copy agreement)

　　Achi, Karok, Wiyot, Tuscarora (semi-copy agreement)

　　Cacua   (agreement type uncertain)

　　However, there are certainly languages that exhibit free word order even in Steele's sense, but
which do not have any form of person agreement for
S_i, A or O.   A number of Australian languages, mostly eastern members of the Pama-Nyungan family, answer
this description.   The best known is Dyirbal (Dixon
1972), but we could add also Yidin^y (Dixon 1977),
Guugu-Yimidhirr (Haviland 1979) and others.

　　Tagalog and a number of other Philippines-type
languages have free word order and no person agreement.   Tagalog does not qualify as a free word order

language in Steele's sense but it does have a freedom
that would cause confusion between A and O if it were
not for the system of prepositions and verb prefixes
that mark the topic-subject and the semantic relations (illustrated in section 2.3.5.).   Strangely
enough Steele lists Tagalog as having person agreement, but this must be an error.[13]

Steele notes that one might argue that if a language has some kind of cross-referencing for subject
(and object), it is free to place the subject and
object in any position in the sentence.   However, as
she points out, if A and O are both third person singular or both third person plural, the cross-referencing does not distinguish which noun is A and which
is O.   In principle this is true but one should add
that elaboration of the third person cross-referencing in terms of number or gender/class will greatly
reduce the number of sentence tokens in which it will
be impossible to distinguish A and O.

It seems startling that a language could have
free word order and no case marking and have to rely
on a system of cross-referencing when such a system
is not going to allow one to distinguish *John saw
Bill* from *Bill saw John*.   It may not happen very
often, outside a linguistics class, that one has to
distinguish between two sentences like these, but it
certainly can happen and one would expect a language
to be able to handle this situation.

Let us look at a few languages that appear to
have this problem.

Takelma (Sapir 1922) is a language that relies
entirely on cross-referencing to distinguish agent
from patient.   Where the critical 3 - 3 combinations
are involved, a suffix *kwa* is employed to indicate a
human O or, in semantic terms, a human patient or recipient.   A sentence of the form NP V will normally
be interpreted as OV, but a sentence of the form NP V-
kwa will be interpreted as A V (Sapir 1922:168-9).

(3.67)   t'ibiṣṬ   t'ayak

          ants   found

          'He found the ants'

(3.68)   t'ibiṣṬ   t'ayakwa

          ants   found:3rd human O

          'The ants found him'

kwa is not a cross-referencing form; it marks O
directly and its presence indicates that any NP present is not O, hence the translation of (3.68).   *kwa*
is not an integrated part of the bound pronoun system
either.   It stands as an exception to a number of
the rules for concatenating morphemes within the verb.
The impression one gets from Sapir's account is that
kwa is an ad hoc addition to the system, an element
added for the purposes of distinguishing the agent
from the patient.

There is at least one other method of distinguishing agent and patient in Takelma.   There is an
agentless passive and the participant expressed with
this construction is necessarily the patient.   An
agent may be expressed in a juxtaposed clause.

(3.69)   ei   salk'omok'imi·n.   p'iyin

           canoe   kicked:to:pieces-passive   deer

           xebe'n

           did

           'The canoe was kicked to pieces.   The deer
           did it'

Presumably the passive, which is used with very great
frequency in Takelma texts, can be used to distinguish
the agent from the patient in any critical case and
serves to distinguish A from O in those instances
where *kwa* will not help (e.g. *dog bites snake* v.
snake bites dog).

The use of the passive as a disambiguating
device is not confined to Takelma.   The passive may
be used to disambiguate 3 > 3 combinations in Dakota
(Boas & Deloria 1939) and other languages.   Morphemes with a function similar to *kwa* also occur in
some other American Indian languages.   Compare, for
instance, the use of *k'-* in Washo (see section 2.5.2.).

In Hixkaryana (Derbyshire 1979:87) there is a
system of cross-referencing pronouns but no case marking for A and O.   The OVS word order serves to
distinguish A from O most of the time but S can be
fronted to produce SOV.   In a clause of the pattern
NP V the NP could be S_i, A or O.   The ambiguity is
resolved by the use of a verb prefix y- when the preceding NP is O and a prefix n(ɨ) in any other case.

(3.70)   toto yahos†ye

          man   3>3:grabbed

          'It grabbed the man'

(3.71)   toto nahos†ye

          man   3>3:grabbed

          'The man grabbed it'

Mohawk is a free word order language that relies
on cross-referencing rather than case marking to distinguish A from O.   However, for clauses that cannot
be disambiguated by the cross-referencing system or
by semantic clues, a strict SVO word order is invoked
(Mithun & Chafe 1979:10-11).   Thus to express 'Kor
hit Sak' (Kor and Sak are names of males) one says
the following:

(3.72)   Kor   wahó:-ienhte'   Sak

          Kor   he:him-hit   Sak

          'Kor hit Sak'

Tiwi, like Gunwinggu, is an Australian language
that has a cross-referencing system but no case marking to distinguish agent from patient.   It allows
considerable freedom of word order, certainly such
freedom as would appear to introduce ambiguity, but
it employs SVO as a 'normal' order.   Writers of
grammars of languages that have free word order and
cross-referencing but no case marking usually fail to
inform readers how one deals with the 'John hit Bill'
problem.   Osborne, however, explains very clearly
how the problem is handled.   We quote the relevant
section in full.

>'It is commonly believed that structural
>identification of subject and object is
>achieved either by case inflexion or by fixed
>word order, and that therefore languages
>which are without one must have the other.
>Tiwi, however (like many other Australian
>languages), has neither case inflexion nor
>fixed word order, and yet manages to avoid
>structural ambiguity, and it is thus a matter
>of some interest to observe how this is
>achieved.   SVO and OVS both occur.   How are
>they distinguished?

The means which are used are as follows:
(1) *normality of order*, (2) *phonological
signals*, (3) *concord*, (4) *selectional
restrictions*, (5) *knowledge of the cultural/
situational context*.

As already stated, Tiwi word order
although not fixed is not entirely free.
Every structure has a normal order, and de-
partures from this are governed by bracketing
rules and other constraints. SVO is a normal
order and OVS an inverted one, and for this
reason, given no other structural cues of any
kind, a native speaker of Tiwi will interpret
a sentence such as jərəkati juuṇai kuɹupurani
as 'Jərəkati found Kuɹupurani' not 'Kuɹupurani
found Jərəkati'. When any danger of structural ambiguity arises the normal order is
always reverted to in order to avoid this.

Phonological signals too play an important part in the interpretation of sentence
structure, principally as an indication of
inversion. When the order of subject and
predicate is reversed, a distinct pause may
occur following the predicate phrase, signalling that the predicate ends at this point
and that the subject is only added for ampli-
fication. For example, in a sentence such as
kuɹupurani juuṇai, jərəkati 'Jərəkati found
Kuɹupurani', the pause after the predicate
phrase signals the bracketing, showing
kuɹupurani to be object and jərəkati subject.

Concord between the verb and the nominals
related to it as subject and object is another
of the main means of signalling structure.
As verbs include information about the person,
number and gender of both subject and object,
subject and object nominals which differ in
any one of these respects can be easily distinguished. For example, in the sentence
waijai ṭuuṇai ṭapara 'Ṭapara found Waijai',
Waijai (the woman) is identified as object,
no matter in what order the words are
arranged, by the initial prefix on the verb,
ṭu-, which indicates third-person singular
subject acting on third-person singular feminine object. Concord is thus a sufficient
means of distinguishing subject and object,
even without the assistance of order and

phonology, except, of course, when subject
and object are of the same person, number
and gender.

Selectional restrictions on the choice
of nominals as subject and object also play
a great part, especially a severe restriction on the use of inanimate nominals as
subject of a transitive sentence. For
example, the sentence jikwani juuŋau purikikini
'Purikikini threw fire', can only be interpreted in one way, no matter in what order
the words are arranged, because the interpretation 'Fire threw Purikikini' is semantically deviant, and precluded by selectional
restrictions.

Finally, knowledge of the cultural/
situational context is of the greatest importance in the structural interpretation of
sentences, and would, in fact, often be
sufficient for interpreting them even if all
other means were absent. Take for instance
the inverted sentence ţapara jipuŋipa
purukupaɹli 'Purukupaɹli hit Ţapara in the
eye'. In this case order, concord and
selectional restrictions all fail to distinguish subject and object (as the order is
inverted and the two nominals have the same
person, number and gender, and are both
human and animate), and let us suppose that
phonological signals of structure are also
absent (as they might be). Disambiguation
is still achieved through knowledge of the
cultural context, as all Tiwi are familiar
with the story of Purukupaɹli and Ţapara,
and thus know in advance who hit who in the
eye'.   (1974:64)

One language has achieved some prominence in the
typological literature because it appears to lack any
means whatsoever for distinguishing A from O.   The
language is Lisu, or at least the Thailand dialect of
Lisu.   This dialect is spoken by a community that
migrated from China to Thailand in the 1930s.   The
community was formed by Chinese Nationalist troops
marrying Lisu women.   Hope refers to the Thailand
form of this language as 'creolized Lisu' (1976, see
also 1974).   As far as we know this dialect of Lisu
is a genuine native language and cannot be dismissed
as a pidgin, although the Lisu are multilingual.[14] In

any case it is not typical of pidgins that they lack
means of distinguishing A from O.

Sentences with A, O and V consist of A or O
followed by a topic marker, then the remaining participant, then the verb.

A topic   O V

O topic   A V

In (3.73) làthyu 'people' is chosen as topic, but
there is no indication of whether it is A or O.   The
sentence has two readings (or the string represents
two distinct sentences).   In (3.74) ánà 'dog' is
topic, but (3.74) has the same propositional possibilities as (3.73), though admittedly one reading is
unlikely.

(3.73)   làthyu nya   ánà   khụ̀-ạ

          people topic dog   bite-declarative

          'People, dogs bite them'

          'People, they bite dogs'

(3.74)   ánà   nya   làthyu khụ̀-ạ

          dog   topic people bite-declarative

          'Dogs, people bite them'

          'Dogs, they bite people'

There is no possibility of adding agent or patient
marking to a participant, nor is there any cross-
referencing.

In commenting on this system, Li & Thompson
(1976a:473) point out that 'this total disregard for
agency or subjecthood in the structure of the language does not impair its communicative function, as
much as might be expected'.   They note that context
and the animacy hierarchy will disambiguate many sentences.   These factors play a part in many languages
of course.   Consider the English sentence *John is
cooking* and *The meat is cooking*.

Li & Thompson characterize Lisu as a 'topic pro-
minent' language, as a language lacking subject formation, as a language organized in terms of topic and
comment.   The topic is chosen presumably as in any
language on the basis of what is given in a particular context.   In sentences involving no presupposed
noun phrases, the topic marker *nya* is allotted accor-

ding to the following hierarchy:

agent > dative > object > instrumental

Thus in the following sentence nya marks swu 'one' as opposed to dè 'knife' (Li & Thompson 1976a:477).

(3.75)   swu   nya   áthà   dè-a̱

        one   topic   knife   forge-declarative

        'Someone is forging a knife'

This use of nya where there is no 'real' topic, is characteristic of subject marking, but as Li & Thompson point out, this subject-marking function of nya occurs only in this rather rare sentence type.

Hope's monograph on Lisu (1974) does not provide an answer to the question of how the Lisu distinguish *John saw Mary* from *Mary saw John* but in the light of the hierarchy given above, one cannot help wondering if the agent isn't chosen as topic unless there is some contextual reason to topicalize O.

From reading grammars one cannot ascertain whether all languages have means of distinguishing an agent from a patient across the board. A language could use different strategies for different situations of course, e.g. cross-referencing for sentences involving a first or second person as agent or patient, and word order for sentences in which both agent and patient were third person. We assume, as almost every linguist does, that all languages can distinguish any agent from any patient, but it is a lamentable fact that grammars do not always make this clear. We imagine that a linguist describing a 'new' language would be anxious to discover how to distinguish *John saw Bill* from *Bill saw John* on his first day in the field. Apparently this is not so. We have asked a number of linguists, some of them missionaries with years of experience in a language, how to distinguish *John saw Bill* from *Bill saw John* in 'their' language. To our surprise, they have often been unable to answer this seemingly elementary question.

We feel that Steele's dismissal of Vennemann's claim that English word order became rigid as inflections were lost is premature. Vennemann in fact saw it as significant not only that English word order became rigid, but that the order it adopted was SVO. There does in fact seem to be a connection between

lack of case marking and SVO order and Steele has
missed this.

Greenberg (1963:96) noted that according to his
sample 'if in a language the verb follows both the
nominal subject and nominal object as the dominant
order, the language almost always has a case system'
(universal 41).   Now if most SOV languages have a
case system and if many languages lack a case system,
as appears from the most casual observation, then the
caseless languages must be spread over the non-SOV
languages among which SVO are the largest group.   In
our sample of 100 languages, 56 are [+case], and 46 of
these are found in SVO, SOV and VSO languages, as
shown below (in this context [+case] means having an [15]
affix or adposition that can be used to mark A or O).

SVO	[+case]	9
	[-case]	26
SOV	[+case]	34
	[-case]	7
VSO	[+case]	3
	[-case]	6

It is obvious from these figures that SVO languages tend to lack case marking for A and O about as
much as SOV languages tend to have case marking for A
or O.   The correlation between SVO and no marking for
A and O is fairly striking particularly when the combination occurs outside the three great SVO blocs:
Europe, southern Africa and southeast Asia.   For
instance, almost all Australian languages have a basic
SOV word order with a good deal of freedom and most
Australian languages have case marking (usually ergative with nouns and accusative with pronouns).   Some
of the northern non-Pama-Nyungan languages lack all
case marking and it is among these that SVO as a basic
order has been reported e.g. Tiwi, Gunwinggu.   The
western Austronesian languages tend to be verb-initial
or SVO.   The verb-initial type has the focus system
as in Tagalog; the SVO languages lack a means of distinguishing A from O apart from word order.   The
Eastern Nilotic language, Bari, differs from its
neighbours not only by being SVO (whereas they are
VSO), but also in that it lacks an S/O case distinction and lacks subject marking and object marking on
the verb (some other Eastern Nilotic languages also
lack object marking).   However, having said this we

must point out that most of the evidence comes from
blocs of languages that are genetically related and/
or in contact (see also section 6.5.1.(e)).

Vennemann (1973, 1975) has suggested that SVO is
a favoured pattern in languages that do not mark the
A/O distinction morphologically since it allows O to
be fronted without causing ambiguity.   In a verb-final language one cannot place O before A without ris-
king ambiguity since the resulting pattern will be the
same as the AO pattern, viz. NP NP V.   This attempt
at explanation has some plausibility, particularly
when one considers that fronting of O (and of various
constituents) is extremely widespread, probably universal.   However, the explanation is weakened by the
fact that a language can lack a morphological means
of distinguishing A and O and yet not have SVO order
(e.g. Yessan-Mayo which is SOV) and by the fact that
a language can be SVO and exhibit a morphological
means of making the A/O distinction (e.g. Slavonic
languages).

3.5   Conclusion

At the beginning of chapter two we raised the
question of whether a morphological distinction between A and O was necessary if a language had free word
order.   We have shown that a language may lack both
a case distinction for A/O and fixed word order.
However, a language without fixed word order can employ order to distinguish A from O by using its basic
unmarked pattern in critical instances.

In the course of chapters two and three we have
discussed various means of distinguishing A from O
morphologically and the various orders of A, O and V
that can be found.   We have answered all the questions raised at the beginning of chapter two bar one,
viz. the question of whether a language can have fixed
word order *and* case marking for the A/O distinction.
The answer to this question proves elusive since there
are degrees of freedom in word order and degrees of O
marking (and to a lesser extent of A marking).   Certainly a number of languages have some accusative
marking and keep to a certain pattern of S, O and V
most of the time, e.g. Spanish, Khamti.   It appears
that languages with fairly rigid word order are a
distinct minority and most of the examples known to us
occur in western Europe, southern Africa and southeast
Asia, i.e. in the SVO 'caseless' areas.   In fact

Spanish and Khamti are exceptions in their areas.
Spanish has some 'new' O marking, more, for instance,
than most forms of Romance; while Khamti is an atypical
Tai language in that it has SOV order and accusative
marking (in the form of an oblique postposition
(Needham 1894)), both features of its Tibeto-Burman
neighbours.   We have not attempted to do statistics
on the apparent correlation between fixed word order
and absence of a morphological means of distinguishing
A and O since it is difficult to quantify 'fixedness'
of word order.   However, it seems that the view often
expressed by the casual observer is vindicated.
There is a correlation between rigidity of word order
and absence of a morphological means of distinguishing
A from O, even if it is not true that *rigid* word order
is necessary if A and O are to be distinguished by
order.

NOTES

[1]Where the term *free* is used, it means free at
the referential level.   It does not imply that the
use of one order rather than another is of no significance.

[2]We do not disagree with Dik's characterization
of German as VSO with a fronting rule, but we prefer
to be as conservative as possible in presenting data
for reference purposes.

[3]An alternative spelling *kunwinjku* is used in
Carroll 1976b with 'voiceless symbols' instead of
'voiced' ones.

[4]Further information appears in Carroll 1976b.

[5]See also sections 2.3.5. and 2.9.2.

[6]Geoff Pullum (pers.comm.) has pointed out to us
that he believes there are about 10 attested OVS languages in the world and about 5 OSV.   He assumes
there are 4,400 languages in the world and that
therefore OVS make up only 0.227% and OSV 0.113%.
He feels that our figure of 1% for these types is
misleadingly high.   We do not seriously dispute his
figures though we usually think of the total number of
languages as being vaguely around 4 to 5 thousand and
wonder how he manages to come up with a definite

figure (whatever the figure is it is dropping rapidly).
We arrived at our sample by going through lists of
languages and language families and drawing out 100
spread evenly over these families.   We gave preference to those languages on which there was a good
description available, hence Dyirbal (OSV) and
Hixkaryana (OVS) were included.   All our figures
should be regarded as approximate and nothing hangs
on a per cent one way or the other.   One per cent and
zero are both suitable approximations for OSV and OVS
and 1% is perhaps less misleading than zero since it
suggests the existence rather than the non-existence
of the type.

When we collected the sample we were unaware of
the existence of the Brazilian OSV languages so OSV
was lucky indeed to get into our sample.   Dyirbal
was the only OSV language known to us and it is a
rather dubious representative of the type since it
displays great freedom of word order.   We are indebted to Derbyshire and Pullum for drawing the existence of the Brazilian object-initial languages to our
notice.

Geoff Pullum has also pointed out to us that
millions of indians have been killed in the Brazilian
area since 1500 and that this has probably reduced
the proportion of object-initial languages from what
it would have been in a pre-1500 sample.

Geoff Pullum also notes that Hupda, which is
related to Nadib, is also OSV.   A checklist of OS
languages appears in Pullum's recent manuscript
'Languages with object before subject: a comment and
a catalogue'.

[7]Our source for Apurinã is two typescript papers
by Wilbur Pickering.   These appear in our bibliography as Pickering 1973a and 1973b.   Our examples
are from 1973a:1.   These papers are referred to in
Derbyshire & Pullum 1979 and Pullum 1980 as
Pickering 1974 (rather than 1973).

[8]An agent-to-the-left tendency *could* be involved
quite apart from topicalization.   One could speculate about why such a tendency should exist.   The
sequence AVO could be said to stand in an iconic relationship with the event described: the action passes
from the agent via the verb to the patient, as in the
primary school description of transitivity.   One of
our students, Peter Bruell, points out that AOV may

equally well be considered iconic, the 'permanent'
entities being presented before the transient, and
within the permanents, the instigator precedes the
patient.   VAO could then be considered weakly iconic.

[9]See also discussion in section 6.5.3.

[10]Des Derbyshire (pers.comm.) has pointed out to
us that in the Carib languages, Makúsi and Arekuna/
Taulipang, a pronominal subject almost always occurs
after V, while a noun subject commonly occurs before
or after the verb.   Derbyshire & Pullum 1979 ana-
lyze these languages as OVS with a fronting rule for
emphasis etc.   If this is the correct analysis, then
one would expect pronouns, which are less likely to
be emphasized, to appear less often in the first
position in the clause than nouns.   These languages
seem to be topic-to-the-right languages and the behaviour of pronouns is consistent with this.   Note in
passing that these languages exhibit ergative marking
and an ergative pattern of word order and affix order:

basic order: $S_i V$ affix order: S_i-V

O V A   O-V-A

In Hixkaryana (Derbyshire 1979:87), the normal order
is OVS, but an *emphasized* free S pronoun may appear
before the verb yielding an SVO pattern.

[11]Steele (1978:595) sees a semantic difference
between these two constructions.   'One of the distinctions between the two possible orders of direct
and indirect objects is roughly this.

Mary threw John the ball

Mary threw the ball to John

In the first John has to be actively participating in
the act; in the second he needn't.

*Mary threw John the ball, but he wasn't looking

Mary threw the ball to John, but he wasn't
looking'

We do not see anything wrong with the starred sentence and in general we do not see that active parti-
cipation is involved in any distinction between the
two types.

[12]In Romanian there are separate bound pronouns
for direct and indirect object, but with neutraliza-

tion in the plural of the first and second persons, also third feminine plural.

[13]Three quarters of the languages of the world have agreement, most of them 'copy' or 'semicopy' agreement.   One would need to examine a sample of non-agreement languages to establish whether some of these have free word order.   If one takes a random sample, there will be so few non-agreement languages in the sample that one could miss the free-word-order/ non-agreement type by chance.   In Steele's sample of 63 languages, 49 had agreement, as we noted in the text.

[14]We are grateful to David Bradley for drawing to our attention the exceptional status of Thailand Lisu.

[15]We counted as [+case] languages having marking on at least one major subclass of nouns, e.g. human nouns.

CHAPTER 4

CO-ORDINATION

4.1 Introduction

In chapters two and three we discussed the ways in which languages use word order and case marking to signal grammatical relations. In our discussion we were concerned with languages as a whole but our material was drawn primarily, though not exclusively, from either simple sentences or main clauses. However, we did point out that in subordinate clauses matters can be a little different. In German, for example, word order in main clauses is verb-second whereas in subordinate clauses it is primarily verb-final. In English, too, there are differences of this kind, so that we find a contrast in word order between simple (or direct) questions and embedded (or indirect) questions. Compare (4.1) and (4.2).

(4.1) a. Was the Prime Minister incapacitated?

       b. Why was the Prime Minister incapacitated?

(4.2) a. The Chancellor asked whether the Prime Minister was incapacitated

       b. The Chancellor asked why the Prime Minister was incapacitated

In (4.1) the subject is not in its usual initial position whereas in (4.2) it occurs in the normal declarative position before the verb.

In chapter five we will be looking at some of the reasons for differences in word order between main and subordinate clauses when we discuss the formation of relative structures. Indeed, the major part of that chapter will be concerned with word order but in our discussion we will also be examining

case marking.   Once more it will be shown to be unrealistic to discuss word order and case marking as
separate issues, since the very effect of word order
differences in subordinate structures, as compared
with main clauses, may be a masking of the grammatical relations normally discernible from basic word
order, so that some case marking may be called on to
allow decoding.

   In this chapter, too, we will be concerned with
word order when we examine the conjoining of structures ranging from constituents as small as prepositions to ones as large as clauses.[1] In this case,
however, explicit case marking is less important since
our main aim will be to investigate the relationship
between word order and the ways in which languages
avoid the repetition of identical material.   Nevertheless, the details of this economizing principle
cannot be examined without some reference to the role
of explicit case marking.   To illustrate this point,
consider the following example of what is known in
the transformational literature as *gapping*.[2]

(4.3)   a.   Do cats eat bats and do bats eat cats?

        b.   Do cats eat bats and bats cats?

In b. the verb is missing from the second clause (or
has been *deleted*) and this is allowed by language
since the hearer will be able to *recover* it from the
occurrence of the verb in the first clause.   Such a
phenomenon is widespread in English, though the extent to which it is used varies considerably.   It
appears to be a feature more of written than spoken
language; it also varies from speaker to speaker
(the two authors, for example, differ greatly in their
use and tolerance of gapping in spoken language,
though this may well be a reflection of an interest
in, and hence familiarity with, the phenomenon on the
part of one of us).

   Gapping can be remarkably complex.   Consider
the following example, in which the second clause has
lost its verb but retains subject, object, indirect
object and two adverbial phrases.

(4.4)   John sends presents to his children every
              year from Paris and Mary flowers to her
              mother every month from Athens

There appear to be two important factors governing

the acceptability of gapping examples. First it is
crucial that there be some balance between the number
of constituents in each clause, and their type.
Thus, language users may find (4.5) more troublesome
than (4.4), since it is our ability to recover the
roles of the nominal constituents in the second
clause that is at issue, and this is facilitated by
our ability to match those roles with the ones in the
full clause that precedes it.

(4.5)   ?John sends presents to his children every
             year from Paris and Mary to her mother

Secondly, it appears from informal work done on gapping in languages with more explicit case marking
that the recovery of explicitly marked roles adds to
the acceptability of the gapped structure as a whole.
This can be seen in languages such as, for example,
Romanian where there is explicit marking of object
NPs high on the animacy hierarchy, and is certainly
true of languages in which subjects and direct
objects are consistently marked as such (for a discussion of gapping in Romanian see Mallinson 1981a).
However, the principle can even be seen in English,
and it is likely that examples such as (4.6), in
which the indirect object appears without a preposition and before the direct object, is less acceptable
than its equivalent (4.4), for some speakers at least.

(4.6)   John sends his children presents every year
             from Paris and Mary her mother flowers
             every month from Athens

Although, as we have pointed out, there is great variation from speaker to speaker in the acceptability of
particular instances of gapping, it is safe to assume
that the lack of explicit indirect object marker
increases the chances in (4.6) of inaccurate processing (for a discussion of the effect of potential ambiguity on the degree to which gapping is tolerated
see in particular Hankamer 1973).

However, our main discussion of word order and
case marking has been in terms of a tradeoff between
them. We concluded, in fact, that there was a lot
of truth in the informal view that languages with
more rigid word order tend to need less explicit case
marking. In the case of gapping, however, this
tradeoff is not the main issue, since the degree to

which the examples we have looked at are acceptable
may well vary according to the degree of case marking,
but this will be so even in a language where fairly
strict word order makes case marking redundant.   Thus
it seems that a study of gapping strategies in language is of relevance to two matters: the degree to
which languages can exploit this avoidance of repetition, and the degree to which explicit case marking
helps in processing missing constituents - though it
is also indirectly of relevance to the tradeoff between word order and case marking in the decoding of
grammatical relations.

In chapter five we will also be concerned with
the ability of languages to avoid repetition and with
the devices they make use of to recover the missing
material.   However, we will see that the tradeoff
between word order and case marking is a much more
real issue in relative clause formation.   It is
partly for this reason that we have chosen to discuss
co-ordinate and subordinate structures separately,
though they also involve distinct strategies for
reducing sentences.

In order to do this, of course, we require some
clear means of distinguishing co-ordination from subordination.   In the remainder of this section we discuss one or two problematical structures that make it
difficult to set up a clearcut distinction.

The most obvious definition of a co-ordinate
structure is one in which constituents of the same
type are joined by *and*, or its equivalents in other
languages.   Unfortunately this definition is far
from satisfactory since first, not all languages have
a morpheme corresponding to *and*; secondly, it begs
the important question of how we know that two constituents *are* of the same type.   To illustrate the
first point, Japanese has a range of postpositions
for conjoining noun phrases but no explicit conjunction for forming co-ordinate clauses.   Instead, the
first clause is participialized, a feature also of
some of the languages of India.   (4.7) is a typical
example of this kind of conjoining device in Japanese,
and (4.8) in Hindi.

(4.7)   Norio ga Tokyo ni ik-i,   Sumie ga
              nom   to go-ing   nom
        Osaka ni iku
              to goes
        'Norio goes to Tokyo and Sumie goes to Osaka'

(4.8)   usne uskii ããkhõ mẽ   dekhkar darwaazaa
        He   poss   eyes   into look-ing door
             band kar diyaa
             shut   did
        'Looking into her eyes, he closed the door'

In other languages, mere juxtaposition is the method
used for conjoining. Thus, in Oykangand, clauses
are simply placed together without a conjunction.

(4.9)   abm   ay in   elkoy idar   lalaŋal
        person I   meat turtle eat-past [uncle-ag]
             uy   idar
             fish eat-past
        'I ate the turtle (and) uncle ate the fish'
                                        (Sommer 1972)

Juxtaposition is also a favoured conjoining device in
Yaqui, although it is an optional rather than an obligatory alternative to the use of a discrete marker.

(4.10) a. ooro-po-te koakte-k   te potam-po
            Oros-in-we turn-realized we Potam-in
                yaha-k
                arrive-realized
            'We turned around in Oros (and) reached
             Potam'
        b. in ačai   bwiika in abači   into
            my father sing   my brother and
                yeʔe
                dance
            'My father is singing and my brother is
             dancing'   (Lindenfeld 1973)

It is, of course, essential in such cases to be certain that we are dealing with a single, compound structure rather than with the mere sequencing of two quite separate, simplex sentences.   Use of non-final intonation at the end of the first conjunct is a reasonably safe criterion and is evident in the following example from English, where juxtaposition has a highly contrastive value.

(4.11)   Them as ask don't get, them as don't ask

          don't want

The second point is particularly troublesome and often gives rise to theoretical circularity.   That is, the very name co-ordination suggests equality between the elements linked, so that there has been a tendency to *assume* that only elements of the same type can be co-ordinated and then to claim that two constituents must be of the same type *because* they can be co-ordinated (or conversely are not of the same type because they cannot be linked in this way).   This point we discuss in some detail in section 4.2.

Another way of defining subordination is to claim that one structure is in some way less important than another and, in the case of co-ordination, on an equal footing.   Unfortunately, militating against this definition is a tendency common to all languages. Thus, while there may be little doubt that the italicized clause in (4.12a) is subordinate to the rest of the sentence (here it is acting as an object of the main clause), in (4.12b) too the second clause is in some way logically dependent on the first.

(4.12)   a.   The policeman believed *the car thief was*

              operating in his area

         b.   The policeman came round the corner and

              the car thief ran away

There is a tendency for language users to attach logical priority to the first of two co-ordinate clauses, the thief's departure in this instance being seen as following the policeman's appearance and/or a consequence of it.   Thus, although *and* has very much the quality of a plus sign to merely link clauses, it has more to it than this.   So strong is our tendency to impose temporal or causal sequencing from left to right that we also without much difficulty imagine a scene where there is some logical connection between the two clauses when they are reversed, as in (4.13).

(4.13)   The car thief ran away and the policeman came
          round the corner

This need to impose such a relationship on co-ordinate clauses is very strong indeed and is sometimes the only way of accounting for examples like (4.14).

(4.14)   My grandmother wrote me a letter and six men
          can fit in the back seat of a Ford

Although originally this classic example was to demonstrate the pointlessness of conjoining clauses between which there was no structural similarity and no semantic link, it usefully illustrates how we can impose an interpretation that does give it some point. One assumes that the speaker has had an argument about the seating capacity of large cars and that a letter from a relation has settled the matter (the interpretation is clearer with heavy stress on *can*). (4.15a) however shows that subordination tends to override the effect of the left-to-right ordering that we have just looked at in relation to co-ordination. Here the italicized clause is acting as subject of the main clause, and can be moved into final position, as in (4.15b), without altering the semantic relationship between the two clauses at all.

(4.15)   a. *That soccer is increasing in popularity*
              in Australia is clear from the latest
              accident figures
          b. It is clear from the latest accident
              figures *that soccer is increasing in*
              popularity in Australia

(it is the relative heaviness of the italicized clause that makes b more normal than a - see section 5.2.4. for further discussion of this point).

    On the other hand, if we ignore the logical prominence of clauses coming first in the sentence, it is clear that true co-ordination involves clauses that could function independently of each other. This is clearly so with the example involving the policeman and the car thief.

Nevertheless, just as the logical precedence of
one clause over another may belie the structural
equality of clauses in a co-ordinate structure, so
too may the use of *and* in English belie the subordination of one clause to another.   This is particularly so with pseudo-imperatives like the first clause
in (4.16a), in reality a disguised conditional with
the same value as the italicized clause in (4.16b).

(4.16)   a.   *Give me your money and* I will give you
                   your freedom

         b.   *If you give me your money,* I will give
                   you your freedom

A further use of *and* that is ostensibly co-ordinating
but on closer inspection can be shown not to be is
that in (4.17).

(4.17)   The child went to the shops and bought some
               potatoes

That this sentence is not what it seems is clear from
the fact that a constraint on question formation from
co-ordinate structures appears to be ignored.   (4.18)
can be formed on (4.17) but (4.20) cannot be formed
on (4.19).

(4.18)   What did the child go to the shops and buy?

(4.19)   John fed the cat and locked up the house

(4.20)   *What did John feed the cat and lock up?

In (4.17) it seems that *and* has less the value of a
co-ordinating conjunction and more that of a subordinating conjunction with a purpose or sequential value.

On the other hand, an ostensibly subordinating
conjunction can have a co-ordinating value.   This
view seems to be shared by a number of linguists, particularly those within the transformationalist school,
who have given different sources to the apparently
quite similar examples in (4.21).

(4.21)   a.   All teachers who recently got a payrise
                   will pay more tax

(4.21)   b.   All teachers, who recently got a payrise,
              will pay more tax

It is the fact that (4.21b) can occur as (4.22b), but
not (4.21a) as (4.22a), that has led linguists to
relate the non-restrictive clause type to a co-ordinate structure.

(4.22)   a.   *All teachers and they recently got a
              payrise will pay more tax

         b.   All teachers, and they recently got a
              payrise, will pay more tax

We have already warned in chapter one against the
dangers of using underlying structures to 'prove'
similarities between structures, but the non-restrictive relative clause does appear to be much more
weakly embedded than its restrictive counterpart (we
return to the restrictive/non-restrictive distinction
in our discussion of relative clause formation in
chapter five).

     Clearly we have to be careful in defining co-
ordination and it would seem that a purely structural
definition is much safer than a semantic one.   We
might then define co-ordinate sentences as ones in
which the two (or more) clauses have grammatical
equality.   However, to claim that there is structural
equality between the two parts of a co-ordinate structure might also seem rash in view of the gapping
examples we looked at earlier.   Since it is the
second, not the first clause, which is vulnerable to
reduction a case might be made for stating that the
first clause is more equal than the second.   However,
we will be examining the ability of a range of languages to reduce clauses in this way and it will be
seen that it is not always the first clause which
remains intact.   In our study in this chapter of co-
ordinate structure reduction we do, in fact, take the
view that co-ordinate structures are structurally
balanced, and that the direction of deletion is determined by a combination of principles, including one
that has more to do with the needs of language users
in processing linguistic material, and with the unde-
sirability of imposing unnecessary loads on short-
term memory, than with structural inequality.[3]

     Finally, to close this introductory section, we
should point out that there are other non-subordina-

ting conjunctions which might be discussed in a more
thorough study of co-ordinate structures - in particular *but* and *or*.   However, *and* itself allows scope
for a very full discussion of the phenomena we are
concerned with here, and the distribution of the other
two conjunctions is rather more limited.   This is
because of their enhanced semantic value over the
rather neutral *and*.   It is this limited semantic content of the conjunction *and* (though, as we have said,
it is more than a mere plus sign) that allows it a
less restricted distribution, and thus makes it an
important part of any discussion of co-ordinate
structure reduction.

4.2   Constituent Co-ordination

So far we have talked mainly about co-ordinate
clauses, rather than other types of constituent but
the main theme of this chapter does revolve around the
conjoining of full clauses and the ways in which repetition within these clauses can be avoided.   Languages do, however, allow the conjoining of constituents
below the level of the clause and it will be useful to
examine the degree to which such conjoining is possible.

Major Constituents

It is perhaps the noun phrase that is most
commonly found in co-ordinate structures, but many
languages also allow the conjoining of other major
constituents - including verbs, verb phrases, adpositional phrases, oblique phrases and adverbs.   The
conjunctions used in such cases are the same in English and other Indo-European languages as those used
to conjoin clauses.   This is not, however, by any
means an Old World monopoly and we give the following
examples from Luiseño by way of illustration.

(4.23)   *Clause*

        Xwaan   heelaq   pi   Mariya   pellaq
                sing   and   dance
        'Juan sings and Maria dances'

(4.24)   *NP*

   Xwaan   pi   Mariya   pellaxkutum

            and   dance-future

   'Juan and Maria are going to dance'

(4.25)   *Verb (Phrase)*

   Xwaan   heelaq   pi   pellaq

           sing   and dance

   'Juan sings and dances'

                              (Hyde 1971)

In other languages there may be a distinct marker for
conjoined clauses, as in Kapampangan.   In (4.26)
noun phrases are linked by *ampo*, and in (4.27) clauses
are linked by *ampong*.

(4.26)   Migkanta la ri Maria   ampo   i   Juan

          sang   they   and   det

          'Maria and Juan sang'

(4.27)   Mestro   ya i   Juan   ampong   estudyante

          teacher be det   and   student

             ya i   Maria

             be det

          'Juan is a teacher and Maria is a student'

                              (Mirikitani 1972)

It is not unlikely, however, that there is some morphological relationship between these two markers.

     Constraints on the conjoining of major constitu-
ents are basically grammatical.   It is clearly very
odd to attempt to conjoin a noun with, for example, a
verb, or an adjective.   However, (4.28) is an example of a noun phrase being conjoined with an adjective, a perfectly natural construction provided they
are both being used predicatively.

(4.28)   My father wants to be a politician and happy

Clearly, if we accept that NPs and adjectives are
different types of category, then a purely categorial
basis to co-ordination is unrealistic.   That functional or semantic parallellism is required is also

clear from examples such as (4.29), in which a prepositional phrase and an adverb have been successfully co-ordinated.

(4.29)   John ate quickly and with good appetite

This example is from a paper by Schachter (Schachter
1974) on co-ordination constraints and his claim is
that such examples can be captured grammatically as
follows.

(4.30)

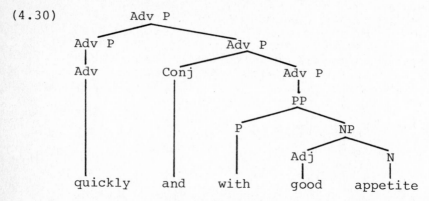

Such a solution seems to us to be cheating since it
involves a quite arbitrary system of node labelling
simply to rescue a purely structural definition of
the constraints on co-ordination.   Presumably one
could extend this system to account for examples like
(4.28) by invoking a category label such as *Predicate
Phrase*, but it would be even more forced if called on
to account for examples like (4.31).

(4.31)   John is a good cook but not very good at
          washing up

On the other hand, two constituents may share the
same category label but resist co-ordination because
they have some semantic incompatibility.   Neil Smith
has suggested the following example.

(4.32)   a.   The queen lurked in the palace
          b.   The queen lived in the palace
          c.   *The queen lurked and lived in the palace

The constraints on co-ordination are much more subtle
than the use of clever labels implies and must

involve some intricate blend of structural, semantic
and pragmatic conditions.[4]

Minor Constituents

   While the constraints on the conjoining of minor
constituents must also take account of semantic com-
patibility, of more importance here is the degree of
freedom minor constituents do or do not enjoy.
Since the degree to which minor constituents such as
prepositions and determiners are free will vary from
language to language much more than is the case with
some of the major constituents we have just examined,
it is likely that there will be more language-specific
constraints in this area. The examples which follow
demonstrate such variation in two related languages –
English and Romanian.

   Although determiners such as the definite and
indefinite article in English are orthographically
distinct, they are not free forms, since they cannot
exist in sentences independently of the noun(phrase)s
they determine. This is why they cannot be conjoined, as in (4.33), in which the Romanian version
is even more disastrous, given the suffixal nature of
the Romanian definite marker.

(4.33)   *Ion   a   vazut   un   şi   animalul

          aux   see-past   a   and   animal-the
                  part

          '*Ion saw a and the animal'

On the other hand, demonstratives in English seem to
tolerate conjoining, whereas Romanian speakers seem
to be much less certain about the acceptability of
examples like (4.34).

(4.34)   ?Aceste   şi   acele   lucruri   sînt

          this-fpl   and   that-fpl   thing-pl   are

          ale   mele

          det   my-fpl

          'These and those things are mine'

   The acceptability of the English translation has
undoubtedly something to do with the fact that demonstratives are phonologically identical in their dependent and pronominal forms, whereas in Romanian a

pronominal marker -a is required, as in (4.35).

(4.35)   Acestea   şi acelea   sînt ale
         this-fpl-pro   that-fpl-pro are   det
         mele
         my-fpl
         'These and those are mine'

    Auxiliary verbs are also a category on the bor-
derline of free occurrence, being more free in English than in Romanian. While all auxiliary forms
may be used in English without the support of a main
verb, in Romanian this is not possible. That auxiliaries cannot be used in Romanian in examples such as
(4.36) thus flows on from their ungrammaticality in
examples such as (4.37), precisely the opposite
judgements being the case for the English translations.

(4.36)   *Ion va   şi poate face   ce   vrea
               will   can   do-inf what wish
         să   facă
         comp do-subj
         'Ion will and can do what he wants to do'

(4.37)   Ion   va   face   ce   vrea să   facă
               will do-inf what wish comp do-subj
         *Nu, Radu va
         no   will
         'Ion will do what he wants to do. No, Radu
         will'

Matters are somewhat complicated by examples such as
(4.38), a reversal of the auxiliary order in (4.36),
and which some speakers of Romanian find quite natural.

(4.38)   Ion poate şi va face tot ce vrea să
              facă
         'Ion can and will do everything he wants to
              do'

(note that this order is also more natural in the
English equivalent, since it is more likely that one
would establish someone's ability to carry out a task
before commenting on their desire to do so - however,
the purely syntactic constraint on (4.36) in Romanian
dominates).   It appears that the modal *poate* is less
clearly an auxiliary - not only does it have an infinitival form in its paradigm (which other auxiliaries
such as markers of future and conditional do not),
but it can also be used with a following subjunctive-
marked complement, as in (4.39).

(4.39)   Pot   să   mă   duc

          can   comp refl lead-subj

          'I can go'

More commonly, though, it is used with an infinitive
following, as in (4.40).

(4.40)   Ion poate veni   dacă vrea

                      come-inf if

          'Ion can come if he wants'

Without wishing to labour the point unnecessarily,
the *poate* paradigm may be seen as straddling the
division between auxiliary and full verb, being perhaps the only verb in modern Romanian to resist the
Balkan areal tendency for infinitival complement
structures to be replaced by ones with a subjunctive
form (see Sandfeld 1930 for a fuller discussion of
Balkan features in general, and Mallinson 1978 for a
discussion of Romanian infinitives).

     It appears that co-ordination can be used as a
criterion for determining the freedom of occurrence
of minor constituents, even if it has limited value
for classifying constituents as being 'of the same
type'.   In the case of prepositions, the two languages allow these to conjoin quite freely, so that
we find examples like (4.41) occurring quite naturally.

(4.41)   Rîndunica   a   zburat   peste   şi
          swallow-det   aux   fly-past   over   and
                                  part

                 printre   pomi
                 through   tree-pl

          'The swallow flew over and through the trees'

With prepositions, however, some language-specific
conditions may arise. For example, they have a dual
status in language: they have their own intrinsic
semantic value as markers of direction, location and
the like, as in the above two examples, but they can
also be regarded as markers of grammatical relations
such as direct and indirect object.

      Comparing English and Romanian again, we find
that there are no problems in English with examples
such as the following, involving the conjoining of
constituents marked as recipients and beneficiaries:

(4.42)   These martyrs gave their lives to and for
          God and their country

In Romanian, however, recipients are marked by inflection (dative case), and benefactives either by dative
case or by preposition (*pentru* 'for'). In (4.43) it is
unclear whether the identical case marking is to be
interpreted as recipient and beneficiary, or merely
as conjoined beneficiaries:

(4.43)   Tărîi   şi   gloriei   le-a
          country-dat   glory-dat 3dat-aux
             jertfit   preotul   propria   sa
             sacrifice-past   priest-det   own-det   poss
             viaţă   part
             life

          'To/for his country and to/for glory did the
          priest sacrifice his own life'

      The only prepositional marking of a clearcut
relational category is the use of the object marker
pe for entities high on the animacy hierarchy and for
marking pronouns as objects. Since the use of *pe*
also involves cross-referencing on the verb, it is

difficult to see how the following two examples could
be conjoined in a way that would directly link *pe* and
the benefactive *pentru*.

(4.44)   Căpcăunul   l-a   mîncat   pe   Radu

          ogre-det   3acc-aux   eat-past   acc
                                   part

          'The ogre ate Radu'

(4.45)   Căpcăunul   a   dansat   pentru   mine

          ogre-det   aux   dance-past   for   me
                                   part

          'The ogre danced for me'

In a language such as Japanese, where case-marking is
by postposition, conjoining in this way is not possible, even among semantically compatible postpositions,
because of the morphologically bound nature of these
markers.   The following example is clearly ungrammatical, even though its English equivalent is quite
natural:

(4.46)   *Sumie wa   Osaka ni   to   kara   iku

                  top   to   and   from   goes

          'Sumie goes to and from Osaka'

(4.46) can be related to (4.47) and (4.48) in which
the postpositions with their directional value are
unconjoined.

(4.47)   Sumie   wa   Osaka ni   iku

                  top   to   goes

          'Sumie goes to Osaka'

(4.48)   Sumie   wa   Osaka kara   iku

                  top   from   goes

          'Sumie goes from Osaka'

Finally, there may be a further constraint on
co-ordination that transcends those we have examined
already.

Government and Concord

When prepositions are more than mere case markers

they may govern different case forms, a problem that
does not arise in English but does in a language with
great reliance on inflections, such as Latin.   In
the following examples, the prepositions govern accusative and ablative case forms respectively, and so
cannot be conjoined without breaking the case-govern-
ment rules of the language.

(4.49)   Romani   in Asiam   transierunt

           nom in   acc   cross-past-3pl

       'The Romans crossed into Asia'

(4.50)   Romani   ex   Asia transierunt

            out of abl

       'The Romans crossed out of Asia'

(4.51)   *Romani   in et ex Asia(m)   transierunt

       'The Romans crossed into and out of Asia'

Unfortunately no native speakers were available at
the time of writing, but it is possible that in (4.51)
Asia would have been more acceptable than *Asiam*
because *ex* is the preposition nearer to the governed
noun.   Since the general meaning of the sentence is
clear from the verb of motion (*in* also occurs with an
ablative case when it has a locational rather than
directional value), native speakers in casual conversation might well have tolerated the technical error.

It appears that proximity is an important factor
in judgements of acceptability on agreement and
government.

There are further instances of this in the conjoining of other constituent types.   In English, the
distance between the first auxiliary italicized in
(4.53) and the full verb it governs is greater than
that between the same elements in (4.52), but (4.53)
would be judged more acceptable.

(4.52)   ?Bill *has* and *will underestimate* the
          opposition

(4.53)   Bill *has* and, if I'm not mistaken which I
          rarely am, probably always *will under-*
          estimate the opposition

Neither of these examples would be acceptable with
the order of auxiliaries reversed, that is, with control by the first auxiliary.

(4.54)   *Bill *will* and *has underestimate* the oppo-
          sition

(4.55)   *Bill *will* and, if I'm not mistaken which I
          rarely am, probably always *has under-
          estimate* the opposition

Whether consciously or unconsciously, though, the control problem is neutralized by using a verb that has
identical stem and past participle forms.

(4.56)   Bill *has* and *will upset* the opposition

The conjoining of nouns is also likely to present
such problems in languages with a grammatical gender
or noun-class system.   Whereas in English there is
no grammatical gender, most Indo-European languages
do have a gender system.   In German, for instance,
adjectives agree with their head noun in case and
gender:

(4.57)   mein   guter   Wein
          masc   masc   masc
          'my good wine'

(4.58)   mein   gutes   Brot
          neut   neut   neut
          'my good bread'

(4.59)   meine   gute   Suppe
          fem   fem   fem
          'my good soup'

However, this patterning has a number of gaps.   Not
only does the agreement of attributive adjectives
with head nouns not occur in certain set phrases, such
as the following proverb:

(4.60)   Gut   Ding   will   Weile   haben

          good   thing   want   time   have-inf

          'Nothing good is done in a hurry'

but there is also neutralization of gender differences
when the adjective follows a definite determiner.
Compare the definite (4.61) with the possessive (4.57).

(4.61)   der   gute   Wein

          masc   -   masc

          'the good wine'

Furthermore, although there is agreement between the
subject of the sentence and the verb, as in (4.62),
there is no agreement between subjects and predicative
adjectives.   (4.62) and (4.63) demonstrate this
neutralization, in comparison with the forms in (4.57),
(4.58) and (4.59).

(4.62)   Sie   waren   fleißig

          pro   were   hardworking-Ø

          'They/you were hardworking'

(4.63)   Mein   Brot ⎫
          Mein   Wein ⎬   ist gut
          Meine   Suppe⎭

             masc ⎫
             neut ⎬   is good-Ø
             fem ⎭

Such neutralization is also found in Russian, as in
the following example from Corbett 1979.

(4.64)   ja beruś   za   sledujuśčix   ženixa   i

          I   take-refl   for following   groom   and

              nevestu

              bride

          'I set about the following groom and bride'

The plural form is neutral with respect to feminine
and masculine agreement.   Where, as in this example,
there is a conjoining of noun phrases of different
gender or word class, two options appear to be open
to languages: first, there may be a syntactically

unmarked form that is automatically used in such
cases.   That this form is often, in Indo-European
languages at least, the equivalent of the masculine
plural, is an unfortunate fact these days and one
wonders in all seriousness whether the tendency to
replace English words in -*man* with ones ending in
woman or *person* (as in *chairman* - *chairwoman*, *chair-*
person) might be repeated in the forms used for agreement in other languages where the masculine is the unmarked form.   In the Romance languages, agreement is
always with the masculine if at least one of the conjuncts is masculine, as in the following examples from
French, Italian and Spanish:

(4.65)   Ce   garçon   et   cette   fille   sont
           masc   masc   fem   fem

               beaux/*belles

               masc   fem

           'This boy and this girl are beautiful'

(4.66)   Aquel   muchacho   y   esta   muchacha   son
           masc   masc   fem   fem

               buenos/*buenas

               masc   fem

           'That boy and this girl are beautiful'

(4.67)   Quello   ragazzo   e   quella   ragazza   sono
           masc   masc   fem   fem

               belli/*belle

               masc   fem

           'That boy and this girl are beautiful'

A second option is for agreement to be with either
the semantically dominant or the nearer conjunct.
In unpublished research carried out by Mallinson, it
was clear that speakers of Romance languages used
both of these principles when asked to relax the offi-
cial rule.

       A further option open to speakers of a language
where neutralization is not possible is to use structures that avoid the problem altogether.   Many languages have a noun-class system far more complex than
the simple two- or three-gender pattern of Indo-Euro-

pean languages.   In Xhosa, for example, a Bantu language with a rich noun-class system on roughly semantic grounds, Voeltz 1971 demonstrates that extraposition can be employed to remove one of the conjuncts
out of a position where it would control agreement.

In (4.68) there is no agreement problem since
the two conjuncts both belong to the 1/2 class.[5]
In (4.69), however, the nouns belong to the 5/6 and
7/8 classes respectively, and neither 5/6 nor 7/8
agreement is acceptable.   (4.70) involves the extraposition of the second conjunct and agreement with
the 5/6 noun is then acceptable.

(4.68)   Umfana   nomfazi bayagoduka

          young man   and-woman   1/2 go home
             1/2   1/2

          'The young man and the woman are going home'

(4.69)   *Igqira   nesanuse $\begin{cases} a\text{yagoduka} \\ \text{5/6 go home} \\ \\ zi\text{yagoduka} \\ \text{7/8 go home} \end{cases}$

           doctor   and-diviner
             5/6   7/8

          'The doctor and the diviner are going home'

(4.70)   Igqira liyagoduka   nesanuse

          doctor   5/6 go home and-diviner
          5/6   7/8

          'The doctor is going home, and the diviner'

Xhosa has no general unmarked plural agreement form
for its adjectives, but some speakers do use a neutral animate form to avoid agreement clashes of this
kind and this might be an instance of speakers
following natural gender.   (4.71) is the form some
speakers can use for (4.69), with 1/2 agreement.

(4.71)   Igqira   nesanuse bayagoduka

          5/6   7/8   1/2

          'The doctor and the diviner are going home'

There are also some cases of morphological neutralization.   In (4.72) the 1a/2a and 1/2 prefixes happen
to be identical (though there are instances where

they would not be).

(4.72)   Abanakwethu   noodadewethu   *ba*yagoduka

          brothers-in-law   and-sisters   1/2
          1/2   1a/2a   1a/2a

          'My brothers-in-law and my sisters are going
             home'

In (4.73) the distinct prefixes for 7/8 and 9/10
classes (*zi-* and *zin-* respectively) are neutralized
by a phonological rule that reduces geminate nasals
(thus, *zinn-* becomes *zin-*)

(4.73)   Izandla   neendlebe   *zin*cinane

          hands   and-ears   7/8 be small
          7/8   9/10   9/10

          'The hands and ears are small'

These last two examples are a precise parallel of the
English phenomenon illustrated by (4.56), in which
morphological neutralization of distinct forms can
add to acceptability, and demonstrates that overriding language-specific constraints there are perhaps universal devices that speakers make use of, in
casual speech at least.

     What the examples in this last section as a
whole demonstrate is that there are more subtle constraints than those imposed by mere grammatical
labelling on the degree of co-ordination that languages will tolerate, and that some of these constraints collapse in the face of a desire to communicate, particularly when the minor grammatical features of government and agreement are to some extent
redundant.

4.3   Co-ordinate Structure Reduction

4.3.1.   A Traditional Approach and Some Criticism

     So far we have examined examples of clause co-
ordination and also, in rather more detail, the co-
ordination of constituents below clause level.   Despite the highly productive nature of constituent co-
ordination, however, there is a well-established
tradition - common to traditional and transformational
grammar alike - of deriving such co-ordination from
full-clause equivalents.   In traditional grammar it

is common to find a relationship established between
examples like (4.74) and (4.75).

(4.74)   Cats like cheese and mice like cheese

(4.75)   Cats and mice like cheese

Rather than being seen as the direct conjoining of
two subject noun phrases with a shared verb phrase,
(4.75) can be viewed as the omission of the first of
two identical verb phrases in the full sentence equivalent.   Such an approach is not unreasonable in the
case of many of the examples of constituent conjoining
we have examined so far, but there are certainly
instances where such an approach is unsuitable.
Writing at the beginning of the century, Fernald comments on this reduction approach as follows:

> 'There are, indeed, some grammarians (as
> Latham) who will say that conjunctions do not
> connect words or phrases, but only sentences,
> and that wherever two words seem to be joined
> by a conjunction the real union is of two
> sentences that might be made out of the one.
> In some cases such a division may be made,
> but in others it becomes ridiculous.'
>   (Fernald 1904:195).

Although enjoying considerable popularity in transformational circles (the reduction approach was
formalized in Chomsky 1957 and adopted by many linguists concerned with conjoining phenomena), there
are, as Fernald points out, a number of instances of
constituent co-ordination that make a reduction
approach untenable as an overall method for dealing
with the co-ordination of constituents below clause
level.   We now examine three types of example.

Distinct Markers for the Two Types of Conjoining

As we have seen, there are some languages which
use a different conjunction for clause and constituent co-ordination, and any approach which relates the
two types must also account for the change in marker.
Furthermore, as we have also pointed out, not all
languages use a discrete marker to conjoin sentences.
Although the conjoining of sentences involves the
participialization of the first in Japanese, there is
conjoining of constituents below clause level, and
the proponents of a reduction approach must therefore

account for this disparity.   In Japanese there are
three markers for conjoining noun phrases, as illustrated by (4.76) - (4.78).

(4.76)   Norio to   Sumie to   Tasaku ga   terebi

                 and   and   nom   T.V.

          o   mita

          acc watched

          'Norio, Sumie and Tasaku watched T.V.'

(4.77)   Norio ni,   Sumie ga   terebi o   mita

                 and   nom   T.V.   acc watched

          'Norio and Sumie watched T.V.'

(4.78)   Norio ya,   Sumie ya   Tasaku ga   terebi

                 and   and   nom   T.V.

          o   mita

          acc watched

          'Norio, Sumie and Tasaku watched T.V.'

-*to* is used to conjoin noun phrases when these are
the only participants involved - that is, Norio,
Sumie and Tasaku were watching television, but no-one
else not mentioned.   Both -*ni* and -*ya* are used when
other conjuncts are left unmentioned, -*ya* being further used when there are more than two conjuncts mentioned, -*ni* being restricted to two only.   Any rule
attempting to relate all these forms, and their uses,
to clausal co-ordination would have to be very
complex.

Non-existence of Full Clause Equivalents

     Just two examples from English will suffice to
illustrate this serious problem for a reduction
approach.   (4.79) is perfectly well-formed but (4.80)
is extremely unnatural.

(4.79)   Your son and his daughter are quite a happy

          pair

(4.80)   *Your son is quite a happy pair and his

          daughter is quite a happy pair.

This constraint is surely universal - it would only be possible to use examples such as (4.80) in a language whose speakers had an extremely odd view of the nature of the individual.

Symmetric Predicates

A wide range of languages have structures of this kind, with a similar semantic range of verbs and adjectival predicates.   Once more it is a matter of the full form being itself ungrammatical.   Such examples as the following from English and German involve a conjoined subject NP but cannot be realistically derived from corresponding conjoined intransitive sentences with singular subjects.

(4.81)   John and Mary met

(4.82)   *John met and Mary met

(4.83)   Ein Mädchen und ihr Freund   treffen sich
          A   girl   and her friend   meet   refl

          im Cafe
          in the cafe

(4.84)   *Ein Mädchen trifft sich im   Cafe
           A   girl   meets refl in the   cafe

           und ihr Freund trifft sich im   Cafe
           and her friend meets   in the cafe

Rather, such examples can be related to (4.85) and (4.86), where a singular subject NP shares the action with the comitative-marked NP in the predicate.

(4.85)   John met with Mary

(4.86)   Ein Mädchen trifft sich mit ihrem
          A   girl   meets refl with her

          Freund im   Cafe
          friend in the cafe

This phenomenon also occurs in Romanian, and is likewise marked with a reflexive form of the verb.

(4.87)   Maria   s-a   întîlnit   cu   Ion
                   refl-aux meet-past with
                     sg   part
         'Maria met with Ion'

(4.88)   Maria   şi   Ion   s-au   întîlnit
                 and   refl-aux meet-past
                               pl   part
         'Maria and Ion met (each other)'

(4.89)   *Maria   s-a   întîlnit
                   refl-aux meet-past
                     sg   part
         '*Maria met'

The class of predicates involved includes the equivalents of verbs such as *collide* and *converge*, and
adjectives such as *similar* and *identical*, although it
is not necessarily the case that all languages sharing
this pattern of structures will have precisely the
same range of predicates involved.   In Oykangand,
the range of such predicates is very restricted, but
at least demonstrates that the symmetric predicate is
not peculiarly Indo-European.

(4.90)   James, Ian ul,   ow-onbaʀ idndamay ul
                      they-2   face together   they-2
         'James and Ian look alike'

(4.91)   James il ow-onbaʀ idndamay iŋun Ian-an
                he face together   [him   -dat]
         'James looks like Ian'

Japanese also has examples, as illustrated by the
following, where the symmetric predicate is *discuss*.

(4.92)   Sensei   to   gakusei wa   mondai   o
         teacher and student top   problem acc
              hanashi atte iru
                 be discussing
         'The teacher and the student are discussing
             the problem'

(4.93)   Sensei   wa   gakusei   to   isshoni
          teacher   top   student   with   together
              mondai   o   hanashi atte iru
              problem   acc   be discussing
          'The teacher is discussing the problem with
          the student'

In each language such a device also serves to highlight or topicalize one of the NPs involved, so that
the subject NP and comitative NP can be reversed, as
for example in Japanese.[6]

(4.94)   Gakusei   wa   sensei   to   isshoni
          student   top   teacher   with   together
              mondai   o   hanashi atte iru
              problem   acc   be discussing
          'The student is discussing the problem with
          the teacher'

Symmetric predicates are a common feature in language
and usually any language with such structures will
have a comitative marker for the noun phrase marked
in English by *with*.   However, there is some variation in the methods used to form the verb in such
structures.

      A number of Indo-European languages use a refle-
xive marker to intransitivize the verb, as we saw
with Romanian and German, but other languages use
special particles to intransitivize structures.   In
Thai, for example, (4.95) is acceptable as a transitive but can occur as a symmetric predicate in (4.96)
by addition of the particle kan, or by a comitative
marker as in (4.97).

(4.95)   puk   phóp   dæ:ŋ
                 meet
          'Puk met Dang'

(4.96)   puk   lǽ?   dæ:ŋ   phóp   kan
                 and   meet
          'Puk and Dang met'

(4.97)   puk phóp kàp dæ:ŋ

        meet with

    'Puk met with Dang'

Once again there is some connection with reflexive
usage and one finds kan used with a reciprocal reflexive value in examples such as (4.98).

(4.98)   puk lǽ? dæ:ŋ ti   kan

        and   hit refl

    'Puk and Dang hit each other'

4.3.2.   Reduction by Proform

    Despite the problem examples just discussed, the
reduction approach to constituent conjoining still
enjoys a good deal of popularity, reflecting perhaps
a widespread awareness among linguists of the tendency of languages to avoid repetition by the omission
of identical constituents.   However, such omission
is not the only way that languages avoid repetition
and a common feature is the use of *proforms* to the
same end.   Not only in conjoined structures, but
also in other types of complex sentence, and also
across sentence boundaries, a second mention of an NP
can be replaced with a personal pronoun.   Matching
examples such as (4.99) from English are (4.100) and
(4.101) from French and German.

(4.99)   *John* enjoys *cricket* although *he* doesn't

        play *it* very often

(4.100)   Moi, je préfère *Jean* parce qu'*il* est plus

        franc que Dominique

    'As for me, I prefer *Jean* because *he* is

    more outspoken than Dominique'

(4.101)   *Karl* hat *Marie* gern   weil   *er*   *sie*

        [be   fond of] because he   her

    charmant   findet

    intriguing finds

    '*Karl* likes *Marie* because *he* thinks *she*'s

    intriguing'

Such a method of avoiding repetition is fairly common
and is well-represented in the Romance languages,
although there are some members of the family, such as
Italian and Romanian, where the subject pronoun is
represented in the verb.

(4.102)   Il   chianti   è   il   piu   famoso dei
           det   chianti   be   det   more   famous of-the

           vini   italiani.   Anzi,
           wine-pl   italian-pl   Indeed,

           rappresenta   l'Italia   in   campo
           represent-3s   det-Italy   in   field

           vinicolo
           wine-making

           'Chianti is the most famous of the Italian

           wines.   Indeed, *it represents* Italy in

           the field of wine-making'

(4.103)   Ion   n-a   vǎzut   piesa.   Cu
           not-aux see-past play-det   with
                            part

           toate   acestea,   înţelege   tema
           all   this-pl-pro understand-3s   theme-
                                                 det

           'Ion didn't see the play.   All the same,

           he understands the theme'

In addition, it is also possible to regard examples
such as the following as involving replacement of
(part of) the predicate by a proform.

(4.104)   John likes spaghetti and *so* does Bill

(4.105)   John likes spaghetti and Bill does *too*

In each case the italicized element replaces the verb
and its direct object, *do* carrying the tense - here
present, but in (4.106) past.

(4.106)   John saw the cat and Bill did *too*

Examples such as the following from Japanese and

Yaqui also seem to involve proforms.

(4.107) Norio wa   terebi o   mita, Sumie mo
                top   acc watch   and
         sō shita
         so did
         'Norio watched television and so did Sumie'

(4.108) Maria kaa yepsak   ta   peo ala
                not arrive-   but   opp
                     realized
         'Maria did not arrive but Peter did'[7]

It seems, however, that in many apparent cases of
predicate proforms, mere deletion of the verb and the
rest of the predicate is involved, the auxiliary
alone being retained. The German example (4.109)
matches its English translation, but such a phenomenon will be restricted to languages which allow their
auxiliary verbs independent existence.

(4.109) Walter muss nicht gehen, aber Peter
         'Walter must not   go,   but   Peter
              muss (gehen)
              must (go)'

Thus, whereas all languages allow pronouns to stand in
place of full NPs, not all languages allow the use of
proforms to stand in place of verb phrases. Once
again we see an instance of a potentially universal
pattern that is subject to language-specific constraints - specifically, in this case, the relative
degree of freedom given to auxiliary verbs to stand
alone as representatives of the verb phrase they can
be interpreted as replacing. Even though pronouns
are a common device for replacing repeated noun phrases (and to a lesser extent for replacing verb phrases) they do however provide less interest for cross-
linguistic investigation than the omission of repeated constituents.

4.4   The Typology of Co-ordinate Structure Reduction

4.4.1. The Theoretical Options

     In chapter one we discussed some of the hazards

of adopting a model-bound approach to the investigation of cross-linguistic data.   This warning against
too heavy a reliance on particular theoretical stances also applies to the treatment of conjoined structures and other devices employed by language to avoid
repetition.   Returning to the use of proforms that
we looked at in the last section, we can view such
devices in two ways.   Model-specifically proforms
involve the *replacement* of all but one occurrence of
an identical constituent by the appropriate form.
Model-neutrally, they are merely *used* in order to
avoid repetition.

The treatment of proforms during the 1960s was
usually transformational, but there came later a rea-
lization that at least some pronouns could not realistically be derived in this way.   In the following
example the first and second person pronouns have no
antecedent, the identity of *I* being whoever the speaker happens to be, and that of *you* being whoever is
being addressed.   A transformational approach would
need a special transformation for every speaker and
one for every hearer.

(4.110)   I like you

Other examples providing problems for a transformational approach include instances of the Bach-Peters
paradox.   In (4.111), the antecedent of each of the
underlined pronouns is an NP containing the other
pronoun, so that an infinitely long derivation would
be required to avoid having any pronouns at all in
deep structure.[8]

(4.111)   The pilot who shot at *it* hit the MiG that
            chased *him*

The alternative favoured in the late 1960s and in the
1970s was an interpretive approach which introduced
pronouns directly into structures and then assessed
them for possible co-reference.   However, it is
important to realize that merely introducing anaphoric pronouns into structures does not solve some of
the descriptive problems that the transformational
approach was intended to solve.   Whichever approach
is adopted, a description of the following examples
must satisfactorily account for the fact that some
uses of anaphoric pronouns are possible and others
not:

(4.112)   When John got home he felt sick

(4.113)   When he got home John felt sick

(4.114)   John felt sick when he got home

(4.115)   *He$_j$ felt sick when John$_j$ got home[9]

In each of these examples it is of course possible to
see *he* and *John* as not referring to the same person,
but any approach to the description of pronouns in
English must account for the unacceptability of
(4.115) against the acceptability of (4.114) when *he*
and *John* are taken as co-referential.   That is, any
description must account for the distribution of
backwards anaphora, irrespective of the derivational
history of the pronoun involved.   Solutions have been
proposed to account for the distribution of backwards
and forwards pronominalization in transformational
terms (see, in particular, Langacker 1969, Ross 1969a
and Baker 1978 for a mechanical transformational
approach).   Jackendoff 1972 includes an early but
quite thorough attempt to convert this process
approach into a static interpretive one.

     A similar theoretical option is available in
accounting for the distribution of reduced conjoined
structures where repeated elements are omitted.
Transformationally the missing elements will be present in deep structure and deleted under identity
with other constituents in the complex structure;
from an interpretive viewpoint the 'gaps' are built
directly into structures and then assessed for identity with constituents in the remainder of the complex structure.   Once again, the former approach in
the 1960s gave way to the interpretive approach in
the 1970s and the current concern with realism in
grammatical descriptions is reflected in a typical
psycholinguist's attitude to this theoretical option:

     'The underlying relation is captured by non-
     realization of underlying arguments in sen-
     tences, rather than by their realization
     followed by deletion.'   (Maratsos 1978:253).

However, it is again important to point out that,
whichever approach has the most adherents, the description used must still account for the grammatica-
lity ratings on relevant examples.   Thus, the
following examples can be derived transformationally
or interpretively, but either way only the first

example is possible, in which omission or deletion of
the identical verb has worked forwards or to the
right; the second example, in which the gapping of a
verb has worked backwards, or to the left, is quite
unacceptable:

(4.116)   My brother bought some cherries and my

            sister___some eggs

(4.117)   *My brother___some cherries and my sister

            bought some eggs

In English, gapping (by which we mean the loss of an
identical verb) is forwards, not backwards, but in
languages other than English a case might be made for
claiming that gapping works backwards. This appears
to be the case in Japanese, as illustrated by (4.118)
and (4.119).

(4.118)   Taro   wa   inu o, sensei   wa   ki   o

            top   dog acc teacher top tree acc

            mita

            saw

            'Taro saw the dog, and teacher the tree'

(4.119)   *Taro wa   inu o   mita,   sensei   wa

            top   dog acc saw   teacher top

            ki   o

            tree acc

Then there are languages such as Mandarin and Thai
which totally resist the deletion of verbs. An example such as the following from Thai is quite ungrammatical:

(4.120)   *sómcha:j tòp   ma:li læ? damroŋ atcha:

                     stop   and

            S   V   O   S   O

            'Somchay stopped Mali and Damrong Atcha'

Since English is relatively lacking in markers for
indicating grammatical relations other than by word
order yet allows gapping to a remarkable degree it
cannot be the isolating status of Thai and Mandarin

which constrains gapping.   The English translation
of (4.120) has no more relational clues for English
speakers than does the Thai for Thai-speakers.

Sanders 1976 (an approach to reduced conjoined
structures we will be returning to) also points to
the morphological diversity of languages following
similar patterns of reduction, as well as to the diversity in word order among languages avoiding repetition in identical ways.   Thus, although it is theoretically rather tempting, it is empirically quite
unjustified to suggest that case-marking alone forms
a clear basis for predicting the acceptability of
reduced conjoined structures.

As for those languages which do tolerate gapping
or other instances of reduction in conjoined structures, a number of systems have been devised by linguists to account for the patterns that do and do not
occur.   These form the basis of much of the remaining
discussion in this chapter.

4.4.2.   Co-ordinate Deletion

Co-ordinate Deletion is a term used by Koutsoudas 1971 to describe a uniform process for reducing
co-ordinate structures on a cross-linguistic basis.
If such a process can be shown to be valid it will be
an extremely useful addition to typological research
since any grammatical process that works for all languages takes us a little nearer to the goal of a universal set of principles for language.   In this
section we describe the system devised by Koutsoudas
and in the following two sections discuss the theoretical and data-based problems it encounters.

Deriving much from the work of Ross on gapping
(see in particular Ross 1970), Koutsoudas's *Co-ordinate Deletion* captures the four following paradigm
cases of reduction in English.

(4.121)   *Omission of Verb Phrase from Clause 1*

The owl and the pussycat went to sea in a

beautiful pea-green boat

(4.122)   *Omission of Subject NP from Clause 2*

The mesembryanthemum opens in sunshine and

closes when it is cloudy

(4.123)   *Omission of Verb from Clause 2*

War brought employment and peace unemploy-
ment

(4.124)   *Omission of Object NP from Clause 1*

Birds eat, and flies avoid, long-legged
spiders

These are paradigm examples in that a much wider set
of examples might be used to demonstrate the omission
of other constituent types.   Prepositions and adjectives may be deleted but only in company with major
constituents.   Thus, the loss of a preposition in
the following example is unacceptable, but its loss
together with the verb in (4.126) can be seen as a
gapping of a larger section of the verb phrase:[10]

(4.125)   *The inspector looked at the suspect and
the sergeant looked___the lawyer

(4.126)   The inspector looked at the suspect and the
sergeant___the lawyer

Also, discussion of word order in language often
reduces to a discussion of the ordering of S, V and O,
whereas a larger number of constituents has to be
taken into account.   The following example clearly
is a case of gapping, but involves no object NP,
merely an adverbial after each verb:

(4.127)   Primroses bloom annually and other plants
every other year

However, to make the discussion more manageable, we
leave aside such problems and concentrate on the
reduction of major constituents.

Like Ross' pattern of gapping, Koutsoudas' more
general pattern of reduction in conjoined structures
is related to dominant word order, but also to the
ways in which trees branch in the structures underlying the different word orders.

Staying with word order alone for the moment, we
can account for the fact that in Japanese, an SOV
language, gapping of the verb is from the first
clause, while in English it is from the second, Eng-

lish being an SVO language.   On the other hand,
English *appears* to lose object NPs from the first
clause and Japanese from the second.[11] Compare examples (4.128) and (4.129) with the patterns of their
English translations.

(4.128)   Sumie   wa   inu   o,   Norio   wa   kì   o
                   top   dog   acc   top   tree   acc
           S   O   ∅   S   O

           mita

           saw
           V

           'Sumie saw the dog and Norio the tree'
            S   V   O   S ∅   O

(4.129)   Sumie   wa   inu   o   nadete,   Norio   wa
                   top   dog acc pat+ing   top
           S   O   V   S   ∅

           tataita

           hit
           V

           'Sumie patted, and Norio hit, the dog'
            S   V   ∅   S   V   O

To complete the pattern, the following two examples
demonstrate the omission of subject and verb phrase
respectively.

(4.130)   Sumie   wa   inu   o   nadete,   neko   o
                   top   dog   acc   pat+ing   cat   acc
           S   O   V   ∅   O

           tataita

           hit
           V

           'Sumie patted the dog and hit the cat'
            S   V   O   ∅   V   O

(4.131)   Sumie   to   Norio   wa   inu   o   mita
                   and   top   dog acc   saw
           S   ∅   S   O   V

           'Sumie and Norio saw the dog'
            S   ∅   S   V   O

In these four examples we have labelled constituents
in terms of S, V and O but Koutsoudas' rules handle
V+O/O+V as a single constituent verb phrase (we return to this matter in section 4.5).   Koutsoudas'
reduction principle does in fact hang on the branching of structures, rather than on mere word order.
His rule is as follows:

(4.132)   Co-ordinate Deletion (Optional)

           Given a co-ordination in which each con-
           junct includes a constituent which is
           identical to the corresponding constituent
           of each other conjunct, all but one of
           these identical constituents may be deleted,
           the undeleted constituent being that of the
           first conjunct if it is a left-branching
           constituent, and that of the last conjunct
           if it is a right-branching constituent.
                                   (Koutsoudas 1971:347).

     As illustrated by the diagrams below, English
and Japanese appear to follow the same pattern of
reduction: those constituents which branch to the
right are deleted from the first clause, and those
that branch to the left from the second clause.[12]

(4.133)   *English*

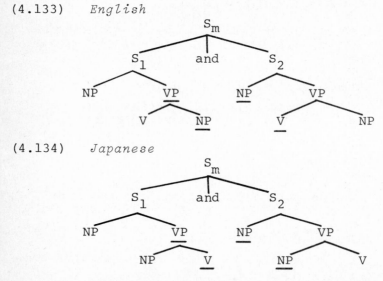

(4.134)   *Japanese*

Geometrically, both English as an SVO language and
Japanese as an SOV language fit the following pattern,
determined by constituent structure, not by the labels

of the constituents involved (it will be seen that the direction of subject NP deletion and verb phrase deletion in both languages is identical, this being a consequence of the fact that English and Japanese are both subject-initial languages).

(4.135)

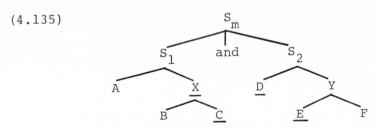

Koutsoudas examines some thirty languages and all appear to conform to the single principle.

Thus, all SVO languages which delete repeated material will delete object NPs from S_1 and verbs from S_2 and this is borne out by Latvian, as in (4.136) to (4.138); on the other hand, SOV languages which delete material will delete object NPs from S_2 and verbs from S_1, and this is borne out by Korean, as in (4.139) to (4.141).

(4.136) puika redzēja suni

boy   saw   dog

'The boy saw the dog'

(4.137) meitene dzirdēja suni

girl   heard   dog

'The girl heard the dog'

(4.138) puika redzēja, un meitene dzirdēja

boy   saw   and girl   heard

suni

dog

'The boy saw and the girl heard the dog'

(4.139) sonyəni suleḷiḷ kḷəsta

boy-nom cart-acc pull-past

'The boy pulled· the cart'

(4.140)   sonyəka   suleɬ̵ɬ   miləsta
           girl-nom   cart-acc   push-past
           'The girl pushed the cart'

(4.141)   sonyəni   suleɬ̵ɬ   kɬ̵lko   sonyəka
           boy-nom   cart-acc   pull+ing   girl-nom
                 miləsta
                 push-past
           'The boy pulled and the girl pushed the cart'

Other languages examined by Koutsoudas include VSO
languages such as Arabic, and VOS languages such as
Toba Batak, as well as a wide range of SVO languages.
These include Estonian, Romanian, Swahili and Zulu
while SOV languages are represented by, among others,
Turkish, Susu and Telugu.

        Data from Keenan 1978a appears to confirm some
of Koutsoudas' pattern for a number of VOS languages.
Malagasy deletes a final subject from the first
clause, parallelling loss of object NP in English and
verb in Japanese.

(4.142)   misotro   taoka   sy   mihinam-bary   Rabe
           drink   alcohol   and   eat-   rice
             V   O   Ø   V   O   S
           'Rabe is drinking alcohol and eating rice'

A VSO language such as Welsh also appears to follow
Koutsoudas' directionality principle. In the following example, the subject noun phrase is deleted from
the middle of the second clause, parallelling the
deletion of a verb from the same position in English:

(4.143)   Gwelodd   Gwen   Wyn   a   tarodd   Ifor
           saw   and   hit
             V   S   O   V   Ø   O
           'Gwen saw Wyn and hit Ifor'

As Koutsoudas points out, not all languages will
allow widescale reduction of conjoined structures.
Sanders & Tai 1969 put forward a universal principle
that a language allows deletion of objects *and* verbs
or neither, but not one without the other.   Koutsoudas lists a number of languages which conform to this

principle and allow neither of these two types of
reduction - including Toba Batak as a VOS language,
SVO languages such as Hausa and Indonesian, and SOV
languages such as Maninka and some dialects of Turkish.   The important point is, however, that if a
language does allow such reduction it should conform
to the pattern of Co-ordinate Deletion.

The pattern can be represented by a table such
as the following which demonstrates the direction of
deletion to be expected in those languages which do
not resist reduction of conjoining.   Each of the
logical options for S, V and O order is listed - Free
Word Order languages are discussed later.

Table 2

Table of possibilities for languages allowing Co-ordinate Deletion

	Single Constituent Reduction			Double Constituent Reduction		
Basic Word order Type	Initial (=S in SVO)	Medial (=V in SVO)	Final (=O in SVO)	Medial + Final (= VO in SVO)	Initial + Medial (= SV in SVO)	Final + Initial (=O+S in SVO)
	I	**II**	**III**	**IV**	**V**	**VI**
1) SOV+SOV	SOV+ØOV	SOV+SØV	SOØ+SOV	SØØ+SOV →[S+S]OV	SOV+ØØV →SO[V+V]	SOØ+ØOV →S[O+O]V
2) SVO+SVO	SVO+ØVO	SVO+SØO	SVØ+SVO	SØØ+SVO →[S+S]VO	SVO+ØØO →SV[O+O]	SVØ+ØVO →S[V+V]O
3) VSO+VSO	VSO+ØSO	VSO+VØO	VSØ+VSO	VØØ+VSO →[V+V]SO	VSO+ØØO →VS[O+O]	VSØ+ØSO →V[S+S]O
4) VOS+VOS	VOS+ØOS	VOS+VØS	VOØ+VOS	VØØ+VOS →[V+V]OS	VOS+ØØS →VO[S+S]	VOØ+ØOS →V[O+O]S
5) OVS+OVS	OVS+ØVS	OVS+OØS	OVØ+OVS	OØØ+OVS →[O+O]VS	OVS+ØØS →OV[S+S]	OVØ+ØVS →O[V+V]S
6) OSV+OSV	OSV+ØSV	OSV+OØV	OSØ+OSV	OØØ+OSV →[O+O]SV	OSV+ØØV →OS[V+V]	OSØ+ØSV →O[S+S]V

4.5   Criticism of Koutsoudas' Co-ordinate Deletion

If all languages available conformed to the pattern in this table, it would represent an extremely
important contribution to language typology and universals since it would embody a principle cutting
across the apparent typological distinction between
languages in their reduction of co-ordinate structures.   As Koutsoudas makes clear, there are languages which do *not* allow such reduction to take place,
but these are not a problem since the universal principle of co-ordinate deletion is intended to capture
the pattern of reduction when it does take place;
the rule is *not* a claim that all languages *do* allow
wholesale reduction.   However, such an approach hangs
critically on the interpretation of available data
(as well as on data not yet available but against
which the principle may have to be tested ultimately),
and also on the validity of theoretical assumptions
made in erecting the formula.   In both cases, the
co-ordinate deletion rule encounters serious difficulties, and these we now examine.   We begin with
theoretical criticism of Koutsoudas' approach, and in
section 4.5.2. discuss recalcitrant data.

4.5.1.   Theoretical Arguments Against Co-ordinate
Deletion

(i)   *Constituent Structure and Branching*

In order to make the principle work, Koutsoudas
commits himself to an approach which treats constituent structure in binary terms.   That means, in an
SVO language like English, a pattern of branching as
in (4.144).[13]

(4.144)

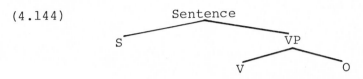

Such an approach to sentence structure hangs on the
validity of a verb phrase constituent and it might be
said that the concept of verb phrase, inherited from
the traditional notion of *predicate*, is merely a linguist's convenience with little empirical justification.

If one were to seek some justification for a VP

node, it would come from an analysis of such supra-
segmental features as intonation, which might confirm
the inherent unity of the VP constituent.

Such a pattern of binary constituent structure
might be regarded as reasonable in SOV languages, too.
Thus:

(4.145)

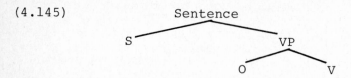

Of the remaining four language types, only two allow
such an analysis - those with subjects in final position: VOS and OVS.   In each case, the verb phrase
can be assumed and allows a binary analysis of the
three elements V, S and O.

(4.146)

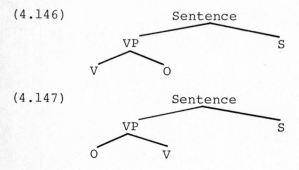

(4.147)

A binary analysis involving a VP constituent is simply not available for the other two language types,
however.   In VSO and OSV languages, the two elements
forming a potential VP constituent are separated by
the S constituent.   The only way to impose a binary
branching on such languages is to adopt some artificial pattern that pairs S with either O or V.   For
example, (4.148) would be the pattern for a VSO language in which the S constituent was paired with O.

(4.148)

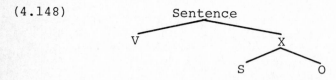

Precisely what we are going to label this constituent
X is not quite clear, and the same problem arises

with the alternative analysis for VSO languages, in which V and S are paired; similarly we would pair S with either O or V in the remaining type, the OSV language.

The onus is on supporters of Koutsoudas' approach to convince linguists concerned with anything other than an SVO language that the binary approach embodied in the concept of the verb phrase is something more than a traditional, ethnocentric device for analyzing sentence structure.

One might, of course, posit for VSO and OSV languages an underlying word order different from surface order, an underlying VP being broken up by the movement rules already needed to move constituents into positions of prominence. Such rules are a reasonable way of accounting for examples like the following in English, in which the object appears in initial position (a rule of *topicalization*, in transformational terminology).

(4.149)   *People with long hair* I really can't stand

                   O   S   V

However, such a rule is useful for accounting for *non-basic* word orders in English and there is no reason to derive the *dominant* SVO order by means of such rules (see our discussion in chapter one for further comment on the ploy of giving languages an underlying order that is different from the dominant order on the surface).   In the same way, it is quite artificial to attempt to retain the binary analysis by appealing to quite unwarranted movement rules in languages other than English.   That is, there seems to be little justification (except as a device to get out of a tight corner) for deriving a basic word order of, say, VSO from an underlying order of, say, SVO.

Another alternative is to treat *all* languages on a non-binary basis.   Thus, an SVO language would have the following pattern:

(4.150)   Sentence

                   S   V   O

This would mean that the two problem language types would be as follows:

(4.151)   *VSO*

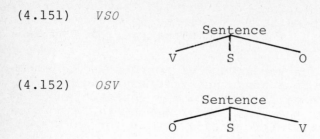

(4.152)   *OSV*

This system would be more natural but would not allow
the Koutsoudas deletion principle to be sensitive to
the direction of branching; rather it would have to
be reformulated in terms of *position*.   Thus, it might
be claimed that initial constituents were removed from
the second clause and final constituents from the
first clause, with medial constituents also removed
from the second clause.   As can be seen from columns
I, II and III of the table, this accords with the prediction of Koutsoudas' directionality principle without the disadvantage of an unmotivated binary division
of clauses into their main constituents.

     Sanders 1976 discusses the reduction of conjoined
sentences in terms of position rather than branching
and it is clear, as he suggests, that there are functional principles governing the choice of favoured
'ellipsis-sites'.   One such principle appears to be
that languages avoid the removal of constituents from
either initial position or final position in the
entire conjoined structure.   However, this does not
explain why medial position in the first clause should
be less favoured than medial position in the second
clause.   That is, why if D is the most-favoured
ellipsis-site in (4.153), followed closely by C and E,
is B less favoured than E?

(4.153)   ABC + DEF

     If indeed position B *is* highly resistant to
ellipsis (or reduction), the conversion of Koutsoudas'
branching approach to one based on position encounters
a serious problem.   If sentences are divided on a
trinary basis, as in the patterns of (4.150) to
(4.152), then all examples in columns IV, V and VI of
the table will involve the loss of two constituents
each, not the loss of a single, branching constituent.
For example, SVO languages will involve reduction as
follows:

(4.154)

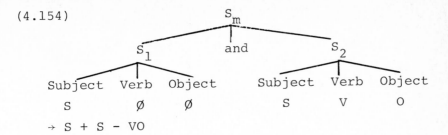

→ S + S - VO

All patterns in column IV would involve reduction as in (4.155).

(4.155)   AØØ + DEF

The problem for a revised Koutsoudas approach is this: according to his pattern, medial constituents should be removed from the second clause, as in column II. Yet when a medial constituent is removed along with a final constituent *both* are removed from the *first* clause.   If removal of any constituent from ellipsis-site B is highly unfavoured why does it occur in all patterns of column IV?

(ii)   *Regrouping*

A further reason for doubting the validity of the co-ordinate deletion approach is the need for rules that *regroup* the output of reduction.   Of the four paradigm cases in English, for example, only two appear to involve restructuring.   The result of gapping a verb from the second clause or removing an object NP from the first clause is in each case still a sentence with one full clause and the remains of another.   Thus:

(4.156)   *Gapping*

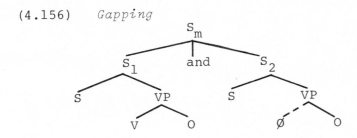

(4.157)   *Object NP Reduction*

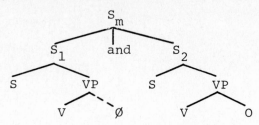

However, the result of removing a subject NP or a
verb phrase is a *single* clause structure.   That is,
regrouping of (4.158) as (4.159) and (4.160) as
(4.161) is an unavoidable part of the co-ordinate
deletion approach.

(4.158)   *Subject NP Reduction*

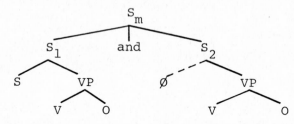

(4.159)   *Regrouping*

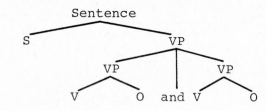

(4.160)   *Verb Phrase Reduction*

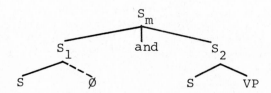

(4.161)   *Regrouping*

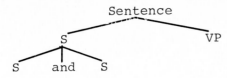

   Such a system of regrouping rules will clearly
be required for two of the four paradigm patterns in
each of the five language types other than SVO.

(iii)   *Multiple Conjunct Reduction*

   Whether one adopts a binary or non-binary
approach to the reduction of conjoined structures,
and whether or not one is prepared to countenance the
regrouping that we have just described, it is clear
that the reduction approach as a whole is in some
instances going to involve rather complicated rules
for deleting material under identity.   As a final
theoretical nail in the coffin of a rigid reductio-
nist approach, consider the implications of attempting to account for examples such as (4.162) in this
way.

(4.162)   Arthur, Bill, Charlie, David, Ernest, Fred,

           Graham, Harry, Ivan and James followed

           Katie, Laura, Mary and Nora

Since the number of participants as subjects and the
number of participants as objects are unequal, a
respectively interpretation is not available.   This
means that rather than some ten or so underlying full
clauses before reduction, as in (4.163), one must
assume a high degree of vagueness as to precisely who
was following whom.   A vast number of alternative
underlying structures must be posited for the various
permutations of who was following whom;   and even in
an example in which the subjects and objects could be
paired, by attaching *respectively*, a remarkable
amount of regrouping of constituents would be necessary to derive it from an underlying structure like
(4.163).

(4.163)   Arthur followed Katie, Bill followed Laura,

           Charlie followed Mary......

One could, of course, extend such examples to the

other five language types but it would serve little
purpose to illustrate the problems there.   Extreme
as the above example might be, it serves to demonstrate the unwieldy nature of an approach that opts
for *reduction* solutions to examples of constituent
conjoining.   There seem, then, to be some serious
theoretical problems with the approach favoured by
Koutsoudas, attractive though his system is.   First,
it involves an assumption that all languages are subject to a binary constituent analysis, no matter how
unworkable this is in the case of some languages; and
if an approach like Sanders' is used instead to avoid
the binary analysis, the branching basis to the co-
ordinate deletion rule is lost.   Secondly, the need
for a regrouping rule in half the paradigm cases of
reduction complicates the derivation of what are
ostensibly quite simple instances of constituent conjoining.   This section has, however, been concerned
with only theoretical problems for Koutsoudas'
approach.   We now provide cross-linguistic data that
shows not only that we must abandon the co-ordinate
deletion approach of Koutsoudas (attractive though it
is) but also that we must find some alternative to a
reduction approach at all for a large range of
examples.

4.5.2.   Problems with Data

      Koutsoudas, Sanders and Tai (Koutsoudas 1971,
Sanders & Tai 1969, Tai 1969) claimed that, even
though not all languages engage in wholesale reduction of this kind, a rule could be established that
languages allow the reduction of both objects and
verbs, or they allow neither.   In an SVO language,
if (4.164) is not possible, nor too is (4.165), and
vice versa.

(4.164)   SVØ + SVO

(4.165)   SVO + SØO

Similarly, in a VSO language an ungrammatical (4.166)
would entail (4.167) also being ungrammatical.

(4.166)   VSØ + VSO

(4.167)   VSO + ØSO

Such entailment is extended by Koutsoudas in a foot-

note to include a ban on the conjoining of finite
verbs.   Thus in a VSO language which did not allow
either object reduction or verb reduction, the following pattern would also be ruled out:

(4.168)   VØØ + VSO → V + V - SO

Such a set of constraints is shared by Swahili, and
Koutsoudas provides examples to show that (4.169) is
as unacceptable a pattern as (4.164) and (4.165).

(4.169)   SVØ + ØVO

Thus:

(4.170)   *mvulana aliona   na   alipiga   mti

           boy   saw   and   hit   tree
            S   V   V   O

           'The boy saw and hit the tree'

However, in the same footnote in which he discusses
finite verb conjoining in Swahili, Koutsoudas also
includes examples that show there is no constraint on
the reduction of conjoined structures resulting in
conjoined subjects.   That is, (4.172) can reduce to
(4.171).

(4.171)   mvulana na   msichana waliona mti

           boy   and   girl   saw   tree
            S   S   V   O

           'The boy and the girl saw the tree'

(4.172)   mvulana aliona mti na   msichana aliona

           boy   saw   tree and   girl   saw
            S   V   O   S   V

                mti

                tree
                 O

           'The boy saw the tree and the girl saw the

           tree'

The pattern is as in (4.173).

(4.173)   SVO + SVO → SØØ + SVO → S + S - VO

Why does Swahili allow the reduction of conjoined
clauses in some cases, but not in others?   A possible solution is to regard (4.171) not as the reduction of two constituents but as the reduction of a
VP.   However, this fails to account for (4.174),
which is a perfectly grammatical structure but would
involve reduction of both subject and verb from the
second clause to give a conjoined object.

(4.174)   mtoto alitaka uzi   na   sindano

           child wanted   thread   and   needle
            S   V   O   O

           'The child wanted thread and a needle'

The pattern would be:

(4.175)   SVO + SVO → SVO + ∅∅O → SV - O + O

Clearly this means that a verb *can* be reduced, provided it is removed along with an adjacent subject.

      A similar set of data is found in Thai.
(4.176) involves reduction to give conjoined subjects,
(4.177) conjoined objects and (4.178) both conjoined
subjects and objects.

(4.176)   sómcha:j læ̂? ma:li tòp   damroŋ

                     and   slapped
              S   S   V   O

           'Somchay and Mali slapped Damrong'

(4.177)   sómcha:j tòp   damroŋ læ̂? ?atcha:

                     slapped   and
              S   V   O   O

           'Somchay slapped Damrong and Atcha'

(4.178)   sómcha:j læ̂? ma:li tòp   damroŋ læ̂?

                     and   slapped   and
              S   S   V   O

           ?atcha:

              O

           'Somchay and Mali slapped Damrong and Atcha'

Furthermore, unlike Swahili, Thai *does* allow the conjoining of verbs, though Koutsoudas claims it does

not.

(4.179)   sómcha:j   khâ: lǽ?   fǎŋ   ma:li
                      killed   and   buried
              S   V   V   O

           'Somchay killed and buried Mali'

Perhaps the most damaging data of all from Thai is in
examples such as the following. Thai does not allow
loss of verbs (gapping) but *does* allow loss of object
NPs.   (4.180) closely parallels its English translation and even has the same intonation breaks after
each verb.

(4.180)   sómcha:j   tòp   lǽ?   damroŋ   tè?
                      slapped   and   kicked
              S   V   S   V

           ma:li

             O

           'Somchay slapped, and Damrong kicked, Mali'

In fact, intonation is yet another area presenting
problems for Koutsoudas.   If, as he suggests, object
reduction in an SVO language is equivalent to verb
reduction in an SOV language, and verb reduction in
an SVO language is equivalent to object reduction in
an SOV language, then the two language types should
have similar intonation patterns.   However, native
speakers of Japanese consistently claim there is no
intonation break between the second object and the
verb in (4.181) - whereas we saw above that an intonation break does occur in the object NP reduction
examples of SVO languages.

(4.181)   Taro   wa   inu   o,   sensei   wa   ki   o
                  top   dog   acc teacher top   tree acc
              S   O   S   O

           mita

           saw
            V

           'Taro saw the dog and teacher the tree'

     We believe that the above data from Swahili and
Thai seriously undermines Koutsoudas' approach.   In
particular, it demonstrates that the occurrence of

gapping and object NP reduction cannot be related in
the way claimed, since Thai allows one but not the
other.   A more fundamental problem, however, is the
occurrence in Swahili of sentences with conjoined NPs.
Despite all the restrictions claimed for languages in
the way that they can reduce conjoined structures, it
appears to be a virtual universal that languages have
conjoined NPs.   If any language does have restrictions on clause reduction but has no restrictions on
NP conjoining (and such languages abound) an account
of co-ordinate structure reduction in that language
in Koutsoudas' terms will involve either (a) a very
complex reduction pattern or (b) a simple reduction
principle with a lot of exceptions.   The solution to
this problem is clear.   It is necessary to distinguish two types of conjoined structure that involve
less than two *full* clauses.

(1)   Examples in which the conjoining can be
        handled directly by constituent conjoining
        of the type captured by rules like:

                NP → NP and NP

                V → V and V

(2)   Examples in which no such recursion is
        possible and in which the structures have
        'missing' constituents, but are still
        recognizable as one full clause plus one
        part clause.

Since direct conjoining of constituents will
handle two of the four paradigm cases of reduction in
English, this leaves only two cases where reduction
is involved.   (4.182) and (4.183) will be instances
of constituent conjoining and (4.184) and (4.185)
will involve some form of reduction.

(4.182)   *NP → NP and NP*

(=(4.121))   The owl and the pussycat went to sea in

                a beautiful pea-green boat

(4.183)   *VP → VP and VP*

(=(4.122))   The mesembryanthemum opens in sunshine

                and closes when it is cloudy

(4.184)   *Deletion of Verb*

(=(4.123))   War brought employment and peace unem-

               ployment

(4.185)   *Deletion of Object NP*

(=(4.124))   Birds eat, and flies avoid, long-legged

               spiders

In section 4.6 we extend this compromise approach
to a range of languages in an attempt to determine
whether it is applicable to languages other than English.   In doing so we will also be examining a number of other attempts at constructing a typology of
conjoined structure reduction.   It will be shown
that, although not dependent on an artificial branching pattern in the way that Koutsoudas' approach
was, they nevertheless do involve reduction in examples where we have demonstrated that direct constituent conjoining is a realistic alternative.   Furthermore, we will demonstrate that most reduction of conjoined structures is forwards despite Koutsoudas'
claim that deletion occurs in both directions.   Since
some instances of backwards reduction can be eliminated by direct constituent conjoining this will leave
a smaller number of instances of apparently backwards
conjoining to account for.

4.6   A Compromise Approach to Reduced Conjoining

4.6.1.   Some Alternatives to Koutsoudas' Branching

          Approach

The claim that forwards deletion is the norm in
the reduction of conjoined structures is a view
shared by Sanders 1976, Harries 1973 and Hankamer
1971, all attempts at devising a typology of co-ordinate reduction.   In the paper by Sanders that we
referred to in our criticism of Koutsoudas 1971 (see
section 4.5.1.) it is claimed that favoured ellipsis-
sites tend to be in following rather than initial
clauses, and this seems to be a not unreasonable phenomenon to expect in human language.

First of all, it accords with the pattern we
have already seen in pronominalization, which is
always possible in a forwards direction and comparatively rare in a backwards direction.   This is hardly surprising if one considers that human short-term

memory will cope more readily with a pattern that
gives full mention of a constituent before referring
to it less specifically (with a potentially ambiguous
pronoun).   And as Sanders himself points out, presenting a 'gap', or ellipsis, before the full constituent imposes an unnecessary load on short-term memory.

That such considerations play an important role
in processing conjoined structures was implied in our
discussion of agreement in section 4.2.   In those
languages which have unmarked agreement for conjoined
NPs of distinct genders, or neutralization of agreement (the former in the Romance languages, the latter
in German), the load on memory is reduced, since
speakers require no processing time to determine the
dominant conjunct and select the appropriate agreement.   Where selection has to be made because unmarked forms or neutralization are not available, selection will tend to be in terms of the nearer, or
more recent, conjunct.

As Harries (1973:152) also points out, pronominalization and deletion are related processes and since
pronominalization can only work forwards in conjoined
structures one would expect a similar constraint on
deletion.   Thus, whatever the principle allowing
backwards pronominalization, examples such as the
following are not grammatical.

(4.186)   *He$_j$ came home and John$_j$ felt sick

(4.187)   *He$_j$ felt sick and John$_j$ came home

We now examine two attempts to tie conjoined structure reduction to forwards deletion only.

Harries 1973

Harries 1973 is also very critical of Koutsoudas'
approach to reduced conjoining.   In particular, she
claims that *co-ordinate deletion* fails to account for
the existence of 'split co-ordination', as in the
following examples from Hindi and Hungarian, respectively.[14]

(4.188)   Jon-ne safarchand kharida aur kela

                   apple   bought   and banana
            S   O   V   O

            bhi

            also

           'John bought an apple and (also) a banana'

(4.189)   János (egy) almát   vett   és   (egy)

                   a   apple-acc bought and a
            S   O   V

            banánt

            banana-acc
            O

           'John bought an apple and a banana'

In each case reduction is from SOV + SOV by loss of S
and V from the second clause.[15] The only way Koutsoudas' reduction pattern could account for this would
be by resorting to reordering or *scrambling* rules to
finish up with the appropriate order, from an underlying SVO order.   This is particularly unmotivated
in the case of Hindi which, although having some
freedom in its surface ordering, is otherwise an
archetypal SOV type - it has, for example, prenominal
adjectives and genitives and uses postpositions.

     To resort to underlying SVO order to make a prin-
ciple work is highly unsatisfactory.   As Pullum puts
it, 'Harries' deletion rule generates the pattern SOV
+ O directly from SOV + SOV without any unsupported
scrambling rules, which is its great strength;   to
turn again to the ad hoc manipulations of 'underlying
order' that characterized such discussions as that of
Ross (1970) and Koutsoudas (1971) is a sad retro-
gression'   (Pullum 1974:96).

     However, one example from Hindi provides prob-
lems for Harries since (4.190) involves the apparent
loss of an object from the first clause.

(4.190)   Jon-ne   kharida   aur   Bill-ne   safarchand
                     bought   and   apple
           S   V   S   O

           khaya
           ate
           V

           'John bought and Bill ate an apple'

Harries attempts to capture the SV + SOV pattern by
positing an underlying order SVO + SOV with subsequent regrouping of constituents to give a surface
SOV order in the second clause.   A second alternative is to see such examples as resulting from loss
of a medial O from the first clause of an SOV + SOV
structure.   The problem with the first approach is
that it represents an unnatural and unmotivated
ordering of underlying constituents, whereas the
second involves B as an ellipsis-site, despite its
resistance to ellipsis, especially in SOV languages.
Thus the following pattern is normally ruled out for
languages such as Hindi and Japanese.

        ABC + DEF   →   *AØC + DEF

In fact, Pullum points out that examples such as
(4.190) from Harries are actually not acceptable in
Hindi and thus he presents a simple solution to an
otherwise intractable problem.   Once again we can
see the dangers in discussing phenomena from a wide
range of languages, and the reader is reminded of
our discussion of data reliability in section 1.1.3.

        Although Harries now needs no artificial
reordering rules or underlying word orders distinct
from actual word order, she nevertheless does need
a system of regrouping rules in order to account for
examples which ostensibly involve ellipsis-sites in
initial clauses.   In addition to the cases of split
co-ordination in Hindi and Hungarian both languages
also allow the reduction of SOV + SOV to SO + OV.
Thus, in Hindi:

(4.191)   Jon-ne safarchand aur kela   kharida
                  apple   and banana bought
          S   O   O   V

'John bought an apple and a banana'

and in Hungarian

(4.192)   János (egy) almát   és (egy) banánt
                  a   apple-acc and a   banana-acc
          S   O   O

          vett
          bought
          V

'John bought an apple and a banana'

In order to avoid admitting the loss of constituents from the first clause, Harries must resort to
regrouping rules that are even more complex than
those proposed by Koutsoudas.   Yet there is a simple
solution to examples like (4.191) and (4.192) - they
are simply instances of the direct conjoining of NPs,
as we proposed for SVO languages like English.

Thus, the need for regrouping follows from a
subservience to the reduction approach that Fernald
warned about as long ago as 1904.   Furthermore, it
is also the case that Harries needs a greater number
of regrouping rules than Koutsoudas since her aim is
to avoid admitting that backwards reduction can occur
at all.

Hankamer

Hankamer 1971 is also an attempt to restrict
conjoined structure reduction to a forwards direction.   His approach is summed up as follows:

    '...in order to account for certain empirical
    facts it is necessary to postulate a universal
    rule of Co-ordinate Deletion which effects
    deletion under identity from left to right in
    co-ordinate structures;   and that there is no
    rule which deletes from right to left in co-

ordinate structures.'   (Hankamer 1971:14)

Hankamer's solution to apparent cases of backwards reduction is a rule called *delay*, defined as
follows:

'Chomsky-adjoin to the right of the co-ordinate
node a copy of some constituent which occurs
in final position in all conjuncts, and then
delete the original constituents.' [16]

This turns structures like (4.193a) into structures like (4.193b).

(4.193)   a.

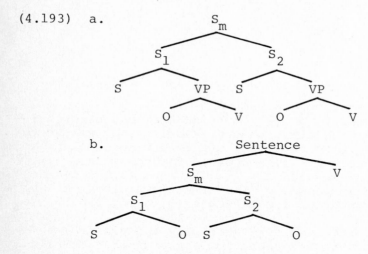

b.

Although intended as an alternative to the Koutsoudas
approach, which can survive only by an ad hoc manipulation of scrambling rules and unmotivated underlying word orders, *delay* does, in fact, like Harries'
approach, itself resort to an empirically untestable
process of adjunction, and a clever manipulation of
deletion and scrambling rules to boot.   Above all,
if delay is to account for examples with the pattern
in (4.193b), this assumes that native speakers feel
there is some kind of intonation break between the
second object and the verb.   This would match the
pattern English speakers readily attribute to corresponding English examples where the object is removed
from the first clause, or rather *appears* to be - that
is, in examples such as (4.194) (=(4.124)).

(4.194)   Birds eat, and flies avoid, long-legged
             spiders

However, as we pointed out in discussing our revision
of Koutsoudas' approach, this assumption does not
accord with the facts.   Japanese speakers do not feel
that such an intonation break exists, and it therefore seems reasonable to accept that the pattern
SO + SOV is indeed the result of backwards deletion
of an identical verb, in that language at least;
(4.195) thus seems a reasonable way of representing
such examples.

(4.195)

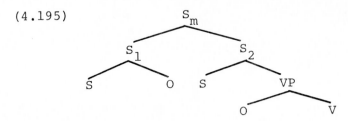

Or, if we take a non-VP approach:

(4.196)

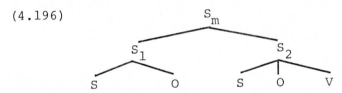

In view of this conclusion, which seems to us unavoidable, notwithstanding the reasonableness of such an
approach as *delay* to the corresponding English example, it is necessary to admit that backwards reduction is a valid phenomenon in at least some cases.
It seems to us to be merely a case of a widespread
linguistic generalization occasionally bowing to language-specific constraints, in this case the status
of Japanese as a strictly verb-final language.

On the other hand, some such rule as delay does
seem to be appropriate for languages like English,
and also for verb-initial languages, such as Tagalog.

In English and Tagalog, an object NP can be left
out under identity with an object NP in a co-ordinated clause.   Thus, parallelling examples like (4.194)
are Tagalog examples like (4.197), with the pattern
VS and VSO.

(4.197)   Binaril   ng sundalo at   hinalikan   ng
           O:shot   soldier   and   kissed
           topic

              guro   ang babae
           teacher   girl

           'The soldier shot, and the teacher kissed
           the girl'

The alternative to reduction in this way is to
remove the object NP from the second clause. However,
this gives rise to ungrammaticality in both languages.

(4.198)   *Binaril   ng sundalo ang babae at
           O:shot   soldier   girl   and
           topic

              hinalikan   ng guro ø
           kissed   teacher

           '*The soldier shot the girl and the teacher
           kissed Ø'

As Sanders 1976 points out, final position in
the conjoined structure is not a favoured ellipsis-
site.   This is understandable, since in both English
and Tagalog the second verb would look as though it
were acting intransitively in such a case.   Each
language thus avoids the problem by shifting the
ellipsis-site.   However, in English at least, there
is not an absolute ban on such reduction and one
finds examples like (4.199) as well as (4.200).

(4.199)   The queen may abdicate and the prince
           definitely will

(4.200)   The queen may, and the prince definitely
           will, abdicate

Examples such as (4.199) demonstrate two points.
First, final position is not always vetoed as a site
for deletion from conjoined structures.   Secondly,
what we have been referring to as object NP reduction
should more properly be referred to as reduction of
post-verbal constituents.   Certainly, as we pointed
out at the beginning of section 4.4.2., one can be
misled by dealing with paradigm examples.   Nevertheless, it is certainly the case that examples such as
(4.200), and others involving deletion of post-verbal

constituents cannot be seen as merely the removal of
such constituents from the end of the first clause –
they seem to involve a structure that *shares* the
remaining identical constituent with the remains of
each of the two clauses.   Whether one handles it by
delay or by a rule that derives (4.200) via an intermediate form (4.199), or even by a rule called *Right
Node Raising*[17] in the transformational literature, it
is clear that such examples do not involve mere deletion under identity.

Hudson 1976 recognizes the distinction between
such examples (we will refer to them as Right Node
Raising since that is what they are commonly known as
in the literature) and other instances of reduced
conjoining.   He adopts the view that there are three
reduction rules in English conjoining - Conjunction
Reduction, Gapping and Right Node Raising, as illustrated by three of our paradigm examples from section
4.4.2.

(4.201)   a.   *Conjunction Reduction*

The owl and the pussycat went to sea in

a beautiful pea-green boat

b.   *Gapping*

War brought employment and peace unem-

ployment

c.   *Right Node Raising*

Birds eat, and flies avoid, long-legged

spiders

Of these, most people would probably agree that
(4.201a) sounds most natural, whereas examples such
as (4.201b) are slightly bookish, and those like
(4.201c) even less natural in colloquial English.
This difference in acceptability and usage does, we
feel, give strong support to Hudson's claim that
they are distinct types of structure.   However, as
we have shown, *Conjunction Reduction* examples like
(4.201a) are more sensibly derived by the direct co-
ordination of major constituents.[18] Whether Right
Node Raising is a valid approach to examples such as
(4.201c) or not, certainly such examples are not
merely instances of reduction of an object NP from
the *first* clause;   and since we can abandon conjunction reduction as a basis for deriving examples like

(4.201a) and thus eliminate the need for a rule that
removes a VP from the first conjunct, it appears that
ellipsis in the first rather than the second clause
is *not* a reduction pattern of English.

　　We can eliminate conjunction reduction in many
languages in this way and thus see ellipsis (in the
form of gapping and delay/Right Node Raising) in conjoined structures as more normally occurring in
second clauses.   However, there may be occasional
instances where this universal tendency is baulked by
language-specific constraints - as is the case with
verb-ellipsis in Japanese, where the verb-final condition overrules the psychologically more natural
forwards reduction.

4.6.2.　　Free Word Order Languages

　　To continue our survey of such reduction on a
cross-linguistic basis we turn now to so-called Free
Word Order languages (FWO languages).　　Such languages can be expected to present problems for all the
approaches to conjoined structure reduction we have
examined.　　In a useful article, for example, Rosenbaum 1977 presents a critical discussion of the
approaches of Koutsoudas (and Ross), Hankamer, and
Harries, demonstrating the failure of any of them to
account for the facts of a number of Mayan languages,
in particular the Valley dialect of Zapotec.

　　As Rosenbaum points out, these languages allow a
number of word orders and also allow in most cases
what appears to be backwards verb gapping.　　The
following table sums up the patterns for a number of
languages (the table is taken from Rosenbaum 1977:393
and is adapted to include the data he presents from
Zapotec).

Table 3

Language	Occurring orders of main constituents						Verb deletes to	
	VSO	VOS	SVO	OVS	SOV	OSV	Right	Left
Tojolabal	X	X	X	X	X	X	X	X
Cakchiquel	X		X	X	X		X	X
Ixil	X		X	X	X		X	X
Tzeltal	X	X	X	X	X	X	X	X
Tzotzil	X	X	X	X	X	X	X	X
Valley Zapotec	X*		X	X	X		X	X

(* = backwards deletion does not occur with this order)

To sum up Rosenbaum's criticism of earlier approaches
very briefly, none of them can readily account for
the apparent widescale occurrence of backwards gapping and in particular of the following patterns in
Valley Zapotec.

(4.202)   SO + SVO

(4.203)   OS + OVS

Examples of two of the Zapotec patterns are as follows:

(4.204)   makU   bizie,   ne   xwain   jumE   been

           Markos   well,   and   Juan   basket made
             S   O   S   O   V

           'Markos made a well and Juan a basket'

(4.205)   bizie   abel,   ne   yuu   been   makU

           well   Abel,   and   house   made   Markos
             O   S   O   V   S

           'Abel made a well, and Markos a house'

Rosenbaum concludes his discussion with a new typology that distinguishes between *Forward-Deletion* languages and *Forward-and-Backward-Deletion* languages.
It seems inescapable that at least some languages allow backwards deletion and the languages in the table
above are clear candidates for membership of the second club.   As an example of a language belonging to
the first type, Rosenbaum selects Quechua, which is
discussed in all the approaches we have examined.
Quechua is an interesting language since it has quite
free word order but apparently no examples of backwards deletion of verbs.   Thus, (4.206) and (4.207):

(4.206)   Juanito   rik"un   alquta,   uyarintaq   misita

                     sees   dog-acc   hears-and   cat-acc
             S   V   O   V   O

           'Juanito sees the dog and hears the cat'

(4.207)   *Juanito rik"un,   tiyucataq   uyarin   alquta

                     sees   Tiuca-and   hears   dog-acc
             S   V   S   V   O

           'Juanito sees and Tiuca hears the dog'

                            (Pulte 1971)

For those linguists who favour a forwards-only
approach, Quechua is a godsend, whereas for linguists
like Koutsoudas and Ross it presents serious problems.
To cope with the existence of any language lacking
ellipsis-sites in the first clause, such linguists
must resort to what can only be described as fiendish
rule orderings, with careful selection of underlying
orders.   Such an approach would be extremely ad hoc,
and it is much more reasonable to accept that Quechua,
like for example Cherokee, is a language with fairly
free word order that simply cannot gap backwards.

If one considers that one FWO language normally
presents no more interpretation problems for its
users than any other, it is rather odd that some FWO
languages avoid backwards reduction of constituents.
If any language type allowed large-scale backwards
reduction it would almost certainly be a language with
less restricted ordering, since it would presumably
have relational clues to help in the decoding of the
'original' unreduced structure.   Languages like Quechua are an anomaly among FWO types, whereas languages like Tojolabal and other Mayan languages which
allow wholesale backwards gapping should not be surprising in view of their free word order.   What is
clear is that one would not expect to find a language
which allowed *only* backwards reduction.   We can,
then, say that forwards reduction is the norm in language, and that occasional backwards reduction (as in
Japanese) is a necessity imposed by particular features of a language (the particularly strict verb-final
condition in Japanese) or a luxury that other features
of the language (free word order in the Mayan languages) tolerate to a greater or lesser degree.

However, before finishing with *Backward-and-For-
ward* languages, one point still needs to be cleared
up.   Rosenbaum 1977 presents the following pattern
for Valley Zapotec verb-reduction:

(4.208)   (i)   VSO + SO   (ii)   *SO + VSO

              (iii)   SVO + SO   (iv)   SO + SVO

               (v)   OVS + OS   (vi)   OS + OVS

              (vii)   SOV + SO   (viii) SO + SOV

In his discussion of earlier approaches to gapping he
admits that (4.208) (ii) matches the directionality
view that initial verbs cannot be removed from initial
clauses.   However, having dismissed the directiona-

lity approach with further evidence, he then fails to
account for why this pattern is not acceptable in
Valley Zapotec when all the other backwards patterns
are acceptable.   We feel that a solution to this is
quite simple.   In the other three cases of backwards
reduction, the resultant pattern leaves the same constituent beginning each clause, whereas in the out-
lawed pattern the first clause begins with the subject and the second clause with the verb.   There is
clearly a relationship between this unacceptable
order and the importance of focus in what Rosenbaum
shows is a basically verb-initial language.   If the
first clause begins with a subject, the subject will
be taken by the hearer to be in focus, so that the
ensuing verb-initial clause breaks the anticipated
pattern.   In forwards reduction of a verb-initial
string, the resultant pattern (4.208)(ii) is quite
acceptable and this can be accounted for in one of
two ways.   Either all forwards gapping is acceptable,
a not unreasonable assumption; or, the lack of congruity between the verb-initial first clause and the
subject-initial second clause is overridden by the
verb-initial clause setting the pattern, that is the
neutral, unmarked pattern, for the whole sentence.

The other Mayan languages discussed appear to
have no such constraint on gapping backwards in verb-
initial patterns and one can only assume that in
these languages verb-focus is not as dominant as
it is in Valley Zapotec.   Finally, one might conjecture that any language which did have the same pattern
of gapping as Valley Zapotec but also allowed the
remaining two word orders of OSV and VOS, might be
expected to allow only one of these to gap backwards.
That is, in the following two hypothetical patterns,
(i) is ruled out because of the lack of congruity
between the initial constituent in the first and
second clause, whereas (ii) is not, having an initial
object in both clauses:

(4.209)   (i)   VOS + VOS   → *OS + VOS

             (ii)   OSV + OSV   →   OS + OSV

However, this is pure conjecture and suffice it to
say that in languages which allow reduction of constituents in conjoined sentences the dominant patterns are those which involve *forwards* reduction,
backwards reduction occasionally being allowed as
either a language-specific necessity, as in Japanese,
or as a luxury in FWO languages.

4.6.3.   Object-initial Languages

Before summarizing the results of our survey it would be valuable to comment on language types that are very much in the minority.   Our discussion so far has been primarily in terms of SOV and SVO languages, though we have also included some material from verb-initial languages such as Tagalog and Malagasy. In recent years, however, a number of object-initial languages have come to light, as we pointed out in chapter three.   Unfortunately, little information on conjoined structures in OSV languages of the Amazon basin is available.   Pickering 1973b considers gapping in Apurinã and finds that it simply does not occur, either forwards or backwards.   Unfortunately this paper provides no data about other kinds of reduction in conjoined structures.   Des Derbyshire has however provided the authors with valuable material on the OVS language Hixkaryana.

A number of patterns in Hixkaryana could be interpreted as involving some kind of conjoined structure reduction.   However, the equivalent of English gapping does not seem to occur - there are no patterns of the form OVS + OS - but since there are no patterns of the form OS + OVS, Hixkaryana is no problem for any of the approaches to reduction we have discussed.

The existence of examples like (4.210), in which the subject is 'missing' from the first clause appears to involve backwards reduction.

(4.210)   mawu   wono;   horoto
           howler-monkey he-shot-it; spider-monkey
           O   xarha   wono,   V   Waraka   O
               also   he-shot-it,   Waraka
                       V   S

           'Waraka shot a howler-monkey and a spider-

           monkey'

However, it is possible that one could account for such an example in other ways.   There might be grounds for claiming that the constituents O and V formed a verb phrase constituent, though one should be wary of such an assumption.   Alternatively, one might see the two clauses as subjectless, the final constituent *Waraka* being added as an afterthought, to clarify the identity of the hunter.   Particularly

interesting is (4.211) in which it appears that a
subject has been removed from final position.

(4.211)   thetxe   yarɨye   Waraka.   buru

           his-wife   ħe-took-her   his-son
           O   V   S   O

              xarha   yarɨye

              also   he-took-him
                       V

         'Waraka took his wife and his son'

    However, it appears from the intonation pattern
that we are dealing here with two separate sentences.
The absence of a discrete subject in the second
clause does not necessarily militate against this
analysis because, like Italian (see example (4.102)),
the subject may simply be seen as incorporated within
the verb.   Other patterns of conjoining do occur and
seem to confirm that constituent conjoining does take
place.   That is, one finds patterns of the type
OV + VS, and OVS + S and, as we have demonstrated,
such examples are best considered as *not* reduced from
full clause structures (for further discussion of conjoining in Hixkaryana, see Derbyshire 1979:45-6).

4.7   Summary

    If one examines again the table we provided to
capture Koutsoudas' approach to reduced co-ordination
(Table 2, p.226), it is clear that many of the paradigm instances of reduction can be eliminated.   *All*
examples in columns IV, V and VI can be handled by
the direct conjoining of constituents.   Of the
remaining 18 patterns, only six involve removal of
elements from the first clause - those in column III,
which we reproduce here.

(4.212)

	Basic Word order Type	Final (=O in SVO)
1)	SOV + SOV	SOØ + SOV
2)	SVO + SVO	SVØ + SVO
3)	VSO + VSO	VSØ + VSO
4)	VOS + VOS	VOØ + VOS
5)	OVS + OVS	OVØ + OVS
6)	OSV + OSV	OSØ + OSV
		III

Of these six patterns predicted by Koutsoudas, two
may well be susceptible to an analysis that will
allow direct conjoining of VPs. This we suggested
was a possibility for Hixkaryana, and seems to be a
reasonable approach to the VOS language Malagasy.
(4.213) exemplifies full clause conjoining and (4.214)
a missing subject.

(4.213)   Misotro   taoka   Rabe *ary* mihinam-bary

           drink   alcohol   and eat   rice
             V   O   S   V   O

           Rabe

             S

       'Rabe is drinking alcohol and Rabe is

        eating rice'

(4.214)   Misotro   taoka   *sy*   mihinam-bary   Rabe
           drink   alcohol and   eat   rice
             V   O   V   O   S

       'Rabe is drinking alcohol and eating rice'

     Keenan 1978a claims that reduction of the subject
from the first clause leads to the regrouping of the
remaining constituents into a conjoined VP with a
special *and*-marker reserved for constituent conjoining. This seems to us to be an ideal example to be
handled by direct constituent conjoining of VPs.

     Thus, only four out of the original 36 patterns
in Koutsoudas' plan can be seen as involving backwards reduction, and in both SVO and VSO languages

the intonation points to some kind of delay or Right
Node Raising treatment.   Along with the Tagalog
examples presented earlier, it appears that Welsh, as
a VSO language, displays an intonation pattern that
matches such an analysis.   The symbol # in the
following example represents a break in intonation
that neatly parallels equivalent English examples
(Gwen Awbery, pers.comm., Alan Thomas, pers.comm.).

(4.215)   Gwelodd   Gwen # a   rhybuddiodd   Ifor#   y

           saw   and warned   the
           V   S   V   S

           dyn

           man
           O

           'Gwen saw, and Ifor warned, the man'

Of the non-FWO languages available for consideration
it would seem that only a strict SOV language like
Japanese clearly invites a backwards reduction analysis, though one would imagine that any OSV language
that did allow gapping or other reduction might pattern with Japanese if it was rigidly verb-final.

    Turkish is also a verb-final language and exam-
ples like (4.216) appear to involve a pattern of
gapping like that in Japanese.

(4.216)   Mehmet   yumurtayɨ,   Hasan   patlɨcanɨ   yedi

                    egg   eggplant   ate
           S   O   S   O   V

           'Mehmet ate the egg and Hasan the eggplant'

However, Turkish has a freer word order than Japanese
and allows final objects, as in (4.217), which can be
handled by the delay pattern, and is in fact done so
by Hankamer 1971.

(4.217)   Mehmet   piṣirdi,   Hasan   yedi   yumurtayɨ

                    cooked   ate   egg
           S   V   S   V   O

           'Mehmet cooked and Hasan ate the egg'

    The foregoing rather detailed discussion of
reduced conjoined structures has, we hope, served
several purposes.   Not only has it presented a large
quantity of apparently disparate data that can be

fitted into a variety of patterns but it also shows that selection of a favoured model for dealing with such diversity can be based on what turn out to be both factual and theoretical misconceptions.   In particular the directionality approach that links the occurrence of forwards or backwards deletion to the order of constituents or their direction of branching is subject to a great deal of manipulation, since an inherent part of such an approach is the use of unmotivated and ad hoc orderings of rules and the positing of unreasonable underlying word orders.   As we pointed out in chapter one the positing of underlying word orders that are different from surface word orders is a theoretical convenience but can not be regarded as having any testable psychological reality. What is particularly clear in reading the literature on the reduction of conjoined structures is that many linguists have become tied to an inherent circularity. Following what was, as we pointed out, a traditional system of positing reduction wherever possible, linguists may become blind to the pointlessness of putting material into underlying structure just so that it can be transformationally removed.

Furthermore, although the aim of any typologist should be to devise a potentially universal pattern to capture all the language types available, such a universal pattern should not ignore recalcitrant data. The attempt to impose a geometrical principle on the direction of gapping and other reduction makes no allowance for languages which may break such a geometrical principle.   The tendency for languages is to reduce in a forward direction but this is only a tendency, not a watertight universal and lends itself to an approach on the part of the typologist that recognizes the requirements of speakers to avoid the unnecessary burden on short-term memory that backwards reduction of any kind involves.   There are of course languages which do allow backwards reduction but this is normal in only two kinds of language: those like Japanese in which a language-specific feature (in this instance strictly verb-final status) overrides the tendency; and Free Word Order languages like the Mayan group, where speakers are more used to deviation from a set word order pattern - though Quechua demonstrates that even FWO languages may rigidly follow the universal tendency to reduce in a forwards direction.   Above all, it appears that *no* language indulges in backwards reduction and backwards reduction only, and this should be seen as significant.

NOTES

[1] In this chapter we use the terms *co-ordination*, *conjoining* and *conjunction* interchangeably.

[2] *Gapping*, a term apparently first used by Ross (see for example Ross 1970), refers to the transformational deletion of a verb from a conjoined structure. However, the term has been somewhat abused in the literature, being taken by some to refer to the omission of *any* constituent in a conjoined structure, under conditions of identity. Nevertheless, even the more proper restriction of the term to *verb* deletion presents problems.

First, the very term itself suggests a 'gap' in the structure and there is little doubt of the aptness of the term for examples such as (4.3b). However, as we shall see in sections 4.3 and 4.4, the apparent loss of a verb may not involve any discernible gap in the intonation pattern. Furthermore, in other languages the term may be used to refer to the omission of another type of constituent from the position that a verb would hold in English. Again, see section 4.4 for discussion.

Secondly, even in English *gapping* may be used to refer to the omission of much more material than a verb. In the following example the gap involves a verb *and*, for most speakers, also an adverb.

John raced quickly to the phone and Mary to the

   telex machine

For a discussion of the size of the gap and its possible interpretations see in particular Jackendoff 1971.

Finally, note that we use the term *gapping* to refer to examples such as those just discussed, but in so doing do not commit ourselves to the transformational approach that the term is normally associated with. A gapped example is one about which there would be a consensus among linguists that a verb had been left out, irrespective of the model used to describe the phenomenon.

[3] By *direction of deletion* we mean the following: where identical material is removed from the second of two clauses, deletion is in a *forwards* direction;

where identical material is removed from the first
clause deletion is *backwards*.

Once more we stress that our use of the term
deletion does not necessarily restrict us to a transformational approach (see note 2 above).

[4]Purely morphological identity can also be used
as a basis for conjoining, usually with comic effect.
For example:

She went off in a red dress and a blue fit

For a discussion of the literary value of such conjoining see Mallinson 1977.

[5]In Xhosa, as in other Bantu languages, noun
classes are designated by numbers.   Generally the
classes relate to a semantic division in the real
world.   However, as in more familiar languages which
have a gender system, the noun-class/real world match
is not always a perfect one.

[6]Note the morphological identity of *to* ('with')
and *to* ('and') in (4.92) to (4.94).   It is far from
unusual for languages to use the same morpheme in
such cases, as witnessed by the following entry in
the LDS questionnaire (Comrie & Smith 1977:19).

> 1.3.1.4.   Is the means used for expressing co-
> ordination and accompaniment
> (comitative) the same?

[7]Lindenfeld (1973:129), the source of our data
on Yaqui, expresses uncertainty about the precise
value of *ala*, but it does appear to stand in place of
a whole predicate.   It may however be the case that
ala simply means something like 'contrariwise'.

[8]For a further discussion of such examples of
the Bach-Peters Paradox see Dik 1973 and other references cited there.

[9]In (4.115) we have adopted the device of using
referential indices (the subscript j) to represent
the coreference of *he* and *John*.   Such an example is,
of course, perfectly grammatical if *he* and *John* are
not coreferential.

[10]However, in such an example a strong case can
be made for treating *look at* as a *phrasal verb*.   For
a clearer instance of gapping more than just a verb

see the example in note 2 to this chapter.

[11]Just as we have, for the sake of simplicity,
decided to discuss only paradigm cases of reduction,
so too have we limited our discussion to structures
in which only two conjuncts are involved.   Where
three or more conjuncts are involved, all but one conjunct may be reduced.

[12]In (4.133) and subsequent examples involving
tree-diagrams we use the symbol S_m to refer to the
matrix sentence node.

[13]In (4.144) and other examples we use the full
label *sentence* rather than the more usual S.   This
is to avoid any confusion with S as a symbol for
subject.   Also, our mixing of *categorial* labels
(such as VP) and *functional* labels (such as S(ubject)
and O(bject) might offend some.   We have adopted
this approach for greater simplicity in our diagrams.

[14]Our Hindi informant claimed that some of
Harries' examples were incorrect.   (4.188) is our own
version of Harries' equivalent example with *kharida*
('bought') instead of her *bech lia* (which Harries
glosses as 'sold').   This comment on the unreliabi-
lity of Harries' data tends to support Pullum's
comment on (4.190).

[15]See also our comments in chapter three on the
uncertainty among linguists about basic word order in
Hungarian (p.132), which we take to be SVO.

[16]Hankamer's attractive notion of *delay* is somewhat spoiled by his use of esoteric transformational
descriptive devices.   For a simple explanation of
the geometry of *Chomsky-adjunction* see Huddleston
1976:189-92.

[17]For a description of Right Node Raising see
Hudson 1976 and Postal 1974.

[18]Hudson 1976 also expresses dissatisfaction
with a reduction approach to examples such as (4.201a).
However he chooses to work in that paper within a
transformational framework in order to make his
points to linguists who might not be impressed by a
non-transformational approach.

CHAPTER 5

RELATIVE CLAUSES

5.0   Introduction

      In chapter four we distinguished between complex
structures of two main types - those involving subordination, and those in which the relationship between clauses is a co-ordinating one.   As we pointed
out, the distinction is by no means a clear one and
even in the most obviously co-ordinating structures
there is usually some semantic relationship (often of
a temporal or causal nature) between clauses, despite
the structural independence of each.[1]

      On purely structural grounds it appears that
separability is an important criterion in distinguishing co-ordination from subordination.   Whereas in
examples such as (5.1) the two clauses can exist as
independent simple sentences, in the case of (5.2)
the italicized clause is structurally dependent on
the other clause and cannot exist independently unless it is amended in some way.

(5.1)   The cats have broken six eggs and we will be

            having omelettes for tea

(5.2)   Toy trains are for adults *who haven't com-*

            pletely grown up

The result of splitting (5.2) into separate clauses
is either (5.3) or (5.4), depending on whether or not
who is seen as a disposable linking word, like *and*.

(5.3)   Toy trains are for adults.   *Who haven't

            completely grown up

(5.4)   Toy trains are for adults.   *Haven't comple-
         tely grown up

Nevertheless, it would be a mistake to claim that
separability was a fool-proof criterion.   (5.5) is
an instance of co-ordination but the italicized part
cannot be separated from the first clause.

(5.5)   Chocolate is good for adults and *fruit for*
         children

This, as we saw in chapter four, is an example of
reduction.   (5.5) can be related to a fuller example
(5.6), which *can* be separated.

(5.6)   Chocolate is good for adults and fruit is
         good for children

On the other hand, the subordinate clause cannot be
filled out in this way.   (5.4) cannot be related to
a non-reduced version;   (5.7) would not be a complex
sentence equivalent to (5.4).

(5.7)   Toy trains are for adults, adults haven't
         completely grown up

In the case of (5.8), the two clauses *can* be separated, it seems.

(5.8)   The king is annoyed about some jam tarts
         (that) the knave has eaten

(5.9)   The king is annoyed about some jam tarts.
         The knave has eaten

However, the second clause is only acceptable because
eat in English can be used both transitively and intransitively.   This subterfuge simply disguises the
fact that in (5.8) *that* is an integral part of the
second clause (but can be left out) and that the
whole of the second clause functions as a modifier of
some jam tarts, a constituent of the first clause.

     A similar example, involving a complement clause,
is (5.10).

(5.10)   The doctor believes *(that) all his patients*
           are hypochondriacs

It is only because *believe* can also be used both
transitively and intransitively that (5.10) can
apparently be separated, as in (5.11).

(5.11)   The doctor believes. All his patients are
           hypochondriacs

However, (5.11) is not equivalent to (5.10), where
the italicized clause is functioning as an object of
the first clause.

An important difference between the relative
clauses in (5.2) or (5.8) and the complement clause
in (5.10) is that the marker *that* can be seen as *part*
of the relative clause, but merely an element introducing, or marking the onset of, the complement
clause.   A thorough discussion of subordination
would be concerned with both these clause-types but
we discuss only the relative clause.   It is precisely
because the relative marker is more than a mere empty
marker of the onset of the relative clause that it is
pertinent to the themes of this book.   The element
referred to as the relative marker, or relative pronoun, does introduce the relative clause and identify
it as such, but it also in many languages clearly
acts as a substitute for one of the NP participants
in the clause.   For this reason, a study of relative
clauses is very relevant to the study of those devices
languages use for identifying grammatical relations:
word order and case marking.   Since in many languages
the relative marker appears at the beginning or end
of its clause it will occupy a position other than
that of the participant it stands for; it is the
interrelationship of word order and case marking that
will help the language user to recover the function
of the participant that the relative marker stands
for, even though the normal word order and case marking systems of the language may be upset by the formation of relative structures.

Accordingly, the greater part of the chapter
will be concerned with relative clauses, though we
will also make reference on occasion to complement
structures.   Our main concern will be to demonstrate
the range of devices and strategies languages make
use of in forming relative clause structures; to
relate their structure to the notions of case marking

and word order discussed in chapters two and three;
and to establish where possible perceptual principles
that may be at work in the formation of these structures.

5.1   Definitions of Relative Clauses

Traditional English grammar books commonly dub
the relative clause the *adjectival* clause, since its
function is that of qualifying a *head* noun in the way
that an adjective does.   In (5.12) the italicized
material is a relative clause, and in (5.13) an adjective, but it is clear that the function of each is to
add further information about the head noun *sheep*.

(5.12)   Sheep *that have long fleeces* survive better
            in winter

(5.13)   *Long-haired* sheep survive better in winter

Furthermore, in both cases the italicized material is
essential to the definition of *sheep* since the statement is not that sheep in general survive better in
the winter but that those that have long fleeces or
are long-haired do.   It is possible to paraphrase
(5.13) as (5.14), with a relative clause.

(5.14)   Sheep *that are long-haired* survive better in
            winter

Such a paraphrase relationship has proved irresist-
ible to many linguists and the result has been a
carrying over of the semantic relationship to a
structural one, with transformations such as *relative
clause reduction*.[2] However, whether one does or does
not subscribe to a reduction approach, the depleted
or reduced relative structure is a common feature in
language and any comprehensive review of relative
clause structure across languages should give some
space to those structures which function in the same
way as full relatives but which have fewer of the
clausal attributes associated with examples such as
(5.2), (5.8) and (5.12).

A further type of relative clause which deserves
some consideration is the *non-restrictive* relative,
as opposed to the *restrictive* relative exemplified so
far.   In (5.15a) the italicized clause is parenthetical and does not restrict the reference of the head

in the way that the restrictive equivalent does in
(5.15b).

(5.15) a.   All teachers, *who have been sacked*, are to
            attend a protest meeting
       b.   All teachers *who have been sacked* are to
            attend a protest meeting

In (5.15a) we assume that *all* teachers are to attend
a protest meeting, whereas in (5.15b) only those who
have been sacked will attend.

Most linguists confine detailed discussion to
the restrictive relative and in this chapter we also
concentrate on this type.   However, we do devote
some space to non-restrictives in section 5.5.

One particularly important study of relative
clauses (RCs) is that of Keenan & Comrie 1977, 1979
(henceforth referred to as K & C).   They define the
RC as follows.

> 'We consider any syntactic object to be an RC
> if it specifies a set of objects (perhaps a
> one-member set) in two steps: a larger set
> is specified, called the *domain* of relativi-
> zation, and then restricted to some subset of
> which a certain sentence, the *restricting*
> sentence is true.   The domain of relativiza-
> tion is expressed in surface structure by the
> head NP, and the restricting sentence by the
> *restricting clause*, which may look more or
> less like a surface sentence depending on the
> language'.   (Keenan & Comrie 1977:63-4).

Clearly, such a definition serves to encompass those
structures across language which may bear little
resemblance to English relative clauses but which,
nevertheless, have the same role of *defining, qualifying, specifying* or merely *modifying* a head noun.
This view is shared by the author of another important
study of RCs:

> 'What is a relative clause?   For the purposes
> of this chapter, a relative clause is any
> clause with approximately the semantic struc-
> ture and function of a relative clause (res-
> trictive or non-restrictive) in English.   I
> shall sharpen this rough criterion somewhat
> by saying that a relative clause is a sub-
> ordinate clause that modifies a constituent

external to it by virtue of containing a constituent that is in some sense semantically
equivalent to the modified constituent.'
                              (Andrews 1975:13).

Neither Andrews' definition nor the concluding
sentence of K & C's definition sets a lower limit on
the degree to which the RC can resemble a simple sentence or full clause and still be an RC (even an adjective may in these terms be regarded as an RC).
Ostensibly an RC proper, the German participial
structure in (5.16) may not behave in the same way
that full clausal RCs behave yet it can still be regarded as matching these definitions.

(5.16)   Der   *in   seinem   Büro   arbeitende*   Mann

          the   in   his   office   working   man

          'The man working in his office'

Such structures are considered RCs by many linguists
but their behaviour does not follow the patterns that
can be established for most languages.   In terms of
word order, for example, they break the normal rule
for SVO languages by appearing to the left of their
head, while *clausal* RCs in German appear as expected
to the right of their head.   Compare (5.17).

(5.17)   Der   Mann   *der   in   seinem   Büro*   arbeitet

          the   man   REL   in   his   office   works

          'The man who is working in his office'

We return to such structures in our discussion of
word order in section 5.2.

Another instance of RCs not being what they
appear to be is demonstrated by Australian languages.
The following examples from Walbiri (Hale 1976) are
typical of many languages of Australia.

(5.18)   ŋatjulu-ḻu   ɸ-   ṇa   yankiri   pantu-ṇu,

                I-erg   aux-I   emu   spear-past

          kutja-lpa   ŋapa   ŋa-   ṇu

          comp-aux   water   drink-past

          'I speared the emu *which was/while it was*
          drinking water'

(5.19)   ŋatjulu-ḷu   kapi-ṇa   wawiri   pura-mi,

         I-erg   aux-I   kangaroo   cook-nonpast

      kutja-npa   pantu-ṇu   njuntulu-ḷu

      comp-aux   spear-past   you-erg

      'I will cook the kangaroo *you speared*'

(5.20)   ŋatjulu-ḷu   Ipa-ṇa   kaḷi   tjaṇṭu-ṇu,

         I-erg   aux-I   boomerang   trim-past

      kutja-∅-npa   ya- nu- ṇu   njuntu

      comp-aux   walk-past-hither you

      'I was trimming a boomerang *when you came up*'

In (5.18) the normal Head-RC relationship is a possible interpretation but, as the translation shows, it
is also possible to see the RC as 'specify[ing] the
temporal setting of the event depicted in the main
clause'.   In (5.19) this temporal interpretation is
not available, whereas in (5.20) *only* the temporal
interpretation is possible.

    Hale terms these structures *adjoined relatives*,
though in some instances they have interpretations
which make it clear they are not RCs in the normal
sense of that term.   Apart from the temporal interpretation they may, for example, have a conditional
interpretation, and 'specify a condition under which
the predication embodied in the main clause could
refer to an actual event, process or state'.   (1976:
79).[3] This is the case with (5.21).

(5.21)   ŋatjulu-ḷu   kapi-ṇa   maliki   ḷuwa- ṇi,

         I-erg   aux-I   dog   shoot-nonpast

      katji-∅-ŋki   yaḷki-ṇi   njuntu

      comp-aux   bite-nonpast   you

      'I will shoot the dog, if/when it bites you'

      or

      'I will shoot the dog that bites you/that is
        going to bite you'

Apart from this semantic difference between adjoined
and ordinary relatives, syntactic evidence for a
distinction comes from the fact that adjoined rela-

tives can occur before the main clause (normal RCs
can be moved away from their head, but only to clause
final position - see section 5.2.4. for discussion of
extraposition).   Furthermore, they need not contain
a participant coreferential with a participant in the
main clause.   (5.22) is an optional variant on (5.18)
and (5.23) on (5.20).

(5.22)   yankiri-ḷi kutja-lpa ŋapa ŋa-ṉu,

          ŋatjulu-ḷu φ-ṉa pantu-ṉu

          'The emu which was drinking water, I speared
              it'

          or

          'While the emu was drinking water, I speared
              it'

(5.23)   kutja-φ-npa ya-nu-ṉu njuntu,

          kaḷi lpa-ṉa tjanṭu-ṉu

          'When you came up I was trimming a boomerang'

Hale considers whether there is any value in relating
the adjoined relative to the normal embedded type.
As we have seen, there are considerable differences
and in no case can the adjoined relative be seen as
functioning as a single unit with its head.   The
best one can do is to relate the two types on an historical basis, with evolution as represented by the
pattern in (5.24) (where 'attraction' refers to the
attraction of an adjoined structure from a peripheral
position to one where it flanks the head).   Such a
pattern implies a claim that embedded RCs are phylo-
genetically a late development, and that the embedded
relative is a universal structure towards which all
languages are moving.

(5.24)   *Initial Stage*
          Adjoined relatives only
          First Intermediate Stage
          Adjoined relatives with optional attraction
          Second Intermediate Stage
          Adjoined relatives with obligatory attraction

Final Stage

Reanalysis of the attracted relative as an
embedded relative

(Hale 1975:15).

We make no further comments on such structures
except to deliver a warning against juggling recalcitrant data to make a near-universal into a complete
one (for further examples and discussion of adjoined
structures in Australian languages see Hale 1976, and
for a similar analysis of some RCs in Hindi and
Marathi see Andrews 1975:93ff).

Participial and adjoined relatives are two types
of structure that present problems for linguists
attempting to establish universal principles of relative clause formation. One such principle is the
relating of head and RC order to word order in particular languages. We have seen that participial RCs
precede their head in German, whereas one would expect RCs to follow their heads in verb-second languages, which is indeed the case in German with its
clausal RCs.

The first of our two main sections (5.2) will be
concerned with an important relationship between RCs
and word order - the position of RCs before or after
their heads. We will attempt to account for the
choice particular languages make by following, but
expanding on, a cognitive principle put forward by
Kuno 1972. We will also examine the distribution of
extraposed RCs and again find some perceptual motivation for the data we have gathered.

In the second main section (5.3), we will turn
to the other major problem in establishing universal
principles of RC-formation - the relationship between
case marking and RC structure. In particular, any
account of RC-formation in language will have to
demonstrate how language users can recover the role
in the subordinate clause of the NP that is coreferential with the head. For example, in (5.25) the
italicized marker stands for the direct object of the
RC, whereas in (5.26) the italicized element is
acting as subject. It is the case marking of Latin
which helps recovery of the grammatical relations
that may otherwise be disguised (by the changes in
word order brought about in the formation of RCs).
However, we will also see that again word order is
relevant to the task of recovering grammatical rela-

tions, working often in conjunction with explicit
case marking, rather than in opposition to it.

Latin

(5.25)   Miles   qui   victoriam

         soldier   REL   victory-acc
         -sg.nom   [+masc+sing
                    +nom]

         reportavit puellam amat

         win-past   girl-acc love-pres

         'The soldier who won the victory loves the
         girl'

(5.26)   Puellae   quas   rogavi

         girl-pl.nom REL   ask-past
                      [+fem+plural
                       +acc]

         cras   respondebunt

         tomorrow   reply-future

         'The girls whom I asked will answer tomorrow'

This perceptual priority - the recovery of grammatical relations - is paramount, and is summed up as
follows by Keenan.

> 'Any language which has relative clauses must
> provide some strategy to identify the role
> that the head noun plays in the subordinate
> sentence, or else the relative clauses would
> be intolerably ambiguous - we would not be
> able to distinguish the referents of "the girl
> that John loves" and "the girl that loves
> John". We stress that identifying the posi-
> tion relativized into by the head noun is
> logically important, for only if the position
> is known can we clearly determine the sentence
> which must be true of the objects specified by
> the head noun, and thus understand the reference
> of the entire relative clause.'
>   (Keenan 1974:479).

Nevertheless, we will see that languages are not
always successful in allowing unequivocal recovery of
grammatical roles, though one must assume that languages that did allow their users to encounter such
problems would not survive long in that form if

speakers could not tolerate at least some ambiguities, or counter them with other devices.

5.2   Order of Head and Relative Clause

5.2.1.   Major Trends

Relative clauses invite discussion in connection with word order in at least two ways - the order of constituents within the RC, and the position of the RC in relation to its head.   In the latter case there are three options: the head precedes, the head follows and the head is surrounded by the RC.   This last option is quite uncommon and apart from illustrating it we will have very little to say about it.[4] The other two orders are widespread.

Head-internal

(5.27)   *Crow* (Andrews 1975)

   Mary-sh   shiká:ka-m   hi: -liche-é:sh

      nom   boy   spec   meet-sort-of det

   'The boy who Mary is dating'

(5.28)   *Bambara* (K & C)

   tye   ye   ne   ye   so   min   ye   san

   man   Past I   Past horse REL   see buy

   'The man bought the horse that I saw'

Head-RC

(5.29)   *Hebrew* (K & C 1972)

   ha- iša   še- Yon   natan   la et   ha-

   the woman REL John   gave   to - her   the

    sefer

    book

   'The woman that John gave the book to'

(5.30)   *Luganda* (Walusimbi 1976)

   ekitabo   kye   n-a-   gula   kirungi

   book   REL   I-past-buy   good

   'The book that I bought is good'

(5.31)   *Batak* (K & C)
          boru-boru   na   manussi   abit   i
          woman   REL   wash   clothes   the
          'The woman who is washing clothes'

(5.32)   *Vietnamese* (Clark 1974)
          ông   mà   mua   sách   dó   di
          man   REL   bought   books   det   go
          'The man who bought the books is going'

(5.33)   *Samoan* (Chung 1978)[5]
          'O   fea   le   tamāloa   na
          pred   where?   the   man   past
             maitau-ina   tupe?
             count- trans   money
          'Where is the man who counted the money?'

RC-Head

(5.34)   *Japanese* (Kuno 1973)
          Kore   wa   watakushi   ga   kaita   hon   desu
          this   top   I   nom   wrote   book   is
          'This is a book that I have written'

(5.35)   *Basque* (K & C)
          emakume-a   -ri   liburu-a   eman   dio-n
          woman   the dat   book   the   give   has REL
             gizon-a
             man   the
          'The man who has given the book to the woman'

(5.36)   *Fore* (Scott 1978)
          naga'tái   ntagara   kánaye
          [na-ka-'tá-íɴ   yagara:'   kana-y-e]

            me-see-past-he(emph)   man   come-he-
                                                      indic

          'The man who saw me is coming'

(5.37)   *Tigre* (Palmer 1961)

ʾət   ʾäfuhu   la   ʿälät   kətfät

in   his-mouth   REL   it-was   piece

'The piece that was in his mouth'

(5.38)   *Sherpa* (Givón 1979)

mi- la   ţyeŋka   bin-dup   pumpetsa-ti

man-dat money   give-ing   woman-top

'The woman who gave the man money'

Among the languages we have used to illustrate the order Head-RC in examples (5.29) to (5.33) are three SVO languages (Hebrew, Luganda and Vietnamese), while the other two languages (Batak and Samoan) are both verb-initial.   On the other hand, all five examples of RC-Head order are SOV languages.   In fact, there seems to be a very strong correlation between basic word order and Head/RC order, which can be stated as follows:

VO languages have Head-RC order
OV languages have RC-Head order.

Several of Greenberg's universals also point to such a correlation, including universal 24:

'If the relative expression precedes the noun either as the only construction or as an alternative construction, either the language is postpositional, or the adjective precedes the noun or both'.

A more direct statement of the word order relationship we are discussing is presented by the table on which this universal is based:

	I (VSO)	II (SVO)	III (SOV)
Relational expression precedes noun	0	0	7
Noun precedes relational expression	6	12	2
Both constructions	0	1	1

	Pr	*Po*
Relational expression precedes noun	0	7
Noun precedes relational expression	16	4
Both constructions	0	2

The table demonstrates that only SOV languages can
have the order RC-Head exclusively, though one SVO
language can have the order RC-Head as an alternative
to Head-RC.   A larger number of languages have the
order Head-RC, including all thirteen SVO languages
and all six VSO languages in Greenberg's sample.
The table above also demonstrates that prepositional
languages have Head-RC order while postpositional
languages show a strong trend towards the order RC-
Head.

Thus, when related to universal 3, which claims
VSO languages are always prepositional, and to universal 4, which claims SOV languages are normally
postpositional, it is clear that universal 24 involves an implicit statement of the predictability of
Head/RC order in these two word order types at least.
Interestingly, not one of Greenberg's universals
makes direct reference to SVO languages and this more
limited predictability of SVO languages is reflected
in his table.   However, in many respects SVO languages follow the pattern for VSO languages and this
can be attributed to their VO status.

Greenberg's sample thus appears to support the
correlation between VO order and Head-RC order, and
between OV order and RC-Head.   However, his is a
rather restricted sample and it might be of interest
to extend it, as we did in chapter three, to test to
what extent his conclusions are borne out by a much
wider range of languages.   This we have done in
table 4.

In table 4 we have collected 150 languages and
shown the order each has for major constituents and
for Head/RC.   The languages are numbered from 1 to
150, but in the second column we have added in paren-
theses the number of any language also used in table 1
in chapter three.   Where possible we have used the
same languages but in some instances information was
not available on Head/RC order.   In other cases our
sample in chapter three included languages with unusual relative structures, in particular Australian

languages, which normally have the adjoined type of
RC that we briefly discussed in section 5.1.   These
we have excluded from table 4.   Table 1 also included
a representative sample of the languages of the Americas, whereas these are poorly represented in table 4.
Many American languages have *headless* RCs and are
therefore not relevant to the aims of table 4.[6]

The sample in table 4 is very much a sample of
convenience, based on what relevant material happened
to be available.   Europe, Africa and southeast Asia
are well represented but the table does not give a
fair illustration of genetic groupings on a world-wide
basis.   Thus, of the 150 languages selected 74 have
the basic order SVO, while 11 more have SVO as an
alternative order;   30 languages have SOV order, a
further 11 having SOV as an alternative order;   the
remaining languages are all verb-initial.

This means that verb-initial languages are as
well-represented as SOV languages, and together
are only as common as the SVO type in our table.
Clearly, in terms of the distribution of word order
types shown in chapter three, this is a most unfortunate bias and shows dramatically what happens when we
fail to sample properly.   Nevertheless, in table 4
the spread of word order types is not the critical
issue.   What *is* important is whether the distinction
between VO and OV languages in terms of Head/RC order
is borne out by the languages selected.

Table 4

Word Order and Head/RC Order

		Word Order	RC–Head	Head–RC
1.	Achenese	SVO		x
2.	Adyghe	SOV	x	x
3.	Ainu	SOV	x	x
4.	Akan	SVO		x
5.	Albanian	SVO		x
6.	Amharic (12)	SOV	x	x
7.	Aoban	SVO		x
8.	Arabic (Iraqi) (13)	SVO		x
9.	Armenian	SVO		x
10.	Basque (43)	SOV/Fr	x	
11.	Batak	VOS		x
12.	Bemba	SVO		x
13.	Berber	VSO		x
14.	Berta	SVO		x
15.	Bikol	V1/Fr		x
16.	Bongo	SVO		x
17.	Bulgarian	SVO		x

		Word Order	RC–Head	Head–RC
18.	Burmese (47)	SOV	x	
19.	Burushaski	SOV	x	
20.	Cambodian (52)	SVO		x
21.	Chamorro	SVO/VSO		x
22.	Chibcha	SOV	x	
23.	Chichewa	SVO		x
24.	Chinook	SVO/VSO		x
25.	Czech	SVO		x
26.	Dagbani	SVO		x
27.	Danish	SVO		x
28.	Dutch	SVO		x
29.	Dzamba	SVO		x
30.	Easter Island	VSO		x
31.	Efik	SVO		x
32.	Ehona	SVO		x
33.	English (1)	SVO		x
34.	Estonian	SVO		x
35.	Fijian	VOS		x

		Word Order	RC–Head	Head–RC
36.	Finnish (33)	SVO	x	x
37.	Fore (65)	SOV/Fr	x	x
38.	French (3)	SVO		x
39.	Fulani (27)	SVO		x
40.	Fur (19)	SOV		x
41.	Galla (14)	SOV	x	x
42.	Ge'ez	VSO		x
43.	Georgian (40)	SVO		x
44.	German (2)	V2	x	x
45.	Gilbertese	VOS		x
46.	Greek (Classical) (7)	SVO/SOV	x	x
47.	Greek (Modern)	SVO		x
48.	Guaraní (98)	SVO/Fr		x
49.	Hausa (16)	SVO		x
50.	Hawaiian	VSO		x
51.	Hebrew (Modern) (11)	SVO		x
52.	Hindi (10)	SOV	x	x
53.	Hittite (10)	SOV	x	x

	Word Order	RC–Head	Head–RC
54. Hottentot	SOV	x	x
55. Hungarian (34)	SVO/Fr	x	x
56. Iban	SVO		x
57. Icelandic	SVO		x
58. Ilocano	V1/Fr		x
59. Ilonggo	V1/Fr		x
60. Irish (4)	VSO		x
61. Italian	SVO		x
62. Jacaltec (90)	VSO		x
63. Japanese	SOV	x	
64. Javanese	SVO		x
65. Kalagan	VSO		x
66. Kannada (78)	SOV	x	
67. Kanuri (17)	SOV	x	
68. Kapampangan	V1		x
69. Kapingamarangi	SVO/VSO		x
70. Kashmiri	SVO		x
71. Kenga	SVO		x

	Word Order	RC–Head	Head–RC
72. Kera	SVO		x
73. Khamti (51)	SOV		x
74. Khasi (54)	SVO		x
75. Khmu (53)	SVO		x
76. Kihung'an	SVO		x
77. Kinyarwanda	SVO		x
78. Kivunjo	SVO		x
79. Korean (38)	SOV	x	
80. Koyo	SVO		x
81. Lao	SVO		x
82. Latin	SOV/Fr		x
83. Lelemi	SVO		x
84. Lenakel (63)	SVO		x
85. Lingala	SVO		x
86. Luganda	SVO		x
87. Lunyole	SVO		x
88. Maasai (23)	VSO		x
89. Malagasy (57)	VOS		x
90. Malay	SVO		x

		Word Order	RC-Head	Head-RC
91.	Mandarin (44)	SVO/SOV	x	x
92.	Maori	VSO		x
93.	Marathi	SOV/Fr	x	x
94.	Margi	SVO		x
95.	Maya	SVO		x
96.	Mba	SVO/SOV		x
97.	Minang-Kabau	SVO		x
98.	Mongolian (37)	SOV	x	
99.	Moru	SVO/SOV		x
100.	Nahuatl (Classical)	SVO		x
101.	Nguna	SVO		x
102.	Norwegian	SVO		x
103.	Nubian (21)	SOV	x	x
104.	Palauan	SVO	x	
105.	Persian	SOV		x
106.	Piro (100)	SOV	x	
107.	Polish (6)	SVO		x
108.	Portuguese	SVO		x
109.	Pukapukan	VSO/VOS		x

		Word Order	RC–Head	Head–RC
110.	Quechua (99)	SOV/Fr	x	x
111.	Rashad	SOV		x
112.	Rennellese	SVO/VSO		x
113.	Romanian	SVO		x
114.	Roviana	VSO		x
115.	Rukai	VSO		x
116.	Russian	SVO		x
117.	Samoan	VSO		x
118.	Sandawe	SOV/Fr	x	x
119.	Sango	SVO		x
120.	Serbian	SVO		x
121.	Shatt	SVO		x
122.	Sherpa	SOV	x	
123.	Shona	SVO		x
124.	Sinhala	SOV	x	
125.	Slovenian	SVO		x
126.	Songhai	SVO		x
127.	Spanish	SVO		x
128.	Squamish (96)	VSO		x

	Word Order	RC–Head	Head–RC
129. Sri Lanka Malay	SOV	x	
130. Sri Lanka Portuguese	SOV	x	
131. Swahili (29)	SVO		x
132. Tagalog (59)	V1/Fr	x	x
133. Tamil (76)	SOV	x	
134. Telugu (77)	SOV	x	
135. Thai (49)	SVO		x
136. Tibetan (Classical) (45)	SOV	x	x
137. Tigre	SOV	x	x
138. Tongan (60)	VSO		x
139. Turkish (36)	SOV	x	x
140. Twi	SVO		x
141. Tzeltal	VOS		x
142. Uduk	SVO		x
143. Vai	SVO		x
144. Vietnamese (55)	SVO		x
145. Welsh	VSO		x
146. Yapese	VSO		x
147. Yiddish	SVO		x

		Word Order	RC–Head	Head–RC
148.	Yoruba	(28)	SVO		x
149.	Zande		SVO/VSO		x
150.	Zapotec	(94)	VSO		x

The sample in table 4 yields the following conclusions:

Only 6 SVO languages allow the order RC-Head,
and of these only 1 (Palauan) does not have
Head-RC as an alternative order.

Among verb-initial languages only 2 allow the
order RC-Head, and both these languages
(Kapampangan and Tagalog) have Head-RC as an
alternative order.

Among the SOV languages only 16 have the order
RC-Head exclusively, while 17 allow Head-RC as
an option and 4 allow *only* Head-RC order.

The correlation between VO order and Head-RC order is therefore very strongly supported by table 4.
The correlation between OV order and RC-Head order is
also evident but no more reliable than Greenberg's
figures demonstrated.   The best one can say here is
that there is more chance that an SOV language will
have the order RC-Head than a VO language.

We now examine some exceptions to the trends and
then discuss some possible explanations.

5.2.2.   Exceptions to the Trends in Table 4

As we pointed out in our discussion of basic
word order in chapter three, other linguists have en-
larged on Greenberg's sample but have not achieved
precisely the same results that we have.   One important reason for this is a lack of agreement on basic
word order in particular languages.   Such languages
include Hungarian, Tagalog, Diola-Fogny and Tongan
(see p.132) but it is likely that other languages will
also be controversial.   In table 4 we have also included languages about which there is some uncertainty but the implications for the table in this chapter
are different from those for our table in chapter
three.   As far as the distribution of basic word
order types is concerned, assigning SVO status to
Hebrew, rather than VSO order, will substantially
reduce the percentage of VSO languages, given their
smaller numbers, but will make little difference to
the percentage of SVO languages.   Hungarian would be
less troublesome since the two possible basic orders
(SVO and SOV) are usually well-represented in any
sample.   When, however, SVO and VSO languages are
grouped together as VO languages, indecision over the
status of Hebrew will have no effect on the correla-

tion between VO order and Head-RC order, while indecision over Hungarian will determine whether it goes
against the trends in table 4 or follows them.

One way of achieving a more clearcut pattern is,
of course, to carefully select only those languages
over which there is general agreement. On the other
hand, it is precisely such controversial languages
which are most interesting. They may well provide
some insight into *why* it is that the correlation between basic order and Head/RC order is far from watertight.

In this section we discuss several languages
which go against the trends in table 4. First we
examine a number of languages in which contact has
played an important part, and then we discuss several
languages where a different solution must be found
for their exceptional behaviour.

5.2.2.1.   The Effects of Language Contact

(a)   *Turkish and Persian*

Although some linguists have patterned it with
strict verb-final languages such as Korean and Japanese, Turkish has some features which distinguish it
from the more rigid verb-final language type. As we
saw in chapter four, Turkish allows gapping in the
second rather than the first clause in a co-ordinate
structure, and in simple sentences the order SVO can
occur.   The following examples are a problem for any
linguist attempting to group Turkish with Korean and
Japanese.

(5.39)   Ahmet   yumurtayɨ   pişirdi,   Mehmet
                 egg   cooked
         S   O   V   S

         patlɨcanɨ

         eggplant
              O

         'Ahmet cooked the egg and Mehmet the egg-
         plant'

(5.40)   Hasan   yedi   yumurtayɨ
                 ate   egg
         S   V   O

         'Hasan ate the egg'

It is therefore perhaps no surprise to find that, in
addition to its RC-Head order, Turkish also allows the
order Head-RC.   Compare (5.41) and (5.42).

(5.41)   *RC-Head*

mekteb-e   gid-en   oğlan

school-dat   go-part   boy

'The boy who goes to school'

(5.42)   *Head-RC*

bir   adam   vardi   ki   ismi   Hasan   idi

a   man   there was REL name   was

'There was a man whose name was Hasan'

While the postnominal RC is not widely used, it
is nevertheless possible in Turkish and there have
even been moves to have it adopted as the only type of
relative structure.   Heyd 1954 describes how linguists in Turkey tried to convince the country's fourth
national language congress that this was one method of
westernizing and simplifying the language.   The reaction was a negative one, the congress stating that
'it was neither necessary nor possible to change the
syntax of our language by any interference' (Heyd
1954:96).   Indeed the trend has been in this direction, with a move towards linguistic 'purity', and
the use of the Head-RC order actually discouraged.
Yet this does not remove the fact that both structures
are possible in the language.

The occurrence of an alternative Head-RC order in
Turkish is generally agreed to have been through the
influence of Persian and, as Lehmann points out
(1978c:401), acceptance of the *ki* relative construction may have been eased by the occurrence already in
the language of a morpheme *ki* that marked the onset of
other subordinate structures.

As for Persian itself, this language too is predominantly SOV yet allows some VO features.   (5.43)
and (5.44) illustrate verb-medial ordering as an alternative to verb-final ordering.   (5.45) illustrates
Head-RC order (all three examples are from Kuno 1972).

(5.43)   jān   be-xāna   raft

John   to-home   went

'John went home'

(5.44)   jañ   raft   be-xāna
          John went   to-home
          'John went home'

(5.45)   mardi   ke   mixāhad   bā   šomā   sohbat
          man   REL   wants   with   you   talk

               konad   dam-e   dar   ast
               do   near-of door   is

          'The man who wants to speak with you is at
           the door'

Persian thus allows features that are a mix between OV and VO types and one might look to borrowing
from other languages (such as the VSO Classical Arabic) as a reason for this mixed status.

(b)   *Languages of Ethiopia*

A particularly interesting exception to the
trends in table 4 is Amharic.   As the table shows,
this language has SOV order but allows both orderings
of Head/RC.   Of course, one is always at the mercy
of one's sources and not all linguists who have written on Amharic have recognized that both orders are
possible, stating merely that the RC precedes the head.
If this were so it would undoubtedly reinforce Greenberg's conclusions but would at the same time disguise
the very mixed status of this language.   As Bach
1970 shows, Amharic has predominantly SOV order but
also has prepositions, while ordering the genitive
expression before the noun (thus presenting a conflict between universals 4 and 2).

As Amharic is by no means a clearcut SOV language, Bach claims that the underlying order is either
VSO or SVO, with transformational reordering of constituents to account for surface OV ordering.   As we
pointed out in chapter one, there is little value in
this approach since underlying structures are empirically quite untestable.

What one must accept is that Amharic is a mix of
VO and OV features.   The general view is that, as a
Semitic language, Amharic was originally VSO but was
influenced by Cushitic SOV languages.   Tigre has
also been influenced in this way, to a lesser extent
but enough to allow both RC-Head and Head-RC orders.
For a discussion of such contact see Bender et al.

1976 and also Gragg 1972.

On the other hand, the Cushitic language Galla allows both orders for its RCs, as illustrated by (5.46) and (5.47).

(5.46)   *RC-Head*

kan   kalēsa   gale   namtičča   an   arge

REL   yesterday   arrived   man-def   I   saw

'I saw the man that arrived yesterday'

(5.47)   *Head-RC*

namtičča   kan   kalēsa   gale   an   arge

man-def   REL   yesterday   arrived   I   saw

'I saw the man that arrived yesterday'

One might also assume, therefore, that some Cushitic languages at least have been affected by contact in the complex areal situation of Ethiopia.

(c)   *The Indian Linguistic Area*

The Indian area is a classic example of convergence, with prolonged contact between Dravidian and Indo-Aryan languages in particular leading to a good deal of borrowing at the syntactic level. While Dravidian languages are strongly SOV, Indo-Aryan languages tend to be less so. However, the Indo-Aryan language Sinhala appears to have only prenominal RCs, and this must be a result of its isolation from the Indo-Aryan languages on the mainland and its prolonged contact with Tamil. Since it has also hardened as an SOV language, however, Sinhala is only an anomaly to anyone who is aware of its genetic affiliation. Precisely the same can be said of Sri Lanka Portuguese and Sri Lanka Malay, which are also SOV and have the order RC-Head but are languages resulting from contact between SVO languages and Dravidian.

Hindi, on the other hand, displays less subservience to the SOV norm. It has many features of SOV languages but allows postnominal RCs, as in example (5.48).

(5.48)   us   aadmii   ne   jo   miir   hai   ek
          that   man   erg   REL   rich   is   a
          makaan   khariidhaa
          house   bought
          'The man who is rich bought a house'

Hindi also has prenominal RCs, as illustrated by
(5.49).

(5.49)   yi   merii   likhii   huii   kitaab   hai
          this me-gen   written   have   book   is
          'This is a book I have written'

One might speculate that the Indo-Aryan languages
were at one time relatively free in their word order,
though like Latin favouring SOV order, and that the
move away from SOV order was impeded by contact with
Dravidian languages.

Lightfoot (1979:382-4) warns against the dangers
of glibly blaming foreign influence for syntactic
change but is willing to admit some genuine cases.
One such instance involves the Indo-Aryan language
Konkani, which has two types of RC.   One is a native
Indo-Aryan structure and the other a Dravidian structure borrowed from Kannada.   The native Indo-Aryan
RC is giving way to the borrowed structure in the
Saraswat Brahmin dialect of Konkani, but what makes
it so interesting is that the RC structure borrowed
from Kannada was itself originally taken into Kannada
from Indo-Aryan.   As the author of the paper Lightfoot is drawing on puts it:

    'Thus we find a curious phenomenon in which
    the borrowing of a borrowing replaces an
    original which was the model for the first
    borrowing.'
                    (Nadkarni 1975:674).

Intimate contact between languages will inevitably involve some degree of borrowing and the degree
to which the Indo-Aryan languages of the Indian subcontinent have been influenced by Dravidian varies
considerably.   Nevertheless, one must be careful not
to overestimate the importance of contact.   Aitchison 1979 shares Lightfoot's scepticism, and regards
as oversimplified the view that Hindi is a language
whose growth away from OV status has been stunted by
contact with Dravidian.[7]

Clearly there will be some examples of languages which break a typological trend because of contact with other languages. However, to claim that an exception to a trend *is* a result of contact assumes either extra-linguistic knowledge about the movement of peoples or a knowledge of the history of the languages involved. Such information may not always be available and in any case, as we have seen with Sinhala, contact may indeed result in a language *following* a trend. As an SOV language with RC-Head ordering, Sinhala obeys the trends in table 4, whatever the history of its contact with Tamil.

5.2.2.2.   Factors other than Language Contact

(a)   *Mandarin Chinese*

Bach's treatment of Amharic is an attempt to account for surface inconsistency of type in terms of underlying structure and transformations. Such an approach is always tempting to some linguists and has also been resorted to for another hybrid language, (Mandarin) Chinese. Tai 1973 considers Head/RC order in this language and concludes that the mixed status Chinese demonstrates (SOV and SVO) can be handled by an underlying SOV order, with a transformational rule of NP-V inversion to handle surface structure SVO order.

In Chinese, RCs can both precede and follow their heads, as illustrated by (5.50) and (5.51).

(5.50)   *RC-Head*

wo   you   yige   xihuan   meiguo   dianying

I   have   one   like   american   movie

de   meimei

REL   younger sister

'I have a sister who likes American movies'

(5.51)   *Head-RC*

wo   you   yige   meimei   xihuan

I   have   one   younger sister   like

meiguo   dianying

american   movie

'I have a sister who likes American movies'

In (5.51) the relative marker *de* is missing, and this
appears to be a feature of the less frequent postnominal RC.[8]

Although the RC-Head order is more common, Tai
claims that an underlying order Head-RC is warranted,
with a transformation reversing this order in examples like (5.50).   Tai's motivation comes from a
desire to avoid backwards pronominalization in Chinese (for details see Tai 1973:661-2) but also reflects Bach's 1965 approach to RC-Head ordering in
Japanese that we discussed in chapter one (pp.29-30)
and which he also follows for Amharic.

Tai's handling of Chinese is clearly one more
attempt to bring consistency to a language which simply is not a consistent type.   We regard the positing
of one word order in underlying structure and transformations to account for a different surface order
as quite vacuous.   One must simply accept that Mandarin Chinese displays features of both SVO and SOV
languages.   Li & Thompson suggest, furthermore, that
the mixed SVO/SOV status of Mandarin is to some extent at least a result of internal development, with
the reanalysis of some complex sentence structures
into simple sentence structures (for further details
see Li & Thompson 1974b).

(b)   *Philippines-type Languages*

Like other Philippines languages, such as Ilo-
cano and Kapampangan, Tagalog is verb-initial and
thus might well be expected to pattern with VSO languages such as Welsh in taking the order Head-RC.
However, Tagalog also allows the order RC-Head.
This option is demonstrated in (5.52) (from Schachter
& Otanes 1972:123) and in (5.53) (provided by our
informant).

(5.52) a.   babae-ng   nagbabasa   ng[9]   diyaryo

             woman REL   read   paper

       b.   nagbabasa   ng diyaryo-ng   babae

             read   paper   REL   woman

             'Woman reading a paper'

(5.53) a. Sinuntok   ng lalake ang babae-ng
           O topic:hit   man   woman REL
           nakaupo sa silya
           sit   loc chair

       b. Sinuntok   ng lalake ang nakaupo sa
           O topic:hit   man   sit   loc
           silya-ng babae
           chair REL woman
           'The man hit the woman sitting in the
           chair'

K & C claim that the RC-Head order is possible when
the RC is 'short' (1979:347).   However, they do not
define what they mean by 'short'.   Certainly (5.54)
is an alternative to (5.53b) and our informant preferred this division of the RC into two parts.

(5.54)   Sinuntok   ng lalake ang nakaupo-ng
         O topic:hit   man   sit   REL
         babae sa silya
         woman loc chair
         'The man hit the woman sitting in the chair'

It appears that there *are* some constraints on the
occurrence of RCs in prenominal position in Tagalog,
and Schachter & Otanes suggest that the RC-Head order
is avoided when it might lead to ambiguity.   On the
other hand, quite complex self-embedding is possible
in prenominal position, as in (5.55).

(5.55)   Sinuntok   ng lalake [ang [humalik
         O topic:hit   man   kiss
         [tinugtog ng piyano-ng] bata -ng]
         play   piano REL   child REL
         babae]
         woman
         'The man hit the woman who kissed the child
         who was playing the piano'

Once again there is no clear evidence that con-

tact with other languages has led to this alternative
order and we must look elsewhere for a reason why
Tagalog does not restrict itself to Head-RC order in
company with VSO languages.   First, however, we look
at three European languages which also allow both
Head/RC orders.

(b)   *German, Finnish and Hungarian*

    In their discussion of relativization strategies,
K & C list German as a language with SVO order but
both Head-RC and RC-Head patterns.   Finnish and Hungarian are also problematical because there is disagreement over basic word order; but they too allow
both orders of Head/RC.

    The following examples show the possible orders
in each language.   Examples are from K & C for German, Karlsson 1972 for Finnish, and Bánhidi et al.
1965 for Hungarian (note that (5.56) is identical with
(5.16) and (5.57) with (5.17)).

German

(5.56)   *RC-Head*

Der   in   seinem   Büro   arbeitende   Mann
the   in   his   office   working   man
'The man working in his office'

(5.57)   *Head-RC*

Der   Mann   der   in   seinem   Büro   arbeitet
the   man   REL   in   his   office   works
'The man who is working in his office'

Finnish

(5.58)   *RC-Head*

a.   Pöydällä   tanssinut   poika   oli   sairas
      on table   having-danced   boy   was   sick
      'The boy who danced on the table was sick'

b.   Näkemäni   poika   tanssi   pöydällä
      I-having-seen   boy   danced   on-table
      'The boy I saw danced on the table'

(5.59)   *Head-RC*

Tyttö   jonka   tapasin   oli   kaunis

girl   REL   met   was   beautiful

'The girl whom I met was beautiful'

Hungarian

(5.60)   *RC-Head*

Acquincum   területén   végzett   ásatások

           area:loc   carry out: excavation:
                       past part   pl

'Excavations carried out in the area of
    Acquincum'

(5.61)   *Head-RC*

Ezek   azok   a   hibák,   amelyek

this:pl   that:pl   the   mistake:pl   REL:pl

   ellen   küzdünk

against   fight

'These are the mistakes that we are fighting
   against'

There appear to be two ways of accounting for
these alternative orders in all three languages.
First, one might claim that the alternative orders of
Head/RC reflect the mixed status of each language -
as was the case with, for example, Amharic and Mandarin.   There is, as we have said, some freedom of
word order in Hungarian and Finnish, and German has
SOV order in subordinate clauses.   However, an alternative, and more useful, way of accounting for the
three languages is one that relates the order of
Head/RC to the ordering of adjective and noun (henceforth Adj and N), a solution, furthermore, which has
the added advantage of accounting for Tagalog, where
the verb-initial status of the language is unassail-
able.

5.2.2.3.   RCs, Participles and Adjectives

In addition to Head/RC ordering, Greenberg also
discussed the ordering of Adj/N.   For example, universal 17 states:

'With overwhelmingly more than chance frequency,
languages with dominant order VSO have the adjective after the noun'.

Of the 6 VSO languages in Greenberg's sample,
Berber, Maasai, Maori, Welsh and Zapotec support such
a correlation.   So too does Biblical Hebrew, though
we have taken our material from the modern SVO language.   On the other hand, the SVO languages in his
sample are mixed in terms of Adj/N ordering - 4 have
the order N-Adj and 8 Adj-N.   The SOV languages in
Greenberg's sample are also far from clearcut - 5 have
the order N-Adj and 6 Adj-N.

Once again it appears that VSO languages are much
more polarized than either SVO or SOV types.   However,
we have seen that verb-initial languages of the
Philippines type may have RCs preceding heads, and it
is also the case that Tagalog allows adjectives to
precede as well as follow nouns.

We might then claim that there is some correlation between the order of Adj and the order of RC in
relation to the head noun.   In view of the agreed
adjectival function of the RC this seems far from unreasonable.   We might consider RCs to be extended
forms of adjectives and thus to behave in similar
ways, except where their clausal nature prevents this.

In his doctoral thesis (1976) Foley discusses the
typology of noun phrases and examines the degree of
bondedness between noun heads and their adjuncts.
Drawing his material primarily from Austronesian languages, Foley demonstrates that there is a scale of
bondedness as follows:

(5.62)

	Articles + Noun
	Deictics + Noun
	Interrogatives + Noun
weaker	Quantifiers/Indefinites + Noun
bondedness	Adjectives + Noun
	Participles + Noun
	Relative Clauses + Noun

In many Austronesian languages modifiers are
linked to their nominal heads by special particles or
ligatures.   In Toba Batak, for example, the top
three positions on the hierarchy do not have liga-

tures but the bottom four positions do.   Thus, in
(5.63) a quantifier is linked to a noun, in (5.64) an
adjective, and in (5.65) a relative clause, all by
the ligature *na*.

(5.63)   huta   na   leban

             village   lig   another

             'another village'

(5.64)   bijang   na   balga

             dog   lig   big

             'a big dog'

(5.65)   baoa   na   mang-arang   buku   i

             man   lig   act-write   book   the

             'The man who wrote the book'

     In Palauan, however, ligatures are used for all
but the top position, while in Malagasy it is only
relative clauses which have a ligature to bind them
to their heads.[10] The relationship between the notion
of bondedness and the occurrence of ligatures is
summed up as follows:

> 'It is claimed that the hierarchy represents
> universal tendencies in the strength of bonds
> between adjuncts and their head nouns.   The
> bond between an article and its head noun is
> much stronger than that between a relative
> clause and its head noun.   Thus, as soon as
> a category has an overt marker of subordina-
> tion, all weaker-bound categories also require
> an overt marker.   To some extent the strength
> of the bond varies inversely with the degree
> of full sentential properties of the subordi-
> nated element, such as tense or aspectual
> inflection of the adjunct.   Thus relative
> clauses are more weakly bound than participles,
> which in turn are more weakly bound than ad-
> jectives.'
>
>   (Foley 1976:20).

As Foley also remarks, one can regard participles as
'specially tightly bound relative clauses'.   However,
participles are also much more adjectival than RCs
proper and thus represent a transitional category
between RC and adjective.   It is not surprising,
then, that participial structures can occur in the

same position as adjectives even if clausal RCs cannot.
In English we find examples such as (5.66) in which
the participle is acceptable in the position normally
reserved for adjectives.

(5.66)   The *sleeping* child looked very peaceful

In examples like (5.67) the italicized material is
even more participial in nature.

(5.67)   The *quickly rotating* shaft caused a fire in
          the engine

While one must be rather sceptical about drawing
universal conclusions from a study of one language
area, Foley's bondedness hierarchy and analysis of
participles as 'tightly bound relative clauses' does
allow us to account for not only Tagalog Head/RC
ordering, but also that of the three European languages we have just discussed. The more participial an
RC is, the more likely it is that it will occur in
those positions occupied by adjectives proper. The
occurrence in Tagalog of prenominal RCs in addition
to postnominal RCs can be correlated with the participial nature of such RCs and the occurrence of adjectives in pre- as well as postnominal position.

In German, Finnish and Hungarian the participial
RC also occurs in prenominal position, and this is the
position occupied by adjectives proper in each language. It is presumably the more clausal nature of
postnominal RCs in these languages which accounts for
their position. One might well be tempted to say
that RCs will appear in the same position as adjectives in a language unless their clausal status forces
them into a position after the head. Thus, any survey of the ordering of Head/RC should also take into
consideration the ordering of Adj/N *and* the degree to
which RCs are clausal in structure.

Considerations such as these, together with the
tendency shown by table 4 for even SOV languages to
have RCs following their heads, lead us to conclude
that the *normal* position for clausal RCs is *after* the
head. Those languages in which the RC precedes the
head will be of two types:

Those in which the RC is participial in structure

Those which have other features militating
     against the order Head-RC, whatever the inter-

nal structure of the RC.

German, Finnish, Hungarian and Tagalog appear to be
languages of the first type while Japanese appears to
be a language of the second type.   We discuss Japanese in section 5.2.3.

As a final comment on the correlation between
basic word order and Head/RC order, before we examine
a possible explanation for such a correlation, we now
turn to the polarization of VSO languages that we
noted earlier.

5.2.2.4.   Vennemann and Language Drift

A clue to the consistency of VSO languages in
opting for the order Head-RC lies in Greenberg's
universal 6:

'All languages with dominant VSO order have
SVO as an alternative or as the only alternative basic order'.

Since both VSO and SVO orderings are linked with the
order Head-RC, any VSO language tending towards the
SVO type will maintain this Head-RC order.   On the
other hand, a number of the exceptions to the major
trend were among SOV languages and here again the
trend was broken by languages without consistent word
order.   SOV languages are only clearcut RC-Head languages if they are rigidly SOV (Korean, Mongolian and
Japanese are strong examples of this), whereas languages which are not rigidly SOV may also allow the
order Head-RC.   Turkish is such a language, allowing
some structures of the Head-RC type but also allowing
elements to occur after the verb.   The less consistently an SOV language has its verb in final position,
the greater the chance it will behave like a VO language and have the order Head-RC.   The same applies
mutatis mutandis to SVO languages, which sometimes
have the features associated with OV languages.

We can show this transition, and polarization, of
VSO languages as follows.

VSO	SVO	SOV
VO		OV
HEAD-RC		RC-HEAD

Vennemann 1973 considers VSO languages to be advanced stages of SVO languages which in turn have developed from SOV order.

> 'Once again, then, I must conclude that VSO
> languages are "old" SVO languages because
> while SVO languages may have some RN [= RC-Noun]
> constructions holding out from the old SOV days
> in their initial phase, these constructions
> have long since died out by the time the SVO
> language is ready to become VSO.'
>   (Vennemann 1973:35).

Vennemann claims that English is an SVO language that is still undergoing a change from SOV status - a change that he claims has been going on for some 1200 years and is still not yet complete.   He thus claims that the occurrence of RCs and extended adjectival structures after the head is the beginning of a general shift of *all* adjectival modifiers from prenominal to postnominal position.

Although this notion of language change in progress is attractive it involves an assumption that English will eventually undergo the change from Adj-N to N-Adj, a development that is by no means certain. However, even if Vennemann's claims are valid, they represent merely an account of historical development and nothing more.   They do not provide an *explanation* for the ordering of Head/RC in different language types, any more than claiming participial RCs pattern with adjectives rather than with clausal RCs can be regarded as explaining *why* adjectives appear in the positions they do and *why* clausal RCs tend to follow their heads.

5.2.3.   A Possible Cognitive Explanation for Head/RC
Ordering

A particularly appealing explanation for the polarization of VSO languages is put forward by Kuno 1972.   Kuno's claim is that VSO languages take the order Head-RC because of limitations on short-term memory and that these same limitations also lead to the order RC-Head in strict SOV languages.   He suggests that the processing of complex sentences is facilitated or hindered by the degree of self-embedding involved and that certain orders of constituents will increase or diminish the ability of the hearer/reader to recover sentence structures.   The claim is that a *push-down store* in processing stores an expec-

tation of what constituents are able to appear at any
point in the production of a sentence and that the
greater the number of possible structures that could
occur at a particular point the greater will be the
burden on short-term memory.   Languages thus tend to
avoid self-embedding since this increases the burden
on language users.

To illustrate the push-down principle with a simple example, an English sentence like (5.68) will present no processing problems since there are severe
limits on what type of constituent can occur at any
point (examples (5.68) to (5.83) are mainly adapted
from Kuno 1972).

(5.68)   Mary killed Bill

The expectations at each point in this sentence are
represented as follows:

(5.69)   *Input Substring*   *Pushdown*
                                Received   *Store*

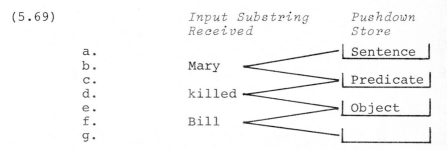

a.		Sentence
b.	Mary	
c.		Predicate
d.	killed	
e.		Object
f.	Bill	
g.		

In (5.69) the words on the left represent the lexical
items of the sentence in the order they are presented
to the hearer, while the diagonal lines to the constituent type on the right represent the expectations the
hearer has of what type of constituent can follow, or
is yet to come.   Thus, the occurrence of an NP *Mary*
in initial position in English gives the hearer the
expectation of a predicate;   this expectation is borne
out by the occurrence of *killed*;   in turn, the transitive verb *killed* raises the expectation of a following object, confirmed by the occurrence of *Bill*.[11]

Turning now to relative clauses, in (5.70) we
have a simple sentence with no great burden on short-
term memory, while in (5.71) we have an RC embedded
into it.

(5.70)   The cheese was rotten

(5.71)   The cheese that the rat ate was rotten

(5.72) represents the limited expectations involved in
processing (5.70), while (5.73) shows the complications that can set in with even single level self-
embedding.[12]

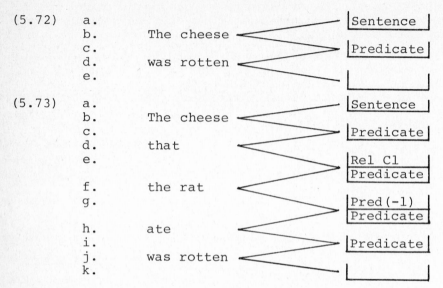

(5.72)   a.   Sentence
          b.   The cheese
          c.   Predicate
          d.   was rotten
          e.

(5.73)   a.   Sentence
          b.   The cheese
          c.   Predicate
          d.   that
          e.   Rel Cl
                                                      Predicate
          f.   the rat
          g.   Pred(-1)
                                                      Predicate
          h.   ate
          i.   Predicate
          j.   was rotten
          k.

In (5.73) the expectation that a predicate will follow
the subject NP *the cheese* is disconfirmed by the
occurrence of *that*.   This relative marker leads to
the expectation that an RC will follow, an expectation
that increases the load on memory since the predicate
of the main clause subject is still to come.   The
occurrence of *the rat ate* confirms the expectation of
a relative structure, and *was rotten* completes the main
clause that the whole sentence began with.   At no
point in the processing of this sentence are there
ever any more than two expectations.   However, in
processing the more complex (5.74) there will be as
many as three expectations at a time and the pattern
in (5.75) shows this set of expectations for the
italicized material.

(5.74)   *The cheese that the rat that the cat* chased
          ate was rotten

(5.75)   a.
         b.   The cheese
         c.
         d.   that
         e.
         f.   the rat
         g.
         h.   that
         i.
         j.   the cat
         k.
                etc.

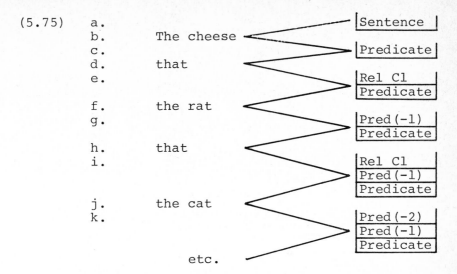

Thus, at point k. the hearer will be expecting the remainder of the second (most deeply embedded) RC, with the remainder of the first RC and the remainder of the main clause still to come.

On the other hand, an example such as (5.76) has a potentially infinite sequence of RCs but never becomes unprocessable.

(5.76)   The cat chased the rat that ate the cheese
              that...

(5.77) is an example of this type but with only three clauses.   (5.78) represents the expectations available to the hearer and at no point in the processing of (5.77) is the burden on short-term memory very great.

(5.77)   The cat chased the rat that ate the cheese
              that was rotten

(5.78)   a.
          b.   The cat
          c.
          d.   chased
          e.
          f.   the rat
          g.
          h.   that
          i.
          j.   ate
          k.
          l.   the cheese
          m.
          n.   that
          o.
          p.   was rotten
          q.

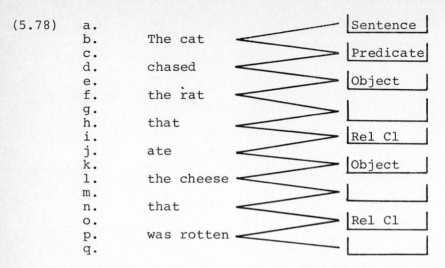

     Turning now to Japanese, Kuno attempts to explain
why the translation of the difficult to process (5.74)
as (5.79) presents no problems for speakers of this
language.[13]

(5.79)   [[[Neko   ga   oikaketa] nezumi ga   tabeta]
            cat   nom   chased   rat   nom   ate

          chiizu   wa   kusatte-ita]
          cheese   top   rotten   was

          'The cheese that the rat that the cat chased

          ate was rotten'

Kuno gives (5.80) as a rough constituent structure
for (5.79) (note that he is content with a VP node for
Japanese, whereas we tended to steer away from such an
analysis in chapter four; however, the distinction is
not critical here).

(5.80)

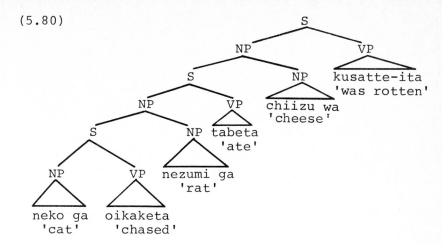

He suggests that such examples would be horribly in-comprehensible if push-down memory expectations were as represented by (5.75) for the English equivalent. However, they are acceptable in Japanese and this can be accounted for in terms of (5.81).

(5.81)

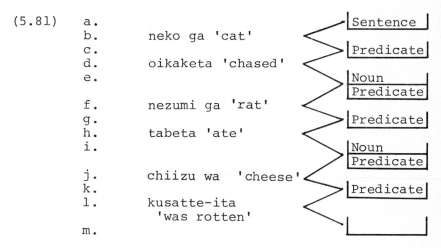

The hearer will initially interpret *neko ga* as sub-ject of a main clause and expect the remainder of a simple sentence; the occurrence next of a predicate *oikaketa* normally taking an object will lead to re-analysis of *neko ga* as subject of an RC, with an ex-pectation of a head following *oikaketa* (plus a main clause predicate still to come); *nezumi ga* confirms the expectation and is interpreted as the subject of the main clause; the occurrence of *tabeta*, another verb normally taking an object, leads to the reanalysis of *nezumi ga* as subject of another RC; the occurrence of *chiizu wa* is taken to be head of the RC *nezumi ga tabeta* and the subject (or topic here) of a main clause; this expectation is confirmed by the occurrence of an intransitive verb *kusatte-ita*.

Thus, at no point in the processing of such an example are the expectations of the hearer greater than two, and this can be attributed to the structure of the Japanese sentence and the speaker's 'knowledge' of this structure. A combination of features leads to a reduction in processing difficulties in Japanese sentences with multiple-embedded RCs, compared with equivalent English translations:

Japanese NPs are explicitly case-marked

Japanese RCs involve deletion rather than pro-nominalization of the coreferential NP

Japanese RCs are prenominal.

Kuno claims that this avoidance of processing difficulties is a motivation for the occurrence of RCs before their heads in Japanese. He also claims that VSO languages favour postnominal RCs for the same reason and demonstrates the degree of self-embedding that would result if Japanese had postnominal RCs and VSO languages had prenominal RCs. In (5.83) we show the implications in terms of self-embedding for SOV and VSO languages with each order of Head/RC. The three examples in each case are a schematic translation of the English examples in (5.82).

(5.82) a. The boy that loved Mary died

OR

The boy that Mary loved died

b. The boy that loved Mary hated Jane

OR

The boy that Mary loved hated Jane

c. Jane hated the boy that loved Mary

OR

Jane hated the boy that Mary loved

(5.83)   *SOV Prenominal*

    a. [Mary loved] boy died
        (left-embedding)

    b. [Mary loved] boy Jane hated
        (left-embedding)

    c. Jane [Mary loved] boy hated
        (self-embedding)

    SOV Postnominal

    a. Boy [Mary loved] died
        (self-embedding)

    b. Boy [Mary loved] Jane hated
        (self-embedding)

    c. Jane boy [Mary loved] hated
        (self-embedding)

    VSO Prenominal

    a. Died [loved Mary] boy
        (self-embedding)

    b. Hated [loved Mary] boy Jane
        (self-embedding)

    c. Hated Jane [loved Mary] boy
        (self-embedding)

    VSO Postnominal

    a. Died boy [loved Mary]
        (right-embedding)

    b. Hated boy [loved Mary] Jane
        (self-embedding)

    c. Hated Jane boy [loved Mary]
        (right-embedding)

Clearly there will be some self-embedding in both
language types, whatever the order of Head/RC.   However, the number of instances will be reduced with
Head-RC order in VSO languages and RC-Head in strict
SOV languages.

    Kuno goes on to consider SVO languages such as
English and concludes that there will be some degree
of self-embedding with Head-RC order but that other
devices are available to such languages to avoid this
self-embedding.   From the patterns in (5.84) it is
clear that in fact prenominal position presents fewer

instances of self-embedding than postnominal position,
yet it is in postnominal position that SVO languages
generally position their RCs.

(5.84)   *SVO Prenominal*

    a. [Loved Mary] boy died

       OR   (left-
                                       embedding)

       [Mary loved] boy died

    b. [Loved Mary] boy hated Jane

       OR   (left-
                                       embedding)

       [Mary loved] boy hated Jane

    c. Jane hated [loved Mary] boy

       OR   (self-
                                       embedding)

       Jane hated [Mary loved] boy

    SVO Postnominal

    a. Boy [loved Mary] died

       OR   (self-
                                       embedding)

       Boy [Mary loved] died

    b. Boy [loved Mary] hated Jane

       OR   (self-
                                       embedding)

       Boy [Mary loved] hated Jane

    c. Jane hated boy [loved Mary]

       OR   (right-
                                       embedding)

       Jane hated boy [Mary loved]

    The following table sums up the patterns to be
found in verb-initial, verb-medial and verb-final
types and demonstrates the degree to which self-
embedding occurs, depending on whether RCs are prenominal or postnominal.

Table 5

Head/RC Order and Self-embedding

		V-initial	V-medial	V-final
Prenominal RC	NP	V RC–NP	RC–NP V *OR* V RC–NP	RC–NP V
	NP , NP	V RC–NP RC–NP	RC–NP V RC–NP	RC–NP RC–NP V
Postnominal RC	NP	V NP–RC	NP–RC V *OR* V NP–RC	NP–RC V
	NP , NP	V NP–RC NP–RC	NP–RC V NP–RC	NP–RC NP–RC V

   The incidence of self-embedding can be reduced in
verb-initial languages by adopting the order Head-RC,
while in verb-final languages the order RC-Head is the
perceptually more advantageous order.   Table 5 also
demonstrates that verb-medial languages present a
degree of self-embedding whichever order of Head/RC is
adopted, and the choice is therefore less clearcut
than in verb-initial and verb-final types.   The fact
that verb-medial languages tend to have Head-RC order
apparently supports the view that Head-RC order is the
unmarked order and is only abandoned if there is overwhelming pressure to take RC-Head order, as is the
case in verb-final languages like Japanese.

   The devices which English as a verb-medial language has available to avoid the problems of self-
embedding with postnominal RCs include extraposition
and raising.   Such rules allow heavy material to be
moved from clause-medial to sentence final position,
and the value of extraposition in this respect is
demonstrated by (5.85), where the two self-embedding
patterns of (5.84) postnominal RCs are neatly avoided.

(5.85) a.   Boy [loved Mary] died

            ⟶

            Boy ∅ died [loved Mary]

            'The boy died that loved Mary'

            OR

            Boy [Mary loved] died

            ⟶

            Boy ∅ died [Mary loved]

            'The boy died that Mary loved'

     b.   Boy [loved Mary] hated Jane

            ⟶

            Boy ∅ hated Jane [loved Mary]

            'The boy hated Jane that loved Mary'

            OR

            Boy [Mary loved] hated Jane

            ⟶

            Boy ∅ hated Jane [Mary loved]

            'The boy hated Jane that Mary loved'

Thus it appears that on balance postnominal RCs need not be a serious problem for SVO languages in terms of self-embedding.

However, Kuno's paper does not consider all word order types and it might therefore be useful to look beyond the VSO, SOV and SVO types he examines.

(a)   *Philippines-type Languages*

We have seen that Tagalog allows prenominal RCs, even though it is a verb-initial language. As in the case of German, Finnish and Hungarian we took this to be because such RCs are participial and thus tend to pattern with adjectives in these languages. Nevertheless, in Tagalog at least, prenominal RCs appear to be acceptable even with multiple self-embedding.

As we have seen, multiple self-embedding in English is perceptually difficult for language users and examples such as (5.74) (repeated here as (5.86)) are simply not acceptable.[14]

(5.86)   The cheese [that the rat [that the cat

        chased] ate] was rotten

This example compares very unfavourably with the simpler example (5.71) (repeated here as (5.87)) which has only *one* level of self-embedding.

(5.87)   The cheese [that the rat ate] was rotten

In Tagalog, postnominal RCs present no more problems than do their English equivalents, since in both cases each RC only begins when the preceding clause has finished.

(5.88)   Sinuntok   ng   lalake ang babae-ng

        O topic:hit   man   woman REL

          humalik sa   bata na   tumugtog

          kiss   loc child REL   play

          ng piyano

            piano

    'The man hit the woman who kissed the child

        who was playing the piano'

In (5.89) the same clauses are in prenominal position
and the result is a greater degree of self-embedding
than one would imagine could be tolerated.   Our informant found such examples 'bookish' yet by no means
unintelligible.

(5.89)   Sinuntok   ng lalake [ang [humalik [sa
          O topic:hit   man   kiss   loc

              tumugtog   ng piyano-ng] bata -ng] babae]
          play   piano REL child REL woman
          'The man hit the woman who kissed the child
          who was playing the piano'

        Since it is highly unlikely that Tagalog speakers
are cognitively distinct from speakers of other languages one must assume that other features of the
language allow examples such as (5.89) to be successfully processed.   Presumably it is the presence of
case markers and relative markers between constituents which is critical.   In English multiple self-
embedded sentences, processing is aided by the retention of the optional relative markers.   Compare
(5.90) with (5.91).

(5.90)   The girl that the man that the cat chased
              kissed died

(5.91)   The girl the man the cat chased kissed died

Nevertheless, neither example is particularly easy to
process and this is because there is no element to
break up the sequence of verbs stacked up at the end
of the sentence.   In the Tagalog example (5.89) the
verbs are separated by case markers and the NPs are
separated by relative markers.   Thus it appears that
Tagalog, like Japanese, has other features which
allow language users to tolerate prenominal RCs and
even, in the case of Tagalog, when they are involved
in multiple self-embedding.

(b)   *VOS Languages*

        Since these languages were not included in Green-
berg's sample Kuno did not discuss them in perceptual
terms.   However, VOS languages could be expected to
present the same problems of self-embedding as other

verb-initial languages.   Thus, what is true of the
VSO language Welsh and the Philippines-type language
Tagalog should also be true of a VOS language such as
Fijian.   In each language the pattern of constituents
would be the same in *categorial* terms, as represented
by (5.92).

(5.92)   V - NP - NP

    In all three languages there are potentially the
same problems of self-embedding for prenominal RCs.
Thus we find with little surprise that in Fijian the
RC does follow the head.   The following example is
from Keenan 1978a.

(5.93)   na   gone   yalewa   ka   a   raica   na

          art   child   woman   REL   past   see   art

              tagane

              man

          'The girl who saw the man'

          OR

          'The girl whom the man saw'

Fijian as a VOS language shares with Welsh as a VSO
language a paucity of explicit case marking and this
accounts for the fact that (5.93) is ambiguous.
Furthermore, even if Fijian allowed prenominal RCs it
would not be able to indulge in the degree of multiple
self-embedding we found in Tagalog, precisely because
there would be no case marking morphemes to rescue
such examples in the way we saw in examples such as
(5.89).

(c)   *Object-initial Languages*

    In the case of the best-documented language of
the OVS type Hixkaryana apparently has no RCs of the
type we have been discussing.   Instead the language
uses nominalized structures, as illustrated by
(5.94). [15]

(5.94)   nomokno harha (xofrye), K-

          he-came   back   (sloth)   us(incl)

              anihnoh-nye-   nhi -yamo

          destroy-nomzn   past-collective

          'The sloth/one who was destroying us all has

          come back'

Superficially it seems that RCs in Hixkaryana do
follow their heads and one might take this as confirmation that Head-RC order is the norm.   However, as
Des Derbyshire has pointed out to us, the nominalized
structure follows the head but 'is phonologically
dislocated from it'.   This confirms that we are
dealing with quite a different type of structure from
the normal embedded type that we have been discussing;
in (5.94) the RC is in apposition to *xofrye*, rather
than subordinate to it.

     On the other hand, if an OVS language did have
the usual embedded type of RC we have found in the
major word order types of language, what might we
expect?   We might expect OVS languages to require an
extraposition rule that would shift heavy object NPs
into final position; and even though Hixkaryana has
headless, nominalized RCs, such a rule does appear to
exist.   In (5.95) the nominalized structure
amryehxomo komo is in opposition to *hawana* but is
separated from it by the remainder of the main clause.

(5.95)   hawana   heno komo yonyekon   hati,

          visitor dead coll he-ate-them hsy,

              amryehxemo   komo

          ones-that-went-hunting   coll

          'He (jaguar man) used to eat the visitors

          who had gone hunting'

It is not unlikely, therefore, that an OVS language
with truly embedded RCs would allow extraposition of
these RCs qualifying an object.   That is, one would
not be surprised to find patterns such as (5.96).

(5.96) $O_{[+RC]}VS \rightarrow OVS[+RC]$

However, this must remain mere speculation in the

absence of information on languages with normal embedded RCs.   Indeed, Derbyshire's view is that nominalized or headless relatives are 'very common in Brazilian languages, and not only those that are object-
initial.   It seems to be an areal trait that cuts
across both genetic affiliations and basic word-order
typologies, and it is often the only strategy' (pers.
comm.).   It is not surprising, then, to discover that
Apurinã, an OSV language that is better documented
than most, has nominalized RCs as well.   (5.97) is
taken from Pickering 1973a.

(5.97)   pixena   anakory   ny-syka-ro -ko   ãtokoro

           cat   litter   I -give-her-will   the girl

               "nota   nyrekaka-na" sãkiretakaro

               "I   want them"   said-who

           'I will give the kittens to the girl, the

           one who said "I want them"'

Although the glossing and translation of (5.97)
give the impression that we are dealing here with an
ordinary embedded RC, the most likely analysis is
that, as in Hixkaryana, the relative structure is in
apposition to *ãtokoro* and phonologically dislocated
from it.

Were, however, an OSV language to be discovered
that had embedded, rather than nominalized RCs, one
might speculate on what the Head/RC order might be.
OSV languages share with SOV languages verb-final
status and thus might be expected to have the order
RC-Head, provided that the O and S constituents were
case-marked.   As we saw in Kuno's discussion of this
order in strictly verb-final languages such as Japanese, the case-marking of nominal constituents, plus
the clause-final position of the verb and its known
valency all combine to decode what would in an
uncase-marked language with prenomimal RCs be horren-
dously difficult to process (see, in particular, pp.
304-6).   Yet there might still be pressure for RCs
to be prenominal: there would be less self-embedding
with RC-Head order in an OSV language in precisely
the same way as applies in Japanese.   Again, all
this is mere speculation.

The foregoing examination of language types not considered by Kuno lends support to his major claim - that the ordering of Head/RC in language can be correlated with the perceptual needs of the language user. Between the two extremes - Head-RC in VSO languages and RC-Head in SOV languages - are a variety of language types which generally prefer the order Head-RC. Only languages with non-clausal RCs will pattern with SOV languages like Japanese in taking the order RC-Head, and Tagalog appears to be such a language.   In Tagalog it is the participial nature of the RC which allows it to occur in the same positions as adjectives, which themselves can occur prenominally as well as postnominally.   Similarly, German has both clausal and participial RCs and it is only the participial kind which occur prenominally, the position also occupied by adjectives.

Of the remaining language types with embedded RCs, VOS languages appear to pattern with VSO languages - clausal RCs give rise to less self-embedding in postnominal position.   Finally, SVO languages generally have the order Head-RC as the lesser of two evils for their clausal RCs and also tend to have access to devices which reduce the degree of self-embedding.   One such device is extraposition and this we now examine.

5.2.4.   Extraposition

In section 5.2.3. we referred to Kuno's claim that extraposition was a device SVO languages have available to them to avoid excessive self-embedding of RCs.   Although the term has been used to refer to the placing of any constituent in final position (as does Hankamer 1971 in his discussion of Turkish - see section 4.7 above), it is normally reserved for attributes separated from their heads - usually subordinate clauses, but also some prepositional phrases in English.

(5.98)   *Some friends* came to stay last week *whom we hadn't seen for years*

(5.99)   There were *no details* given *of the extent of the contamination*

Such examples should be distinguished from those like (5.100), in which a *whole* constituent has been dis-

placed to the right, leaving behind a dummy subject
it.

(5.100)   *It* is quite obvious *that life under the*
           Caesars must have been grim

    Two further examples of *full* constituent dis-
placement are *complex NP shift* and *dislocation*.   In
(5.101b) the complex or *heavy* object NP has been moved
into final position and in (5.102b) the object NP has
been *right-dislocated*, leaving behind an appropriate
pronoun.

(5.101) a.   John donated *all the money he had saved*
             while a professor with no lecturing to
             do to his favourite charity
        b.   John donated to his favourite charity *all*
             the money he had saved while a profes-
             sor with no lecturing to do

(5.102) a.   I can't stand *that bloke*
        b.   I can't stand him, *that bloke*

    Given the stance we have adopted towards over-
formalized theoretical approaches to cross-linguistic
study (see section 1.3), we stress that our use of
terms such as *displacement* or *movement* of constituents
from their *normal* position in a sentence is merely a
terminological convenience.   Certainly linguists
differ as to whether the b. examples above can be regarded as derived from the a. examples (or, more
accurately, from the structures underlying the a.
examples), or whether the italicized material is gen-
erated *in situ*.   In the case of examples (5.98) -
(5.100) there would again be a difference of opinion
over the derivation and many linguists would suggest
that a term like *extraposition* committed them to a
transformational approach.   However, such discussions over terminology disguise the central problem,
which is: can the subordinate structure still be
interpreted as 'belonging' to the head from which it
is separated?   Our use of *extraposition* in this chapter is an acknowledgement of this relationship between head and modifying structure, not an acceptance
of any transformational derivation for such examples. [16]

Another distinction to be made is that between
premeditated displacement of constituents and *afterthoughts*. This latter term refers to the speaker's
ability to patch up structures that are information-
ally unclear (see also section 3.3 for discussion of
this point). The following example is clearly an
afterthought, the speaker clarifying who was being
referred to after an initial assumption that his identity was self-evident.

(5.103)   You remember that bloke we saw last week...

the one with the long beard and the

miserable expression on his face

In other cases it is quite clear that the heavy final
constituent was premeditated. In (5.101b) the placing of a heavy object-NP in final position was clearly intended from the start - otherwise the speaker
would have been intending to break the subcategorization feature associated with *donate* that prevents it
from being used intransitively. That is, for most
speakers at least, the following example is unacceptable.

(5.104)   ?John donated to his favourite charity

Extraposition is a device which may or may not
be seen as premeditated, however. In examples such
as (5.105), it is unclear without some indication of
the stress and intonation pattern whether the italicized RC was premeditated or merely added as an afterthought.

(5.105)   Three policemen called on us last week, *who*

were more interested in my electric

train set   than finding stolen property

In this section we will assume that all such examples
are instances of extraposition proper. Whether the
italicized material in (5.105) is premeditated or not
it is still analyzable as modifying *three policemen*
and thus can be regarded as an RC separated from its
head.

In addition to his perceptual explanation for
Head/RC order in language, Kuno also discusses the
incidence of extraposition and its relationship with
word order types. As he points out, extraposition

is an important device in SVO languages since for
them the choice of Head/RC ordering is far from clearcut on perceptual grounds.   We have suggested that
SVO languages have Head-RC ordering *in spite of* the
greater degree of self-embedding involved, so it is
not unreasonable to claim that extraposition is a device to rescue the resultant self-embedding.

　　　　Nevertheless, there are some comments that one
might make about Kuno's claims, attractive as they
are.   First of all, even though SVO languages with
Head-RC order do give rise to self-embedding not all
SVO languages have access to extraposition to compen-
sate for this.   Hayon 1973 for example claims that
Hebrew does not allow examples such as (5.107), even
though the unextraposed version (5.106) is quite
acceptable.

(5.106)　　hu　　natan　　'et　　harove　　šehu　　nika

　　　　　he　　gave　　the　　gun　　　REL　　cleaned

　　　　　　lə'aħiv

　　　　　　brother:dat

　　　　'He gave the gun that he cleaned to his

　　　　brother'

(5.107)　　*hu　　natan　　'et　　harove　　lə'aħiv　　　šehu

　　　　　he　　gave　　the　　gun　　　brother:dat　　REL

　　　　　nika

　　　　　cleaned

　　　　'He gave the gun to his brother that he

　　　　cleaned'

On the other hand, Ziv & Cole 1974 demonstrate that
extraposition *is* sometimes possible in Hebrew, but
that it is subject to a constraint related to definiteness.   (5.108) can occur as (5.109) but (5.110)
has no equivalent (5.111).

(5.108)　　baxur　　exad　　*shepagashti*　　*etmol*

　　　　　guy　　　one　　REL/met　　　　yesterday

　　　　　betrinoz　　　nixnas　　lekan　　karega

　　　　　at Treno's　　entered　　to here　　just now

　　　　'A guy that I met at Treno's yesterday just
　　　　came in'

(5.109)   baxur exad nixnas lekan karega
           shepagashti etmoʒ betrinoz
           'A guy just came in that I met at Treno's
           yesterday'

(5.110)   ha baxur *shepagashti etmoʒ   betrinoz*
           the guy REL I met   yesterday   at Treno's
           nixnas lekan   karega
           entered to here just now
           'The guy that I met yesterday at Treno's
           just came in'

(5.111)   ??ha baxur nixnas lekan karega
           shepagashti etmoʒ betrinoz
           ??'The guy just came in that I met at
           Treno's yesterday'

    Cambodian and Thai are SVO languages which do
not allow extraposition. In Cambodian (5.113) is
not a possible version of (5.112) and we could elicit
no examples at all which involved separation of an RC
from its head.

(5.112)   pʰaɛːnkaː daəl ratʰapʰibal ban
           plan   REL   government   past
           yolprəm trov   ban   rɔkkʰəːn
           approve passive past   find
           'A plan which the government approved (of)
           was found'

(5.113)   *pʰaɛːnkaː trov   ban   rɔkkʰəːn daəl
           plan   passive past   find   REL
           ratʰapʰibal yolprəm
           government   approve
           'A plan was found which the government
           approved (of)'

    It is also true, however, that Cambodian spea-
kers cannot accept examples involving multiple self-

embedding, and avoid structures whose English equivalents are acceptable.   (5.114) *is* possible but it
will be noticed that there is no relative marker between *mɔnuhsrei* and *lok* (it is represented in the
gloss by ∅).

(5.114)   tʰei   ban   kʰən   mɔnuhproh   daəl

             past   see   man   REL

         mɔnuhsrei   lok   pʰlae: krotʃ

         woman   ∅ sell classifier   orange

         ban   tʰaəp

         past   kiss

      'Thel saw the man whom the woman that sold

      oranges kissed'

Such an example with a second *daəl* would be quite ungrammatical and suggests that *lok* corresponds to participial usage in English.   A better translation for
(5.114) might therefore be: *Thel saw the man whom
the woman selling oranges kissed.*   On the other hand,
(5.115) is not possible with or without the second
relative marker and strongly suggests that in Cambodian there is a constraint on the stacking of adjacent verbs from different clauses.   The reader might
consider whether the English translation is acceptable - we find it difficult but certainly not in the
category of examples like (5.74).

(5.115)   *kʰɲom   ban   kʰən   mɔnuhproh   [daəl

       I   past see   man   REL

        mɔnuhsrei   [(daəl)   tʰei   ban   kʰən]

        woman   REL   past   see

        ban   tʰaəp]

        past   kiss

      'I saw the man that the woman that Thel saw

      kissed'

Thus, while it is true that not all SVO languages
have extraposition, those that do not have such a
device merely *avoid* multiple self-embedding altogether.
As for single level self-embedding, this appears to
be tolerated even by a language like Cambodian which

has more of an aversion to multiple self-embedding
than English.

Turning now to VSO languages, Kuno showed that
such a basic word order was much more suited to Head-
RC order than to RC-Head order.   Nevertheless, there
would still be some examples of self-embedding and in
all verb-initial languages a pattern such as (5.116)
can be expected to occur regularly.

(5.116)   V-NP$_{[RC]}$-NP

However, such a pattern appears to be no real problem
for speakers, anymore than it is in English patterns
such as (5.117).

(5.117)   NP$_{[RC]}$-V-NP

Furthermore, extraposition seems to be uncommon
in verb-initial languages, a fact which reflects not
so much a contentment with self-embedding but rather
an antipathy towards unnecessary ambiguity.   To
illustrate first from English, consider an example
like (5.118), a ready source of humour.

(5.118)   *A piano* was bought by a woman *that had three
            legs*

Since the agent (*a woman*) could also be interpreted as
the head of the italicized RC which follows it, it is
only knowledge of human anatomy that makes the
message clear.   For this reason extraposition from
subject heads is much more common with intransitive
structures like (5.119) and agentless passives like
(5.120).

(5.119)   *The child* has confessed *who was responsible
            for the mess in the bathroom*

(5.120)   *A suggestion* was put forward *which received
            a good deal of support in the Lords*

Gwen Awbery (pers.comm.) confirms that potential ambiguity militates against extraposition in a VSO language like Welsh.   Thus the pattern in (5.121) would
give rise to the ambiguous (5.122) while extraposition
from the subject head of an intransitive structure
like (5.123) would be quite vacuous, since no self-

embedding is involved anyway.

(5.121)   V S$_{[RC]}$O

(5.122)   V S O + RC

(5.123)   V S$_{[RC]}$

In Tagalog, our informant confirmed that it is the permutation of *whole* NPs that is used to avoid self-embedding, not extraposition of RCs.   Thus (5.124) can occur as (5.125) but not as (5.126).

(5.124)   Tumugtog   ang lalaki-ng   sinuntok

            A topic:play   man   REL hit

            sa   babae   ng piyano

            loc   woman   piano

            'The man who hit the woman was playing the
            piano'

(5.125)   Tumugtog   ng piyano ang lalaki-ng

            A topic:play   piano   man   REL

            sinuntok   sa   babae

            hit   loc   woman

            'The man who hit the woman was playing the
            piano'

(5.126) a. *Tumugtog   ang lalaki-ng   ng piyano

            A topic:play   man   REL   piano

            sinuntok sa   babae

            hit   loc   woman

        b. *Tumugtog   ang lalake   ng piyano-ng

            A topic:play   man   piano REL

            sinuntok sa   babae

            hit   loc   woman

            'The man was playing the piano who hit
            the woman'

In (5.126a) the RC has been separated from its relative marker -*ng*; in (5.126b) the relative marker has moved with the RC and the result is an anomalous sen-

tence.   (5.126b) is unacceptable because pianos don't
usually hit women.   Had the *ng*-marked object topic
of the main clause been *human*, the RC could have been
interpreted as modifying this NP - thus demonstrating
again the ambiguity resulting from applying extraposition in sentences with more than one NP in the main
clause in *any* language.   An added factor in the restriction of extraposition to languages of the SVO
type is thus the perceptual requirement that structures be no more ambiguous than necessary.   What is
more, ambiguity such as we have just examined is often
avoided in SVO languages by a judicious use of variable relative markers.   Returning to our humorous
example (5.118), the ambiguity could be avoided by
selection of a relative marker with nonhuman reference,
as in (5.127).

(5.127)   A piano was bought by a woman *which* had

              three legs

Only those languages with variable relative markers of
this kind will have the ability to disambiguate potentially confusing examples that arise from extraposition.

     Kuno's 1972 paper is also concerned with SOV lan-
guages like Japanese, and attempts to account for a
ban on extraposition in this and other *strict* SOV languages.   This term *strict* is important since there
are SOV languages which do allow extraposition.
(5.128) is a perfectly well-formed extraposed version
of (5.45), which illustrated the Head-RC order in
Persian in section 5.2.2.1.

(5.128)   *mardi* dam-e dar   ast   *ke   mixāhad   bā*

           man   near   door   is   REL wants   with

           šomā   sohbat   konad

           you   talk   do

           'There is a man at the door that wants to

            speak with you'

In an SOV language, extraposition could give rise to
ambiguity on a level with other languages.   In
(5.128) it is presumably because one knows that doors
do not speak that the extraposed RC is interpreted as
modifying *mardi* not *dar*.   Kuno claims in fact that
the ban on extraposition in Japanese is quite a dif-

ferent one.   It is in fact a two-part constraint:

RCs cannot cross their heads

Sentences must end with a main verb.

However, the evidence for this twofold ban is both
circumstantial and contradictory.   First, it is possible for sentences in Japanese to end with constituents other than verbs and one finds examples such as
the following in the spoken language.

(5.129)   Yō chan, mō   sundano   gohan

           already finished meal

'Yō chan, the meal is already finished'

One does not however find extraposed RCs in Japanese,
as Kuno quite rightly claims, but it is circumstantial to claim that this is because RCs cannot cross
their heads.[17] Because RCs in strict SOV languages
do occur only to the left of their heads and *cannot*
occur after the main verb does not necessarily mean
that there is any motivated link between the two
facts.

We suggest that another perceptually-motivated
explanation is available that accords with the two
facts, and that it takes something like the following
form:

(5.130)   *Since extraposed structures are modifying*
           clause-like structures that have been
           moved away from their heads, they require
           some feature(s) that will serve as a per-
           ceptual clue to this function and thus aid
           in the recovery of the grammatical relation
           they hold to the main clause

Since Japanese and some other SOV languages not only
have their RCs in prenominal position, but also tend
to have no relative markers (Andrews 1975 claims it
is rare for *any* SOV language to have relative markers
on its prenominal RCs), then the extraposition of
such structures will mean that there are no perceptual clues for the hearer to trace the origin of the
extraposed clause or to identify it as an RC at all.

The informal statement in (5.130) might also be
claimed to be circumstantial, and the complete absence of any language with extraposed RCs from prenominal position would mean there would be no way of

deciding between our approach and Kuno's.   However,
it can be shown that recovery *is* an essential perceptual factor governing extraposition in languages where
it is quite a normal device.

English Extraposition

As we have seen, ambiguity can be a problem in
some cases of extraposition in English.   Even more
of a problem appears to be the danger of misbracketing
during processing if the relative marker is left out.
(5.131) can occur as (5.132) - that is, without an
overt relative marker.

(5.131)   The man who(m) Bill saw was my long lost

brother

(5.132)   The man Bill saw was my long lost brother

Although this phenomenon is quite widespread in English there are some limits on its occurrence.   Where
the relative marker replaces the subject of the RC
the marker cannot be left out.[18]

(5.133)   The man who fell downstairs was my brother

(5.134)   *The man fell downstairs was my brother

If one considers these examples from the viewpoint of
bracketing during processing, it is clear that there
is a perceptual basis to this constraint.   (5.134)
has the structure shown in (5.135) but it will be interpreted as (5.136), since it appears to be a processing strategy that the sequence NP-V in English
will be interpreted as a main clause.

(5.135) $_{S_1}[NP_{S_2}[\phi \; V \; \ldots\ldots$

(5.136) $_{S_1}[NP \; V \; \ldots\ldots$

With (5.132), however, misbracketing of this kind on
the part of the hearer/reader is avoided.   It will
be bracketed correctly as (5.137), because of the sequence of two NPs in initial position.[19]

(5.137) $_{S_1}[NP_{S_2}[NP \; V \; \ldots\ldots$

When examples such as (5.131) and (5.133) are extraposed we find that *both* must retain the relative marker.

(5.138)   *The man* was my long lost brother *Bill saw*

(5.139)   *The man* was my brother *fell downstairs*

Furthermore, the same constraint on extraposition
applies to reduced relative clauses such as the following.   (5.141) is an alternative form for (5.140)
but it cannot extrapose;   (5.142) is unacceptable,
whereas (5.143) is perfectly acceptable.

(5.140)   A patient who was recovering from a major
               operation phoned the insurance company

(5.141)   A patient recovering from a major operation
               phoned the insurance company

(5.142)   *A patient phoned the insurance company
               recovering from a major operation

(5.143)   *A patient* phoned the insurance company *who
               was recovering from a major operation*

In perceptual terms, either the displaced RC will be
taken to modify the wrong head (here *the insurance
company*) or it will be felt to tag unnaturally onto
the main clause.[20]

     Misbracketing also appears to be the explanation
for a ban on the loss of the complement-marker *that*
under certain conditions.   It is generally accepted
that examples such as (5.144) are ungrammatical
because they will be misbracketed as (5.145) instead
of (5.146).   The complement marker must be retained
in such examples, as in (5.147).

(5.144)   *Syntax is becoming more trendy is clear
               from the numbers studying it

(5.145) S_1 [Syntax.....

(5.146) S_1 [S_2 [Syntax.....

(5.147)   That syntax is becoming more trendy is clear
           from the numbers studying it

However, *that* can be deleted when complement clauses
of this type are extraposed.   (5.149) would be for
many speakers quite an acceptable alternative to
(5.148).

(5.148)   It's clear from the numbers studying it
           that syntax is becoming more trendy

(5.149)   It's clear from the numbers studying it
           syntax is becoming more trendy

On the other hand, the extraposition of *that*-
clauses in English is not the displacement of a subordinating structure - rather it is the displacement
of an entire constituent, the *it*, as we have said,
being merely a dummy subject marker.   Furthermore,
the presence of *it* serves as a perceptual warning
that an extraposed complement clause is yet to come
and thus helps avoid misbracketing the complement
clause as something other than a displaced constituent of the main clause (for a discussion of the circumstances in which the *that* marker can be removed
from extraposed complement clauses in English, see
Bolinger 1972).   In Japanese there are no relative
markers, so that the occurrence of an RC in extraposed position would provide none of the perceptual
clues necessary for processing it *as* an RC displaced
from its head.

We stress, however, that our analysis is no less
circumstantial than Kuno's.   The choice between a
constraint on prenominal RCs crossing their heads and
one that is sympathetic to the needs of language
users in recovering unmarked RCs must ultimately
depend on finding languages which have prenominal RCs,
allow extraposition and have explicit markers identifying the extraposed RC as such.   The existence of
such languages would favour our analysis, while a
failure to find any such language would leave the
matter unresolved. [21]

What we can say in conclusion, however, is that
Japanese has less need of extraposition than English
because its prenominal RCs involve it in fewer instances of self-embedding and this might account for
the absence of such a device in this and other strict

SOV languages.   Nevertheless, extraposition is not a
necessary feature of SVO languages either and languages with an antipathy towards self-embedding may
simply *avoid* such perceptually complex structures
rather than rescuing them by means of devices like
extraposition.

5.2.5.   Summary

     In section 5.2 we have been concerned with the
ordering of RCs and their heads in a variety of language types.   From the languages we have examined it
is apparent that RCs tend to follow rather than precede their heads, and that this can be attributed to
a number of factors.   First, Head-RC order appears
to be perceptually simpler for language users in all
but SOV languages because such an order leads to
fewer instances of self-embedding, or, as is the case
with SVO languages, devices such as extraposition are
available to reduce the occurrence of self-embedded
structures.   However, we have also stressed that
this constraint on self-embedding is to some extent
marginal since all languages appear to tolerate some
degree of self-embedding.   In the case of an SOV
language like Japanese there appears to be some value
in Kuno's claim that the order RC-Head is perceptually simpler for language users, given that other
features of a language militate against the more normal Head-RC order.   A number of languages with the
order RC-Head also appear to have participial RCs -
that is, RCs of less than clausal status.   Drawing
on the work of Foley 1976 we have suggested that such
languages will take the order RC-Head if adjectives
also precede their heads, since participial RCs are
structurally more related to adjectives than to clausal RCs.   Thus, there will be languages which have
the order RC-Head but are not SOV in basic word
order, and Tagalog is such a language.

     We have also examined a number of languages
where evolution (from internal or external pressures)
has resulted in mixed types.   Languages such as
Amharic demonstrate that the division between SOV and
VO languages is not always clearcut and this is confirmed by the optional ordering of RC-Head and Head-
RC in a number of languages which straddle the bor-
derline between OV and VO orders.

     Finally, we have examined the incidence of extra-
position in a number of languages and concluded that
although it is a useful device for languages which

exhibit a high degree of self-embedding, it is not a
necessary device in such languages.   Furthermore,
while an SOV language such as Japanese has no extraposition at all, it does indulge in self-embedding to
some extent.   We ended by discussing Kuno's claim
that Japanese resists extraposition because of a constraint on RCs crossing their heads and main clause
verbs.   Our conclusion was that an alternative perceptual explanation was available - in a language
with no explicit relative markers, the displacement
of an RC away from its head would lead to processing
difficulties.   This perceptual basis to constraints
on extraposition is supported by a constraint on the
omission of relative markers in extraposed RCs in
English, a language with a propensity for omitting
such markers.

We now turn to the relationship between RCs and
case marking.

5.3   RCs and Case Marking

5.3.0.   Preliminary Remarks

Since English, as we have seen, can in many instances dispense with its relative markers it is
important not to overrate their value in decoding RCs.
Furthermore, in Japanese there are no relative markers as such and the NP coreferential with the head
is merely omitted rather than pronominalized or replaced by a marker of some kind.

In fact, Japanese RCs *are* marked but only indirectly.   As Kuno says:

'Relative clauses (and for that matter, all
subordinate clauses) in Japanese are strictly
verb-final, and therefore, verbals signal the
end of clauses.   There is therefore no need
for relative pronouns, whose main function
seems to be to mark the clause boundary of
embedded clauses'.
                          (Kuno 1978:88).

It must be said that the marking of clause boundaries is not by any means the *only* function of relative pronouns (RELs).[22] If it were, this would not
explain why many languages, ranging from the comparatively uninflected English to the highly inflected
Latin, have RELs that are explicitly case-marked.
To claim that the relative marker functions in the
same way as the complementizer, which marks the boun-

dary of nominal clauses, is to ignore the fact that
the same languages which case-mark their relative
markers do not so mark their complementizers.   Why
should a language be redundant in the formation of
one type of clause boundary marker, but not another?

As we pointed out in section 5.0, the relative
marker also acts as a replacement for an NP in the
relative clause, the NP which is coreferential with
the head.   In examples like (5.150), *whom* can be seen
as a replacement for the object NP missing from the
italicized RC.

(5.150)   Sir Lancelot dallied with the maiden *whom*

King Arthur rescued

It would not seem unreasonable to claim that the relative marker itself in (5.150) helps to recover the
role of the missing object NP, in addition to marking
the onset of the subordinate structure as a whole.
Nevertheless, it must also be recognized that (5.150)
can also occur as (5.151), (5.152) and (5.153) with
little or no effect on the ability of language users
to recover the role of the missing NP.

(5.151)   Sir Lancelot dallied with the maiden who
King Arthur rescued

(5.152)   Sir Lancelot dallied with the maiden that
King Arthur rescued

(5.153)   Sir Lancelot dallied with the maiden King
Arthur rescued

As we have seen, the recovery of grammatical
relations in language involves an often quite delicate tradeoff between explicit case marking and rigidity of word order.   Generally speaking, the greater
the flexibility of word order in a language, the
greater the need to mark the roles of NPs explicitly.
Conversely the more fixed word order is in a language,
the more redundant explicit case marking will be.

This tradeoff is also at issue to a limited
extent in relative clause formation.   Thus, it would
seem on a cursory examination to be quite understandable that a heavily case-marked language such as
Latin should have variable, case-marked RELs, while
an isolating language such as Cambodian has invari-

able RELs.   Since in Latin word order is fairly free
there would be a need to identify the role of the NP
replaced by the marker.   On the other hand, Cambodian has very strict word order and so case marking
would not be required to identify the role of the NP
the marker replaces.   However, English does have
case marking of its RELs (*who, whom*), in spite of its
status as a fairly strict SVO language, and thus
appears to be some kind of anomaly.   This feeling is
reinforced when we recall that in examples such as
(5.150) the object role of the REL was evident even
without case marking (as in (5.152)), with the 'wrong'
case marking (as in (5.151)) or even with the REL
omitted (as in (5.153)).

It is not only English which is redundant in
using case-marked RELs.   Consider the free word order, heavily case-marked language Latin, and one of
the examples we used in section 5.1 (example (5.26),
repeated here as (5.154)).

(5.154)   Puellae   quas   rogavi

          girl-pl.nom   REL   ask-past
                    [+fem+plural
                    +acc]

       cras   respondebunt

       tomorrow   reply-future

     'The girls whom I asked will answer

     tomorrow'

In (5.154) the case marking of *quas* is also to some
extent redundant because the inflection on the subordinate verb (*rogavi*) shows that the relative marker
cannot refer to the subject of the clause.   *-avi* is
first person singular, while a marker relating to
puellae, the head, would take a third person plural
verb.   Furthermore, *rogavi* would involve an object
NP in its clause and there is no available NP in the
clause other than the relative marker that can fill
this role.

What then seems to be critical in the recovery
of the role of the NP replaced by the REL is not explicit case marking of the REL, but three things in
combination:

(a)   the use of an identifiable relative marker to
      mark the onset of the clause

(b)   the positioning of that marker alongside its head in the superordinate clause

(c)   the speaker's knowledge of the *valency* of the verb in the subordinate clause.

Thus it appears that even in a language where case marking is an essential feature to overcome the difficulties in role recovery brought about by free word order, it is possible to identify the role of the REL without explicit case marking of the REL; instead there will be strategies to identify that role *indirectly*.

In this section we examine the degree to which case marking of RELs themselves is redundant in a range of languages, and demonstrate that there is once more some tradeoff between case marking of nominal constituents and the order of these in allowing language users to recover the role of the NP that the REL stands for.

5.3.1.   Role Recovery in Relative Clauses

(a)   *SVO Languages*

Whereas it is not unreasonable to imagine that languages have the same order in both main and subordinate clauses, it is unreasonable to expect such consistency as a matter of course.   One need go no further than German to find an example of a language with different orders for the two clause types.   In this language, subordinate clauses are verb-final while main clauses are verb-second.   Compare (5.155) and (5.156).

(5.155)   Er *möchte*   gehen

          he wants   go:inf

          'He wants to go'

(5.156)   Er   sagte,   daß   er   gehen   *möchte*

          he   says   that   he   go:inf   wants

          'He says that he wants to go'

Further afield, Kashmiri is mainly SVO but does have SOV ordering in subordinate clauses (Hook 1976).

(5.157)   ra:man kh'av bati
               erg   ate   food
           'Ram ate food'

(5.158)   tsě   yus   mě wakhun^u dyututh
           you-erg which me   lesson   gave
           'The lesson which you gave me'

And Hebrew, now an SVO language, does have the biblical VSO order in some relative clauses, though Hayon
1973 claims that VOS order is even more natural.

(5.159)   hamore   šehe'ric   dan 'oto,   met   (VSO)
           teacher admired   him-acc died
           'The teacher that Dan admired died'

(5.160)   hamore   šehe'ric   'oto   dan, met (VOS)
           teacher admired   him-acc   died
           'The teacher that Dan admired died'

    It does not seem unreasonable to account for such
inconsistency historically.   Subordinate clauses may
well reflect an earlier word order of the language as
a whole, though lack of documentary evidence in historical analysis should make us rather wary.[23] If a
'lag' in development is the reason, the next question
is: why do subordinate rather than main clauses lag
behind?

    It is clear from English alone that subordinate
clauses are the poor relation when it comes to avail-
ability for application of rules.   Thus, subject-
auxiliary inversion occurs in main clause questions
but not embedded questions.

(5.161)   Who has John fired?

(5.162)   Bill asked who John has fired

Topicalization is also restricted.   Compare (5.163)
and (5.164).

(5.163)   Beans he just couldn't stand

(5.164)   *He claimed that beans he just couldn't
               stand

(For a long list of phenomena occurring in main but
not subordinate clauses in English see Green 1976,
and for discussion of Ross' Penthouse Principle that
'leaks' in word order rigidity start in higher clauses see Aitchison 1979.   It would seem that such a
principle is a language-general phenomenon).

However, we need to distinguish between two kinds
of order in subordinate clauses - where the order of
constituents is fixed and, more important, where the
order of constituents varies.

Whatever the normal order of constituents in a
clause, the result of relative clause formation may
drastically alter it.   Since SVO languages have
postnominal RCs, and these have a relative marker in
initial position (alongside the head), the degree of
deviation from basic order will depend on which NP is
relativized.   Thus, where the subject NP is relativized, there will be no change in order.   (5.165a)
will become (5.165b), the REL merely occupying the
same position as the NP it stands for.

(5.165) a.   Head - S V O

             →

        b.   Head - REL V O

             'The man *that saw the policeman*'

Any other NP will, if relativized, vacate its normal
position.   The object NP in (5.166a) will give way
to a REL in clause-initial position, resulting in a
verb-final clause.

(5.166) a.   Head - SVO

             →

        b.   Head - REL S V

             'The man that the policeman saw'

Word order in simple sentences (or main clauses) and
RCs will be different in such examples, yet not random.   Word order in RCs is predictable and allows
recovery of the 'original' structure.   Just as the
object status of the first NP in (5.163) is clear, so
too is the status of the REL in (5.166b) obvious - it
is a marker representing a relativized object.

Object NPs in clause-initial position in English
main clauses can be decoded because the subject NP is

still in its normal pre-verbal position and the invariable REL in (5.166b) can be identified as replacing
an object because the subject NP (*the policeman*) is
in *its* normal position.

As we have also àlready pointed out, the relative marker cannot be removed when it stands for the
subject of the RC.

(5.167)   The man *(that) chased the cat drank the

           milk

This is because the hearer would otherwise bracket
the two constituents *the man* and *chased* as respectively subject NP and verb of a single clause.   It is
not because the subject role of *that* would be undeco-
dable.   The absence of any NP before the verb in
such an example would in itself be a clue that the
missing NP was itself the subject of the relative
clause.

It seems, then, that SVO languages allow their
users to invoke *perceptual strategies* for decoding
structures in which word order is different from the
norm of a simple sentence.   It is the knowledge of
what constituents can occur with a particular verb
plus the knowledge that subjects tend to occur pre-
verbally which allows the hearer to decode grammatical
roles in the absence of explicit case marking when
normal order is altered.

In Cambodian, a more strictly SVO language, decoding of case roles in RCs is similar to that in English.   As there is no explicit case marking, the
following sentence is, like its English translation,
decoded (as to Agent and Patient roles) by word order
alone.

(5.168)   mɔnuhproh   ban   kʰəɲ   mɔnuhsrei

           man   past   see   woman

           'The man saw the woman'

This lack of case marking extends to RC formation,
there being an invariable marker *daəl* in clause-
initial position, whichever role is relativized.
The following three examples demonstrate respectively
the relativization of subject, object and oblique NPs.

(5.169)   tʰel   ban   kʰəɲ   mɔnuproh   daəl   ban
           past   see   man   REL   past
           viəj   mɔnuhsrei
           hit   woman
           'Thel saw the man who hit the woman'

(5.170)   tʰel   ban   kʰəɲ   mɔnuhproh   daəl
           past   see   man   REL
           mɔnuhsrei   ban   viəj
           woman   past   hit
           'Thel saw the man that the woman hit'

(5.171)   tʰel   ban   kʰəɲ   mɔnuproh   daəl   mɔnuhsrei
           past   see   man   REL   woman
           nijiəj   ciamuəj
           speak   with
           'Thel saw the man whom the woman speaks
           with'

It is knowledge of the valency of the verb and of the
positions normally occupied by NP roles that allows
unequivocal decoding in such examples. And even
when there is some optional order, as in passive
structures, there is no decoding problem since, as
the following pair of examples illustrate, the agent
is either marked by preposition or by position between passive marker and verb.

(5.172) a.   tʰel   ban   kʰəɲ   mɔnuhproh   daəl   trov
             past   see   man   REL   pass
             viəj   doj   mɔnuhsrei
             hit   by   woman
        b.   tʰel   ban   kʰəɲ   mɔnuhproh   daəl   trov
             past   see   man   REL   pass
             mɔnuhsrei   viəj
             woman   hit
             'Thel saw the man who was hit by the
             woman'

There is no danger of this being interpreted as
Thel saw the man that the woman was hit by.   In
(5.173) it also appears to be ordering predictability
that allows loss of the indirect object marker.

(5.173)   tʰel   ban   kʰən   mɔnuhproh   daəl

             past   see   man   REL

        mɔnuhsrei   ban   oj   krotʃ   (tow)

        woman   past   give   orange   to

        'Thel saw the man that the woman gave an

        orange (to)/to whom the woman gave an

        orange'

What is clear is that Cambodian seems to be happy
with the stranding of prepositions whereas English
allows prepositions to migrate along with the NP
attracted to initial position.   That this migration
does not take place in Cambodian is not surprising.
The invariable marker *daəl* takes on no features of
the constituent it stands for, just as with *that* in
English - it does not need to do this because role
recovery is possible without it.   English also has
variable markers (who, whom) in addition to the invariable *that* and it is these *wh*-words alone that can
allow migration of the preposition, as in the translation of (5.173).

     Thus, in SVO languages with fairly strict word
order and no explicit case marking of NPs, recovery
of the role of the relativized NPs is neatly achieved
as follows: the relative marker may not give a
direct clue to the case relation of the NP it replaces, but the fixed nature of word order plus a knowledge of the valency of the subordinate verb will
make it clear which NP is missing.   Variations in
word order from the norm to be expected in a main
clause (resulting for example in a transitive verb
appearing clause-finally) will present no problems
since the language user will perceive that this ordering is *because* a particular NP has been relativized.

(b)   *SOV Languages*

     Strict verb-final languages tend to have expli-
citly case-marked NP constituents (with a concomitant
freedom of order among such constituents).   These
languages, as exemplified by Japanese, have no relative markers as such to mark the onset of an RC, the

final position of the verb acting as a clause boundary
to separate RCs from their heads.   Thus the main
strategy for recovering the role of the NP relativized
is once again in part a knowledge of the valency of
the verb in the RC *plus* recognition of which NPs have
not been removed (with explicit case marking rather
than word order allowing such recognition).

The missing subject NP in (5.176) can be recovered quite readily from this knowledge speakers have
(unconscious) access to.   (5.176) is the complex sentence formed from embedding (5.175) into (5.174).

(5.174)   Sensei   wa   neko   o   mita

          teacher   top   cat   acc   saw

          'The teacher saw the cat'

(5.175)   Neko wa   chiizu o   nusunda

          cat   top   cheese acc   stole

          'The cat stole the cheese'

(5.176)   Sensei   wa S_2[chiizu o   nusunda]

          teacher   top   cheese acc   stole

           neko   o   mita

           cat   acc   saw

          'The teacher saw the cat which stole the

          cheese'

Similarly, the indirect object NP in the RC in (5.179)
can be recovered as the 'missing' role.   (5.179) is
formed by embedding (5.178) into (5.177).

(5.177)   Inu wa   kodomo o   kanda

          dog top   child   acc   bit

          'The dog bit the child'

(5.178)   Sensei   wa   kodomo ni   purezento   o

          teacher   top   child   dat   present   acc

           ageta

           gave

          'The teacher gave a present to the child'

(5.179) Inu wa $_{S_2}$[sensei ga   purezento o
         dog top   teacher nom present   acc
         ageta] kodomo o   kanda
         gave   child   acc bit
         'The dog bit the child to whom the teacher
         gave a present'

Such a delicate decoding system may however break down
at some point and speakers must rely on context to
recover roles in examples such as (5.180).   Here the
direction-marked NP can be either *ni* (*to*) or *kara*
(*from*); that is, the RC can have either (5.181) or
(5.182) as its source.

(5.180) [kisha ga   kita] machi ni   jishin
         train nom came   town   loc earthquake
         ga   okotta
         nom happen
         'An earthquake took place at the town to
         which/from which the train came'

(5.181) kisha ga   machi kara kita
         train nom town   from came
         'The train came from the town'

(5.182) kisha ga   machi ni kita
         train nom town   to came
         'The train came to the town'

This is the kind of example where Japanese is perhaps
just a little bit too economical.[24] Nevertheless a
tactic for avoiding such problems is available.
Speakers either recast examples without relative
clauses, or they adopt pronoun retention (in (5.183)
it is *soko*) to give the postposition something to
attach to (though this is slightly odd for many speakers).

(5.183)   [Soko   kara   kisha   ga   kita] machi   ni
          there   from   train   nom   came town   loc
          jishin   ga   okotta
          earthquake   nom   happen
          'There was an earthquake at the town $\{{from \atop *to}\}$

          which the train came'

This pronoun-retention strategy is restricted to oblique cases and appears to be motivated as an ambigu-
ity-avoiding device.

(c)   *Verb-initial Languages*

   (i)   *VSO and VOS*

     Such languages are often not too richly case-
marked and so one might expect serious problems in
sorting out NP roles.   What distinguishes verb-initial languages from subject-initial VO languages is the
positioning of both the main NP constituents in the
clause after the verb.   Absence of a case marker will
render structures of the pattern (5.184) potentially
ambiguous, with a reading as either (5.185) or (5.186).

(5.184)   Head - REL V NP

(5.185)   Head - REL V Subject

(5.186)   Head - REL V Object

     Such problems can arise in VOS languages, as
exemplified by Fijian (examples from Keenan 1978a).
With limited case marking, the formation of examples
such as (5.187) will allow two interpretations, the
RC corresponding to the simple sentence in either
(5.188) or (5.189).

(5.187)   Na   gone   yalewa   *ka*   *a*   *raica*   *na*
           art   child   woman   REL   past   see   art
               tagane
               man
           'The girl *who saw the man*'
           or
           'The girl *whom the man saw*'

(5.188)   A   raica   na   tagane   na   gone   yalewa
           past   see   art man   art child woman
           'The girl saw the man'

(5.189)   A   raica   na   gone   yalewa   na   tagane
           past   see   art child   woman   art man
           'The man saw the girl'

Since the marker *ka* is not marked for coreference with
its antecedent or with the NP it replaces, there is no
way of recovering from (5.187) whether it is the subject or object that has been relativized.   While
Fijian examples such as this one are ambiguous, other
VOS languages (for example Gilbertese) have *pronoun
retention* to aid in role recovery.   Thus (5.190) can
be relativized as (5.191) without ambiguity through
the optional retention of the pronoun *ia*, which is coreferential with its antecedent.

(5.190)   E   ore-a   te   mane   te   aine
           3sg hit-3sg art   man   art   woman
           'The woman hit the man'

(5.191)   Te   mane   are   oro-ia   te   aine
           art   man   REL   hit-him   art   woman
           'The man that the woman hit'

     A further method of avoiding such problems is a
condition that only subjects can be relativized, as
illustrated by Malagasy.   (5.192) occurs but not
(5.193).

(5.192)   ny   mpianatra   izay   nahita   ny   vehivavy
           the   student   REL   saw   the   woman
           'The student that saw the woman'

(5.193)   *ny   vehivavy   izay   nahita   ny   mpianatra
           the   woman   REL   saw   the   student
           'The woman that the student saw'

It is only possible to relativize objects if they are
converted to subjects.   (5.194) shows how an 'original' object can be relativized in this way.

(5.194)   ny   vehivavy   izay   nohitan'ny   mpianatra

        the   woman   REL   seen   the   student

        'The woman that was seen by the student'

The VSO language Welsh also has potential ambiguity problems and (5.195) can be interpreted in two ways.

(5.195)   y   bachgen   a   welodd   y   ferch

        the   boy   REL   saw   the girl

        'The boy who saw the girl'

        or

        'The boy whom the girl saw'

That is, the logical structure of the RC matches either (5.196) or (5.197).

(5.196)   Welodd   y   bachgen   y   ferch

          V   S   O

        saw   the boy   the girl

        'The boy saw the girl'

(5.197)   Welodd   y   ferch   y   bachgen

          V   S   O

        'The girl saw the boy'

Of course, such ambiguity in both VOS and VSO languages only arises where the selection restrictions of the subordinate verb allow ambiguity. If the verb is *eat* and one of the two NPs has inanimate reference, it will be clear which role the REL replaces. Also, since sentences are rarely spoken in isolation, context will serve to disambiguate examples like (5.187) in Fijian and (5.195) in Welsh. Where ambiguity is not eliminated in this way, there may be resort to another construction. The following examples were suggested to us as a means of avoiding the ambiguity in (5.195).

(5.198)   y   bachgen sydd   wedi   gweld   y
           the   boy   REL-is after   seeing   the
                 ferch
                 girl
           'The boy who saw the girl'

(5.199)   y   bachgen y   mae'r   ferch   wedi
           the   boy   REL is the   girl   after
                 ei   weld
                 his   seeing
           'The boy whom the girl saw'

However, as Gwen Awbery put it when suggesting these
examples, ambiguity is something Welsh speakers 'just
learn to put up with'.

   (ii)   *Philippines-type Languages*

   Tagalog differs from Fijian and Welsh in having
more explicit marking of the roles NPs have in clauses.   As we demonstrated in section 2.3.5., it is
always clear from the marking of topic and registra-
tion in the verb which NP has which role.   Whether
or not this intricate system could avoid the ambiguity
just demonstrated in Fijian and Welsh is however
hypothetical since, like Malagasy, Tagalog may only
relativize the (topic-)subject.   The following examples from K & C (1979:347) clearly demonstrate this.

(5.200)   *babae-ng   sumampal   ang   lalake
           woman REL   slapped   man
           'The woman whom the man slapped'

(5.201)   babae-ng   sinampal   ng   lalake
           woman REL   slapped   man
           'The woman who was slapped by the man'

   The voice system allows objects and indirect objects to be relativized indirectly by promoting them
to subject.   In (5.200) the object NP has been
directly relativized and is ungrammatical, whereas
(5.201), in which the object is a derived subject, is
perfectly well-formed.

As a final comment on verb-initial languages, we might briefly consider the redundant nature of the relative marker. In Japanese there is no nominal relative marker and this is a feature of other SOV languages, the verb itself signalling the boundary of the RC. In English we saw that the marker was redundant in most cases, with only the subject REL being retained. In verb-initial languages too there might be some instances where the marker can be left out. In fact, in Tagalog, the relative marker is essential and is clearly very important as a boundary marker. It is only the use of this marker that allows Tagalog speakers to cope with self-embedding and the reader is referred to example (5.89) (p.312) for illustration of this point.

In Welsh, however, some omission of relative markers is possible. The marker *a* may be left out in rapid speech, though matters are complicated by the mutation rules of Welsh. (5.195) can occur as (5.202), though the mutation form *welodd* must be retained even though the controlling *a* has been removed (without a preceding *a* the verb form should have been *gwelodd*).

(5.202)   y   bachgen   welodd   y   ferch

           the   boy   ∅ saw   the   girl

           'The boy who saw the girl'

           or

           'The boy whom the girl saw'

However, it appears not to be possible to omit the *y* REL. (5.204) involves relativization of an indirect object and cannot be reduced in the way (5.195) was with the *a* REL.

(5.203)   Dyma'r   bachgen   y   rhoddais   y

           here-is-the   boy   REL   I-gave   the

               llyfr   iddo

               book   to-him

           'Here is the boy I gave the book to'

This constraint on *y* deletion is rather odd, since this relative marker appears to be no less redundant than *a*. In (5.202) the clause boundary-marking role of the REL is just as important, though the retention

of *welodd* may signal the absent REL.   However, in
(5.203), *iddo* (*to him*) is an instance of pronoun
retention - the relativized NP leaves behind a pronoun to aid in recovery of its role, which may be disguised by the use of the *y* or any other relative marker not directly case-marked.

Indeed, there appear to be examples in English
where pronouns are retained to aid in recovery of the
role of the NP the marker replaces, though many would
claim that such examples are ungrammatical.

This perceptual value of pronoun retention is
commented on by Bever & Langendoen (1972:36) in their
study of the history of relative clause formation in
English:

> 'Obviously, the retention of the shared nominal
> in sentences like [(5.204)] serves to remind
> the speaker and hearer of the grammatical source
> of the relative pronoun in a situation where the
> syntactic complexity is so great that it is
> both easy to forget and hard to tell what that
> source is.'

(5.204)   The choir limped through the anthem (that)

the organist couldn't make up his mind

at what tempo *it* should be played

Once more it would seem that we can relate the occurrence of some examples to the perceptual requirements
of the language user.   For this reason it is not
surprising that some typologies of RC-formation have
taken a perceptual line.   It appears, for example,
to be an underlying theme of the Accessibility Hierarchy of Keenan & Comrie 1977.

5.3.2.   RC-structure and the Noun Phrase Accessibi-
            lity Hierarchy

Appearing first as an 'underground' paper in
1972, Keenan & Comrie 1977 (augmented by a mainly
data paper in 1979) has justifiably been seen as an
important contribution to the typology of RC-formation.   Listing and illustrating the major strategies
involved in such structures, including the order of
Head/RC, the retention of pronouns, and case marking,
K & C are particularly concerned with the accessibility of particular roles within the subordinate
clause to being relativized.   Essentially, their

claim is that there exists a hierarchy of relativizable relations within clauses and that there is a
non-random selection by languages of which of the positions on the hierarchy can be relativized.   The
hierarchy is shown in (5.205) and three constraints
underlying this non-random selection are shown in
(5.206).

(5.205)   *Accessibility Hierarchy*

SU > DO > IO > OBL > GEN > O Comp

[SU = subject;   DO = direct object;
   IO = indirect object;   OBL = oblique
   (NPs in prepositional phrases in English,
   but see K & C 1977:66 for clarification);
   GEN = possessor;   O Comp = object of
   comparison;   > = 'more accessible than'].

(5.206)   *The Hierarchy Constraints (HCs)*

1.   A language must be able to relativize
      subjects

2.   Any RC-forming strategy must apply to
      a continuous segment of the AH

3.   Strategies that apply at one point of
      the AH may in principle cease to
      apply at any lower point

K & C's papers are very accessible (*sic*) but we
have included the following range of examples to demonstrate the constraints on the relativization of
roles in a range of languages (all examples from
K & C 1977 and 1979).

(a)   *Subjects Only*

Malagasy is severely restricted in its NP accessibility to direct RC-formation.

(5.207) a.   ny   mpianatra   izay   nahita   ny   vehivavy
              the   student   REL   saw   the woman
              'The student that saw the woman'

        b.   *ny   vehivavy izay nahita   ny   mpianatra
              the woman   REL   saw   the student
              'The woman that the student saw'

(5.207) c. ny   vehivavy   izay   nohitan'ny   mpianatra

the   woman   REL   seen   the   student

'The woman that was seen by the student'

Only by promoting the relativized object in b. can
relativization take place at all, c. being an example
where a derived subject is relativized (these examples
are the same as (5.192) - (5.194)).

(b)   *Subjects and Objects Only*

In Welsh there are two relativization strategies
but one of these is restricted to subjects and objects
only.   (5.208) is ambiguous (this example is the same
as (5.195)).

(5.208)   y   bachgen   a   welodd   y   ferch

the   boy   REL   saw   the   girl

'The boy who saw the girl'

or

'The boy whom the girl saw'

(c)   *Subjects, Objects and Indirect Objects Only*

Literary Tamil has one strategy for these positions, and another for other positions on the hierarchy.   (5.209a) to (5.209c) show the participialization strategy for SU, DO and IO respectively.   In
(5.210) the retention of a pronoun helps decode the
relativization of an instrumental.

(5.209) a. Jān   pāṭu-kiṟ   -a   peṇmaṇi(y)-ai

John   sing pres   part   woman   acc

kaṇ-ṭ   -ān

see past   sg-3rd-masc

'John saw the woman who is singing'

b. Anta   manitan   aṭi-tt   -a

that   man   hit past   part

peṇmaṇi(y)-ai   jān   kaṇ-ṭ   -ān

woman   acc John see past sg-3rd-
masc

'John saw the woman that that man hit'

(5.209) c.   Jā̱n   puttakatt-ai(k)   koṭu-tt   -a
             John   book   acc   give pasᴸ   part
             peṉmaṉi(y)-ai   nā̱n   kaṇ-ṭ   -ē̱n
             woman   acc   I   see past sg-1st
             'I saw the woman to whom John gave the
             book'

(5.210)   Eṉṉa(k) katti(y)-ā̱ḷ   koṟi(y)-ai   anta
          which   knife   with   chicken acc   that
            maṉitaṉ   kolaippi-tt   -ā̱n
            man   kill   past   sg-3rd-masc
          anta   katti(y)-ai   jā̱n   kaṇ-ṭ   -ā̱n
          that   knife   acc John see past sg-
                                                3rd-
                                                masc

          'John saw the knife with which the man
              killed the chicken'
          (literally: with which knife the man killed
              the chicken, John saw that knife)

(d)   *No Restriction*

As a final illustration, English can relativize
on *any* of the positions in the hierarchy;   so too can
Urhobo.   (5.212) shows relativization of O Comp,
which appears to be aided by pronoun retention.

(5.211) a.   The man who likes children (SU)
        b.   The man that children like (DO)
        c.   The man to whom I gave a present (IO)
        d.   The man with whom I shared a cab (OBL)
        e.   The man whose children left home (GEN)
        f.   The man than whom no one is more respected
                in this town (O Comp)

(5.212)   oshale   na   l-   i Mary rho   n-   o
          man   the REL   big   than him
          'The man that Mary is bigger than'

As we have seen, there are clearly some perceptual principles underlying the choice of RC-forming
strategies in language and it is not surprising to
find K & C claiming some psychological motivation for
their hierarchy and its constraints.   They sum this
motivation up as follows:

> *'The AH directly reflects the psychological
> ease of comprehension*.   That is, the lower
> a position is on the AH, the harder it is to
> understand RCs formed on that position'
>   (Keenan & Comrie 1977:88).

However, they hasten to add that '...this psychological interpretation cannot fully account for HC_1, that
subjects must, in general, be relativizable.   It
only justifies the claim that subjects are easier to
relativize than any other position on the AH, but it
would allow in principle that, in some language, no
position on the AH be relativizable' (89).

Commenting further on this psychological motivation, K & C cite experimental evidence that ease of
comprehension diminishes as one descends the hierarchy (for references see K & C 1977:90).   On a purely
data-based chart of RC strategies, they also show
that pronoun retention is more likely at the bottom
end of the hierarchy, and we have seen how Japanese
and even English resort to such a strategy for coping
with difficult instances of role recovery (see also
the Welsh example (5.203) and the Easter Island example (5.191)).   The progressive difficulty of decoding RCs as one descends the hierarchy would seem to
provide some motivation for the use of *extra* strategies at the lower end, or the restriction of *direct*
relativization to positions at the top end of the
hierarchy.

Nevertheless, it would not be surprising if there
were some details of languages yet to be encountered
which worked against the precise details of the hierarchy as formulated by K & C, in spite of its overall
attractiveness.

In their 1977 paper K & C consider several apparent counterexamples to the AH.   Among these is an
apparent counterexample to the second constraint that
prohibits RC-forming strategies from applying to a
discontinuous segment of the hierarchy.   Hausa
appears to invoke pronoun retention for subject RELs
and oblique RELs, but not for object RELs (and only
optionally for indirect objects); however, K & C

demonstrate that the retained pronoun is merely a
clitic on subjects, an agreement strategy that also
appears in simple sentences, and that therefore Hausa
does not have a discontinuous RC-forming strategy of
pronoun retention.

Much more interesting however is the Australian
language Dyirbal. This ergative language appears to
break the first constraint that a language must be
able to relativize subjects. As an ergative language, Dyirbal distinguishes between the subjects of
transititve verbs (ergative) and the subjects of intransitive verbs and the objects of transitive verbs
(absolutive). In Dyirbal an ergative NP can only be
relativized if it first becomes absolutive, as illustrated by (5.213) to (5.215). The ergative-marked
subject in (5.213) is anti-passivized into an absolutive in (5.214), and then relativized, as in (5.215).

(5.213)   bayi   yuṛi   baŋgul   yaṛaŋgu
           det-abs   kangaroo-abs   det-erg   man-erg

           bagan
           spear
           'The man speared a kangaroo'

(5.214)   bayi   yaṛa   bagalŋaɲu   bagul
           det-abs   man-abs   spear-a/p   det-dat

           yuṛigu
           kangaroo-dat
           'The man speared the kangaroo'

(5.215)   bayi   yaṛa   bagal-ɲa   -ŋu   bagul
           det-abs   man-abs   spear-a/p   REL   det-dat

           yuṛigu   banagaɲu
           kangaroo-dat   return
           'The man who speared the kangaroo is
           returning'

One solution would be to have a special hierarchy that put ABS higher than ERG:

ABS > ERG > IO .....

However, K & C claim there is little support for this

from other ergative languages.   Instead, they suggest
that the absolutive be seen as the subject in both
transitive and intransitive sentences in Dyirbal,
since the absolutive does have the most subject-like
qualities in basic transitive sentences.

       Criticism has come from a number of linguists,
both against the hierarchy in RC-formation and against
the hierarchy as a pattern for other structures and
their constraints.   For example, Hale, Jeanne &
Platero 1977 observe that in Hopi RC-formation is limited to subjects, but only when the complex NP is
itself a subject.   This they regard as a 'curious'
limitation on accessibility and one unlike any found
elsewhere in language.   On the other hand, Chung &
Seiter 1980 criticize the hierarchy as a universal
pattern for pronominalization accessibility, since
many Polynesian languages of the ergative type break
the hierarchy in this respect.

       There will no doubt be an increasing number of
counterexamples to the Accessibility Hierarchy as
formulated by K & C 1977, and against the constraints
in particular.   However, it does appear that as a
general principle there is some value in the hierarchy as a reflection of accessibility of roles in RCs
and that the pattern of relativizability can to some
degree be correlated with the perceptual requirements
of language users.   The Accessibility Hierarchy can
be seen as reflecting not a watertight universal but
rather a strong universal tendency that the lower
down a scale of relativizable roles in subordinate
clauses the harder recovery of the role will be;   and
so the greater the likelihood that languages will
either resist relative clause formation at or below a
certain point or will invoke extra or distinct strategies to allow the hearer to decode the message.

5.3.3.   Givón's Approach to RC-formation

       A study of RC-forming strategies on a cross-
linguistic basis would not be complete without some
consideration of Givón's approach to typology.   In
his 'On Understanding Grammar' (1979) - a loosely-knit
collection of chapters on a variety of linguistic
themes - Givón devotes considerable space to relative
structures in his chapter 'Semantic Case and Pragmatic
Function'.   With apologies for couching his remarks
in the model-specific but highly useful terminology
of TG, he examines the *case-recoverability problem*,
which he defines as follows:

'When the strategy used in the neutral sentence
pattern for recognizing the case function of
arguments vis-à-vis the verb is tampered with
by transformations, the language resorts to
remedial strategies for recoding those case-
functions'
                            (Givón 1979:146).

Givón also points out that what he terms 'semantic-
pragmatic-contextual redundancies' will often remove
the need for such remedial strategies, and that languages do in any case tolerate some degree of ambiguity and perceptual confusion.   However, the need to
recover case-functions directly from structure will
frequently emerge in the absence of such contextual
clues.   As we saw in Fijian (see (5.187)), ambiguity
is allowed to occur, but other languages appear to
restrict their relativization in such a way as to
avoid ambiguity.   Thus, in Malagasy (see (5.192) to
(5.194)), only subjects may relativize, and we have
seen that the same applies to Tagalog.   In *both*
these languages NPs can be promoted to subject (or
topic-subject) status, with a corresponding marking
of the verb to allow recovery of the original case-
function (in a way that is similar to, but richer
than, the method of marking promoted or *advanced* object NPs in English passive structures).

     This type of strategy Givón captures in the
following typological condition (Givón 1979:156).

     'If a language has no other viable recoverabi-
     lity strategy in relativization, and if in
     addition it has a promotion to subject device
     which involves coding the semantic case of the
     subject on the verb, then the language will
     tend to exploit this device in relativization
     by imposing a subject-only constraint and
     thus resorting to verb-coding recoverability
     strategy'.

An alternative but weaker condition is the following.

     'Only languages in which promotion to subject
     results in coding the verb for the semantic
     case of the topic/subject will have the
     subject-only constraint in relativization'.

     Though he prefers the first of these Givón ad-
mits that its ultimate justification will only come
with a clearer definition of 'viable alternative strategy', and with a clearer statement of how overt verb
coding is before it can be regarded as available for

use in decoding relative structures.

Languages of the Malayo-Polynesian type discussed by Givón might be seen as using a verb-coding
and promotion-to-subject strategy and thus not requiring direct relativization of other roles.   Alternatively such languages might be seen as resorting to
promotion-to-subject and concomitant verb-coding
because there is no direct relativization of other
roles.   It is unnecessary to attempt to decide between these two perspectives - *both* perspectives
involve a recognition that two features of a language
can be related, and are more than mere coincidence.

In this respect, Givón's approach to a typology
of RC-formation shares a philosophy with the work of
Kuno and K & C.   Kuno's functional explanation for
Head/RC order in SOV and VSO languages, and K & C's
claim that languages adopt special strategies for
relativizing lower (that is, more difficult) members
of the Accessibility Hierarchy are, like Givón's conditions, a recognition that languages are far from
being unmotivated in the strategies they select, a
particularly strong motivation being to aid the hearer in decoding the transformed structure.

5.3.4.   Summary

In section 5.3 we have endeavoured to show that
there is once more a tradeoff between fixed word
order and case-marking and that languages use one or
the other to allow their users to decode non-basic
structures such as relative clauses.   However, both
fixed (or predictable) word order and explicit case
marking are *indirect* methods of decoding roles in
RCs.   The role of the relativized NP is discoverable
not from its position or its morphological shape, but
rather from the position or morphological shape of
the *remains* of the clause left behind when the relativized NP is deleted or pronominalized.   Languages
thus demonstrate a normally quite nice balance between redundancy and parsimony - they do enough, but
not much more than necessary, to allow their users to
successfully decode the non-basic structure, in this
instance the decoding of roles whose direct identity
is disguised by the subordination of RCs to their
heads.

5.4 Headless Relatives

Our final comment in section 5.3 involved an assumption that the normal RC has a head in the superordinate clause.   However, as we have already seen, there are some oddities.   In section 5.1, for example, we pointed out that a number of Australian languages have *adjoined* relatives, structures which can only with great difficulty be analyzed as being embedded into a nominal head.

A further oddity, but one that is much more widespread, is the *headless* RC, and although we do not have space here to discuss such constructions to the extent we have examined embedded RCs, some comment should be made about what in some language areas is the normal form that RCs take.   As we pointed out in our comments introducing table 4 (p.275), headless RCs are quite typical of the Americas.   They appear to be the norm in the Carib group, which includes the OVS language Hixkaryana and the OSV language Apurinã, and they are also found in other languages throughout North and South America.

Andrews (1975:64ff) discusses headless RCs and distinguishes two types - *free* relatives and *internal head* relatives.   The former are quite common in language and are represented in English by examples such as (5.216).

(5.216)   *What he was doing* was quite illegal

In the italicized clause (the whole of which functions as subject of the main clause), *what* is an amalgam of head and relative marker (something that is clearer if *what* is expanded into the somewhat more archaic *that which*).   Internal head relatives also occur in English, though they are less common. (5.217) is an example of this type.

(5.217)   *What jewellery the thief left behind* wasn't
               worth worrying about

In such structures the head appears within the RC and cannot be separated from it.

Despite these differences between headless and embedded RCs in English, such examples present no serious problems when it comes to decoding the role of the *pivotal* NP.[25] In (5.216) it is the object that has been relativized, and this is also the case in

(5.217).   Just as with embedded RCs, it is a combination of two factors which will aid in role recovery:

(a)   the valency of the verb - both *doing* and
        left behind expect an object

(b)   the identification of the remaining NPs by
        virtue of their predictable positions - in
        each of these two examples the subject is
        identifiable by its position before the verb,
        he also taking the subject form in (5.216).

Headless RCs in an SVO language like English thus present no problems for the language user and the presence of a relative marker (*what*) is particularly important for decoding their structure.   However, other languages with headless relatives have no such nominal markers, and this is particularly so in SOV languages.   To conclude this section we examine data from three SOV languages which can form RCs without a head in the superordinate clause.

Navajo

Although it has pre-nominal embedded RCs, this language also has many examples of internal head RCs. (5.219) demonstrates the formation of such a structure from the simple clause in (5.218).   It is the verb which signals the occurrence of an RC, with a relative affix (here -ę́ę).[26]

(5.218)   tł'éédą́ą́'   ashkii   athą́ą́'
            last:night   boy   imp:3:snore
            'The boy was snoring last night'

(5.219)   tł'éédą́ą́'   ashkii   athą́ą́'-ę́ę
            last:night   boy   imp:3:snore-REL

                 yádootłih
                 fut:3:speak

            'The boy who was snoring last night will
                 speak'

There are essentially two problems in the analysis of such examples.   First, how do we know that ashkii ('boy') is part of the headless RC and not the head of an ordinary embedded RC?   In this example it is the position of ashkii after the adverbial

tl'éédą́ą́' (itself a part of the RC) which determines
the internal head analysis, though there will be
examples in which the position of the pivotal noun at
the periphery of its clause will allow either analysis.   Secondly, we have the usual problem of identifying the role of the pivotal NP within the RC since
this SOV language has no nominal relative marker, a
dearth of case marking and some freedom of word
order.   In an example such as (5.220) two interpretations are possible.

(5.220)   ┼ị́ị̀'   ashkii   ┼ééchąą'í   bishxash-ę́ę̣

           horse boy   dog   3:perf:3:bite-REL

               yizta┼

               3:perf:3:kick

           'The horse kicked the dog which bit the boy'

           or

           'The horse kicked the boy who the dog bit'

Either ashkii ('boy') or ┼ééchąą'í ('dog') can be
taken as the pivotal noun.

Wappo

     In this languages there is some direct case mar-
king of NPs.   The subject is normally marked by the
suffix -*i*, while the object case is unmarked, as in
(5.221).

(5.221)   chic-i   čiča   ị̧a -ta?

           bear-subj bird   kill-past

           'The bear killed the bird'

However, this subject marker does not occur in subordinate clauses.   In (5.222) the complement clause
contains a subject NP *ce k̂ew* ('that man'), unmarked
for its grammatical function.

(5.222)   ?ah [ce   k̂ew   ?omehwiliš   mehwiliš]

           I   that man story   tell

               hațishkhi?

               know

           'I know that the man tells the story'

It is the absence of such marking in subordinate clauses which convinces Li & Thompson (1976b:452-3) that
Wappo has headless RCs.   Since in (5.223) ce kew
('that man') is unmarked for subject, it must be part
of the RC; if it was the subject of the main clause
and head of an embedded RC it would have a subject
marker.

(5.223)   [ce   kew ?ew   ʈohtih] ?i pehkhi?
           that   man fish catch   me look at
           'The man who was catching a fish was
              looking at me'

As a result of this differential treatment of subject
marking in main and subordinate clauses, Wappo faces
the same problem as Navajo in the decoding of roles
in its headless RCs.   The result is ambiguity in
examples such as (5.224).

(5.224)   ?ah [ce   kew ?ew   ʈum-tah] naw-ta?
           I   that man fish buy-past see-past
           'I saw the man who bought the fish'
           or
           'I saw the fish that the man bought'

Either ?ew ('fish') or ce kew ('that man') can be
taken as the pivotal NP.

Murinypata

     In Wappo it appears from Li & Thompson's data
that subject marking does not operate on the RC as a
whole; since the whole internal head RC in (5.223)
is subject of the main clause one might have expected
subject marking on the last element of the RC, here
the verb ʈohtih ('catch').   In the Australian language Murinypata, such marking does take place.   The
whole of the nominalized RC in (5.226) receives the
ergative marking that the simple NP mutᵛiŋga ('old woman') receives in (5.225) (examples from Walsh 1976).

(5.225)   mutᵛiŋgaɹɛ   ŋayi panŋibaḍ
           old woman-erg   me   hit
           'The old woman hit me'

(5.226)   [mutᵞiŋga   paŋanduwi   mundakŋayya]

           old woman-abs   arrive   earlier

           -ɹɛ   ŋayi   panŋibaḍ

           -erg   me   hit

           'The old woman who arrived earlier hit me'

Furthermore, the case marking system in this language
also allows us to confirm that we are indeed dealing
with headless RCs.   In (5.228) it is clearly the
head that has been omitted, not the coreferential NP
in the subordinate clause.   Mutᵞiŋga has the ergative marking -ɹɛ since it is the agent in the subordinate clause.   If it was a true head, it would be
subject of the main clause and would take the zero
absolutive form, as in (5.227).

(5.227)   mutᵞiŋga   paŋanduwi   mundakŋayya

           old woman-abs   arrived   earlier

           'The old woman arrived earlier'

(5.228)   [mutᵞiŋgaɹɛ   ŋayi   panŋibaḍ]   paŋanduwi

           old woman-erg   me   hit   arrived

           mundakŋayya

           earlier

           'The old woman who hit me arrived earlier'

     Once again, as we saw with embedded RCs, langua-
ges vary in the degree to which they aid their users
in the decoding of grammatical relations within subordinate structures.   Since SOV languages will tend
to have at least some freedom in the position of
their nominals, then it is the SOV language with explicit case marking that will involve the least ambiguity in its RC structure, embedded and headless
alike.[27]

5.5   Non-restrictive RCs

     Our final short discussion revolves around a
type of RC which is often neglected in the literature.
Although linguists recognize a distinction between restrictive and non-restrictive clauses, the non-restrictive type is usually ignored after a short mention.

     A clear semantic distinction exists between Eng-
lish examples such as the following.

(5.229)   All teachers *who last week got a payrise*
           will pay more tax

(5.230)   All teachers, *who last week got a payrise*,
           will pay more tax

In (5.229) the italicized clause is an essential part
of the definition of *which* teachers will pay more tax,
while in (5.230) it merely adds extra information -
here the range of teachers covered by the head is
fully specified by the quantifier *all*.

This semantic distinction, as we pointed out in
section 4.1, is taken by many linguists to justify
distinct derivations for restrictive and non-restrictive RCs.   Since it is clear that non-restrictive
RCs are less intimately wedded to their heads than
restrictive ones, and since the semantic distinction
is reflected in structural differences in English,
this approach is not unreasonable.   However, there
is a serious danger that distinct derivations will be
established by linguists for restrictive and non-
restrictive clauses even in languages where the structural distinctions are lacking.   In this section we
examine some of the criteria that might be used to
motivate distinct derivations for the two types.

In English, only non-restrictive RCs can qualify
sentential heads, as shown by the following examples.

(5.231)   Jim called me a lexicalist, which made me
           cry

(5.232)   *Jim called me a lexicalist which made me
           cry

Only if the sentential head is first nominalized can
the restrictive RC qualify it.   This is demonstratd
by the clefted structure in (5.233).

(5.233)   It was his calling me a lexicalist that
           made me cry[28]

The parenthetical nature of non-restrictive
clauses is borne out in many languages by the special
intonation pattern given to them.   The non-restrictive is separated by a drop in intonation between the
head and the first element of the RC, whereas inton-

ation treats head and restrictive RC as a single unit.
This intonation break is represented orthographically
by commas (see (5.230) and (5.231)), but such a criterion is unreliable; German, for example, uses
commas to separate both types of RC from their heads.

In English the relative marker may be deleted in
some cases, but never from a non-restrictive RC.
Note too that some speakers of English cannot have
the invariable marker *that* with the non-restrictive
type.

(5.234)   *Non-restrictive*

All teachers, *that/who(m)/*ø the minister

disciplined, are now on strike

(5.235)   *Restrictive*

All teachers that/who(m)/ø the minister

disciplined are now on strike

In English the non-restrictive alone can modify
a proper name, though the restrictive clause can also
be used if the proper name is given a determiner.

(5.236)   *Non-restrictive*

I saw John, who is now in the army

(5.237)   *Restrictive*

*I saw John who is now in the army

(5.238)   I saw the John who is now in the army

(not the one you know who joined the navy).

Some languages mark the distinction between the
modifying restrictive and the non-modifying non-
restrictive in other ways.   In Romanian there is a
rule that nouns governed by prepositions (there are
one or two prepositions that do not trigger this
rule) cannot take a definiteness suffix unless they
are further modified.   Compare (5.239) and (5.240).

(5.239)   Soldatul   a   pus   mina   sub
           soldier-the   aux   place-pp   mine-the   under
               pod
               bridge-∅
           'The soldier placed the mine under the
           bridge'

(5.240)   Soldatul   a   pus   mina   sub
           soldier-the   aux   place-pp   mine-the   under
               podul   turnant
               bridge-the   turning
           'The soldier placed the mine under the
           swing bridge'

This rule is blocked if the modifier is a restrictive
relative clause, but not if the clause is a non-
restrictive.

(5.241)   *Restrictive*
           Soldatul   a   pus   mina   sub
           soldier-the   aux   place-pp   mine-the   under
               podul   care   a   fost   bombardat
               bridge-the REL   aux   be-pp bombard-pp
               de   rachete
               by   missile-pl
           'The soldier placed the mine under the
           bridge which was bombarded by missiles'

(5.242)   *Non-restrictive*
           Soldatul   a   pus   mina   sub
           soldier-the   aux   place-pp   mine-the   under
               pod,   care   a   fost   bombardat
               bridge-∅ REL   aux   be-pp bombard-pp
               de rachete
               by missile-pl
           'The soldier placed the mine under the
           bridge, which was bombarded by missiles'

Some Bantu languages demonstrate further morpho-syntactic differences between the types. Compare the distinct forms of the prefix on the italicized verb in (5.243) and (5.244), from Bemba (Walusimbi 1976).[29]

(5.243)   *Restrictive*
           Ababemba   *bà-à-ishile*   beekala   mu   Lusaku

                      come   live   loc

           'The Bemba who came live in Lusaka'

(5.244)   *Non-restrictive*
           Ababemba   *ábà-à-ishile*   beekala   mu

                      come   live   loc

           Lusaka

           'The Bemba, who came, live in Lusaka'

Walusimbi 1976 also claims that in Luganda a syntactic distinction is made between restrictives and non-restrictives in that the latter are postposed (in some but not all dialects).

(5.245)   *Restrictive*
           ekikopo   *kye   nagula   jjo*   kyatise

           cup   REL   buy   yesterday   break

           'The cup which I bought yesterday broke'

(5.246)   *Non-restrictive*
           ekikopo   kyatise   *kye   nagula   jjo*

           cup   break   REL   buy   yesterday

           'The cup, which I bought yesterday, broke'

Such a distinction is quite odd since many linguists would claim that non-restrictives rarely if at all can be separated from their heads, by, for example, extraposition. This is the view taken by Ziv & Cole 1974 in relation to Hebrew and English.

(5.247)   *Aba   sheli nixnas   lekan   karega,
          father   my   entered   to here   just now
             shehu   atsma'i
          that he(is)   independent
        '(*)My father came in, who runs his own
          business

The reader might like to consider whether the English
translation is really unacceptable.   Certainly we
feel it is less acceptable than the unextraposed version (*my father, who runs his own business, came in*)
but so too are some extraposed restrictives.   There
are speakers of English who do find extraposed non-
restrictives perfectly natural, especially when they
are in the nature of parenthetical afterthoughts.
(5.248) seems quite normal.

(5.248)   Take the aluminium industry, for example,
             which is bloody big business nowadays

One of the authors also heard the following example
on a religious radio programme recently, as part of
a scripted lecture.

(5.249)   He saw Columba before the battle, who had
             appeared.....

Finally, restrictive RCs can *stack* on a single head
but non-restrictives cannot.

(5.250)   *Restrictive*
          I saw the man who was laughing who you
             pointed out to me

(5.251)   *Non-restrictive*
          *I saw Bill, who was laughing, who you
             pointed out to me

    It is quite clear that not all languages will
make the same structural distinctions between restrictive and non-restrictive relative clauses.   In some
instances this follows from the nature of the relative structure itself.   Only those languages with
nominal relative markers will be able to distinguish

lexically in the way English does between markers
which introduce restrictives and those which introduce non-restrictives (see (5.234) and (5.235)). It
is no surprise then that Japanese should lack such
formal means of differentiating the two types, since
like other SOV languages it omits, rather than prono-
minalizing or replacing, the coreferential NP in the
RC.   The following examples from Kuno 1973 are cited
by Andrews 1975 to illustrate the structural similarity between restrictives and non-restrictives.

(5.252) a. watakushi ni eigo   o   osiete

            I   to English acc teaching

                iru Mary

                be   Mary

            'Mary who is teaching me English'

        b. watakushi ga   sitte   iru Mary

            I   nom knowing be

            'The Mary that I know'

(5.253) a. honyuu-doobutu de aru kuzira

            mammal   is   whale

            'The whale, which is a mammal'

        b. nihon-kai ni sunde   iru kuzira

            Japan sea in living be   whale

            'The whales that live in the Japan sea'

Because of a typographical error, (5.253b) is
labelled non-restrictive, whereas it is clearly intended to be restrictive, to match the non-restrictive example in (5.253a).   However, it is also clear
from the example itself that it is restrictive, since
we know that whales are not restricted to Japanese
waters (it wouldn't be a very safe place for them to
live!).   Confirmation that (5.253a) is indeed the
non-restrictive example Kuno and Andrews claim it to
be comes from our knowledge that *all* whales are mam-
mals.

    Clearly, such knowledge of the world will aid
language users in decoding precisely the message intended, despite a lack of structural differences between restrictive and non-restrictive RCs.   However,
there will be instances where both interpretations

are possible - in (5.252a and b), for example.

Such languages will, of course, have other means
available for communicating an unambiguous message.
In Korean, for example, the conjoined structure in
(5.254) avoids the ambiguity between a restrictive
and a non-restrictive interpretation that a relative
clause structure would give rise to - though one could
hardly call this example economical (Yang 1972).

(5.254)   na   ka   cinkong   chəngsoki   lɨl

           I   nom   vacuum   cleaner   acc

           sa -ass -ta   kɨlante   kɨ   cinkong

           buy past stat   and   the vacuum

           chəngsoki   ka   kocang-na   -ass -ta

           cleaner   nom out of order past stat

      'I bought a vacuum cleaner and the vacuum

      cleaner was out of order'

      (Compare: 'I bought a vacuum cleaner which
                was out of order'

      and   'I bought a vacuum cleaner, which
                was out of order')

Finally, one must point out that some languages (including Navajo - see Andrews 1975:20) make no distinction between restrictives and non-restrictives even
at a semantic level.   And even languages which do
distinguish between the types may not readily exploit
the difference.   Killean 1972 claims that in modern
Arabic non-restrictives are comparatively rare, even
though the distinction exists.   However their use is
increasing under the influence of French and English.

5.6   Summary

In this chapter we have discussed data on relative clauses from a number of languages representing
different word order types.   Our aim has been to
demonstrate once more that it is possible to establish
a link between the degree of explicit case marking
and the degree to which word order is fixed or free
in any particular language.   We have seen (section
5.3) that such a tradeoff allows language users to
recover grammatical relations even in those structures - here relative clauses - which are at variance
with the form taken by simplex *kernel* sentences.

This need to decode structures, which might lead to increased explicitness in the representation of grammatical relations in RCs, is however counterbalanced by a tendency for language to be parsimonious. Thus we find that in some instances there may be ambiguity - where this tendency towards parsimony overrides the needs of language users. However, we have also seen that languages employ remedial strategies (in particular, pronoun retention) to aid the hearer where relations are particularly opaque.

The role that perceptual strategies play in the recovery of grammatical relations is parallelled by an apparent link between the ordering of Head/RC and the perceptual needs of language users. We have examined Kuno's claim that RC-Head or Head-RC ordering can be related to basic word order because of the limitations on human short-term memory, and we have found this claim to have some merit (section 5.2.3.). Nevertheless, the importance of such a functional explanation for the order of constituents in certain language types should not be overstated, and in our final chapter we examine some other attempts to explain the distribution of language features.

NOTES

[1]However, in gapping examples such as those discussed in chapter four the truncated clause does of course become structurally dependent on the other clause by virtue of its reduction to less than full-clause status.

[2]There is a considerable amount of literature on relative clause reduction, including a welcome degree of scepticism on the value of directly relating examples such as (5.12) and (5.13) by rules such as *whiz-deletion* and *modifier-shift*. See in particular Bolinger 1967 for a discussion of examples which defy such an approach.

[3]Andrews 1975 cites Klokeid 1970 to the effect that another language with adjoined structures, Mabuiag, allows a *causal* interpretation in some instances.

[4]See, however, note 27 below.

⁵Some linguists have expressed doubts about the use of the *trans* gloss for the suffix -cia (here realized as -ina).   See Tsunoda 1980 for comment.

⁶For some discussion of headless relatives see section 5.4.

⁷See also Klaiman 1976 for a discussion of the view that the Indo-Aryan language Bengali is shifting *towards* the OV type rather than being slowed down in its move *away* from OV status.

⁸According to Tai (1973:661), post-nominal RCs appear to be more likely '...when the head noun is indefinite and in a predication built on the existential verb *you*'.

⁹In our Tagalog examples in this chapter we have again avoided glossing *ang* and *ng*.   See discussion of examples (2.20) to (2.23) in section 2.3.5. for comment.

¹⁰However, Foley does point out that the boundaries between the categories on the hierarchy are not rigid, '[they] are, in fact, rather vague.   The categories more or less merge into each other'.   (Foley 1976:19).

¹¹We do of course stress that we are referring to an *unconscious* expectation on the part of the hearer.   We are not claiming that the language user consciously works out the options available at any point in a sentence.

¹²In this chapter we follow Kuno in using the term *self-embedding*, though other linguists might prefer the term *centre-embedding*.

¹³However, not all native speakers of Japanese would share the view that (5.79) is a completely natural sentence.

¹⁴It is interesting that comprehension, if not acceptability, of such examples increases when relations between major constituents are more obvious. In the following example, knowledge of the usual behaviour of policemen, terrorists and bombs helps to make clear who is doing what, despite the multiple self-embedding.

The bomb that the terrorists that the policeman
   arrested planted exploded.

[15]This example is from Derbyshire 1979:26, but
with the gloss modified as suggested by Derbyshire
(pers.comm.).

[16]There are, furthermore, many examples where
extraposition cannot easily be formulated in terms of
a movement rule.   Gazdar 1980 uses the following
example to show that some 'extraposed' examples have
no unextraposed equivalents.

   A man just came in and *a woman* went out *who were*

      similar in all kinds of ways.

[17]See Miyake & Mallinson 1981 for detailed discussion of examples which some might claim were extraposed RCs in Japanese.

[18]As Bever & Langendoen 1972 point out, however,
such relative marker deletion is possible in certain
examples for some speakers.   In examples such as the
following, misbracketing of the type depicted in
examples (5.135) and (5.136) fails to alter the interpretation.

   There is a boy ∅ wants to see you

This also appears to be the principle allowing some
speakers of English to accept examples such as the
following:

   I knew a man from Dunstable could hold his

      breath for fifteen minutes.

[19]It is intonation and stress which presumably
prevent patterns of the form NP-NP-V from being
momentarily analyzed by the hearer as instances of
topicalization in a single clause sentence, as in
Yoghurt I loathe.

[20]Note that (5.142) does have an interpretation
equivalent to:

   A patient phoned the insurance company *while*

      recovering from a major operation.

Here the *-ing* structure is taken to be an adverbial
phrase of time.

Some speakers may however also accept (5.142) as
an example of extraposed reduced relative clauses.
One must assume that here the participial form of the
verb acts itself as a marker of RC onset.

[21]See again Miyake & Mallinson 1981 for discussion of extraposition in Navajo, an SOV language with
RCs explicitly marked by an affix.   See also section
5.4 below for Navajo RCs.

[22]It is somewhat controversial to use *relative
pronoun* as a blanket term for relative markers.
Such a term is not unsuitable for languages like
English and Latin with their variable relative markers but is inappropriate for languages with invariable relative markers.   We use the term *relative
marker* from this point, and also the abbreviation
REL.

[23]In the case of German, for example, it is
highly likely that SOV order in subordinate clauses
reflects some degree of influence from (Classical)
Latin.

[24]However, Tasaku Tsunoda (pers.comm.) suggests
that Japanese speakers will tend to assume that the
ni ('to') interpretation is intended rather than the
kara ('from') interpretation.   These case-marking
particles thus can be hierarchically ordered in terms
of their recoverability.   See section 5.3.2. for
further discussion of such a hierarchy.

Tasaku Tsunoda has also provided us with another
example open to two interpretations.   In the following sentence, the 'missing' REL (that is the NP which
would occur as a relative marker in a VO language)
can be either of the two *ga*-marked NP constituents
that one finds with *nom-nom* verbs such as *suki-*
('like').

    [Taro ga   sukina]   Hanako ga   kita

        nom   like-adn   nom   came

   'Hanako, whom Taro likes, came'

   or

   'Hanako, who likes Taro, came'

[25]By *pivotal* we mean the NP in the RC which
would in an embedded RC be relativized.

[26]Navajo examples in this section are from
Platero 1974 and Andrews 1975.

[27]It appears that Crow examples such as (5.27)
(p.271) should be handled in the same way as examples
in this section.   That is, the label *internal head*
is somewhat inappropriate since it implies that the
RC surrounds the head.   In fact, in such examples
the pivotal NP is *not* the head - the head is simply
missing.

[28]However, in not all languages can non-restrictive RCs modify sentential heads.   See de Rijk's
(1972) discussion of Basque, for example.

[29]Our source unfortunately provided no glosses
for examples (5.243) to (5.246);   like other Bantu
languages, however, Bemba and Luganda have a rich
prefixing system on verbs and nouns alike.   The
essential point in (5.243) and (5.244) is that there
are different prefixes on the verb in each example.

CHAPTER 6

ON EXPLANATION AND THE TYPE

6.0   Introduction

Our aim up to this point has been to display the
non-randomness of variation across languages in four
selected areas: agent/patient marking, basic word
order, co-ordination and relative clause formation
(the latter as an example of subordination).   We have
also sought to make significant generalizations and
to explain the distribution of the data.   In this
chapter we want to focus attention on the nature of
explanation and to consider attempts at explaining
not so much the skewed distribution of the data but
more the correlations between what at first blush
might seem to be unrelated features.

There are two sides to language - one synchronic,
the other diachronic.   If we take as a sample a number of languages, each considered as it is at a particular point in time, and if we compare them, we are
making what we could call a *synchronic comparative
study*.   If we choose these languages so as to minimize the possibility of resemblances between them
being due to a common origin or to direct or indirect
contact, then the pattern of similarities and differences we find must be explained in terms of the nature of language itself.   We can study the distribution of the various means of expression of a semantic
entity or opposition or the various semantic functions
of a formally defined entity.   What is perhaps more
interesting is to try to correlate the distribution
of the features that we study.   In chapter three,
for instance, we demonstrated that there was a correlation between case marking and word order;   in chapter four we demonstrated that strategies for co-
ordination reduction were to some extent related to
word order, and in chapter five we pointed out correlations between word order and case marking on the

one hand and the type and position of various kinds of
relative clause on the other.

Word order has been at the centre of many discussions of correlations between language features, and
Greenberg showed that the order found in a number of
constructions correlated with the basic order of S, O
and V.   In fact on the basis of Greenberg's work
there has arisen the notion of the *word order type*.
Thus one speaks of a language as an SOV language and
the label signifies that the language not only has
SOV word order but that it has a cluster of correlated
properties (see next section).[1]

If one were to confine one's study to synchrony,
there are certain aspects of language that would not
be revealed.   One would not be able to learn of the
effects of phonetic reduction, changes in part-of-
speech, semantic shifts, and the like.   This information must be gleaned from a comparison of synchronic
states in the history of a language or language family
or from internal or comparative reconstruction.   If
one makes a number of diachronic comparisons (e.g.
Old Norse - Modern Icelandic; Archaic Chinese -
Modern Chinese; Classical Arabic - Modern Arabic),
one can make generalizations about recurrent types of
change, try to establish principles of change or constraints on change, and raise questions about the
evolution of language - whether it shows a constant
drift in a given direction, for instance, or whether
all change is cyclic.

There is one fundamental difference between synchrony and diachrony and that is that synchrony involves principles embodied in the knowledge of speaker-hearers.   Diachrony, on the other hand, if
indeed one can establish principles of diachrony, is
not necessarily part of such knowledge.

In the following sections we will discuss the
notion of the *word order type* as an example of *types*
in general, pointing out that the establishment of
the type represents a significant success in typology,
a significant advance over mere listing or cataloguing.   The existence of types raises the question
of how they come to exist.   It also raises the
questions of how they are maintained over time and if
one type can change into another.   We discuss these
questions, turning in the final section to the problem of explanation itself.   We point out that watertight explanations are practically impossible in linguistics, but this does not mean we cannot provide

some kind of satisfying and illuminating account of
aspects of synchrony and diachrony.

6.1   The Word Order Type

Greenberg 1963 demonstrated that there were correlations between various features of ordering.   For
example, universal 2 stated:

> 'In languages with prepositions, the genitive
> almost always follows the governing noun,
> while in languages with postpositions it almost
> always precedes'.

In particular he demonstrated that a number of language features of order correlated with the position of
S, and more particularly of O, with respect to V.
The following are some of the correlations, together
with the figures Greenberg gave to support them.

Universal 3

'Languages with dominant VSO order are always
   prepositional'

Universal 4

'With overwhelmingly greater than chance frequency,
   languages with normal SOV order are postpositional'

	VSO	SVO	SOV
N Post	0	3	11
Prep N	6	10	0

Universal 17

'With overwhelmingly more than chance frequency,
   languages with dominant order VSO have the
   adjective after the noun'

	VSO	SVO	SOV
NA	6	8	5
AN	0	5	6

Universal 22

'If in comparisons of superiority the only order,
   or one of the alternative orders is standard-
   marker-adjective, then the language is postpositional.   With overwhelmingly more than chance
   frequency if the only order is adjective-marker-

standard, the language is prepositional'.

In this instance, Greenberg has framed his universal
in terms of a correlation with postpositions versus
prepositions, but he has given figures relating stan-
dards, markers and .adjectives to basic word order as
well as to adpositions.   The basic word order and
the position of adpositions are shown to be correlated in universals 3 and 4.

	Preposition	Postposition
Adj-Marker-Standard	13	1
Standard-Marker-Adj	0	10
Both orders	0	1

	VSO	SVO	SOV
Adj-Marker-Standard	5	9	0
Standard-Marker-Adj	0	1	9
Both orders	0	1	0

Universal 24 (already covered in detail in chapter
five but repeated here for the sake of completeness):

'If the relative expression precedes the noun
either as the only construction or as an alter-
nate construction, either the language is postpositional, or the adjective precedes the noun
or both'.

On the basis of the figures cited below, one would be
entitled to assume that if a relative precedes its
head noun then the language is always postpositional,
but Greenberg has framed universal 24 to cater for
Chinese, a language outside his sample; Chinese is
prepositional, has the adjective before the noun and
has relatives before the head noun (though, as we
pointed out in section 5.2.2., Chinese also allows
some relatives to follow the head).

	Preposition	Postposition
Relative N	0	7
N Relative	16	4
Both orders	0	2

	VSO	SVO	SOV
Relative N	0	0	7
N Relative	6	12	2
Both orders	0	1	1

(See also section 5.2, especially 5.2.1. and 5.2.3.).

Greenberg listed 45 universals in all, but it is this short list (2, 3/4, 17, 22 and 24) that has received most attention in the extensive literature that has flourished on the subject.   Universals 2, 22 and 24 have been 'rewritten' (with some loss) as direct correlations with the position of O relative to V.

One spurious correlation has been added to the list.   Universal 17 points out that VSO languages have the order Noun-Adjective (NA).   It does not point out any correlation between AN and OV nor between NA and VO yet such a correlation is often claimed (see, for instance Lehmann ed. 1978).   Greenberg's sample does not support such a correlation, nor do the extensive lists in his appendix.   Greenberg himself may have been responsible for injecting this false universal into the literature, for in his discussion of the universals (1963:100) he claims that NG (Noun-Genitive) VS VO NA are harmonic, as are the opposite orders GN SV OV AN.   However, he points out that languages with GN SV OV NA are also common because of the 'general dominance of NA order'.

The following table summarizes the correlations on the short list.   The figures to the right of each entry indicate the number of languages in Greenberg's sample of thirty that exhibit the correlation.   The figures at the far right indicate the total number of languages that exhibit the correlation with VO or OV out of the number of languages for which it was possible to obtain clear evidence one way or the other (on this last point see the discussion at the end of this section).

Note that VO represents a conflation of VSO and SVO.   We treat VSO and SVO together simply to provide a basis for the discussion of the Greenbergian literature where such a conflation often appears.

Table 6

Word Order Type Consistency

VSO SVO (VO)		SOV (OV)		
N Genitive	11	Genitive N	10	21 out of 25
Prep N	16	N Post	11	27 out of 30
N Adj	14	Adj N	6	20 out of 30
Adj Mkr Std	14	Std Mkr Adj	9	23 out of 25
N Rel	18	Rel N	7	25 out of 29

Along with this short list of correlations has arisen the concept of the word order type.   A language is said to be *consistent* if it exhibits all the correlations.   Thus one speaks of a consistent SOV (or OV) language and one means that it has SOV as its basic word order, preposed genitives, postpositions, preposed adjectives, standard-marker-adjective and preposed relative clauses.   It is obvious from the figures given above that the inclusion of noun/adjective order has blurred the notion of the consistent type.   On the figures shown for the five correlations, only 40% of languages can be expected to be consistent.   If the noun/adjective correlation is omitted the figure rises to 60%.

Lumping together VSO and SVO as VO also blurs the notion of the type.   Greenberg's figures indicate that VSO and SOV are polar opposites.   SVO emerges as something of an in-between type.   See for instance the figures quoted under universal 4 and universal 22.

The significance of the figures 40% and 60% becomes apparent if we consider that if the relationship between word order and the other features was random and only half the VO languages exhibited NG, half the OV languages GN, and so on, then the chances of a language having a particular basic word order plus the set of five features shown under it in the table would be 1 in 32 (there are 64 possible types if all languages can be categorized as *X* or *not X* for each parameter).

The following sentences illustrate the items on the list.   The first set of sentences is from Thai, a consistent SVO language.   The second set is from Japanese, a consistent SOV language (compare Lehmann 1973a:55.   See also Lehmann ed. 1978 for illustrations from Sinhalese (SOV) and Irish (VSO)).

Thai: *SVO*

SVO

(6.1)   pùk   pə̀ət   pra?tuu

Pook   open   door

'Pook opens the door'

NG

(6.2)   khruu   khɔ̌ɔŋ   pùk   pìt   praʔtuu
         teacher   of   Pook   close door
         'Pook's teachèr closes the door'

NA

(6.3)   khruu   rák   nákrian   dii
         teacher like   student   good
         'A teacher likes good students'

N Rel

(6.4)   phǒm   mɔɔŋduu   mǎa   thîi   kàt   dèk
         I   see   dog   that   bite   child
         'I saw the dog that bit the child'

Prep N

(6.5)   suwilai   yùu   nay   krungthêɛp
         Suwilai   live   in   Bangkok
         'Suwilai lives in Bangkok'

Adj-Marker-Std

(6.6)   phǒm   khít   wâa   phǒm   dii   kwàa   khun
         I   think   that   I   good   than   you
         'I think I'm better than you'

Japanese: *SOV*

SOV

(6.7)   Taro   ga   inu   o   mita
         Taro   nom   dog   acc   saw
         'Taro saw a dog'

GN

(6.8)   Taro   ga   kinjo   no   hito   no   inu   o
         Taro   nom   n'hood   gen   man   gen   dog   acc
            mita
            saw
         'Taro saw his neighbour's dog'
         (lit. Taro neighbourhood's man's dog saw)

AN

(6.9)   Taro   ga   ookii   inu   o   mita
          Taro   nom   big   dog   acc   saw
          'Taro saw a big dog'

Rel N

(6.10)   Taro   ga   niku   o   tabeta   inu   o   mita
          Taro   nom   meat   acc   ate   dog   acc   saw
          'Taro saw the dog that ate the meat'

N Post

(6.11)   Taro   ga   mado   kara   inu   o   mita
          Taro   nom   window   from   dog   acc   saw
          'Taro saw a dog from the window'
          (alternatively *mado yori*; compare the follow-
             ing)

Std-Marker-Adj

(6.12)   Inu   ga   neko   yori   ookii
          dog   nom   cat   than   big
          'The dog is bigger than the cat'

We should point out that it is not always easy
to determine whether a language is SOV, GN, etc.   We
have already alluded to the problem of determining
basic word order in chapter three.   In some languages there is no morphologically separate class of adjectives; the translational equivalent of English
adjectives are either nominal or (intransitive) verbal.   One could classify languages as *head-modifier*
or *modifier-head*, but not all types of modifier
occupy the same position in relation to the head.
Moreover in some tokens of noun phrases it is unclear
which of two nominals is the head and which the modifier or whether neither is a modifier.   It is not
uncommon to find that even in languages with a morphologically defined class of adjectives, some adjectives appear before the noun and others after.   Such
languages can be characterized as AN/NA.   These need
to be distinguished from languages that appear to
allow a good deal of freedom of order in noun phrases.
A number of Australian languages seem to be like this,
e.g. Ngiyambaa (Donaldson 1980), Kalkatungu (Blake
1979c), both languages where there does not seem to

be any morphologically distinct class of adjectives.
Some Australian languages tend also to postpose adjectives so that a sentence such as *The big dog bit
the snake* may appear with the order *dog snake bit big*.
In some languages comparison is indicated by 'X is
big, Y is little'.   Such languages obviously cannot
be characterized in terms of adjective-marker-stand-
ard or standard-marker-adjective.   Similarly, languages with expressions of the form 'X is large, sur-
passes Y' cannot be so classified (Greenberg 1963:88).

As we noted in chapter five, it is not always
clear what counts as a relative clause.   Some Australian languages have what Hale 1976 calls an 'adjoined
relative clause'.   This construction covers the
function of relative clauses in English, but it need
not contain a participant that appears also in the
main clause and when this is the case (but not only
then) the construction covers the function of adverbial clauses of time.   If such a construction is
accepted as a relative clause, a further difficulty
remains.   The adjoined relative clause appears before or after the main clause, not as part of a noun
phrase, so such languages can not be characterized as
Rel N or N Rel (see also section 5.1).

Australian languages tend to be difficult to
classify in Greenbergian terms on many points.   They
tend to exhibit considerable freedom of order not
only of sentence constituents but also of what we
might expect to be phrase constituents.   One commonly finds the following:

(i)   fairly free word order, with SOV being
        common

(ii)   lack of evidence for a morphological class
        of adjectives; head-modifier and modi-
        fier-head with adjective-like modifiers,
        the former predominating

(iii)   GN and NG

(iv)   adjoined relative clauses

(v)   comparisons of the form: X big, Y little

(vi)   suffixes or postpositions for case relations
        but also adpositions (expressing in par-
        ticular the orientation of one entity
        with respect to another) that occur be-
        fore or after the noun to which they
        refer (see (6.17)).

6.2   Explaining the Type

There have been several attempts to explain the word order type either by positing general principles that relate the correlations that make up the type or by positing diachronic links between the correlated features.

6.2.1.   Greenberg

Greenberg himself offered both types of explanation.   Commenting on the fact that prepositions, NG, VS, VO and NA are harmonic, he says (1963:100), 'We have here a general tendency to put modified before modifier, and the most highly "polarized" languages in this direction are those of type 1 [=VSO], with NG and NA, a considerable group of languages'.   Greenberg then goes on to point out that the Turkish type, the type that has come to be thought of as the classic SOV type, is based on harmony between postpositions, GN, SV, OV, and AN, i.e., it is based on a modifier-modified order.   As we saw in the previous section, Greenberg also noted that many SOV languages had NA, which he related to the general dominance of NA.   He suggested that noun-adjective dominance may arise from the same factor as that which makes subject-verb the dominant order, the tendency for the comment to follow the topic.   However, the modified-modifier principle makes NA harmonic with VS, but the topic-comment principle makes NA analogous with SV.

Some of the examples of NA among SOV languages may reflect the verbal origin of the 'adjectives'. This seems to be the case in the Yuman languages where 'all the adjectives and quantifiers...are of verbal origin' (Langdon 1977:260).

Greenberg (1963:99) also saw that there was a connection between the position of the adposition and genitives.   Adpositions expressing location are often derived from nouns as in *back of the hut*, where an original head noun (*back* in this instance) is reinterpreted as an adposition.   If the head precedes the originally dependent genitive, it becomes a preposition.   If the head follows, it becomes a postposition.   Thus the position of the genitive in relation to the head can determine the position of an adposition derived from a noun.   We are interpreting Greenberg's brief remarks on this subject in terms of an historical development, as a diachronic explanation for a synchronic relation.   Of course the whole

notion of harmony, of modifier-modified or modified-
modifier, raises questions of diachrony, as we shall
see below.

6.2.2.   Vennemann

Vennemann 1973 proposed a principle of natural
serialization to account for the word order type.
The natural serialization principle states that the
operator-operand relationship tends to be expressed
by unidirectional serialization.   'Operator-operand'
is simply 'modifier-modified' and the principle is
that a language tends to use the order modifier-
modified throughout or the order modified-modifier
throughout.   Two things should be noted about this
principle, which incidentally is really a generalization of Greenberg's taken over without acknowledgement and rephrased in less familiar terminology.
First of all, the principle is simply a generalization
which is itself in need of explanation, and secondly,
the generalization is based on assumptions about modifiers and modifieds that are not altogether uncontro-
versial.   Presumably we can take it that adjectives
modify nouns and that genitives modify nouns (but see
section 6.2.3.).   Vennemann assumes that O is a modifier of V, as does Greenberg.   Vennemann argues
that 'semantically, the application of an operator
results in a specification of the operand predicate,
and, syntactically, the application of an operator to
an operand results in a constituent of the same general syntactic category as that of the operand...object
application delimits the extension of a transitive
verb, and syntactically, the operation of applying an
object noun phrase to a transitive verb results in a
verb rather than a noun phrase' (1974c:81).   We do
not disagree with this, but we draw attention to it,
because it is by no means obvious, unless one is used
to working in a verb-centred framework, and if one
accepts a verb-centred framework, then one must
accept that S is also a modifier of the verb (Greenberg seems to take this for granted;   see previous
section).

What is more controversial is Vennemann's assumption that 'noun phrases are operators on prepositions,
which are transitive adverbials, because the result
of the operation is a prepositional phrase, i.e. an
adverbial, rather than a noun phrase' (1974c:81).
Although one can see a correspondence in form between
some adverbs and some prepositions (*He walked up.*

He walked up the stairs) and although one can ascertain that some prepositions derived historically from
adverbs, there is no clear synchronic relationship
between prepositions and adverbs.   A prepositional
phrase is exocentric [PP = P + NP], whereas a noun
phrase [NP = (A)N] and a verb phrase [VP = V(NP)] are
endocentric.   Jackendoff 1973 also takes prepositions
to be transitive adverbials.   He has a rule of the
type PP → P(NP), with the preposition/adverb as the
head of an endocentric construction.

Like Greenberg, Vennemann attempts to explain
some correlations that characterize the type in terms
of certain types of historical development.   Presumably the principle of natural serialization is intended by Vennemann to be a sufficient explanation for
the word order type, so one might ask why there is
any need for another type of explanation.   Perhaps
the particular historical developments should be considered mechanisms by which the general principle
comes to be realized.

Vennemann (1973:31) attempts to explain the correlation between OV and postpositions on the one hand
and VO and prepositions on the other by reference to
the fact that verbs are the historical source for
some adpositions.   In English, for example, the preposition *concerning* derives from the verb *concern* and
since verbs precede O in English, an adposition deriving from a verb will precede its object, i.e. it
will be a preposition.   Similarly in German
betreffend is a postposition because it derives from
a verb and verbs in participial constructions follow
O.   As noted in sections 3.1.4. and 5.2.2., German
employs SOV order in subordinate clauses.

Andersen (1979:25) gives a number of examples of
postpositions arising from participles in Sanskrit,
an OV language.   The sequence NP-acc V-participle is
reinterpreted as NP-acc postposition.

NP-acc	ādāya	'having taken NP' → 'with NP'
NP-acc	uddiśya	'having shown NP' → 'for NP'
NP-acc	ārabhya	'having begun NP' → 'since NP'
NP-acc	gṛhitva	'having taken NP' → 'with NP'
NP-acc	muktvā	'having freed NP' → 'except NP'[2]

Craig (1977:117) gives examples of prepositions
derived from verbs in Jacaltec, e.g. *ul* 'in' derives
from the verb *huluj* 'to come'.

In Chinese, southeast Asian languages, west African languages and various others it is common to find
some prepositions that are homophonous with verbs.
These prepositions are synchronically derivable from
verbs in most cases.   In Thai, for instance, we find
words like tɛ̀ɛ 'from' that occur only as prepositions
as in (6.13).   Then we find words such as càak which
can occur as verbs as in (6.14) and as prepositions
as in (6.15).

(6.13)   thân bin tɛ̀ɛ   krungthêɛp

          he   fly from Bangkok

          'He flies from Bangkok'

(6.14)   thân càak

          'He   leaves'

(6.15)   thân bin càak krungthêɛp

          he   fly from Bangkok

          'He flies from Bangkok'

It might be thought that càak is a dependent infinitive in (6.15), but against this it could be pointed
out that no 'real' preposition can be used with càak
in (6.15) nor with many analogous forms in other constructions.   Since there seems to be widespread evidence of prepositions deriving from verbs synchronically and diachronically, Vennemann's explanation has
some force.   Given the tendency for some verbs to
develop into prepositions, a fact itself requiring
explanation, then the correlation between VO and prepositions is explained as the synchronic product of a
diachronic development, without invoking the principle of natural serialization.   It would take us too
far from our theme to explain the naturalness of the
verb → preposition tendency.   Let us cite a single
example as a token.   In both southeast Asia and west
Africa and probably elsewhere, one finds a construction such as the following one illustrated from Thai.

(6.16)   phǒm sòng nangsʏ̌y hây   khun

          I   send book   give you

          'I sent a book to you'

hây is a verb and can appear in the frame A hây O
(kàp) Recipient (*Agent give Object (to) Recipient*).

In (6.16) it is a dependent verb lacking A and O
(since they have been specified in the higher clause)
and lacking tense and aspect specification (since
these must match whatever the higher verb bears).
hây is ripe for reinterpretation, if it has not
already been reinterpreted, since it lacks some verb
characteristics and is filling a position that is
also occupied by 'real' prepositions.

Vennemann also attempts to explain the correlation between the position of the genitive and the adposition in historical terms, as did Greenberg (see
section 6.2.1.).   In English the compound preposition *because of* derives from the following construction:

by   cause   of   NP

In this construction *cause* is the head and the postposed genitive prepositional phrase the modifier.
The construction has given rise to a preposition because the genitive phrase followed the original head.
Instances of this type of change are not hard to find.
Anttila (1972:149) gives examples from Hungarian and
Baltic Finnic.   In Finnish, a noun *kohta* 'place,
spot' in the adessive case *kohdalla* 'on the place'
could be modified by a preposed genitive: *talon
kohdalla* 'on the spot of the house'.   The form
kohdalla has now become a postposition, the original
dependent genitive now becoming the head.   Of course
the English compound prepositions *on top of*, *in front
of* and so on all derive from original head nouns
(*top*, *back*, *front*) with postposed genitives *of NP*.

This kind of explanation will account for the
position of a number of local adpositions involving
extension of the meaning of nouns meaning 'head',
'back', etc., but there is a further reason why adpositions are likely to occur on the opposite side of a
head noun from the genitive.   In a prepositional
language an adnominal prepositional phrase follows
its head: *the man on the platform*.   If it did not,
then the addition of a prepositional phrase to the
head of a prepositional phrase would result in a
centre-embedded construction that is difficult to process.   For instance, instead of *to the man on the
platform*, the result would be *to the on the platform
man*.   This is not too difficult to understand, but
the addition of a third prepositional phrase would
certainly result in a difficult construction.   Now
if we consider the origin of the 'new' genitive markers in English and Romance, we find that they were

both prepositions meaning 'from'.   In Old English
the phrase ða *men of Lundenbyrig* means 'the men from
London', but *of* later weakened to acquire its present
'genitive' meaning.[3]   There are examples of this kind
of semantic extension in other parts of the world.
In Australia, for instance, a number of languages
have genitive markers that seem to derive from locative forms, e.g. Warluwara *-pa* from *-*mpa*, Pitta-Pitta
*-*ŋa* from *ŋka.[4]   What is involved in all these instances is the development of an abstract relationship
marker from a more concrete one.   Whenever genitives
derive from local adpositions, they will simply take
their place with other adnominal adpositional phrases
(cf. Greenberg 1963:99).   Thus in English we have
with the supporters of the king instead of **with the
of the king supporters* for the same reason we have
with the supporters from Norwich instead of **with the
from Norwich supporters*.

In a postpositional language, an adnominal postpositional phrase precedes its head and so a postpositional genitive will precede also.

If we accept these lines of development we have
prepositions giving rise to new prepositions and
postpositions giving rise to new postpositions.

(a)	preposition	postposition
(b)	postposed prep phrase	preposed post phrase
(c)	a prep → genitive	a post → genitive
(d)	postposed genitive	preposed genitive
(e)	head becomes new prep	head becomes new post

If this were the only development possible, obviously
prepositions would perpetuate prepositions and postpositions would perpetuate postpositions.   But of
course other developments are possible.   Prepositions can become prefixes and postpositions suffixes.
An adnominal affix-marked phrase is free to precede
or follow its head.

In any language the number of adpositions that
have the function of expressing the orientation of
one entity with respect to another is quite a large
proportion and where we know the origin of these adpositions it usually turns out that they were originally nouns meaning 'head', 'back', 'backside', etc.
(often in an oblique case).[5]   The genitive explanation is promising therefore in terms of numbers.   If

it is correct, it offers a partial answer to the
question of how adpositions came into being and how
they took up the positions they did.   However, we
should not overlook the fact that an adposition can
develop from a noun or adverb without a specific genitive construction being involved.   For example, in
Thai the word thîi occurs as a noun meaning 'place'
and as a preposition meaning 'at'.   The latter meaning seems to have derived from the former historically.   In Thai the modifier follows the head and
phrases of the pattern thîi NP have been reinterpreted as *preposition NP* rather than *head NP modifier NP*.
For example, thîi bâan, originally 'home place' has
become 'at home' (cf. Li & Thompson (1974b:205) on the
origin of postpositions from nominals in Chinese).

   In this same language we find an NG construction,
leekhǎathîkaan khɔ̌ɔŋ khanǎkammakaan 'secretary of the
committee' where khɔ̌ɔŋ 'of' has developed from a noun
meaning 'thing, goods, possessions'.   khɔ̌ɔŋ has
become a preposition for the same reason thîi has,
namely because it derives from a head + modifier construction in which khɔ̌ɔŋ was originally the head:
things X → *of* X.   The fact that the genitive phrase
is postposed is in accordance with the principle
noted above that prepositional adnominal phrases are
postposed to avoid centre-embedding.[6]   In Thai then
we can see a development from head modifier to preposition, including prepositional genitive marker.   To
the extent that developments like this are common they
would account for correlations between NA and PREP
and between NA and NG.

   In some languages there are distinct constructions for *alienable* and *inalienable* possession.   One
would expect phrases meaning 'back of', 'head of' etc.
to belong to the inalienable pattern.   In Australian
languages it is usually the case that the expression
of whole-part relationships is by simply expressing
the whole and the part without any indication of a
case relationship between them.   One would expect
these 'constructions' to underlie any new adpositions
based on nouns.   In Malak-Malak (Birk 1976:106), for
instance, 'a man's dog' is muyiɲ yiɲa-nö (dog man-of)
but 'a man's head' is yiɲa puntu (man head).   Note
that the order is different in the two constructions.
If words for 'back', 'head', etc. were to develop
into adpositions, one would expect them to become
postpositions, at least if they followed the whole-
part pattern rather than the ordinary possessive pattern.   It is also possible for adverbs, themselves

often deriving from nouns in oblique cases, to become
adpositions.   In Kalkatungu, for example, 'behind'
is uṯi-ŋka, uṯi being a stem that does not occur in
combination with affixes other than -ŋka, a locative
allomorph, as here.   The appropriate analysis of
uṯiŋka is that it is an adverb, but it can be used
adjacent to a noun in the locative, either before or
after, and is thus a kind of 'ambiposition'.

(6.17)   juru   iŋka-ṉa   kunti-pia uṯiŋka

            man   go-past   house-loc back

(6.18)   juru   iŋka-ṉa   uṯiŋka kunti-pia

            'The man went behind the house'

One could imagine an adverb becoming an adposition
without the genitive/possessive pattern being involved.[7]   In theory uṯiŋka could be influenced by the
whole-part pattern;   in practice, Kalkatungu employs
the sequences whole-part and part-whole, so this construction provides no model.

        A genitive can also develop from a verb as is
the case with *bilong* in some English-based pidgins
and creoles.   This development parallels *concerning*
< *concern*, the V + complement sequence of English
yielding a preposition.

        In sum we find Vennemann's attempts at explai-
ning the correlation between OV POSTPOSITION and VO
PREPOSITION and the correlation between NG PREPOSITION
and GN POSTPOSITION to be promising.   We feel that
there is a functional reason for postposing adnominal
prepositional phrases and preposing adnominal postpositional phrases and that this will account for the
position of adpositional genitives.   We feel too
that one has to consider the possibility of nouns
developing into adpositions (in some cases via adverbs) without a genitive construction being involved.

6.2.3.   Keenan

        Keenan (1978b:188) puts forward two principles
of word order that are relevant to the word-order
type.   The *serialization principle* states that 'different functional expressions taking the same class
of argument expressions tend to serialize on the same
side of their argument expressions' and the *dissimi-
lation principle* states that 'functional expressions
taking determined noun phrases [*every man, the men*]

as arguments and functional expressions taking common noun phrases [*man* in *every man*, *men* in *the men*] as arguments tend to serialize on the opposite side of their argument expressions'.

Keenan considers that verb phrases, transitive verb phrases and adpositions are functions taking determined noun phrases as arguments. He also considers that possessive phrases (e.g. *the father of*, *'s father*) are functions of the possessor, which is a determined noun phrase. Thus in *Henry is the father of John* or *Henry is John's father*, the expressions *the father of* or *'s father* can be said to indicate the relation of *John* outside the phrase, i.e. in this instance to *Henry*. Keenan considers adjectives, relative clauses, articles, quantifiers and numerals to be functions taking common noun phrases as arguments.

The phrase 'same class of argument expressions' in the serialization principle refers to the classes *determined noun phrase* and *common noun phrase*. Thus the effect of the two principles is to predict the widespread occurrence of the two following types:

	A	B
Determined NP	S VP	VP S
"	O TVP	TVP O
"	Postposition	Preposition
"	GN	NG
Common NP	AN	NA
"	Rel N	N Rel
"	Article N	N Article
"	Quantifier N	N Quantifier
"	Numeral N	N Numeral

Type A is the well-attested SOV type, type B is the poorly attested VOS type. To obtain a better fit between the prediction and the data, Keenan adds a *subject front* principle to the effect that 'the subject occurs to the left of other major constituents of sentences'. This enables him to predict SVO but only at the expense of the serialization principle, and this also means that VOS (along with VSO, OVS and OSV) will fail the subject front principle. In fact SOV is the only language that satisfies all three principles.   Keenan claims the following:

> 'If we take then the possible word order types
> for human language to be those obtained from
> the set defined by the general principles SP
> [serialization principle] and DP [dissimilation
> principle], namely SOV and VOS, and modified in
> the direction of satisfying Subject Front we
> obtain (pending of course a more rigorous form-
> ulation) a surprising number of correct pre-
> dictions:
> (i)   The possible types are SOV, VOS, VSO and
>   SVO.   Just the well attested cases, with
>   the exception of the one OVS language
>   cited [Hixkaryana].
> Note what a strong prediction (i) in fact is.
> There are 9 function-argument structures con-
> sidered and thus in principle 2^9 = 512 possible
> word order types.   Of which only four are
> predicted to occur, and they do.
> (ii)   The principles predict that the SVO, VSO,
>   and VOS languages will evidence the same
>   serialization in their function-argument
>   structures with the exception of the
>   placement of the Subject.   But all others
>   should be the same, and this is correct.
> (iii) The combined effect of the three princip-
>   les would appear to correctly predict the
>   observed genetic-areal distribution of
>   the word order types'
>   (1978b:191-2).

It is difficult to see how (i) is justified.   VSO
does not obey the subject front principle, and if
deviations from any one of the principles are allowed,
then there is no prediction beyond SOV.   All one can
claim is a scale of markedness: SOV > SVO, VSO,
VOS > OSV, OVS.   (i) also ignores numerous deviations, particularly those involving the position of
the adjective.   In English, for example, the adjective precedes the noun, but in an SVO language the
adjective should follow the noun.   In fact, many of
the 512 possible 'word order types' occur.   (ii) is
also incorrect in the same way.   (iii) is true in
that the observed frequency of the types matches
their markedness as noted.

6.2.4.   Lehmann

Lehmann (1978a, but see also 1973b) proposes a
general 'fundamental principle' that governs the word

order of a consistent language.   The principle is as
follows (1978a:19):

$$\#Q\ V\ (N^{Obj})\ (N^{Mod})\ \#\ \rightarrow \begin{Bmatrix} \#Q\ V\ (N^{Obj})\ (N^{Mod})\ \# \\ \#(N^{Mod})\ (N^{Obj})\ V\ Q\ \# \end{Bmatrix}$$

Q   =   verbal qualifier/modifier
N^{Obj} =   object
N^{Mod} =   noun modifier

The formula is to be interpreted as allowing two
possible sequences.   In each the OV sequence is un-
interrupted.   In OV languages nominal modifiers precede O (and nouns in general) and verbal modifiers
follow V.   In VO languages nominal modifiers follow
O (and nouns in general) and verbal modifiers precede
V.

The exact status of this principle is unclear.
Taken at face value it is a generalization about consistent VO and OV languages.   However, in the light
of Lehmann's faith in the *type* ('consistency eventually emerges' 1978c:409)), it may be that this principle is meant to represent an optimum grammar.   An
inconsistent language will have special rules for its
inconsistencies.   Diachronically, the principle
should perhaps be thought of as exerting a pull towards consistency.   The original insight in Lehmann's
principle is the focusing on the uninterruptibility
of the OV or VO sequence.   Note that he does not consider the position of S in his formulation.   Obviously in a VSO language, S interrupts the VO sequence.

6.2.5.   Summary

As we have seen, attempts at explaining the type
mostly fall under two heads: (a) establishing a general principle for the ordering of modifiers and modifieds, and (b) establishing some recurrent diachronic
developments.   The first of these attempts is descriptive not explanatory.   Why should languages develop in such a way as to conform to the general principle?   The second is essentially descriptive and
promises to explain the word order type as an accident
of diachronic developments, themselves in need of
explanation.   To these two attempts at explanation
we can add a third.   In chapter five we pointed out,
following Kuno, that limitations of short-term memory
exert a pressure that favours preposed relative clau-

ses in SOV languages (see section 5.2.3.), and in
section 6.2.2. above we made the point that preposed
adnominal prepositional phrases and postposed adnominal postpositional phrases potentially present processing difficulties.   Languages tend to put postpositional phrases before nouns and prepositional
phrases after them.   These characteristic positions
are reflected in the position of adpositional genitives and of adpositions arising from the heads of
genitive constructions.

     Our own feeling is that the word order type is
the reflection of recurrent diachronic developments
and some pressures resulting from potential processing difficulties.   The alternative is to see the
modifier-modified principle as exerting a kind of analogical pressure.   We are suspicious of this because
the items that would play a part in the proposed analogy are not all alike in an obvious way.   It is not
obvious, for instance, that S is a modifier of V as A
is a modifier of N.

6.3   Word Order Change

     It is recognized that word order changes through
time and this phenomenon is of interest in itself.
However, it takes on added interest in the context of
the word order type.   If the order of constituents
within the noun phrase, for instance, is correlated
with the relative order of O and V, then the question
arises of how the type changes over time.   How is a
transition effected from VO to OV or vice versa?   Is
the basic word order changed first, with the position
of genitives and adpositions changing later to become
harmonic with the new order?   Or does the position
of genitives and adpositions become disharmonic with
the basic word order and put pressure on the basic
word order to change?

     In the following subsections we will summarize
recent views of change in basic word order and in
section 6.4 we will take up the question of word order change and the maintaining of the type.

6.3.1.   Reconstructing Word Order

     Not much is known about word order change since
only a few languages or language families have written records extending over more than a few centuries.
However, some linguists have tried to reconstruct the
word order of unattested stages in the history of lan-

guages, the word order of proto-languages (e.g. Lehmann 1974 for Indo-European), and even to construct
typologies of word order change (e.g. Vennemann 1973).
These attempts are fraught with danger and mostly
rest on assumptions that are not necessarily true.

Givón (1971, 1975), Lehmann (1972) and Vennemann
(1973) seem to believe that the position of clitic
pronouns or agreement markers reflects the position
of earlier independent forms.

Vennemann (1974c:80) compares the following French
sentences and notes that the clitic O precedes V while
the noun O follows.

(6.19)   Marie connaît cet   homme

         Mary knows   this   man

         'Mary knows this man'

(6.20)   Marie le   connaît

         Mary him   knows

         'Mary knows him'

Vennemann considers that in the evolution of French
(SVO) from Latin (basically SOV), the change took
place with noun objects but not with pronoun objects.
He believes that if case is marked on nouns, it it
marked on pronouns. As we saw in chapter two, this
is true of accusative marking though not of ergative
marking. He believes that when case marking is lost,
it is lost first on nouns and that SVO order is introduced with nouns to distinguish S and O (see section
3.4 and section 6.4.1.). However, it is very dubious to conclude that the position of a clitic or
bound pronoun reflects the position held at an earlier stage by a free stressable pronoun or a noun.
As we noted in 3.3.2., pronouns sometimes occupy different positions in the sentence from those occupied
by nouns with the same function. Susan Steele
(1977) argues that clitic pronouns in Uto-Aztecan
languages that appear in second position in the clause
moved into that position as they became clitics. We
would prefer to say that unstressed pronouns tend to
assume positions different from those occupied by the
corresponding nouns and that they may cliticize to
neighbouring words when they are in these positions
(see section 3.3.3.). Certainly we endorse Steele's
general argument that one cannot take the position of
clitics, or of cross-referencing agreement markers,

as a guide to the earlier position of the corresponding noun phrases.   Lightfoot (1979:399) notes that
in modern Greek, as in French, the word order is SVO
and clitic Os precede the verb.   However, the clitics
are not conservative.   As he points out, pronominal
clitics developed in pre-verbal position only after
SVO order was well-established.   In fact in Old
French pronominal complements could appear after the
verb as well as before it, so it is not true that the
position of unstressed pronoun complements in modern
French is a direct reflection of Latin order, which
was not *rigidly* SOV anyway.

     Lehmann is well known for his suggestions that
deviations from the consistent word order type may
enable us to reconstruct unattested word orders.   He
points out, for example (1973b:57), that the Austro-
Asiatic family is divided into two separate branches,
the western or Munda branch, and the eastern or
Khmer-Nicobar branch.   The Munda languages are OV,
Relative N, AN and GN.   The Khmer-Nicobar branch is
VO, NA, NG and prefixing.   The Munda languages exhibit VO order in compounds, some examples of NG order
and some prefixes.   Since the Khmer-Nicobar languages are consistently VO, Lehmann assumes that the
Munda languages have deviated from the VO protolanguage.   Lehmann's argument seems persuasive, all
the more so when we consider the Munda languages are
found in contact with SOV (Dravidian) languages.
However, we should point out that the methodology
does not lead to unimpeachable results.   As Lightfoot
(1979:399) notes, English introduced nominals on the
VO pattern in Elizabethan times (e.g. *pickpocket,
turnkey*), but then reverted to OV forms (e.g. *baby-
sitter, cabinet maker, cocktail shaker*), so the OV
forms cannot be said to reflect the Germanic OV order.
One particular problem with using the order of compounds is that a verb-object compound may reflect the
position of a nonspecific object in relation to the
verb and this position will not necessarily be the
position of a specific O.

     Lehmann (1973b:60-61) cites Thai as a typical
SVO language but notes that the general interrogative
marker occurs in clause final position.

(6.21)   khǎw   kin   khâaw   mǎy

           he   eat   rice   query

           'Does he eat rice?'

He sees final interrogative markers as being characteristic of SOV languages and suggests as a 'preliminary statement' that this may reflect a stage when the
language was OV.   This seems a strange statement
when one considers the frequency of 'non-inherited'
interrogative tags in SVO languages (French: *n'est-ce
pas*, Italian: *(non è)vero*, German: *nicht wahr*, Polish:
nie, etc.).   In fact mǎy in Thai is the negative marker like the European examples.   As a negative it
appears before the verb as mây, and any doubts about
the identity of mǎy and mây can be dispelled by reference to the fact that a single root performs the
same pair of functions in related dialects e.g., Lao
bɔ̂ɔ 'not', bɔ̌ɔ 'query'.

   From a range of languages there is evidence to
suggest that some bound morphemes on the verb were
once independent verbs.   In fact it is likely that
progressions of the following types are involved: on
the one hand, the semantic bleaching of a lexical
verb to become a marker of tense, aspect, causative,
etc.;   on the other hand a progression from full verb
to free verb-modifier to bound verb-modifier.   The
evidence comes from the comparison of related languages where one can see the same root at different
stages of an apparent progression in different members
of the family.

   Givón (1971, 1975) suggests that proto-Bantu was
at one stage SOV (present day Bantu languages are
SVO).   Part of the evidence is the presence of the O
bound pronoun in pre-verbal position.   As we noted
above one has to be wary of such evidence.   However,
he supports his case with a number of other points,
one of them being the presence of verb-suffixes, most
of which he thinks are of verbal origin.   This type
of argument can be applied to Indo-European languages.
The verb is marked for tense, aspect, etc. by suffixes and the origin of some of the suffixes is known
to be verbal.   Bopp, for instance, pointed out that
the *-ba-* and *-bi-* of the Latin imperfect and future
respectively are reflexes of forms of an Indo-European verb 'to be': *amabat* 'he was loving', *amabit* 'he
will love'.   In some Romance languages the future
and conditional have been formed by the suffixation
of the verb 'to have', itself inflected, to the infinitive, e.g. Italian *parlerai* 'thou shalt speak'
< *parlare* 'to speak' + *hai* 'thou hast'.   It is natu-
ral that a verb that develops into a function morpheme will become a suffix in an SOV language, since it
will start life off as the main or higher verb in a

configuration of the following type,

(6.22)

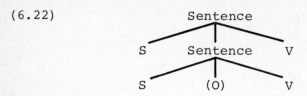

Conversely it is likely that if a verb develops into
a function morpheme in a VSO language it will become
a prefix.   In each case the assumption is that the
originally higher verb becomes unstressed and incorporated into the verb in its original position.   It
seems that the position of markers for tense, aspect,
etc. is a guide to the position of the verb at the
time the bound forms developed, though one would need
to have some idea of the likely origin of the verb
affixes;   not all will have verbal origins.   It is
not uncommon for adverbs and adpositions to become
verbal affixes as in English *look up*, German *auf-
fangen* (gather up) and Indonesian *duduk-i* (see
(2.84)), where -*i* was originally a preposition.

6.3.2.   Ways in which the Basic Word Order Changes

Hyman 1975 discusses proposed explanations for
word order change under four headings: (a) contact,
(b) disambiguation, (c) grammaticalization, and (d)
afterthought.   We shall use the same headings here
except that we will replace 'afterthought' by the wider label *expressivity*, as in Lightfoot 1979.   It is
not accurate to say that contact, grammaticalization
and afterthought or expressivity shifts are *explanations* for word order change.   For instance, contact
with another language may result in the borrowing of
a pattern, but we are still left with the question of
why one particular pattern was borrowed rather than
another, why the borrowing took place at one time
rather than another, why one language was a donor rather than a recipient and so on.   We prefer to speak
of ways in which basic word order changes.   Disambiguation is intended as an explanatory principle but
it does not seem to be a sufficient one, as we shall
see.

(a)   *contact*

Lehmann (1973a:201) mentions that a language may
change its basic word order under the influence of

another language, the influence being exerted by
multilingual speakers.   He cites borrowing of word
order as a possible explanation for the fact that
Akkadian was OV, in contrast with the basic VO structure of Semitic languages.   'It was brought into an
area occupied by speakers of the OV language Sumerian,
and presumably adopted by many speakers of Sumerian.
For in time Sumerian became extinct.   The influence
it may have exerted on Akkadian, however, is our best
explanation of the change in order of the Akkadian
clause'.   Similarly Givón attributes the SOV order of
another Semitic language, Amharic, to prolonged contact with Cushitic (referred to in Hyman 1975:115;
see also Givón 1979:276).   The changes induced by
contact can be dramatic.   Sri Lankan Creole Portuguese is not only SOV but has all the characteristics
of the SOV type.   The source of these typological
features is Tamil (Dravidian SOV) and Sinhala (Indo-
Aryan SOV).   Although this is not an example of a
typological change within a language of successive
generations of Portuguese speakers, the result is a
form of Portuguese (on the basis of lexicon) with a
word order typology radically different from Standard
Portuguese (I. Smith 1978, 1979).   Sri Lankan Malay
is likewise a typical SOV language though 'Malayan
Malay' is an SVO language (I. Smith pers.comm.).

Obviously contact is not a sufficient explanation
for word order change as it leaves unexplained how the
different orders come to exist in the first place.
In one sense we will never be able to answer this
question, but if we allow one word order to change to
another for internal reasons, then there is only one
phenomenon to be explained (one Language with a capital L) and different languages with different orders
are simply specimens of a single phenomenon 'caught'
at a particular point in their cyclic evolution.   Of
course positing internal reasons for change does not
mean precluding contact as a partial explanation for
some instances of change.

(b)   *disambiguation*

Vennemann (1973, 1974a) believes that an avoid-
ance-of-ambiguity principle accounts for one particular type of word order change, namely SOV to SVO (see
also section 3.4).   He claims that SOV order is the
most natural for a language with case marking.   He
assumes that V is weakly stressed relative to S and O,
S typically being topic, O comment, and V the specific
relationship between the topic and comment.   In his

view it is natural for V to stand outside the topic-
comment nucleus, preferably following SO. If V precedes SO, there is no consistent topic-comment serialization. In a VSO sentence, topic (S) precedes
comment (O), but in a VS sentence the topic (S) follows the comment (V).

Vennemann claims that if the morphological distinction between S and O characteristic of SOV languages is lost through phonological change, then the
word order will change to SVO via a 'German period'
or TVX stage (as he calls it), i.e. a type in which a
topic or focus is followed by the verb then the rest
of the clause. SVO becomes the preferred word order
for a language with no morphological distinction between S and O, since it allows O to be fronted without
producing an ambiguous NP NP V sequence.

We have some sympathy for Vennemann's general
argument since there is a clear correlation between
SOV and case marking for the S/O distinction and between SVO and no morphological S/O distinction. However, a number of points need to be made.

It is not true that V in an SOV language is always weakly stressed relative to S and O. It is not
true of Dravidian languages nor of Australian SOV
languages for instance. Also, it is unlikely that
the only way an SOV language loses its case marking
is through phonetic attrition, though this seems to
play a part in some instances of loss of case marking
and loss of transparency in agreement systems. It
is not uncommon to find that related languages and
dialects differ in whether or not they have accusative (or ergative) marking or according to how this
marking is distributed on the pronoun-animacy hierarchy. In most of these cases there is no evidence of
phonetic attrition. Rather it seems that languages
can 'decide' whether to use case marking or not irrespective of phonetic factors. Vennemann is aware
that languages often have accusative marking only for
definite objects or human objects (1975:292), but he
thinks that such incomplete accusative marking is
innovative and will eventually spread to cover all
instances of O.

In English the nominative/accusative distinction
has been lost in nouns, adjectives and determiners.
The loss of marking involved reduction of unstressed
vowels to *schwa*, loss of final *schwa* and loss of
final -*n*. While the first two changes were phonetic
in nature and operated generally, the loss of -*n* was

certainly not phonetic.   It did not occur in plurals
(*oxen*) nor within stems (*heaven*).   It is sometimes
regarded as a morphologically conditioned phonological change, but it is not clear that it was a phonological change at all.   Rather it seems to have been
simply a morphological loss just as the loss of the
dual pronoun forms was.   Phonetic attrition may have
played a part in the loss of the nominative/accusative
distinction in English, but it would be rash to say
that phonetic attrition was the cause of the loss.

Hyman notes that a language may change from SOV
to SVO without losing its case marking (e.g. Russian)
and an SOV language without case marking may change
to SVO, as appears to have happened in the Niger-Congo
languages (quoted in Li & Thompson 1974a:212).

The posited transition of SOV to SVO via TVX is
not well attested, though something like this appears
to have happened in the development of English (see
section 3.1.4.).   There is also some tendency towards verb-second order in late Latin, in the Vulgate
for instance, but data on this kind of transition
from other groups and families is not available.

(c)   *grammaticalization*

Li & Thompson note that the '*bǎ*' construction in
Mandarin, which is an SOV construction, derives from
an earlier SVO construction or more precisely a construction of the form SVOV.   The construction involves a preposition *bǎ*, which marks O (Li & Thompson
1974b:203).

(6.23)   Zhāng-sān   bǎ   Lǐ-sì   piping   le

          Zhang-san   acc Li-si   criticize   perfect

          'Zhang-san criticized Li-si'

bǎ was originally a verb meaning 'take hold of'.
Thus a sentence like (6.23) was earlier a compound
sentence of the type 'Zhang-san took Li-si and criti-
cized him', but *bǎ* was reinterpreted as a preposition
and the compound pattern reinterpreted as a single
SOV clause.

(d)   *expressivity*

In textbook French most sentences are SV(O) in
form like (6.24a).   However, in colloquial French it
is common to find the patterns (6.24b) and (6.24c).

(6.24) a.   Jean a mangé le pain

             'John ate the bread'

        b.   Il a mangé le pain, Jean

             'He ate the bread, John'

        c.   Jean, il a mangé le pain

             'John, he ate the bread'

One could say that the word order in French is changing or that it has changed, if we are sure that only
the (a) pattern is traditional.   Hyman (1975:119,142)
sees the (b) pattern as involving what he calls an
afterthought.   It is true that patterns like (b)
could arise from afterthoughts, from a decision made
'in running' to clarify the reference of the pronoun,
but the frequency of the (b) patterns in French suggests that this is simply the new norm.   Its origin
may lie in afterthought or simply in a marked stylis-
tic variant.   The (c) pattern involves what presumably was a marked topicalization device, but this
topicalization has become or is becoming a new unmarked pattern.   In both cases an originally fancy pattern has lost its novelty and is becoming the plain
pattern.   These examples are interesting in that they
present a plausible path by which a language can
change from SVO (a) to VOS (b), or from SVO (a) to a
new SVO (c) with cross-referencing agreement.   One
imagines that the intonation break, still evident in
slow speech, could disappear in time and the preposed
and postposed phrases be incorporated in the sentence.

It is sometimes claimed that changes in word
order affect main clauses before subordinate ones.
If expressivity is often responsible for changes in
word order, this pattern is entirely to be expected.
There is much less scope for expressivity in subordinate clauses, which, for the most part, carry backgrounded information.

6.4   Word Order Change and the Word Order Type

6.4.1.   Vennemann and Lehmann

It seems to be generally agreed that the OV sequence can alter independently of the order in other
constructions and one gets the impression from reading the literature that in the transition from one
type to another it is the OV sequence that changes
first and exerts a drag-chain effect on the other con-

structions, drawing them into a new harmony with the relative order of O and V.   This seems to have been Lehmann's view at one time (1972).

Vennemann (1974a:352-54) allows for the possibility of the order in 'minor' constructions being affected while the OV sequence remains unaffected. He cites the case of Persian.   Persian, an Indo-European language, was originally SOV, at least according to majority opinion.   It began to drift towards the SVO type (on 'drift' see below), but then drifted back to SOV despite the influence from the prestigious superstratum language, Arabic, which was VSO. Vennemann sees it as significant that the verb position was more resistant to Arabic influence than some other constructions.   For example, in Old and Middle Persian the genitive could occur before or after the head noun.   In Modern Persian genitives always follow the head noun.   Vennemann attributes this ultimate settling for NG to Arabic influence, since in Classical Arabic, a consistent VSO language, NG is the norm.   Whether he is correct in his assumption or not, he is led to reject Lehmann's view that only a change of the basic verb position can bring about a type change, since he sees the possibility of a minor construction changing before OV and being the beginning of a new type.

Lehmann appears to have come over to this view. In the conclusion to his 'Syntactic Typology' (1978c: 400) he mentions that Japanese underwent VO influence from Chinese inasmuch as it adopted a VO type reflexive.   Its SOV order, however, remained unaffected. Lehmann's intention is to illustrate that inconsistency can be introduced through borrowing, but the example also appears to indicate that he now accepts that features of the type other than the order of V and O can change away from consistency and therefore presumably be the beginnings of a new consistency.

In Indo-European, of course, the order of O and V appears to have changed after other 'type changes' had taken place.   Latin, for example, seems to represent a stage between Indo-European with SOV and postpositions and Romance with SVO and prepositions.   It has SOV (though with a lot of freedom) and prepositions.   The 'older' Indo-European languages had postpositions (e.g. Sanskrit *upa* 'near', *pari* 'from') and these have been attributed to proto-Indo-European. Similarly SOV order has been attributed to the protolanguage.   Latin had prepositions (with an odd post-

position: *tenus* 'as far as') and basically SOV word
order though there was a lot of freedom.

I.E.		Latin		Romance
SOV	→	SOV	→	SVO
postpositions		prepositions		prepositions

The ascribing of postpositions to Indo-European is
not well founded.   The elements concerned may have
been ambipositions.   Nevertheless it is true that
prepositions developed in Latin before SVO did, the
latter only developing in the Romance descendants.

     Aitchison 1979 shows on the basis of a study of
Homeric Greek that in the change from OV (assumed for
proto-Indo-European) to VO (attested for Modern Greek)
the first VO feature to appear was probably main verb
+ infinitive complement, followed by prepositions and
postposed relative clauses, with other features such
as the VO order itself being established later.   She
believes that the change began with rightwards movements, such as placing infinitival complements after
the governing verb, which led to the destruction of
the OV constraint, and that eventually a new SVO
order arose.

     Both Vennemann and Lehmann clearly believe in
'drift'.   The term 'drift' goes back to Sapir:

     'The drift of a language is constituted by the
     unconscious selection on the part of its spea-
     kers of those individual variations that are
     cumulative in some special direction.   This
     direction may be inferred, in the main from
     the past history of the language.   In the long
     run any new feature of the drift becomes part
     and parcel of the common, accepted speech, but
     for a long time it may exist as a mere tenden-
     cy in the speech of a few, perhaps of a des-
     pised few.   As we look about us and observe
     current usage, it is not likely to occur to us
     that our language has a "slope", that the
     changes of the next few centuries are in a
     sense prefigured in certain obscure tendencies
     of the present and that these changes, when
     consummated, will be seen to be but continua-
     tions of changes that have been already effected.
     We feel rather that our language is practically
     a fixed system and that what slight changes are
     destined to take place in it are as likely to
     move in one direction as another.   The feeling

is fallacious.   Our very uncertainty as to the
impending details of change makes the eventual
consistency of their direction all the more
impressive'
          (1921:155 - quoted from 1949 reprint).

Sapir was concerned with three examples of drift
in English:

'The drift toward the abolition of most case
distinctions [(a)] and the correlative drift
toward position as an all-important grammatical
method [(b)] are accompanied, in a sense dominated, by the last of the three major drifts
that I have referred to.   This is the drift
toward the invariable word [(c)]'
                              (1921:168).

(a) and (b) of course are the germ of Vennemann's
theory that as an SOV language loses its case marking
through phonetic attrition it aquires SVO order.
Vennemann and Lehmann are concerned in particular
with the drift from one consistent type to another.

Vennemann believes that if a language becomes
inconsistent the principle of natural serialization
will operate to restore consistency.   The inconsistency could be the result of the introduction of SVO
order as the morphological distinction between S and
O is lost, the effect of foreign influence, or some
other factor.   The principle of natural serialization is held to be responsible for drifts toward consistency.

Lehmann seems to believe that if inconsistency
is introduced eventually consistency will again prevail:

'Study of the syntactic changes in the Indo-
European languages then indicates that when
languages change, patterns of the new type are
introduced and gradually become established,
while the language becomes increasingly consistent.   The direction of change may encounter specific interferences, as in the Indian
linguistic area...   In the Indo-European
family as a whole, especially in the Western
languages, the change from OV to VO represents
an internal drift.   In the languages of India
during the past two millenia on the other hand,
syntactic change represents the results of
external influence.   Yet in both groups con-

sistency eventually emerges'
                        (1978c:409).

It is normally accepted that human language is
one unified phenomenon and that it is in a constant
state of change, albeit at different rates at different periods. Under these assumptions, consistency
will eventually emerge at one time or another by accident. If one language type always changes into another, then all languages are, in a sense, in transition. The only significant claim that one can make
about consistent and inconsistent types is in terms of
stability. If we take a large sample of languages,
most of them not closely related to others in the
sample and not geographically contiguous with others
in the sample, then we catch a number of languages
each pursuing its own independent evolution at some
point in time. In such a sample the frequency of
the features and of the types must be a measure of
their diachronic stability. The long running types
are more likely to be caught in our net, the short
run types less likely to be caught. As we noted in
section 6.1, 40% of languages can be expected to be
consistent with their basic word order, if we include
the relative order of A and N. This means that in
its evolution (and we assume, until evidence is
adduced to the contrary, that language evolution is
largely cyclic) a language will be consistent only
about two fifths of the time (see also section 6.5.1.
(e)).

The consistent type is a real phenomenon. There
is something to be explained for, as we noted in section 6.1, the chances of a particular word order
occurring with one of the sets of features that we
consider as constituting consistency if there was only
a random relationship between them would be no more
than 1 in 64. However, the pressures that make for
consistency cannot be so strong that their effect is
noticeable in the short term. As has been pointed
out by several writers, English continues to go on
quite happily being AN when it *should* be NA. In
fact it is not clear what Lehmann means in the passage just quoted when he says that in Western Indo-
European languages consistency eventually emerges.
It certainly hasn't emerged yet, and if all that is
meant is that consistency will eventually emerge,
perhaps after millenia, perhaps after shifts in different directions, then the prophecy is nothing more
than an expression of faith in the cyclic nature of
change.

One problem with the notion of there being a drift to restore consistency is that inconsistency can be eradicated in two ways.   If for example relative clauses in a consistent SOV language 'leak' (to use another of Sapir's terms) from their position in front of their head to a postposed position, the language can achieve consistency either by going forward and switching over to VO *in toto* or by eradicating the innovation.   It would seem preferable to allow for both possibilities.   After all we are dealing with changes that take place over hundreds of years. It is not too hard to see that generations of speakers might be responsive to the pressure of some kind of analogy, but it is difficult to see how they can know which way their language is going.   If the analogical pressure was determined on a numerical basis, it is hard to see how a change of type could ever take place.   The innovation would always be at a disadvantage.

One could of course posit that there is a precedence involved, that basic word order changes before NP order.   Vennemann and Lehmann allow for new orders to be established besides the OV/VO order. This is required by the data, but perhaps it is generally true that the relative order of O and V changes first.   There is at least a superficial plausibility about such a proposal.   After all the order of S, O and V is subject to more expressive variation than is apparent in other constructions and variants are the stuff of which change is made.

Lehmann does believe there may be a precedence involved in the changes that can take place within the NP.   On the basis of English and French evidence he suggests that the order Rel N/N Rel is likely to change before GN/NG before AN/NA before limiting adjectives before adjective numerals (1978a:41) (see, however, Hawkins' views on the stability of GN/NG relative to AN/NA in the next section).

6.4.2.   Hawkins

Hawkins 1979 claims that Vennemann and Lehmann allow for a language to violate synchronic implicational universals in the course of transition from one type to another (see for instance pp.619-20).   This seems to us a remarkable claim.   It would be surprising if anyone held such a paradoxical position. Certainly Hawkins offers no example of such a view

from the work of Vennemann or Lehmann.   In fact he
gives references only to the dates of their papers,
not to specific pages.   If there is a synchronic
implicational universal of the form p ⊃ q, then a language with p cannot lose q and still keep p, and a
language with neither p nor q cannot acquire p unless
it acquires q first.   Some of Greenberg's universals
are statistical and those that are non-statistical are
of course always open to reformulation as statistical
universals in the light of new data.   The non-statistical ones are the most interesting if they can be
maintained.   To take an example, Greenberg's universal 3 states that languages with dominant VSO order
are always prepositional.   We can diagram this universal thus:

A VSO language cannot lose its prepositions without
violating the universal, nor can a language lacking
VSO and prepositions acquire VSO order without first
acquiring prepositions (or acquiring both simultaneously).

        Of the universals that are prominent in Venne-
mann and Lehmann (that is, the set quoted in section
6.1), only 3, the first part of 22, and 24 are non-
statistical.   Now 3, as we have just seen, rules out
the possibility of a language acquiring VSO order
without first acquiring prepositions.   Vennemann
1973 claims that VSO languages arise only from SVO
languages with prepositions (compare section 6.5.1.(f)).
Thus there is no violation of universal 3 in the
course of the proposed transition.   Rather the universal is taken as a constraint on possible transiti-
ons.   As for the other two non-statistical universals, we do not find that Vennemann or Lehmann posit
any specific transition that involves their violation,
nor do they appear to posit any violation of the other
non-statistical universals of Greenberg.

        Hawkins states that, at each stage of their his-
torical evolution, languages remain consistent with
synchronic universal implications (1979:620, 634).
This seems to us a tautology.   It is rather like saying that at every stage of their development children

must have heads, hearts and whatever other properties
are universal among humans.   Hawkins' motivation for
making such a statement seems to be a mistaken belief
that Vennemann and Lehmann have denied this obvious
truth.

Hawkins' positive contribution to the transition
problem is an interesting one.   Working on the basis
of Greenberg's universals and the data in Greenberg's
appendix, he puts forward a number of exceptionless
implicational universals by using multi-valued correlations.   We give, first of all, two examples of how
Hawkins derives his universals and then the complete
list of his universals.

Hawkins considers first of all SOV languages,
and using the data in Greenberg's appendix he notes
the following relationship between AN and GN:

SOV Prep	GN AN	Amharic	
Post	GN AN	numerous examples	
SOV Prep	GN NA	-	
Post	GN NA	numerous examples	
SOV Prep	NG NA	Persian, Iraqw, Khamti, Akkadian	
Post	NG NA	Sumerian, Elamite, Galla, Kanuri, Teda, Kamilaroi and other southeastern Australian languages	
SOV Prep	NG AN	-	
Post	NG AN	-	

This means that within SOV languages, AN ⊃ GN (since
there are no occurrences of AN NG).   The first implicational universal is therefore:

(I)   If a language has SOV word order, and if
       the adjective precedes the noun, then the
       genitive precedes the noun: i.e.
       SOV ⊃ (AN ⊃ GN).

Note that this universal allows the following
three states:

SOV	GN	AN
SOV	GN	NA
SOV	NG	NA

and thus like Greenberg's universal 3 involves a constraint on language change.   A harmonic SOV language
cannot postpose a genitive unless it first postposes
adjectives.   If, however, a harmonic SOV language
changes its word order to SVO, there is no constraint
on changing the order of G and N before changing the
order of A and N.

It is interesting to note in passing that the
languages in the minority categories are ones that
have been in contact with typologically different
languages.   Amharic has been in contact with Cushitic
languages such as Galla (SOV); Persian with Classical Arabic (VSO); Iraqw with Maasai (VSO); Khamti
with various Tibeto-Burman (SOV) languages; Akkadian
with Sumerian (SOV).   Kamilaroi, incidentally, seems
to be AN/NA on the limited evidence available in
Ridley 1875, probably the only source available to
Greenberg.   With reference to VSO languages Hawkins
notes the following data from Greenberg and extracts
his second implicational universal:

VSO Prep NG NA	numerous examples
Post NG NA	-
VSO Prep NG AN	Tagabili and probably other Philippine Austronesian languages; Kwakiutl, Quileute, Xinca
Post NG AN	-
VSO Prep GN AN	Milpa Alta Nahuatl
Post GN AN	Papago (Greenberg 1963:107)
VSO Prep GN NA	-
Post GN NA	-

(II)   If a language has VSO word order, and if
        the adjective follows the noun, then the
        genitive follows the noun: i.e.
        VSO ⊃ (NA ⊃ NG).

This is the mirror image of (I) and like (I) it
implies a constraint on change.   A VSO language,
according to (II), cannot change from NG to GN unless
it first (or simultaneously) changes NA to AN.   However, if it changes NA to AN, then the basic word
order cannot change to SOV since the result would be
the SOV NG AN type forbidden under (I).   Conversely

an SOV language that changes AN to NA is then con-
strained by (II) from changing its basic word order
to VSO, since the result would be VSO GN NA.

Our feeling is that these universals and the constraints on change that they imply are unlikely to
stand up to further sampling (a possibility that Hawkins would probably admit (1979:643)). Multi-valued
correlations of their nature cover a smaller number of
languages than single-valued ones and in fact some of
the occurring combinations of typological features are
represented by so few languages in Greenberg's sample
that one wonders about the significance of occurrence
versus non-occurrence in some of the cells. Presumably no one would posit causal connections between
the order of S, O and V and the order of A and N, G
and N, etc., so exceptions to these universals are to
be expected. However, we must admit that our own
investigations have so far failed to unearth such
exceptions. Rather they have shown that many languages are difficult to type because of indeterminacy
or lack of certain features and that the types and
Hawkins' universals are well founded. The other
universals are as follows:

(III)   If a language has PREP order, and if the
         adjective follows the noun, then the
         genitive follows the noun: i.e.
         PREP ⊃ (NA ⊃ NG).

This is similar to (II) but embraces not only
prepositional VSO languages but also prepositional
SVO and SOV languages. There is an SVO exception to
(III), Arapesh, as noted by Hawkins.

(IV)   If a language has POST order, and if the
        adjective precedes the noun, then the
        genitive precedes the noun: i.e.
        POST ⊃ (AN ⊃ GN).

(V)   If a language has PREP order, and if the
        genitive follows the noun, then the relative
        clause follows the noun: i.e.
        PREP ⊃ (NG ⊃ N REL).[8]

(VI)   If a language has PREP order and either VSO
        or SVO, then it does not have REL N: i.e.
        PREP & (VSO v SVO) ⊃ not REL N.

Mandarin appears to be an exception to this universal, though Hawkins does not mention it in this
context.

(VII)   If a language has PREP word order, and if
          the possessive adjective follows the noun,
          then the descriptive adjective follows the
          noun, i.e. PREP ⊃ (N + POSS ⊃ N + ADJ).

(VIII)   If a language has PREP word order, and if
          the demonstrative adjective follows the
          noun, then the descriptive adjective fol-
          lows the noun, i.e. PREP ⊃ (N + DEM ⊃ N +
          ADJ).

Hawkins tests his universals against data in the
earliest Indo-European language and finds that they
stand up.   His comment on this is curious:

> 'Evidently, impossible word order co-occurrence
> types, on current synchronic evidence, are also
> impossible in diachrony.   And whatever subse-
> quent word order changes these IE [Indo-Europe-
> an] languages underwent are NOT attributable to
> the re-introduction of universal consistency,
> because there was no violation to begin with.'
>   (1979:633).

Hawkins starts with a sample of languages (Greenberg's
sample), draws up implicational universals and then
tests these universals against the earliest Indo-
European languages.   There is no *diachrony* involved.
In sampling languages one can take any period one
likes.   In the nature of things any large sample is
going to be mostly a twentieth century sample.
Greenberg's sample, including his appendix, seems to
include Biblical Hebrew, Classical Arabic, Sumerian,
Elamite, etc. as well as twentieth century material
and there is no reason why it should not.   Hawkins
seems consistently confused about the nature of diachrony.   He talks about invoking 'exceptionless
synchronic implicational universals in a diachronic
context' (1979:641) and '...any synchronic explanation for current word order co-occurrences simultaneously explains the constraints on languages in evolution, given the consistency discovered between synchronic and diachronic data' (1979:644).   Data from
Hittite and Homeric Greek is not diachronic simply
because it is data from earlier centuries.   Diachrony refers to passage through time.   A diachronic
study involves the comparison of two or more different periods in the history of a language or language
family.   Moreover, the phrase 'languages in evolution' seems to imply a distinction between languages
in evolution and those not in evolution.   Surely no
one upon reflection would seriously make such a dis-

tinction except perhaps to point out that some languages at various points in their history change more rapidly than at other times.

Hawkins' motivation in testing his implicational universals against early Indo-European data is to demonstrate that these languages do not contain violations of the universals which could trigger word order changes that re-introduce consistency, but of course a language cannot violate a universal by definition - a violated universal is not a universal. Hawkins presumably fails to see this point, because he considers the early Indo-European data as in some separate diachronic category.

Hawkins presents a number of theoretical arguments against the 'violation of universals' approach which he imputes to Vennemann and Lehmann. As far as we can see they are arguments against a position that no one holds. We quote the first argument in full (1979:641):

> 'First, language universals are by definition exceptionless, or at least exceptions must be rare. If we invoke an exceptionless synchronic implicational universal in a diachronic context, we thus have no grounds for assuming the possibility of violation historically, given that the current synchronic evidence is supposed to be predicting diachronic developments. But even with statistical universals (as in the Lehmann-Vennemann theory), the likelihood of a violation arising historically can presumably be no greater than the (necessarily small) percentage of exceptions on synchronic grounds. Yet trigger-chain theories assume not just that universal violation may SOMETIMES occur: violation is their very cornerstone, and hence must ALWAYS occur. So the more exceptionless the synchronic universal statements are, the more implausible trigger-chain theories become. And even when exceptions exist, these theories will necessarily be at variance with the synchronic facts'.

In this statement Hawkins claims that the Lehmann-Vennemann theory is concerned (generally? exclusively?) with statistical universals. This is at variance with his earlier statement that Lehmann and Vennemann allow languages to break implicational universals of the form p ⊃ q, by acquiring p without acquiring q (1979:619). We agree with the first

part of this statement of course, providing one interprets it to mean that any synchronic state, attested
or hypothesized, must conform to universals.[9] As we
noted above Hawkins uses 'synchronic' and 'diachronic'
in a way that indicates he has misunderstood the
terms. He seems to think synchronic means 'present
day' or 'twentieth century' and diachronic means
'belonging to the past'. We do not share Hawkins'
view that trigger-chain theories are inherently im-
plausible. Even if we confine our study to the order of Post/Prep, Rel N/N Rel, GN/NG, AN/NA and
Std-Mkr-Adj/Adj-Mkr-Std in relation to basic word
order, we are dealing with a situation in which only
40% of languages are consistent. If we consider the
full range of orders of features covered by Greenberg,
then practically no language will ever be consistent.
Inconsistency seems to be normal but this does not
imply violation of universals. It simply involves
statistical universals.

    Hawkins (1979:642) notes that 'a crucial ingre-
dient of the Lehmann-Vennemann theory seems to be the
growth of SVO word order. But SVO is typologically
ambivalent. In both Greenberg's implications and
mine, VSO and SOV can be implicationally antecedent
properties, but not SVO. Nothing correlates with
SVO in a unique and principled way, and hence SVO has
no trigger potential in a historical context: there
are no SVO word order universals to violate'. Hawkins seems to imply some criticism of Lehmann and
Vennemann, but at least while they are dealing with
SOV → SVO they are not positing the violations of
universals that Hawkins imputes to them. It seems
to us that SVO can have some trigger potential.
Consider relative clauses for instance. It is highly marked for preposed relative clauses to occur in
an SVO language (as they do in Chinese) and one could
reasonably hold that a language with SVO and preposed
relatives would be under pressure to change, either
by introducing postposed relatives or by changing to
SOV. Of course it is one thing to talk glibly of
'trigger potential' and 'pressure to change' as we
are doing here, but it is quite another thing to specify the source of the 'trigger potential' or the
'pressure to change'. One has to consider whether
such a pressure is analogical, functional or the result of potential processing difficulties. As we
stated in section 6.2.5., we feel that the word order
type emerges largely as the product of certain types
of recurrent historical change (e.g. verbs becoming

adpositions).   We also allow for the fact that certain combinations of orders may present potential processing difficulties (e.g. preposed relative clauses
in VO languages).   We do not discount analogy entirely, certainly not analogies within the NP, but we
are suspicious of analogies between the verb and its
arguments and between a noun and its modifiers.   It
is probably true to say that the word order type cannot be accounted for on the basis of the evidence
adduced so far in historical studies.   What needs to
be done, among other things, is a massive survey of
recurrent diachronic changes to determine the frequency of certain types of change (e.g. V in a V-final
language becoming a postposition) and so to estimate
the likelihood of such changes being able to account
for the correlations.

Hawkins attempts to explain the word order type
in terms of a *Cross-Category Harmony* principle, which
is essentially an appeal to some kind of analogical
principle.   He makes an operator/operand distinction
in the same way Vennemann does but he rejects the
natural serialization principle.

In a later paper he points out (1980:198) that
Vennemann's Natural Serialization Principle if 'taken
literally' accounts for only two co-occurrence types
of the four operator-operand pairs listed in Greenberg's appendix:

operator-operand	*operand-operator*
OV	VO
AN	NA
GN	NG
N Post	Prep N

and that of the 24 logically possible co-occurrence
types only three in Greenberg's appendix satisfy the
Natural Serialization Principle,

VSO	NA	NG	Prep	19 languages
SVO	NA	NG	Prep	21 languages
SOV	AN	GN	Post	28 languages

These 68 languages represent only 47.89 per cent of
the total in the sample (142).   'These figures',
writes Hawkins, 'present an insuperable argument
against NSP as it stands.   To have over 50 per cent
counterexamples is unpalatable for any theory, even
one which proposes a historical explanation for syn-

chronic exceptions'.   However, we should point out
that 47.89% is significant compared with 1 in 24.
We should also note that these figures are all somewhat misleading in the light of the fact that they
ignore the minority word orders.

Hawkins points out that most languages regularly
have some operators on the noun to the left and some
to the right, some operators on the verb to the left
and some to the right, and so on.   The Cross-Category Harmony principle maintains that 'there is a
quantifiable preference, across languages, for the
ratio of preposed to postposed operators within one
operand category to generalize to other operand categories' (1979:645).   For example, a non-rigid verb-
final language with at least one operator regularly
following the verb is likely to have the order NA.
VSO languages have noun-initial NPs more consistently
than SVO languages in which the subject, an operator
on the verb, precedes the verb and at least one noun
operator precedes the noun, e.g. determiners or numerals.

Hawkins notes that there is a relationship between the frequency of the co-occurrence sub-types and
the number of deviations each exhibits from the predominant serialization.   Consider the following
assignment of operand and operator.

operand	*operator*
V	S,O
N	A,G
Post,Prep	N

If we consider the serialization defined by the operators on the verb and on the adposition, then we
find that there is a decline in the number of attested languages as A and G depart from this serialization - a natural enough distribution if languages tend
to order their operand/operator relations in parallel
ways (figures from fn.24, 1979:645).

SOV	Post	AN	GN	80 languages	(consistent)
SOV	Post	NA	GN	50 languages	(one deviation)
SOV	Post	NA	NG	11 languages	(two deviations)

Hawkins claims the trigger-chain theories of
Lehmann and Vennemann are invalid but he claims that
the Cross-Category Harmony principle expresses an analogical preference for like semantic elements, opera-

tors and operands, to be treated alike and that the
co-occurrence preferences defined by the principle
represent motivation for a language to remain within
or move toward a preferred type.   He says, 'if there
is an independently-motivated need for, e.g., the verb
to shift position, it is expected that this verb shift
will be matched by cross-categorical word order re-
adjustments to the extent predicted by the Cross-
Category Harmony principle' (1979:646).   This seems
to be a restatement of a trigger-chain theory and certainly a restatement, in perhaps an improved and more
accurate form, of the generalizations of Greenberg
and others about modifiers and modifieds.

It is clear that there is some parallelism between the ordering of S, O and V, the order within the
NP, and the position of the adposition.   If this is
an example of analogy it is an interesting one because
the terms that form the basis of the proposed analogy
are not alike in an obvious way.   If this is analogy,
then it is analogy at an abstract level (see also
remarks at the end of section 6.2.5.).   Hawkins sees
this and goes on to suggest that simplicity may motivate the analogical preference.   A language with
greater balance of operators and operands across
different categories can be described by more general
cross-categorical rules.   A disharmonic language
requires more category-particular ordering rules and
thus the grammar of such a language is more complex.
Compare Lehmann's principle, section 6.2.4..   We
should point out that in the absence of an explicitly
formulated grammar it remains unclear how a language
with a balance of disharmonies would be necessarily
simpler than one with an imbalance.   Suppose we have
an abstract rule specifying modifier-modified.   An
SOV language with NA will require one extra ordering
rule.   An SVO language with NA (and everything else
as in a classic SOV language) will require two extra
ordering rules (one for A, one for O), yet the latter
language will have greater cross-categorical balance.

6.5   On Explanation

Suppose John is a few minutes late for his date
with Mary and when she asks him why he is late he
replies, 'Oh, I left home in time, but I stopped at
the chemist's to get some toothpaste'.   We could say
that John has provided an *explanation* for his lateness, and in the situation we have described it is
most probable that Mary would accept John's reply as

a satisfactory and complete explanation.   However,
there is a sense in which John's explanation is far
from complete.   He did not *have to* buy toothpaste at
that particular time.   He did not *have to* buy toothpaste at any time.   He could have left home earlier
so that even after his visit to the pharmacy he could
still have arrived on time.

     In physics one encounters another type of expla-
nation.   There are general laws that hold true
across time and throughout the universe.   Take the
law of gravity, for instance.   According to this law
every body in the universe attracts every other body
with a force proportional to the product of their
masses and inversely proportional to the square of
the distance between them.   This law is held to explain the observation that bodies released above the
earth fall to the earth and to explain the orbiting
motion of the moon around the earth and so on.   In
this case the explanation consists of relating a particular instance to the general law.   If a bomb is
released from a B-52, we expect it to fall to earth.
The bomb is a body, the earth is a body - the law
must apply.   The law is completely general.   It
always applies.   It enables us to make predictions.

     The laws of physics can be said to provide strong
explanations - though in a curious way they are not
explanations at all, at least not in the sense that
John's explanation for his lateness is an explanation.
We chose gravity as an example because the way this
law was taught a generation ago made it seem like
magic.   There was regularity and predictability all
right, but how could one body influence another at a
distance without anything passing in between?   Explanation demands some plausible link between the proposed cause (gravity) and effect (motion).   More
recently physicists have proposed that bodies emit
gravitons, types of uncharged, massless particles
travelling at the speed of light.   The gravitational
pull of one body on another is via the field of these
particles.   This takes the magic out of gravity,
though it leaves it in the same category as most explanations of the universe.   We can appreciate the
regularity, but we are still left with the question
of why the laws of physics are as they are and not
some other way.   Why is the speed of light as it is
and not some other speed?

     In linguistics one does not find general laws.
One can not provide explanations of the law-of-gravity

type.   All one can hope for is an explanation in the
informal, everyday sense, in the sense of a contributing factor or probable contributing cause.   The
reason for this is simply that language is arbitrary
within the limits provided by physiology.   *Arbitrary*
means 'not determined' but it does not necessarily
imply 'random'.   The central point of this book is
that the distribution of case marking, word order,
etc. is anything but random.

Any non-randomness in the data represents something to be explained.   In the preceding chapters
and in the first part of this chapter we have considered the following:

(a)   the distribution of case marking for agent
       and patient

(b)   the distribution of basic word order

(c)   the relationship between agent/patient mar-
       king and basic word order

(d)   the strategies languages make use of in
       avoiding repetition of identical material in
       complex sentences

(e)   the relationship between strategies for rela-
       tivization and case marking and word order

(f)   the correlation between basic word order and
       a number of other features such as the pres-
       ence of postpositions as opposed to preposi-
       tions, these correlations giving rise to the
       basic word order type.

In the following sections we review attempts to
explain these distributions and correlations in the
context of explanation in general.   We shall consider
attempts at explanation under three headings:[10]

(i)   historical
(ii)   functional
(iii) physiological.

6.5.1.   History and Explanation

It has been common practice in linguistics to
offer historical explanations.   For instance, an
unmotivated rule is explained by reference to an earlier stage in which the rule is motivated.   The
origin of various features of languages is explained
in terms of a derivation from some other features
that existed earlier, as for instance in Vennemann's

proposal (discussed in (b) below) that causative
affixes derive from earlier free verbs (1973:21-22).
Resemblances between languages are explained in terms
of a common origin, as in Sir William Jones' much
quoted hypothesis concerning the resemblances between
Greek, Latin and Sanskrit.

Besides explanations for the presence of features within a language and for the presence of
features held in common by a number of languages,
there have also been theories about the nature of
change itself: theories about what actuates change,
about whether change is unidirectional or cyclic,
about what is a possible change, and how types
emerge.

(a)   *The Origin of Unmotivated Rules*

Various features of language can be 'explained'
historically, particularly arbitrary features.   For
example, in Italian adverbs may be formed by adding
the suffix -*mente* to the feminine form of the adjective, at least for those adjectives that have a masculine in -*o* and a feminine in -*a*.   From the point
of view of Italian grammar the fact that -*mente* is
added to the *feminine* is arbitrary.   There is an
historical explanation to the effect that adverbs in
-*mente* derive from Latin phrases of the form adj-
ablative case + *mens* (='mind')-ablative.   Thus in
Latin one would have found phrases such as *certā
mente*, literally, 'with a certain mind', the ablative
case indicating manner.   Now since the Latin word
mens was feminine and since adjectives showed concord
with nouns in number, case and gender, adjectives in
these phrases were feminine.   The word *mens* (in
these phrases, not generally) lost its sense of 'mind'
and the phrases were lexicalized as adverbs, though
the formation of such adverbs is still productive.
In Italian an adverb such as *certamente* 'certainly'
derives historically from *certā mente* and the fact
that the feminine of the adjective is used reflects
the origin of the phrase.   To anyone familiar with
the workings of language, this explanation is a
satisfactory one in the sense that John's toothpaste
explanation is satisfactory.   However, it is not a
strong explanation.   It leaves unanswered such
questions as 'Why is there grammatical gender?   Why
was *mens* feminine?   Why is there concord?   Why did
mens lose its lexical meaning in these phrases?   Why
was *mens* the word to be chosen for these manner phrases?   And so on and so on.   An experienced linguist

can see that semantic bleaching as occurred in the case of *mens* is a recurrent phenomenon.   He can see that the choice of a word meaning 'mind' for manner phrases has an indirect parallel with the use of *lic* 'body' in Old English (thus *quickly* derives from *cwic-lice* 'with a quick body').   The experienced linguist is then in the same position with respect to the explanation as Mary is vis-à-vis the toothpaste. If Mary accepts John's explanation as satisfactory, it is probably because she accepts that people use toothpaste, that there is a chemist on the route from John's and so on.

(b)   *The Origin of Features*

Vennemann (1973:21-22) seeks to explain causative verb formation in diachronic terms.   He considers a hypothetical stage in an SOV language in which there is a lexical verb meaning 'cause'.   Now this verb will take a clausal object yielding a complex sentence of the following form (compare (6.22) above).

(6.25)

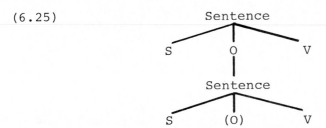

Vennemann suggests that phonological change will turn the upper verb (i.e. the causal verb) into an enclitic and eventually into a suffix.   The causal verb would also have to change in meaning from 'cause' or 'make' or whatever to that meaning that can only be described by a comparison of simple verbs and their causative equivalents.   For example, in Turkish there is a causative verb suffix -*dir*.   If this is added to *öl* 'die' the result is *öldür* 'kill', not 'cause to die'.   We take for granted that linguists accept that this kind of development is a recurrent phenomenon, but it is not clear that a description of the origin of causative verbs explains why they exist.

The example is of some relevance to the themes of the present book since Vennemann suggests that an SVO language like English could not develop causative verbs because the higher and lower verbs would not be contiguous and therefore could not be merged into a complex verb.

(6.26)

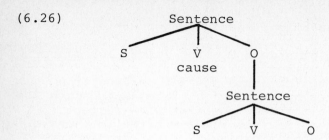

In fact it is only in an SOV language or a VOS one
that the higher and lower verbs would be contiguous.
This suggests that causatives should be found in SOV
and VOS languages, but not in the other types, except
where they are relics of an earlier SOV or VOS period
(as with English *fall/fell*, etc.).   Casual observation suggests that there is indeed a correlation between SOV and the presence of causatives on the one
hand and SVO and the absence of causatives on the
other.   Assuming this is true, can we say that Vennemann's theory of the origin of causatives explains
the correlation?   Briefly, the answer is no.   Consider the following points:

(i)   What is to be explained is a correlation,
        and a correlation implies leakage.   This
        means that a strong explanation is inappli-
        cable.   There is no simple causal connec-
        tion between p and q;   the presence of p is
        not a necessary and sufficient condition
        for the appearance of q.   A language can
        be SOV or VOS and not have a morphological
        causative, and a language can have one of
        the other possible word orders and have a
        morphological causative.

        The leakage can be attributed to the
        presence of relic features.   In the Bantu
        languages, which are SVO, there are produc-
        tive causative suffixes, but the presence
        of these and other suffixes suggests the
        Bantu languages were once SOV.   Similarly,
        a VOS language could arise from an SVO lan-
        guage by the introduction of a topic-to-
        the-right rule and the 'young' VOS language
        could lack a morphological causative because
        of its recent origin in another word order
        type.

(ii)   There is an alternative explanation for part
        of the correlation.   SVO languages tend to

be analytic.   It will be recalled that
Vennemann in the paper where he discusses
the origin of causatives (1973) suggests
that SVO is the natural order for a language without a morphological means of
distinguishing agent and patient.   If SVO
languages tend to be languages going through
a relatively analytic phase, it may be that
the low frequency of causatives is a reflection of their general analytic character.

(iii)   One should not attribute the formation of
morphological causatives solely to the
operation of phonetic attrition on a causative verb that is adjacent to an embedded
lexical verb.   In French and Italian, for
example, a verb that basically means 'make'
or 'do' is used to form causatives.   Since
these are SVO languages the causative verb
will not occur next to the embedded verb
according to Vennemann's schema (6.26).
However, both these languages exhibit a
construction in which the order of the
'embedded clause' is verb-first and therefore the 'lower' verb adjacent to the causative.   Looking at it historically one
can say the embedded clause has been rearra-
nged so that the governing verb and governed
verb come together.   Our example is from
Italian.

(6.27)   Faccio   parlare   Maria   di   questo

         I:make   speak   Mary   of   this

         'I make Mary talk about this'

It might be objected that this is a syntactic causative not a morphological one, but
there are reasons to believe *fare* + infinitive is being treated as one verb.   Clitic
pronouns representing a direct or indirect
object normally precede the verb.   With
fare + infinitive, clitic pronouns, representing the agent or patient of the 'lower'
verb, precede *fare*.

(6.28)   Gli-e-la   faccio   scrivere

         him:to-lig-it   I:make   write

         'I make him write it'

The important point is that a causative verb
and a verb dependent on it can be contiguous
in an SVO language, and therefore probably
in all word order types. These contiguous
verbs can then fall victim to the forces of
phonetic attrition, but note that a language
can be *motivated* to form causatives. Causatives do not arise simply as an accident
resulting from the operation of phonetic
factors.

The process of *grammaticalization* whereby function morphemes arise from lexical items via a process
of semantic bleaching with or without phonetic attrition is a recurrent phenomenon, but neither a description of this process nor the labelling of a particular instance as an example of the general type constitutes an explanation for its occurrence. One
could seek to provide an explanation for grammaticalization in terms of functional utility and one could
seek to provide an explanation for the fact that
phonetic attrition attacks some types of morpheme
more than others in terms of the placement of stress.
There is a language-general principle that the pattern of stresses is determined on the basis of con-
tentive versus relational elements and within conten-
tives according to the demands of the thematic structure. Phrase stress is not entirely arbitrary but
rather it is iconically motivated (the stresses tend
to mirror the importance of the words in the message)
and indeed may be varied over a continuous scale to
reflect attitude.

(c)   *Resemblances between Languages*

Resemblances between languages are often explained as being due to a common origin. English and
German are obviously similar in grammar and vocabu-
lary, more similar 'than could possibly have been
produced by accident'. The explanation for this
similarity is well known. English and German are
both descendants of one and the same language. However, we cannot explain why some words have changed
their meaning in one language but not the other
(*hound/Hund*) while other words have retained the common meaning, why particular verbs have become weak in
one language and not the other (*helfen* is strong in
German, but the English cognate, *help*, has joined the
weak class), and so on. The course of language
change is not determined. We cannot make predictions. All we can do is note recurrent tendencies.

Genetic connections between languages have an obvious significance in language typology. In an effort to ascertain just what the character of language is we try to eliminate genetic factors. We try to sample data from a large number of languages between which there is no known genetic connection. Of course there is always the possibility that languages thought to be genetically distinct are in fact related at some great time depth and indeed a theory of the monogenesis of language is as plausible as any alternative. However, this need not worry us unduly. What we know of the rate of language change suggests that there are unlikely to be resemblances due to common origins going back to time depths measured in tens of thousands of years.

Resemblances between languages may of course be due to contact, either direct or indirect. Any attempt at explaining resemblances as being due to contact is essentially an historical explanation. As with genetically based explanations, explanations in terms of contact are *post hoc*. We cannot lay down 'laws of language contact' - we can only note that there is a rough scale of 'borrowability' running from lexical items (especially words for artifacts, fauna and flora) to bound monophonemic morphemes with an abstract function or functions. We can also make some rather general and uninteresting predictions about the likely direction of borrowing.

As work on language contact continues, it is becoming clear that practically any feature of language can be borrowed (Masica 1976, Heath 1978a). Moreover, convergence can cover such large areas that out of a total of 4 or 5 thousand languages in the world one can probably only find a few score that are independent genetically and free from 'contamination' one by the other (see also (e) below where this point arises).

A particular difficulty for the typologist trying to obtain a sample free from the effects of common genetic inheritance and borrowing is the influence of languages of international communication such as English. The English passive, for instance, seems to be being imitated in Chinese and southeast Asia (with French perhaps having had some influence in Indo-China). On the mainland the scope of the adversative passive seems to have been extended to cover the range of the English passive, while in Malay and Indonesian, the passive, which was formerly

used in a manner analogous to the patient-topic construction in Tagalog, now tends to be the translational equivalent of the English passive.   If this sort
of influence is typical, and one suspects it is, the
long term effect is going to be widespread convergence
towards the international languages.

(d)   *Actuation*

There has been a great deal of discussion in the
literature about the causes of change or the actuation of change.   Most of this is unsatisfactory
since it seeks the cause of change within language
itself.   While we admit that a language may make a
therapeutic change to remedy a problem (e.g. a problem brought about by the operation of blind phonetic
processes) we hold that it is hardly worth seeking
the cause of change within language.   After all if
language is operating at one particular point in time
it does not have to change to operate successfully at
a later point in time.   However, it is possible that
the structure of a language can exert pressure in a
certain direction.   For instance, suppose heterorganic nasal stop sequences change to homorganic ones,
e.g. nb > mb, ng > ŋg.   It cannot be that the difficulty of producing heterorganic sequences caused the
change, since the heterorganic sequences existed for
some time prior to the change.   It could be, however,
that it is true that homorganic nasal-stop sequences
are easier to pronounce, as is often supposed, and
that this provided some pressure for change to proceed in the direction that it did.   It could be that
the ease of producing homorganic sequences provided
the source of the first of such sequences and that
for some reason outside the language system these
sequences were introduced generally.   It is characteristic of phonetic change that it runs in certain
wellknown directions, most changes being reductive
in nature i.e. involving assimilation, weakening or
loss.   The language can provide the stimulus to
change and to a large extent provide the direction of
change, but it cannot be the cause of change.   The
cause must lie outside the system.   It is presumably
social and broadly speaking must be determined by
different social values being placed on variants
arising within the system (see for instance Labov
1977).

The fact that most phonetic change is reductive
does not imply unidirectional change.   For example,
if heterorganic nasal-stop clusters become homorganic,

new heterorganic clusters can arise through new juxta-
positions of morphemes and through loss of interven-
ing vowels (CV̊nVbV > CV̊nbV).

In the case of basic word order, variants are
the norm.   As we suggested in section 6.3.2. (d) it
is likely that when basic word order changes it changes via an expressive variant becoming the new norm.
Lightfoot (1979:384) sees expressivity as a cause of
syntactic change.

> 'A second kind of extra-grammatical cause of
> syntactic change is what one might term "ex-
> pressivity".   This would include the intro-
> duction of novel forms for stylistic effect,
> such as 'topicalized' sentences which are com-
> mon in certain English dialects, where a NP
> occurs in a marked position with heavy stress:
> *Mingus, she heard, but not Miles*.   Similarly,
> 'dislocation' sentences would fall under the
> same rubric: *Mingus, I heard him* and *he played
> cool, Miles*.   These forms are still regarded
> as novel in English and as having a distinct
> stylistic force;   they are common in Yorkshire
> dialects and with British football commenta-
> tors.[11]   However, such forms characteristically
> become bleached and lose their novelty value
> as they become commonly used.   This can be
> illustrated with the parallel dislocation sen-
> tences in French: *Pierre, je le connais* and
> *je le connais, Pierre* were originally stylist-
> ically marked alternants of *je connais Pierre*
> but now they have lost much of their special
> force and have become relatively unmarked
> construction-types, to the point that in simple,
> affirmative main clauses they are the norm and
> the former unmarked type, *je connais Pierre*,
> is vanishingly rare'.

We agree with Lightfoot's characterization of expressivity as a *cause* of change, given Lightfoot's own
admission (p.374) that change is not determined and
that what he calls a cause is but a 'causal factor'.
Lightfoot's description of expressivity refers to
novelty for effect and loss of novelty through common
use.   Both these factors play a part in human behaviour generally, particularly in dress, hair style,
use of make-up and so on.   Why novelty should be
attractive is a question for psychologists to answer.
It is not particular to language use.   Loss of novelty through common use requires no explanation.   Note
that neither in language nor in dress can the form of

the new variant or the time of its appearance be predicted.   Some cynics may point out that in Western
society novelty in dress is consciously promoted by
those with a vested interest in obsolescence, but of
course language is not free from the influence of
Madison Avenue either.   In general, however, language innovation is presumably a spontaneous folk phenomenon.

(e)   *Unidirectional or Cyclic*

As we stated in section 6.4.2. data for typological study can be drawn from any language taken *at
any period of time*.   In our view it makes no difference whether we include Ancient Greek or Modern Greek.
This view is based of course on the assumption that
Language is essentially an unchanging phenomenon, and
that change in individual languages is in the long
term cyclic.   Historical reconstruction is only
possible on the assumption that languages from the
past are based on the same principles as those attested in the present.   We allow of course for language
evolution, but we make the methodological assumption
that language is essentially the same across time and
space.   We assume that language evolution lies beyond
the period for which we attempt reconstruction.

Recently this assumption has been challenged, at
least on one point, by Givón (1979:271-309).   He
points out that 'the majority of language families
known to us exhibit SOV syntax, and so far as we can
tell they were always SOV' (p.275).   He claims that
the 'overwhelming majority of languages and language
families which do not show actual SOV syntax currently, can be nevertheless reconstructed via internal
and comparative methods back to an earlier SOV stage'
(p.275).   Indo-European would be an example of a
language family that was once SOV, at least according
to the most widely held but not unchallenged theory
(Lehmann 1974, Friedrich 1975), but which is now represented predominantly by SVO languages.   Givón
believes that SOV languages were once much more widespread than they are now.   In fact he gives the
impression that he believes the SOV type was once
universal though he does not state this directly.
He states that SOV is the oldest word-order that can
be reconstructed in human language and that there is
a one-way drift from SOV, more particularly, a common
drift SOV > VSO > SVO and a restricted drift SOV >
VSO > VOS.   This drift, according to Givón, is motivated primarily by '*discourse-pragmatic*' considera-

tions: 'the SOV word-order, though seemingly the
earliest attested in human language, is not the one
most *compatible* with the currently extant discourse-
pragmatic evolutionary stage of human language'
(p.276).

There is some evidence for, and some hypotheses
about, change towards SOV but Givón dismisses most of
these as being motivated by massive substratum contact.[12] He admits that there are some reports of a
partial natural drift towards SOV where the motivation seems to be internal, e.g. the *bǎ* construction
in Mandarin (see 6.23)).

Our sample of 100 languages in chapter three contains 41 SOV languages, so there is a preponderance
of this order to be explained anyway.   Givón may be
correct in suggesting that SOV languages were once
more widespread, but we would like to see the evidence for reconstructed word orders spelled out.   We
would like to see how much weight is placed on the
evidence of the position of bound pronominal forms
(which we consider very poor evidence) and how much
on the evidence of the position of verbal affixes
(which we consider promising evidence) - see remarks
in section 6.3.1.   Givón's view is salutary in that
it makes us reconsider the validity of our sample of
100 languages.   We have to admit that the high SVO
figure is based mainly on three areas: Europe,
southern Africa and southeast Asia.   In each of
these areas genetic and areal factors may have boosted the SVO figures to give a skewed distribution and
it is probably true that we have sampled a little
generously in these areas.   Europe contains a number
of SVO descendants of Indo-European (SOV), all genetically related and not free from the direct and
indirect influence of one another, and perhaps exerting influence on the westernmost Uralic languages.
Southern Africa contains a large number of descendants of proto-Bantu or a more remote proto-Congo-
Kordofanian, a language likely to have been SOV on
the evidence of verb suffixation.   Even allowing for
areal pressures helping to spread SVO, it is obvious
that a change from SOV to SVO in any ancestral stage
rich in offspring would have boosted SVO considerably.   In southeast Asia, the Mon-Khmer (or Khmer-
Nicobarese) branch of Austro-Asiatic, Sinitic, Tai
and Austronesian languages are thought to be genetically distinct, though Tai and Austronesian may be
ultimately related (Benedict 1975).   The languages
of China, Indo-China and Thailand show obvious

features of convergence at all levels and Malay-
Indonesian may owe something of its character to in-
fluences from the mainland to the north.   The languages of the area are SVO, but there is no evidence
of earlier OV stages.   The Khmer languages have prefixing morphology suggesting that they have not been
OV within a reconstructable period.   The Tai languages are predominantly analytic and the only bound
forms are transparently new, so there is no evidence
for OV in the morphology.   Mandarin has both SVO and
SOV orders, but the latter is a comparative innovation (Li & Thompson 1974b).   Some other groups whose
genetic affiliation is in doubt, such as the Miao-Yao,
are also analytic SVO types.   The Indonesian languages are SVO and fairly closely related to the other
Austronesian languages, which are predominantly verb-
first.   The verb morphology is partly prefixal and
partly suffixal.[13] There is no clear evidence of an
earlier OV stage.   All in all it seems that there is
no evidence that a survey of east and southeast Asia
taken at an earlier period would have produced more
OV examples and fewer VO.

However, looking at the world as a whole we
allow that a sample taken some thousands of years ago
might have yielded more SOV and fewer SVO languages,
but it remains uncertain whether such a sample would
not have contained relics of earlier SVO languages
(and other word order types).   It could be that
change is indeed cyclic but that samples taken at any
one time tend to be biased because of the wide sprea-
ding of language families and the far reaching effect
of convergence whether through superstratum languages
or chains of contact.

Givón believes that there was an evolution in
word order from (a) O only, to (b) AO, to (c) AOV.
We will not recapitulate in detail his tenuous arguments supporting this thesis, arguments based on
communication among canines and pongids and on the
acquisition of language by humans.   Briefly his argument is as follows.   He envisages an initial stage
in the phylogeny of human language in which the agent
is not specified because its identity is obvious.
Then follows a second stage that allows specification
of agents.   In the third stage the verb is added.
Apparently, in Givón's view, the verb appears after
the AO sequence because it evolved later in time.

Givón points out that 'human language tends to
make the human-agent the most likely topic-theme of

discourse (1979:303) and the agent-topic was eventually syntacticized into a subject. It is unfortunate that Givón omits to discuss ergative languages in this context since they appear to have syntacticized the patient-topic as we saw in chapter two, and what is more, ergative languages have been held to represent an older or more primitive type in certain stadial theories of language evolution (see note on Klimov below).

A serious weakness in Givón's theory is his failure to *account* for the one-way drift from SOV, assuming there is such a drift. He claims that 'whatever evidence we have about the factors motivating the drift from SOV to VSO and SVO...suggest that the factors are *discourse-pragmatic* in nature, involving various topicalization and focusing movement rules. The AGENT-OBJECT-VERB may have been the most suitable word-order at the stage of monopropositional discourse, but somehow it seems that either SVO or V-first are more compatible with topic-oriented, multi-propositional discourse' (p.309). We should point out first of all (see also section 3.2) that there is really very little evidence for saying VSO is widespread. Secondly, Givón ignores Vennemann's hypothesis that SVO is functionally motivated in a language lacking a morphological means of distinguishing agent and patient (see section 3.4). In fact Vennemann claims that SOV is natural (1973:28), but that SVO is natural in the absence of case marking (see also section 6.3.2.). Vennemann concurs with what we believe is the dominant view, namely that language change is cyclic. Thirdly, there is a disturbing notion lurking in Givón's writing that some extant languages may be at a more primitive stage of evolution than others.

Givón sees a social evolution from a *society of intimates*, where all generic information is shared, to a *society of strangers*. The *society of intimates* seems to embrace animals and 'early man's immediate ancestors'; the *society of strangers* is modern, urban society. It is not made absolutely clear, but Givón does seem to lump tribal societies with 'early man's immediate ancestors'. He points out that the move towards the *society of strangers* is a *relative* matter 'and can be observed even now as traditional societies are dissolved under the impact of the urban civilization. But urban civilizations of considerable size must be postulated in certain areas (Meso-America, Mesopotamia, Egypt, India and China) as far

back as perhaps 9000 B.C.   The current variant merely represents the apex of a development which began
long ago' (p.297).   This seems to equate civilization with the society of strangers and hence suggests
a correlation between monopropositional discourse
(for which SOV is most suitable) and uncivilized
tribes on the one hand and multipropositional discourse (for which SVO or VSO is supposed to be more
suitable) and civilization on the other.   Our sus-
picions that indeed this is what Givón is saying are
confirmed by a passage on co-ordination versus subordination (p.298):

> 'Furthermore, there are some languages extant
> to this day - all in preindustrial, illiterate
> societies with relatively small, homogeneous
> social units - where one could demonstrate that
> subordination does not really exist, and that
> the complexity of discourse-narrative is still
> achieved via "chaining" or co-ordination,
> albeit with an evolved discourse function mor-
> phology (Thurman 1978)'.

One is naturally suspicious of claims that languages lack subordination.   Givón does not cite specific examples;   the Thurman reference is to a
U.C.L.A. master's thesis on Chuave.   Obviously one
cannot conclude that subordination does not exist
from the absence of evidence in a grammar.   One
needs a specific report that the phenomenon does not
exist from an investigator who has studied a language
in depth.   Even if one is satisfied that a language
lacks subordination, one cannot be sure that it did
not exist at some stage ancestral to the attested
stage.   Givón could perhaps attempt to show that
lack of subordination exists only among illiterate
societies, but we feel that the phenomenon is probably so rare and the number of literate languages so
small that one could not adduce convincing figures.
One fact we can be sure of is that some preindustrial
societies had languages that exhibited a number of
different kinds of subordination, with the possibility of embedding one type of subordinate within
another.   This is true of the Australian languages
Dyirbal, Kalkatungu, Walbiri and probably many others,
though not all.   Heath (1980b:90) reports that Warndarang and a number of other northern Australian languages had rather limited possibilities for subordination.   If subordination represents an advance in
the phylogenetic evolution of language correlated
with an increase in 'cognitive capacity and sociocul-

tural complexity' one wonders how it develops in the language of one tribe of hunter-gatherers and passes a neighbouring tribe by. Is it that hunter-gatherers are on the threshold of a stage of sociocultural complexity, so that a development in subordination is triggered off here and there? The idea does not seem worth pursuing. If a language lacks subordination, we can never be certain it did not have it at an earlier stage.

In informal speech we may make less use of some syntactic devices and one could imagine that in a society of intimates some construction types would be required so little as not to evolve, or if present to be so little used in performance as to pass from competence. Nevertheless one should be wary of attributing some lacuna to a language not one's own. In sum we remain sceptical about claims for language evolution over the recent past.

Klimov 1973 is another who has advanced a theory of unidirectional development in language. He has suggested that ergative languages represent a stage, though not a necessary stage, in the evolution of accusative languages from active languages. The only typological developments allowable in his schema are active > ergative, ergative > accusative and active > accusative.

active > (ergative) > accusative

It is difficult to say much about diachronic developments involving active languages as data is hard to come by. As for ergative languages, there are some well-substantiated hypotheses about developments from ergative to accusative (e.g. Georgian and Mingrelian (S. Anderson 1977), Lardil and Ngarluma[14]), but there are also hypotheses and data suggesting a development from accusative to ergative. We can trace the evolution of the ergative construction from the passive of an accusative system in the Indo-Iranian languages (though admittedly this was confined to the perfect and/or past) and we have Sandra Chung's plausible hypothesis, based on comparative data, for the evolution of the passive into an ergative in some Polynesian languages (e.g. Samoan (Chung 1977, 1978)).

(f)   *Possible Changes*

In phonology it has long been recognized that some changes are possible (e.g. s → h) while others are unlikely and perhaps impossible (h → s).

In the previous section we noted that Givón proposed that the only possible path for change in word
order for a language developing free from contact was
from SOV.   Similarly we noted that Klimov had proposed that agent/patient marking could proceed only
from active to accusative either directly or via an
intermediate ergative stage.   Vennemann 1973 has
proposed the following schema for possible changes in
basic word order (FWO = Free Word Order):

(6.29)

According to him an SOV language becomes SVO when the
case system is lost through phonetic attrition, the
new pattern being functionally motivated since it
allows the NP NP V sequences arising from object
fronting to be unambiguously interpreted.   An SVO
language can develop a new case system, in which
state it can become FWO, or it can become VSO.
Vennemann constructs the schema on the basis of various types of evidence for earlier orders at unattested stages.   He uses the position of bound pronominal forms as evidence for the position occupied by
the corresponding noun phrase at an earlier period,
but as we have pointed out twice already, this evidence is unreliable.   Another type of argument runs
like this.   While a few SVO languages have preposed
relative clauses as relics from their SOV days, no
VSO language has a preposed relative because 'these
constructions have long since died out by the time
the SVO language is ready to become VSO' (p.35).
Vennemann sees SVO as the only possible immediate
ancestor for VSO.

We will not list all Vennemann's arguments
because the schema can be shown to be at least dubious if not inadequate by reference to data such as
the following:

  (i)   A number of languages seem to be basically
        SOV but to exhibit a good deal of freedom.
        This freedom is not surprising given that
        SOV languages tend to mark the agent/patient
        distinction (see section 3.4).   In Walbiri
        (Hale 1967) SOV order is found in subordi-
        nate clauses, but there is a great deal of
        freedom in independent clauses.   It is a
        general property of languages that they have

stricter word order in subordinate clauses
than in main clauses.   This is true of
Japanese and Turkish for instance.   The
reason seems to be clear enough.   There
is a motivation to focus various parts of
a main clause, but subordinate clauses
represent backgrounded information and
there is usually no motivation to highlight
particular words.[15]

Vennemann does not make it clear how an
FWO language is defined.   Walbiri looks
like a good candidate and the fact that subordinate clauses are SOV suggests that perhaps this is the older order, if any order
can be reconstructed as an 'older' one.
Hale takes SOV to be the basic order synchronically.   Bound pronouns in Walbiri typically appear as enclitics to the first constituent of the clause and do not appear in
any of the positions Vennemann allows for.
In fact Walbiri is a language that tells
against the Vennemann view that pronominal
positions reflect earlier noun phrase positions (see also section 6.3.1.).   In the
face of languages like Walbiri, it would seem
unwise not to allow SOV → FWO.

(ii)   The $b\check{a}$ construction in Mandarin suggests SVO
may be able to become SOV directly, though
admittedly this is not an example of a whole-
scale change of order (see example (6.23))
but only of a change in one construction.

(iii) The Celtic languages seem to have been VSO
for a considerable period.   There is no
evidence for an SVO stage between SOV (assumed for proto-Indo-European) and VSO, though
one cannot be sure that such a stage never
existed.

(iv)   Vennemann's schema is based on Greenberg 1963
and takes no account of VOS, OSV and OVS
languages.

(g)   *Emergence of the Type*

In discussing the word order type we gave some
emphasis to an historical explanation for the phenomenon, pointing out that some correlations reflected
the outcome of recurrent historical trends, e.g.
heads of adpositional phrases becoming genitive markers (see section 6.2.2.).   This seems to us a satis-

factory partial explanation (see also the summary in section 6.2.5.), but it must be remembered that it simply moves the burden of explanation to another sphere.   We still have to explain the recurrent historical trends.

Comrie has suggested that the ergative type of language derives historically from accusative languages via loss of the active voice (Comrie 1976). This origin is then held to account for features of the ergative type, such as the homophony between the ergative marker and an oblique case (this being the earlier marker of a passive agent) and the absence of a passive.   This historical explanation accounts for features of the ergative type, but only in terms of an historical development itself demanding explanation.   We should add that it is possible to account for the ergative type in another way.   The characteristic absence of the passive in ergative languages can be attributed to the fact that it would have little function in a language in which O is the grammaticalized topic.   The homophony between the marker for A and for say INSTRUMENT or LOCATION may simply reflect a semantic entity embracing A and INSTRUMENT or whatever.

6.5.2.   Functional Explanation

Functional explanations are familiar in historical phonology.   Consider, for instance, Martinet's notion that a would-be merger in a phonological system is likely to be inhibited if it carries a high functional load.   The idea behind this claim is that language serves the function of enabling human beings to communicate and that language (or language users) can adopt prophylactic measures to prevent it becoming dysfunctional.   As far as we know no serious investigator has claimed that a language has ever become dysfunctional, but languages do seem to allow mergers that involve large scale oppositions.   We feel that by and large phonological change operates blindly, i.e. without regard to the consequences for the communicative function of language, and that dysfunction is hardly ever a real threat since it is unlikely that all the blind changes are going to conspire to ruin a system of communication.   It would be difficult for changes to ruin a system.   There is after all a lot of redundancy in language.

The notion that language has the function of enabling human beings to communicate arises in connection with the question of case marking and word order raised in chapters two and three.   The basic idea we examined was that languages must have case marking or a principle of word order to distinguish the agent from the patient.   This theory could be disproved if a language were found which had neither.   In the nature of things it is difficult to demonstrate conclusively that a language has neither, unless of course the language in question is one in which a number of investigators have a native or native-like competence.   We mentioned the case of Thailand Lisu in chapter three (section 3.4).   It is a language for which we have at present only one source, the writings of E. Hope (1974, 1976) - see also the report in Li & Thompson 1976a.   However, in cases like these we can never be sure that there is not some unreported feature that enables agent and patient to be distinguished.   Even in what has been reported there is some suggestion of a principle that might serve to distinguish agent and patient, viz. the topicalization hierarchy (see (3.75)).

We support the functionally based theory that a language must have a means of distinguishing agents from patients.   We predict that no natural language will lack some means of making such a distinction. It may not be true to say that the sole function of language is to communicate (Chomsky 1980:230), nor even that communication is *the* most important function of language, but it is true that communication is *an* important function of language.

The discriminatory theory of the distribution of agent/patient case marking is functional in nature in that it suggests that, if a language does not mark the distinction across the board, it will mark the distinction where it is most needed to distinguish the agent and patient (see section 2.8.2.).   The fact that hardly any languages mark both the agent and the patient and the fact that most languages do not mark either the agent or the patient across the board could be taken as evidence to support this theory.   The theory should not be pressed too far. Some languages have a system of agent/patient marking and rules of word order both of which are capable of distinguishing the agent from the patient.   Language is certainly not contrived to fulfill functions by using minimal means.   There is often redundancy and of course redundancy can be seen as functional in that the more redundancy the better the chances of messages being received accurately under adverse conditions (but see also section 5.3 on *parsimony*).

In chapter two we suggested that the discriminatory view of agent/patient marking was insufficient
and that marking in this area could be seen as characterizing semantic, syntactic and thematic (topic/
focus) entities. Under this view marking could be
said to have the function of expressing these relations, but that is obvious and uninteresting. Any
interest in this area lies in assessing the relative
merits of the discriminatory and characterizing theories.

Vennemann's notion that an SOV language that
loses its agent/patient distinction becomes SVO so
that object fronting can still be used without introducing ambiguous NP NP V sequences is an example of
functional explanation. When we consider that a language may lose its case marking and not become SVO,
or, to make fewer assumptions about history, when we
consider that an SOV language without case marking
can exist (e.g. Yessan-Mayo), then we have to accept
that at best disambiguation is a contributory factor.
It is not a sufficient condition to induce a change
from SOV to SVO, and it is not a necessary condition
either. A language can change from SOV to SVO without losing its case marking. This would be true of
the Baltic and Slavonic languages, for instance, and
probably of early Romance.

6.5.3.   Physiological Explanation

The explanation for various language phenomena,
mostly phonetic phenomena, can be found in physiology.
For example, the fact that men speak with a pitch
that is nearly an octave lower than that used by women is a reflection of the fact that the vocal chords
of men are longer and thicker than those of women.
It is natural for men to have deeper voices than
women, though even here the data is not entirely the
product of a physiological constraint. Men can
speak at a higher pitch by speaking falsetto, i.e. by
using only part of their vocal chords, and it is
reported that in traditional Lapp communities men
spoke with a pitch range similar to that used by
women (Collinder 1938:44).[16]

At a number of points in the text we have referred to a physiological limitation that we believe
affects syntax and that is the limited capacity of
our short-term memory. Chomsky has argued that

grammatical competence is independent of short-term
memory limitations.   He envisages a computational
power that can do iterative recursive embedding ad
infinitum.

> 'The language generated by the grammar is
> infinite.   Putting aside irrelevant limita-
> tions of time, patience, and memory, people
> can in principle understand and use senten-
> ces of arbitrary length and complexity.
> Correspondingly, as these limitations are
> relaxed in practice, our ability to use lan-
> guage increases in scope - in principle,
> without bound.   A sentence that is incompre-
> hensible in speech may be intelligible if
> repeated several times or presented on the
> printed page, where memory limitations are
> less severe.   But we do not have to extend
> our knowledge of language to be able to deal
> with repeated or written sentences that are
> far more complex than those of normal spoken
> discourse.   Rather, the same knowledge can
> be applied with fewer extrinsic constraints.
>
> To illustrate with a simple analogy,
> consider a person who knows arithmetic, who
> has mastered the concept of number.   In
> principle, he is now capable of carrying out
> or determining the accuracy of any computa-
> tion.   Some computations he may not be able
> to carry out in his head.   Paper and pencil
> are required to extend his memory.   But the
> person does not have to learn something new
> to carry out a more complex computation,
> using paper and pencil.   Rather he uses the
> knowledge already represented in his mind,
> with access to more computing space than his
> short-term memory provides.   Some computa-
> tions may be too complex even for paper and
> pencil, but these limitations are independent
> of knowledge of arithmetic.   They hold for
> other domains as well.   Therefore a scientist
> interested in determining "arithmetical compe-
> tence" would quite properly disregard these
> limitations, attributing them to independent
> components of the mind'
>   (1980:220-21).

While one can see the force of this argument, we
feel that it is insufficient to account for the
nature of language, in particular it is insufficient

to account for the grammars of particular languages.
Suppose Chomsky is correct in assuming we can in
principle begin a construction, embed another within
it, and another within that and so on.   It is a fact
that languages employ strategies to avoid this.
These strategies are not just a matter of performance,
adjustments made 'in running' to avoid straining
short-term memory.   Rather they are strategies that
are to be learnt as part of the grammar of particular
languages.   Some of these strategies may begin life
as characteristics of performance, e.g. afterthoughts,
but once a new generation learns these patterns and
uses them deliberately they are part of grammatical
competence.

        If one makes a distinction between language com-
petence in general and the rules of a particular language, then it is reasonable to claim that language
competence is independent of short-term memory limitations.   Limitations of short-term memory do not
affect our computational powers, at least in principle, but they affect the rules of particular grammars.   These rules of course lie within the range of
rules allowed by language general competence.   To
take an example.   We could in theory have a sentence
in English of the following form,

(6.30)   That the Builder's Labourer's Federation

                will support the holding of the 1988 Olym-

                pic Games in Melbourne even though they

                will be going on strike during the con-

                struction of the stadium and using the

                built-in deadline as a weapon to gain

                higher wages is quite likely

As we all know this pattern with a long *that* clause
is most improbable.   The preferred pattern would be,
It is quite likely that...   Now one way of describing the *It is likely that*... version is to say that
the *that* clause has been extraposed from a position
as the subject of *is true*.   If we adopt this method
of description we must then assign rightwards movement rules to general grammatical competence.   But
it is surely reasonable to suggest that this particular rightwards movement rule is motivated by short-
term memory limitations.   One could then raise the
further question of whether all rightwards movement
rules are so motivated.   If one felt that they were

all so motivated, one could speculate about whether
rightwards movement rules exist because of short-term
memory limitations.   Our feeling is that this particular computational property probably exists independently of any demonstrable function and indeed that
it is likely to be a property of a wider cognitive
capacity rather than of a specific language capacity.
In fact it remains uncertain whether there is a specific language capacity and Chomsky's argument that
only a specific language competence can account for
rapid acquisition of language on the basis of degene-
rate data is very weak.   Any notion of rapidity must
be subjective and claims concerning the degenerate-
ness of the data remain unsubstantiated.   Children
learn what they are exposed to.

Some may object to the argument based on (6.30)
on the grounds that some recent versions of transformational grammar would not describe an *It is
likely that*... construction in terms of a rightwards
movement rule (see, for example, Emonds 1970).   However, this is irrelevant.   In whichever way one describes the relationship between this pattern and sentences of the type *A quick result is likely*, it is
true that with the former pattern one must associate
the dummy subject *it* with material to the right of
the complement adjective.   It does not follow of
course that semantic interpretation involves placing
the *that*-clause in subject position.   It seems clear
that short-term memory limitations are responsible
for certain grammatical rules or patterns, quite
apart from any claims one wants to make about a language competence that is independent of short-term
memory.   These limitations exert a pressure that
tends to push a language into having certain types of
rule.

Kuno's explanation for the co-occurrence of SOV
and preposed relatives is based on the notion of
short-term memory limitations (see section 5.2.3.).
As we pointed out in chapter five, Kuno's schema can
be extended to cover all word order types and pre-
dicts that preposed relatives will be favoured in
V-final languages and postposed relatives in V-initial
languages.   As can be seen from table 5 in chapter
five (p.309), the occurrence of preposed relatives in
V-initial languages and postposed relatives in V-
final languages would involve a maximum of self-embedding and is likely to be disfavoured if self-embedding presents some processing difficulty.   However,
as we noted in chapter five, single self-embedding

does not seem to present an appreciable difficulty;
it is only the possibility of multiple self-embedding
or of heavy embedding that could be said to exert any
pressure to avoid an embedding pattern. We empha-
size the notion of pressure rather than of cause.
There is no necessary connection between word order
and the position of the relative clause, though there
is high correlation.   Persian for instance is SOV
but has postposed relatives and Tagalog is verb-
initial but allows both pre- and postposed relatives
(though admittedly the preposed relatives are not of
the clausal type).

Vennemann incidentally suggests another reason
why preposed relatives are not favoured in languages
that are not verb-final (1973:34-5).   He claims that
it would be difficult for a hearer to tell where the
relative clause ends and the head noun phrase begins.
Consider the sequence: *The which is responsible for
the milk supply office*...   Vennemann points out that
the listener can have momentary difficulty at this
point in determining whether the head noun is (a)
supply office, (b) *office*, (c) still to come.   The
possibility of confusion of this type may disfavour
preposed relatives in non-verb-final languages, but
we feel that potential ambiguities of this sort are
not likely to arise too often and if they do they
could be resolved by phonological phrasing.   Chinese
is an SVO language, more or less, with preposed relatives, though it is true that such a type of language
is rare.

Short-term memory limitations seem to be responsible for the high incidence of ellipsis-sites (see
chapter four) in non-initial rather than initial
clauses.   As we pointed out in section 4.6, short-
term memory can cope more easily with forwards deletion and pronominalization than with backwards examples of these phenomena.   If a constituent is omitted from an initial clause of a complex sentence, the
listener must hold an unresolved zero in his short-
term memory until he hears a full pattern in a later
clause.   On the other hand omission of a constituent
from a non-initial clause presents no problem if the
constituent has been specified in an earlier clause.
The fact that ellipsis and pronominalization occur at
all simply reflects the fact that speakers tend to
operate with a minimum of specification.   In particular, people do not like to repeat heavy noun phrases in full (e.g. those with participial or relative
complements).   Chapter four was concerned with

avoidance of *repetition* of material that is redundant because it is specified elsewhere in the text, but of course ellipsis and pronominalization are also used to avoid what speakers consider recoverable from the context of situation.

6.6   Finale

If we are interested in understanding language, we naturally try to investigate as many languages as possible.   *A priori* we could expect to find that certain features are common to all languages, i.e. universal, or that some features are much more common than other alternatives.   We could also expect to find universals and non-randomness between features. For instance, we could expect to find that the presence of one feature always involves the presence of another (that there is an implicational relationship), or we could expect to find correlations between features (p tends to imply q, q tends to imply p, p and q tend to imply one another).

In practice, universals are difficult to establish.   This we see as a reflection of the arbitrary nature of language.   In fact the only universals that seem to be well-based are uninteresting ones that reflect the physiological limitations of speaker-hearers or are an essential feature of an oral communication system that enables us to describe experience, e.g. the egressive nature of all or almost all speech sounds in all languages, voicing of some speech sounds in all languages (for carrying power), presence of syntactic rules as opposed to a lexicon, etc.).

On the other hand the non-randomness of the distribution of language features is all but self-evident.   This cries out for explanation, but, as we have argued in section 6.5, no strong explanation is possible.   What then is the point of ascertaining the relative frequency of language features and of classifying languages according to features?

If one knows what is common and what is uncommon and which combinations of features are likely to occur, one feels a certain familiarity with the phenomenon and one feels one knows *how* it works if not *why* it works as it does.   An appreciation of just how language data is distributed enables us to see particular cases in perspective and produces a certain feeling that we understand what is going on.

Perhaps on deeper inspection this feeling proves
meretricious, but up to a point it is satisfying and
certainly a knowledge of distribution is a first step
towards any deeper understanding.

In classifying fauna and flora one chooses features that imply others to arrive at a hierarchical
classification and the result is a typology that
reflects genetic relationship, lines of evolution.
In classifying languages we can use two quite different criteria.   Either we classify according to *roots*
or according to *patterns* or *arrangements*.   It is
generally accepted that the relationship between form
and content is arbitrary (with some exceptions) and
so classification according to common roots reflects
genetic relationship.   We can compare the results of
such a classification with a typology based on patterns or arrangements (accusative v. ergative marking,
order of S, O, V) and see at once that languages
change in pattern-based typology over time.   We mentioned in section 1.1.1. the case of Latin being SOV
while its descendants are SVO.   With fauna and flora
we do not find that one species becomes like another
through contact.   Lions do not grow like giraffes
nor vice versa through sharing a common range.   With
language it is common to find that languages grow to
become similar to their neighbours.   As a result it
is difficult to arrive at a hierarchical typology
with a neat set of implicational rules.   By and
large, patterns or arrangements can change over time
or be borrowed independently of one another.   However, if the patterns are independently borrowable,
which implies they are arbitrarily based, they are
good candidates for typological classification even
if it is difficult to establish clearly defined types.
Any instability in patterns makes them a poor indicator of genetic relationship and a sensitive indicator
of the pressures exerted on language.

Perhaps the most satisfying goal of linguistics
is ascertaining the causal factors responsible for
the non-randomness of the data.   We should not be
put off by the fact that watertight explanations are
impossible to find.   Our aim should be to identify
the pressures or forces that are exerted on language,
whether they be pressures resulting from processing
difficulties or from functional considerations.   A
successful typology should expose non-randomness in a
revealing way, in particular it should bring out as
many correlations as possible.   The results of this
typology are the raw material on which we base our

attempts to find contributory causes.   Experience
suggests that any claims we make about causal factors
are likely to be controversial.   For us, it is this
difficulty that makes linguistics interesting.

NOTES

[1]M.B. Harris (1980:62) writes: '... the description "SVO language" or whatever is simply shorthand
for "language which, in respect of a specifiable set
of morphological and syntactic characteristics, shows
a majority of these characteristics in the form normally correlated with a particular word order".
(Note that under certain circumstances a language
could, by this definition, be in principle designated
"SVO" even if the actual unmarked word order were to
be, say, SOV).'   This is not our usage.   If we say
a language is an SVO language it must have SVO as its
basic word order.   If it does not have the characteristics normally associated with SVO, we would
simply qualify the label.

[2]Andersen (1979:26) also gives examples of adjectives with preposed complements giving rise to
postpositions in Sanskrit.

NP-gen   kr̥ta ('made') → 'NP-gen for'
e.g.   mama kr̥ta   → 'for me'

NP-loc, NP-acc gata- ('gone') → 'into, to, towards
                                  NP'

NP-instr anvita- ('gone along with') → 'accompa-
                                         nied by
                                         NP'

NP-instr sahita ('joined') → 'with NP'

[3]It is interesting to note that Old English *of*
meaning 'from' came to lose its sense of 'from' first
in partitives - hund of scipu 'hundred of ships' -
and in modern English, *of*, rather than *'s*, is still
most favoured with nouns low on the pronoun/animacy
hierarchy while *'s* is favoured at the other end of
the hierarchy.   Compare the following:

year's end   John's book
end of the year   book of John

        your book - book of you

[4]Compare also Early Modern English *'liegemen to the Dane'*, *son to Polonius*, and French *Cette auto est à mon père*.

[5]Examples are easy to find.   French: vis-à-vis, à côté de, en face de, etc.

Jacaltec: -wi'   'on top of'   from wi'e   'head'
          -sattaj   'in front of'   "   sat   'face'

Swahili: mbele   'in front of'   "   mbele   'breasts'

Hausa: gàban   'in front of'   "   gàbā̄   'front'
          kân   'on (top of)'   "   kâi   'head'

Samoan: i tua o   'at the back   "   tua   'back'
                      of'

and so on *ad nauseam*.....

[6]In Cambodian rɔbah 'things, possessions' has developed into a genitive preposition.

[7]In Old English most of the words that are today prepositions could be postposed on occasions, particularly with pronouns.   They could also be used adverbially.   Compare the following,

    Se cyning wið him cenlice feaht
    Se cyning him wið cenlice feaht
    Se cyning him cenlice wið feaht

    'The king fought keenly with/against him'

Lehmann (1978a:33) comments on the fact that while dé occurred in Ancient Greek as a postposition (Oúlumpon dé 'to Olympus') its cognates *to* and *zu* in English and German are preposed.   Lehmann seems to see this settling in preposed position as a development to be expected when a language changes from OV to VO structure (in Old English *to* exhibited the same freedom as wið and eventually settled as a preposition and, more marginally, as an adverb).   Lehmann seems to see the consistency principle at work here. We prefer to look for specific historical developments that give rise to consistency as a more or less accidental result.   If there is a consistency principle that tells speaker-hearers to put adverbs/ ambipositions in preposed positions in VO languages, we wonder why such a principle should exist.

[8]Hawkins' implicational universals indicate that the order of A and N is less stable than that of G and N.   Hawkins suggests an explanation for this.

'The adjective', he claims, 'is syntactically and
semantically less complex than the genitive.   The
latter consists of a whole NP modifying another NP,
in conjunction often with a genitive marker...
If, in the course of its history, a language is going
to change the order of its noun modifiers, ... it can
reorder its adjective with greater ease and with less
drastic restructuring of the NP, than by moving the
whole genitive expression' (1980:208).   As we
remarked in section 6.2.2., it seems that a genitive
marked by a preposition is likely to be postposed and
one marked by a postposition to be preposed so as to
avoid centre-embedding.   This is likely to be part
of the reason for the conservatism of the G/N order
vis-à-vis A/N order.

[9]This is standard methodology of course, but we
are not *entirely* against positing a proto-feature
that is unattested.   It would have been not unreasonable to have allowed for OVS and OSV languages before
they were actually discovered (or introduced into
mainstream linguistics), since these patterns
occurred as variants in the attested types.   One
could have encountered a situation where one wanted
to posit a proto-order OVS or OSV and one could have
pointed out that after all there is no logical reason
why such a basic order should not exist.

[10]In the literature there is often confusion
between description and explanation and many self-
styled explanations are simply generalizations,
explanations by definition or circular appeals to
notions of naturalness.   For a scathing review of
pseudo-explanations, see the first chapter of Givón
1979.

[11]Lightfoot's reference to the popularity of
dislocated patterns with British football commentators is interesting.   There is a marked tendency for
Australian sports commentators to use the right-
dislocated pattern, particularly when they are describing rapidly changing action, and indeed to use
other subject-to-the-right patterns (...*picking up
the ball is Jezza, he turns, he shoots and it's
right through the middle*).   Although the motivation
may be expressivity, it is also likely that the
subject-to-the-right pattern gives the commentators
breathing space to identify the subject.   Fluency is
also maintained by the use of stock phrases in a
manner reminiscent of oral verse.

[12] In 6.3.2.(a) we mentioned the development of Sri Lankan Portuguese creole. In this case an SOV form of an SVO superstratum language has developed among speakers of SOV languages.

[13] The affixes that are likely to be of verbal origin in the Indonesian languages are prefixes (e.g. Indonesian ter-, ber-) and some of the suffixes are probably of adpositional origin (e.g. Indonesian -i (see example (2.84)) and -kan (see example (2.86))). On balance these languages are likely to be reconstructable as VO not OV.

[14] For Lardil and Ngarluma, see Blake 1979a and for Lardil see also Klokeid 1978.

[15] There are fossilized examples of topic and focus rules in some subordinate clause types, e.g. the placing of relative pronouns (topic) in clause initial position.

[16] We are indebted to Claes Christian Elert for this and other references on the Lapps.

REFERENCES

abbreviations used:

BLS : Berkeley Linguistics Society (Proceedings of the nth Annual Meeting of the)

CLS : Chicago Linguistic Society (Papers from the nth Regional Meeting of the)

FL : Foundations of Language

IJAL : International Journal of American Linguistics

IULC : Indiana University Linguistics Club

JL : Journal of Linguistics

Lg : Language

LI : Linguistic Inquiry

TPS : Transactions of the Philological Society

WPLU : Working Papers on Language Universals. Stanford University.

Abraham, W. ed. 1978. Valence, semantic case and grammatical relations. Amsterdam: John Benjamins.

Adams, D.Q. 1972. Relative clauses in Ancient Greek. In: Peranteau et al. eds. 1972, 9-22.

Aitchison, J. 1979. The order of word order change. TPS 1979, 43-65.

Akiba, K. 1977. Conjunction *to* and postposition *to* in Japanese. CLS 13, 1-14.

Alexandrescu, P. 1954. Despre acordul predicatului cu subiectul (on agreement between predicate and subject). Limba Română 3, part 3, 22-6.

Allan, K. 1980. Anaphora, cataphora, and topic focussing: Functions of the object prefix in Swahili. Paper read to the 11th Annual Conference on African Linguistics, Boston University, April 1980 (to appear in conference proceedings, ed. by I.R. Dihoff).

449

Allen, B.J. & D.G. Frantz. 1978.   Verb agreement in Southern Tiwa.
    BLS 4, 11-17.

Andersen, P.K. 1979.   Word order typology and prepositions in Old
    Indic.   In: Studies in diachronic, synchronic and typological
    linguistics, ed. by B. Brogyanyi, vol. 2, part 1, 23-34.
    Amsterdam: John Benjamins.

Anderson, J.M. 1971.   The grammar of case.   Cambridge: University
    Press.

_____.1977.   On case grammar.   London: Croom Helm.

_____.1979.   On being without a subject.   IULC.

_____ and C.Jones eds. 1974.   Historical Linguistics I.   Amsterdam:
    North-Holland.

Anderson, S.R. 1976.   On the notion of subject in ergative
    languages.   In: Li ed. 1976, 1-24.

_____.1977.   On mechanisms by which languages become ergative.
    In: Li ed. 1977, 317-363.

_____ and S. Chung. 1977.   On grammatical relations and clause
    structure in verb-initial languages.   In: Cole & Sadock eds.
    1977, 1-25.

_____ and P. Kiparsky eds. 1973.   A Festschrift for Morris Halle.
    New York: Holt, Rinehart and Winston.

Andrews, A. 1975.   Studies in the syntax of relative and compara-
    tive clauses.   M.I.T. dissertation.

Anttila, R. 1972.   An introduction to historical and comparative
    linguistics.   New York: Collier-Macmillan.

Aronson, H.I. 1972.   Some notes on relative clauses in Georgian.
    In: Peranteau et al. eds. 1972, 136-143.

Awbery, G.M. 1976.   The Syntax of Welsh: A transformational study
    of the passive.   Cambridge: Cambridge University Press.

_____ 1977.   A transformational view of Welsh relative clauses.
    Bwletin y bwrdd gwybodau celtaidd (The Bulletin of the Board of
    Celtic Studies) vol. xxvii, part 2, 155-206.

Babby, L.H. 1973.   The deep structure of adjectives and participles
    in Russian.   Lg 49, 349-360.

_____ 1975.   A transformational grammar of Russian adjectives.
    The Hague: Mouton.

Bach, E. 1965.   On some recurrent types of transformation.
    In: 16th annual roundtable meeting on linguistics and language
    studies, ed. by C.W. Kneedler, 3-18.   Washington, D.C.:
    Georgetown University Press.

_____ 1968.   Nouns and noun phrases.   In: Bach & Harms eds. 1968,
    91-122.

_____ 1970.   Is Amharic an SOV language?   Journal of Ethiopian
    Studies 8, 9-20.

_____ and R. Harms eds. 1968.   Universals in linguistic theory.
    New York: Holt, Rinehart and Winston.

Baker, C.L. 1978.   Introduction to generative-transformational
    syntax.   Englewood Cliffs: Prentice-Hall.

Baltaxe, C.A.M. 1969.   Principles of phonology.   Translation of
     Trubetzkoy 1939 (3rd ed. 1962. Göttingen: Vandenhoeck and
     Ruprecht).   Berkeley: University of California Press.

Bánhidi, Z., Z. Jókay & D. Szabó. 1965.   Learn Hungarian.   Buda-
     pest: Tankönyvkiadó.

Baradja, M.F. 1971.   A contrastive analysis of selected patterns
     of the noun phrases and verb phrases of English and Indonesian.
     U.C.L.A. dissertation.

Barker, M. & A. Mengal. 1969.   A course in Baluchi.   Montreal:
     McGill University.

Bauman, J.J. 1979.   An historical perspective on ergativity in
     Tibeto-Burman.   In: Plank ed. 1979, 419-433.

Bazell, C.E. 1958.   Linguistic typology.   London: School of
     Oriental and African Studies.

Bechert, J. 1976.   Bemerken zu Greenberg's 'Basic order typology'.
     Papiere zur Linguistik 10, 49-66.

_____ 1979.   Ergativity and the constitution of grammatical
     ·relations.   In: Plank ed. 1979, 45-59.

Bell, A. 1978.   Language samples.   In: Greenberg et al. eds. 1978,
     vol. 1, 123-156.

_____ and J.B. Hooper eds. 1978.   Syllables and segments.   Amster-
     dam: North Holland.

Bell, C.A. 1919.   Grammar of colloquial Tibetan.   Calcutta:
     Baptist Mission Press.

Bender, M.L. 1976.   The non-semitic languages of Ethiopia.   East
     Lansing: Michigan State University.

_____ J.D. Bowen, R.L. Cooper & C.A. Ferguson eds. 1976.   Language
     ′in Ethiopia.   London: Oxford University Press.

_____ and M. Eteffa. 1976.   Galla.   In: Bender et al. eds. 1976,
     130-147.

Benedict, P.K. 1975.   Austro-Thai language and culture.   Hraf
     Press (no place of publication given).

Benkö, L. & S. Imre. 1972.   The Hungarian Language.   The Hague:
     Mouton.

Bertkau, J.A.S. 1973.   Comprehension and production of English
     relative clauses in adult second language acquisition and
     child first language acquisition.   University of Michigan
     dissertation.

Bever, T.G. & D.T. Langendoen. 1972.   The interaction of speech
     perception and grammatical structure in the evolution of
     language.   In: Stockwell & Macaulay eds. 1972, 32-95.

Birk, D.B.W. 1976.   The Malak Malak language, Daly River (Western
     Arnhem Land).   Canberra: Pacific Linguistics.

Blake, B.J. 1976a.   On ergativity and the notion of subject: Some
     Australian cases.   Lingua 39, 281-300.

_____ 1976b.   Rapporteur's introduction and summary for the topic:
     ·Are Australian languages syntactically nominative-ergative or
     nominative-accusative?   In: Dixon ed. 1976, 485-494.

Blake, B.J. 1977.   Case marking in Australian languages.
Linguistics Series, 23.   Canberra: Australian Institute of
Aboriginal Studies.

_____. 1979a.   Australian case systems: Some typological and histori-
cal observations.   In: Wurm ed. 1979, 323-394.

_____. 1979b.   Pitta-Pitta.   In: Dixon & Blake eds. 1979, 183-242.

_____. 1979c.   A Kalkatungu grammar.   Canberra: Pacific Linguistics.

_____. 1979d.   Degrees of ergativity in Australia. In: Plank ed.
1979, 291-305.

_____. to appear.   The absolutive: Its scope in English and Kalka-
tungu.

_____ and R.M.W. Dixon. 1979.   Introduction.   In: Dixon & Blake
eds. 1979, 1-25.

Blansitt, E.J. 1973.   Bitransitive clauses.   WPLU 13, 1-26.

Bloomfield, L. 1935.   Language.   London: Allen and Unwin.

_____. 1946.   Algonquian.   In: Linguistic structures of native
America, ed. by H. Hoijer et al., Viking publications in
anthropology, 6.

_____. 1962.   The Menomini language.   New Haven: Yale University
Press.

Boas, F. & E. Deloria. 1939.   Dakota grammar.   Memoirs of the
National Academy of Science, 23.   Washington, D.C.: Government
Printing Office.

Boeder, W. 1979.   Ergative syntax and morphology in language change:
The south Caucasian languages.   In: Plank ed. 1979, 435-480.

Bolinger, D.L. 1967.   Adjectives in English: Attribution and predication.   Lingua 18, 1-34.

_____. 1968.   Aspects of language.   New York: Harcourt, Brace and
World.

_____. 1972.   That's that.   The Hague: Mouton.

Breen, J.G. 1976.   Ergative, locative and instrumental case
inflections: Wangkumara.   In: Dixon ed. 1976, 336-339.

Bresnan, J. 1978.   A realistic transformational grammar.   In:
Halle, Bresnan & Miller eds. 1978, 1-59.

Brettschneider, G. 1979.   Typological characteristics of Basque.
In: Plank ed. 1979, 371-384.

Capell, A. 1962.   Some linguistic types in Australia.   Sydney:
Oceania Linguistic Monographs.

Carroll, P. 1976a.   Gunwinjgu.   In: Dixon ed. 1976, 704-707.

_____. 1976b.   Kunwinjku: A language of western Arnhem Land.
Canberra: A.N.U. Master's thesis.

Catford, I. 1976.   Ergativity in Caucasian languages.   Montreal
Working Papers in Linguistics 6, 37-48.

Chapin, P.G. 1978.   Easter Island: A characteristic VSO language.
In: Lehmann ed. 1978, 139-168.

Chomsky, N. 1957.   Syntactic Structures.   The Hague: Mouton.

_____. 1965.   Aspects of the theory of syntax.   Cambridge, Mass.:
M.I.T. Press.

Chomsky, N. 1973.   Conditions on transformations.   In: Anderson &
    Kiparsky eds. 1973, 232-286.

_____. 1980.   Rules and representations.   Oxford: Basil Blackwell.

_____ and H. Lasnik. 1977.   Filters and control.   LI 8, 425-504.

Chung, S. 1973.   The semantics of *i* in Samoan.   ms, University of
    California, San Diego.

_____. 1976.   On the subject of two passives in Indonesian.   In: Li
    ed. 1976, 57-98.

_____. 1977.   On the gradual nature of syntactic change.   In: Li ed.
    1977, 3-55.

_____. 1978.   Case marking and grammatical relations in Polynesian.
    Austin: University of Texas Press.

_____ and W.J. Seiter. 1980.   The history of raising and relativiza-
    tion in Polynesian.   Lg 56, 622-638.

Clark, M. 1974.   Passive and ergative in Vietnamese.   In: South-
    east Asian linguistic studies, ed. by N.D. Liem, vol. 1,
    75-88.   Canberra: Pacific Linguistics.

Cole, P. ed. 1976.   Studies in Modern Hebrew syntax and semantics.
    Amsterdam: North-Holland.

_____ et al. 1977.   Noun phrase accessibility and island constraints.
    In: Cole & Sadock eds. 1977, 27-46.

_____ and J.M. Sadock eds. 1977.   Syntax and semantics, 8: Gramma-
    tical relations.   New York: Academic Press.

Collinder, B. 1938.   Lautlehre des Waldlappischen Dialektes von
    Gällivare.   Mémoires de la société finno-ougrienne, lxxiv.

Comrie, B. 1975.   The antiergative: Finland's answer to Basque.
    CLS 11, 112-121.

_____. 1976.   Review of G.A. Klimov, Očerk obščej teorii ergativnosti
    (Outline of a general theory of ergativity).   Moscow: Izd-vo
    'Nauka', 1973.   Lingua 39, 252-260.

_____. 1977.   In defense of spontaneous demotion: The impersonal
    passive.   In: Cole & Sadock eds. 1977, 47-58.

_____. 1978.   Ergativity.   In: Lehmann ed. 1978, 329-394.

_____. 1979a.   Review of Dik 1978.   Studies in Language 3, 267-276.

_____. 1979b.   Degrees of ergativity: Some Chukchee evidence.   In:
    Plank ed. 1979, 219-240.

_____. to appear.   'Definite' and 'animate' direct objects: A natural
    class   (typescript 1976 to appear in Linguistica Silesiana 3).

_____ and N.S.H. Smith. 1977.   Lingua Descriptive Studies: Intro-
    duction and questionnaire.   Lingua 42.

Corbett, G.G. 1979.   The agreement hierarchy.   JL 15, 203-224.

Cornyn, W.S. & D. Haigh Roop. 1968.   Beginning Burmese.   New
    Haven: Yale University Press.

Cowan, M.M. 1969.   Tzotzil grammar.   S.I.L. publications in
    linguistics, 18.   Norman, Oklahoma: Summer Institute of
    Linguistics.

Cowell, M.W. 1964.   A reference grammar of Syrian Arabic.   Wash-
    ington, D.C.: Georgetown University Press.

Cowley, R., M.L. Bender & C.A. Ferguson. 1976.   The Amharic
    language: Description.   In: Bender et al. eds. 1976, 77-89.

Craig, C.G. 1976.   Properties of basic and derived subjects in
    Jacaltec.   In: Li ed. 1976, 99-124.

_____ 1977.   The structure of Jacaltec.   Austin: University of
    Texas Press.

Crazzolara, J.P. 1955.   A study of the Acooli language.   Oxford:
    University Press.

Creider, C.A. 1979.   On the explanation of transformations.   In:
    Givón ed. 1979, 3-22.

Crowley, T. 1978.   The Middle Clarence dialects of Bandjalang.
    Canberra: Australian Institute of Aboriginal Studies.

Culicover, P.W., T. Wasow & A. Akmajian eds. 1977.   Formal syntax.
    New York: Academic Press.

_____ and K. Wexler. 1977.   Some syntactic implications of a theory
    of language learnability.   In: Culicover, Wasow & Akmajian
    eds. 1977, 7-60.

Curme, G.O. 1931.   A grammar of the English language. 3 volumes.
    Boston: Heath.

Dalgish, G.M. 1978.   Inaccessibility and demotional nominal marking
    in Iraqw.   Studies in African Linguistics 9, 285-299.

_____ 1979a.   The syntax and semantics of the morpheme ni in
    Kivunjo (Chaga).   Studies in African Linguistics 10, 47-63.

_____ 1979b.   Subject identification strategies and free word order:
    The case of Sandawe.   Studies in African Linguistics 10,
    273-310.

Daniels, P.T. 1976.   S----x and the single manuscript, the joy of
    philology and linguistic morality (evidence for syntactic
    change in Syriac).   In: Steever, Walker & Mufwene eds. 1976,
    69-78.

De Lancey, S. 1980.   An interpretation of split ergativity and
    related patterns.   IULC.

Derbyshire, D.C. 1977.   Word order universals and the existence of
    OVS languages.   LI 8, 590-599.

_____ 1979.   Hixkaryana.   Lingua Descriptive Series, 1.   Amster-
    dam: North Holland.

_____ and G.K. Pullum. 1979.   Object initial languages.   Work
    papers of the Summer Institute of Linguistics, University of
    North Dakota, vol. 23 (revised version to appear in IJAL).

De Rijk, R.G. 1972.   Relative clauses in Basque: A guided tour.
    In: Peranteau et al. eds. 1972, 115-135.

Dešeriev, Ju.D. 1953.   Batsbijskij jazyk.   Moscow: Akademia Nauk.

Dik, S.C. 1968.   Coordination: It's implications for the theory of
    general linguistics.   Amsterdam: North-Holland.

_____ 1973.   Crossing coreference again.   FL 9, 306-326.

_____ 1978.   Functional grammar.   Amsterdam: North-Holland.

Dixon, R.M.W. 1972.   The Dyirbal language of North Queensland.
    Cambridge: University Press.

Dixon, R.M.W. ed. 1976.   Grammatical categories in Australian
        languages.   Canberra: Australian Institute of Aboriginal
        Studies (*and* New Jersey: Humanities Press).

_____.1977.   A grammar of Yidin^y.   Cambridge: University Press.

_____.1979.   Ergativity.   Lg 55, 1-138.

_____.1980.   The languages of Australia.   Cambridge: University
        Press.

_____ and B.J. Blake eds. 1979.   Handbook of Australian languages.
        Canberra: Australian National University Press.

Donaldson, S. 1971.   Movement in restrictive relative clauses in
        Hindi.   Studies in the Linguistic Sciences 3, 45-53.

Donaldson, T. 1980.   Ngiyambaa: The language of the Wangaaybuwan.
        Cambridge: University Press.

Dougherty, R.C. 1970.   A grammar of coördinate conjoined struc-
        tures I.   Lg 46, 850-900.

_____.1971.   A grammar of coördinate conjoined structures II.
        Lg 47, 298-339.

Douglas, W.H. 1964.   An introduction to the Western Desert language
        (revised edition).   Sydney: Oceania Linguistic Monographs.

Eades, D. 1979.   Gumbaynggir.   In: Dixon & Blake eds. 1979,
        245-361.

Ehrenkranz, J. & E.C. Hirschland. 1972.   Latin relative clauses.
        In: Peranteau et al. eds. 1972, 23-29.

Emeneau, M.B. 1956.   India as a linguistic area.   Lg 32, 3-16.

Emonds, J. 1970.   Root and structure-preserving transformations.
        M.I.T. dissertation.

Ferguson, C.A. 1978.   Historical background of universals research.
        In: Greenberg et al. eds. 1978, vol. 1, 7-31.

Fernald, J.C. 1904.   Connectives of English speech.   New York:
        Funk and Wagnalls.

Fillmore, C.J. 1968.   The case for case.   In: Bach & Harms eds.
        1968, 1-88.

_____.1977.   The case for case reopened.   In: Cole & Sadock eds.
        1977, 59-81.

_____ and D.T. Langendoen eds. 1971.   Studies in linguistic
        semantics.   New York: Holt, Rinehart and Winston.

Fodor, J.A. 1970.   Three reasons for not deriving *kill* from *cause
        to die*.   LI 1, 429-438.

Foley, W.A. 1976.   Comparative syntax in Austronesian.   U.Cal.
        Berkeley dissertation.

Foreman, V.M. 1974.   Grammar of Yessan-Mayo.   Santa Ana: Summer
        Institute of Linguistics.

Foster, M.L. 1969.   The Tarascan language.   Berkeley: University
        of California Press.

Fretheim, T. 1976.   Extraposition of relative clauses.   A functio-
        nal approach to a problem of Norwegian syntax.   In: Papers
        from the third Scandinavian conference of linguistics, ed. by
        F. Karlsson, 1976, 121-129.   Academy of Finland Text Linguis-
        tics Research Group.

Friedrich, P. 1975.   Proto-Indo-European syntax.   Journal of IE
    studies, Monograph no. 1.

Fries, C.C. & K.L. Pike. 1949.   Coexistent phonemic systems. Lg 25,
    29-50.

Gamble, G. 1978.   Wikchamni grammar.   Berkeley: University of
    California Press.

Gary, J.O. & E.L. Keenan. 1977.   On collapsing grammatical rela-
    tions in universal grammar.   In: Cole & Sadock eds. 1977,
    83-120.

Gazdar, G. 1980.   Unbounded dependencies and coordinate structure.
    MS, University of Sussex (to appear in LI).

Geytenbeek, B. & H. Geytenbeek. 1971.   Gidabal grammar and dictio-
    nary.   Canberra: Australian Institute of Aboriginal Studies.

Givón, T. 1970.   The resolution of gender conflicts in Bantu
    conjunction: When syntax and semantics clash.   CLS 6,
    250-261.

_____ 1971.   Historical syntax and synchronic morphology.   In:
    CLS 7, 394-415.

_____ 1972.   Pronoun attraction and subject postposing in Bantu.
    In: Peranteau et al. eds. 1972, 190-197.

_____ 1975.   Serial verbs and syntactic change: Niger-Congo.   In:
    Li ed. 1975, 47-111.

_____ 1976.   Topic, pronoun, and grammatical agreement.   In: Li ed.
    1976, 149-188.

_____ 1977.   The drift from VSO to SVO in Biblical Hebrew: The
    pragmatics of tense-aspect.   In: Li ed. 1977, 181-254.

_____ 1979.   On understanding grammar.   New York: Academic Press.

_____ ed. 1979.   Syntax and semantics, 12: Discourse and syntax.
    New York: Academic Press.

Glass, A. & D. Hackett. 1970.   Pitjantjatjara grammar: A tagmemic
    view of the Ngaanyatjara (Warburton Ranges) dialect.   Canberra:
    Australian Institute of Aboriginal Studies.

Gleason, H.A. 1961.   An introduction to descriptive linguistics
    (revised edition).   New York: Holt, Rinehart and Winston.

Gleitman, L.R. 1965.   Coordinating conjunctions in English.   Lg
    41, 260-293 (also reprinted in Reibel & Schane eds. 1969,
    80-112).

Gragg, G.B. 1972.   Sumerian and selected Afro-Asiatic languages.
    In: Peranteau et al. eds. 1972, 153-168.

Green, G.M. 1976.   Main clause phenomena in subordinate clauses.
    Lg 52, 382-397.

Greenberg, J.H. 1960.   A quantitative approach to the morphological
    typology of languages.   IJAL 26, 178-194.

_____ 1963.   Some universals of grammar with particular reference
    to the order of meaningful elements.   In: Greenberg ed. 1963,
    73-113.

_____ ed. 1963.   Universals of language.   Cambridge, Mass.: M.I.T.
    Press.

_____ 1973.   The typological method.   In: Sebeok ed. 1973, 149-193.

Greenberg, J.H. 1974. Language typology: A historical and analytic overview. The Hague: Mouton.

_____ 1978. Typology and cross-linguistic generalizations. In: Greenberg et al. eds. 1978, vol. 1, 33-59.

_____ et al. eds. 1978. Universals of human language. 4 volumes [vol. 1: Method and theory; vol. 2: Phonology; vol. 3: Word structure; vol. 4: Syntax]. Stanford: Stanford University Press.

Gregersen, E.A. 1977. Language in Africa. New York: Gordon and Breach.

Gregores, E. & J.A. Suaréz. 1967. A description of colloquial Guaraní. The Hague: Mouton.

Gruber, J.S. 1965. Studies in lexical relations. M.I.T. dissertation (also IULC, 1970; revised version appears in J.S. Gruber, Lexical structures in syntax and semantics, 1976. Amsterdam: North-Holland).

Guthrie, M. 1967. The classification of the Bantu languages. London: International African Institute.

Haile, B. 1926. A manual of Navaho grammar. St.Michael's Arizona (New York: AMS Press, 1974).

Haiman, J. 1979. Hua: A Papuan language of New Guinea. In: Shopen ed. 1979, 35-90.

Hale, K. 1967. Preliminary remarks on Walbiri grammar. MS, M.I.T.

_____ 1968. Preliminary remarks on Walbiri grammar II. MS, M.I.T.

_____ 1970. The passive and ergative in language change: The Australian case. In: Pacific linguistic studies in honour of Arthur Capell, ed. by S.A. Wurm & D.C. Laycock, 757-781. Canberra: Pacific Linguistics.

_____ 1973a. A note on subject-object inversion in Navajo. In: Issues in linguistics. Papers in honor of Henry & Renée Kahane, ed. by B. Kachru et al., 300-309. Urbana: University of Illinois Press.

_____ 1973b. Person marking in Walbiri. In: Anderson & Kiparsky, eds. 1973, 308-344.

_____ 1975. Gaps in grammar and culture. Lisse: Peter de Ridder Press.

_____ 1976. The adjoined relative clause in Australia. In: Dixon ed. 1976, 78-105.

_____ L.M. Jeanne & P. Platero. 1977. Three cases of overgeneration. In: Culicover, Wasow & Akmajian eds. 1977, 379-416.

Halle, M., J. Bresnan & G.A. Miller eds. 1978. Linguistic theory and psychological reality. Cambridge, Mass.: M.I.T. Press.

Hankamer, J. 1971. Constraints on deletion in syntax. Yale dissertation.

_____ 1973. Unacceptable ambiguity. LI 4, 17-68.

_____ 1977. Multiple analyses. In: Li ed. 1977, 583-607.

Harries, H. 1973. Coordination reduction. WPLU 11, 139-209.

Harris, M.B. 1978. The evolution of French syntax. A comparative approach. London: Longman.

458 REFERENCES

Harris, M.B. 1980. Noun phrases and verb phrases in Romance. TPS 1980, 62-80.

Harris, Z.S. 1942. Morpheme alternants in linguistic analysis. Lg 18, 169-180.

_____. 1945. Discontinuous morphemes. Lg 21, 121-127.

_____. 1946. From morpheme to utterance. Lg 22, 161-183.

Haviland, J. 1979. Guugu Yimidhirr. In: Dixon & Blake eds. 1979, 27-180.

Hawkins, J.A. 1979. Implicational universals as predictors of word order change. Lg 55, 618-648.

_____. 1980. On implicational and distributional universals of word order. JL 16, 193-235.

Hayon, Y. 1973. Relativization in Hebrew. A transformational approach. The Hague: Mouton.

Heath, J. 1972. Uto-Aztecan relative clauses. In: Peranteau et al. eds. 1972, 230-245.

_____. 1976. Substantival hierarchies: Addendum to Silverstein. In: Dixon ed. 1976, 172-190.

_____. 1977. Choctaw cases. BLS 3, 204-213.

_____. 1978a. Linguistic diffusion in Arnhem Land. Canberra: Australian Institute of Aboriginal Studies.

_____. 1978b. Ngandi grammar, texts and dictionary. Canberra: Australian Institute of Aboriginal Studies.

_____. 1980a. Basic materials in Ritharngu: Grammar, texts and dictionary. Canberra: Pacific Linguistics.

_____. 1980b. Basic materials in Warndarang: Grammar, texts and dictionary. Canberra: Pacific Linguistics.

Heilmann, L. ed. 1974. Proceedings of the eleventh international congress of linguists (held in Bologna, 1972). vols. 1-2. Bologna: Il Mulino.

Heine, B. 1976. A typology of African languages. Berlin: Dietrich Reimer.

Henderson, E. 1965. The topography of certain phonetic and morphological characteristics of southeast Asian languages. Lingua 15, 400-434.

Hetzron, R. 1980. Universals of human language: A Monteverdian quartet in 46 movements. Review article of Greenberg et al. eds. 1978. Lingua 50, 249-294.

Hewitt, B.G. 1978. The Armenian relative clause. In: Classification of grammatical categories, ed. by B. Comrie. Edmonton: Linguistic Research Inc.

_____. 1979. Abkhaz. Lingua Descriptive Studies, 2. Amsterdam: North-Holland.

Heyd, U. 1954. Language reform in modern Turkey. Jerusalem: The Israel Oriental Society.

Hinnebusch, T.J. 1979. Swahili. In: Shopen ed. 1979, 209-294.

Hockett, C.F. 1947. Problems of morphemic analysis. Lg 23, 321-343.

Hockett, C.F. 1954.   Two models of grammatical description.   Word
    10, 210-234.

____. 1955.   A manual of phonology.   Supplement to IJAL, Memoir 11.

Hoffman, C. 1963.   A grammar of the Margi language.   Oxford:
    University Press.

Hollis, A.C. 1905.   The Masai.   Oxford: Clarendon Press (reprinted
    by Negro Universities Press, Westport, Conn. 1970).

Hook, P.E. 1976.   Is Kashmiri an SVO language?   Indian Linguistics
    37, 133-142.

Hope, E.R. 1974.   The deep syntax of Lisu sentences.   Canberra:
    Pacific Linguistics.

____. 1976.   Lisu.   In: Phonemes and orthography: Language planning
    in ten minority languages of Thailand, ed. by W.A. Smalley,
    1979, 125-148.   Canberra: Pacific Linguistics.

Hopper, P.J. 1979.   Aspect and foregrounding in discourse.   In:
    Givón ed. 1979, 213-241.

____ and S.A. Thompson. 1980.   Transitivity in grammar and dis-
    course.   Lg 56, 251-299.

Horne, K.M. 1966.   Language typology.   19th and 20th century
    views.   Washington, D.C.: Georgetown University Press.

Huddleston, R. 1976.   An introduction to English transformational
    syntax.   London: Longman.

Hudson, J. 1978.   The core of Walmatjari grammar.   Canberra:
    Australian Institute of Aboriginal Studies.

Hudson, R.A. 1976.   Conjunction reduction, gapping and right node
    raising.   Lg 52, 535-562.

Hurford, J. 1980.   Generative growing pains.   Review article of
    P. Culicover, Syntax.   New York: Academic Press, 1976. *and*
    A. Akmajian & P. Heny, Introduction to the principles of trans-
    formational syntax.   Cambridge, Mass.: M.I.T. Press, 1975.
    Lingua 50, 117-153.

Hwang, S.J.J. 1975.   Korean clause structure: Surface structure and
    deep structure roles.   Norman: University of Oklahoma, Summer
    Institute of Linguistics.

Hyde, V. 1971.   An introduction to the Luiseño language.   Banning:
    Malki Museum Press.

Hyman, L.M. 1975.   On the change from SOV to SVO: Evidence from
    Niger-Congo.   In: Li ed. 1975, 113-147.

Jackendoff, R.S. 1971.   Gapping and related rules.   LI 2, 21-35.

____. 1972.   Semantic interpretation in generative grammar.   Cam-
    bridge, Mass.: M.I.T. Press.

____. 1973.   The base rules for prepositional phrases.   In:
    Anderson & Kiparsky eds. 1973, 345-356.

Jacob, J.M. 1968.   Introduction to Cambodian.   Oxford: University
    Press.

Jacobs, M. 1931.   A sketch of northern Sahaptin grammar.   Seattle:
    University of Washington Press.

Jacobsen, W.H. 1979.   Why does Washo lack a passive?   In: Plank
    ed. 1979, 145-160.

Jensen, J.T. 1977.   Yapese reference grammar.   Honolulu:
    University Press of Hawaii.

Jespersen, O. 1909-1949.   A modern English grammar on historical
    principles. volumes 1-7.   Copenhagen: Ejnar Munksgaard
    (reprinted 1954, London: Allen and Unwin).

Johnson, D.E. 1974.   Toward a theory of relationally-based grammar.
    University of Illinois dissertation.

_____ 1977.   On relational constraints on grammars.   In: Cole &
    Sadock eds. 1977, 151-178.

_____ and P.M. Postal. 1980.   Arc-pair grammar.   Princeton:
    University Press.

Junghare, I.Y. 1973.   Restrictive relative clauses in Marathi.
    Indian Linguistics 34, 251-262.

Kachru, Y. 1965.   A transformational treatment of Hindi verbal
    syntax.   University of London doctoral thesis.

Kalmár, I. 1979.   The antipassive and grammatical relations in
    Eskimo.   In: Plank ed. 1979, 117-143.

Karlsson, F. 1972.   Relative clauses in Finnish.   In: Peranteau
    et al. eds. 1972, 106-114.

Karttunen, F. 1976.   Uto-Aztecan and Spanish-type dependent clauses
    in Nahuatl.   In: Steever, Walker & Mufwene eds. 1976, 150-158.

Keen, S. 1972.   A description of the Yukulta language.   Monash
    University Master's thesis.

Keenan, E.L. 1972.   Relative clause formation in Malagasy.   In:
    Peranteau et al. eds. 1972, 169-189.

_____ 1974.   The logical status of deep structures (logical con-
    straints on syntactic processes).   In: Heilmann ed. 1974,
    vol. II, 477-490.

_____ 1976a.   Towards a universal definition of 'subject'.   In: Li
    ed. 1976, 303-334.

_____ 1976b.   Remarkable subjects in Malagasy.   In: Li ed. 1976,
    247-302.

_____ 1978a.   The syntax of subject-final languages.   In: Lehmann
    ed. 1978, 267-327.

_____ 1978b.   On surface form and logical form.   In: Linguistics
    in the seventies: Directions and prospects, ed. by B.B. Kachru,
    163-204 (special issue of Studies in the Linguistic Sciences).

_____ and B. Comrie. 1977.   Noun phrase accessibility and universal
    grammar.   LI 8, 63-99.

_____ and B. Comrie. 1979.   Data on the noun phrase accessibility
    hierarchy.   Lg 55, 333-351.

Kibrik, A.E. 1979.   Canonical ergativity and Daghestan languages.
    In: Plank ed. 1979, 61-77.

Kiefer, F. 1967.   On emphasis and word order in Hungarian.
    Bloomington: Indiana University.

Killean, C.G. 1972.   Arabic relative clauses.   In: Peranteau et
    al. eds. 1972, 144-152.

Klaiman, M.H. 1976.   Correlative clauses and IE syntactic recon-
    struction.   In: Steever, Walker & Mufwene eds. 1976, 159-168.

Klima, E.S. 1964.   Relatedness between grammatical systems.
Lg 40, 1-20.

Klimov, G.A. 1973.   Očerk obščej teorii ergativnosti (Outline of a
general theory of ergativity).   Moscow: Nauka.

_____. 1979.   On the position of the ergative type in typological
classification.   In: Plank ed. 1979, 327-332.

Klokeid, T.J. 1970.   Research on Mabuiag.   MS, M.I.T.

_____. 1976.   Topics in Lardil grammar.   M.I.T. dissertation.

_____. 1978.   Nominal inflection in Pama-Nyungan.   In: Abraham ed.
1978, 577-616.

_____ and E.A. Arima.   1977.   Some generalizations about antipassives in Inuktitut.   Études/Inuit/Studies 1, 85-95
(corrected copy appears on pp.167-168 of the following issue).

Knecht, L. 1979.   The role of the genitive suffix in relative
clauses in Turkish: A reply to Dede.   BLS 5, 180-197.

Kokora, D.P. 1976.   Relative clause strategies in Koyo: A case of
rule condition solution.   CLS 12, 425-437.

Koutsoudas, A. 1971.   Gapping, conjunction reduction and coordinate
deletion.   FL 7, 337-386.

Kroeber, A.L. & G.W. Grace. 1960.   The Sparkman grammar of Luiseño.
Berkeley and Los Angeles: University of California Press.

Kuipers, A.H. 1967.   The Squamish language.   The Hague: Mouton.

Kuno, S. 1970.   Notes on Japanese grammar (I).   In: Report NSF-27
to the National Science Foundation.   Cambridge, Mass.: Harvard
University Computation Laboratory.

_____. 1972.   Natural explanations for some syntactic universals.
In: Report NSF-28 to the National Science Foundation.
Cambridge, Mass.: Harvard University Computation Laboratory.

_____. 1973.   The structure of the Japanese language.   Cambridge,
Mass.: M.I.T. Press.

_____. 1974.   The position of relative clauses and conjunctions.
LI 5, 117-136.

_____. 1976a.   Subject, theme, and the speaker's empathy - A reexam-
ination of relativization phenomena.   In: Li ed. 1976,
417-444.

_____. 1976b.   Gapping: A functional analysis.   LI 7, 300-318.

_____. 1978.   Japanese: A characteristic OV language.   In: Lehmann
ed. 1978, 57-138.

Kuroda, S-Y. 1969.   English relativization and certain related
problems.   In: Reibel & Schane eds. 1969, 264-287.

Labov, W. 1975.   What is a linguistic fact?   Lisse: Peter de
Ridder Press.

_____. 1977.   Sociolinguistic patterns.   Philadelphia: University of
Pennsylvania Press.

Lakoff, G. 1970.   Irregularity in syntax.   New York: Holt, Rinehart and Winston.

_____ and S. Peters. 1969.   Phrasal conjunction and symmetric
predicates.   In: Reibel & Schane eds. 1969, 113-142.

Lakoff, R. 1971.   If's, and's, and but's about conjunction.   In: Fillmore & Langendoen eds. 1971, 115-149.

_____ 1972.   Another look at drift.   In: Stockwell & Macaulay eds. 1972, 172-198.

Langacker, R.W. 1969.   On pronominalization and the chain of command.   In: Reibel & Schane eds. 1969, 160-186.

_____ 1977.   Studies in Uto-Aztecan grammar.   Volume 1: An overview of Uto-Aztecan grammar.   Arlington: University of Texas and Summer Institute of Linguistics.

Langdon, M. 1977.   Syntactic change and SOV structure: The Yuman case.   In: Li ed. 1977, 255-290.

Larsen, T.W. & W.M. Norman. 1979.   Correlates of ergativity in Mayan grammar.   In: Plank ed. 1979, 347-370.

Lastra, Y. 1968.   Cochabamba Quechua syntax.   The Hague: Mouton.

Lawler, J. 1977.   A agrees with B in Achenese: A problem for Relational Grammar.   In: Cole & Sadock eds. 1977, 219-248.

Lê, T. 1976.   Syntax and semantics in Fillmorean theory (a study of Vietnamese case grammar).   Monash University doctoral thesis.

Lehmann, W.P. 1972.   Proto-Germanic syntax.   In: Towards a grammar of proto-Germanic, ed. by F. van Coetsem & H.L. Kufner, 239-268.   Tübingen: Niemeyer.

_____ 1973a.   Historical linguistics: An introduction (second edition).   New York: Holt, Rinehart and Winston.

_____ 1973b.   A structural principle of language and its implications.   Lg 49, 47-66.

_____ 1974.   Proto-Indo-European syntax.   Austin: University of Texas Press.

_____ 1975.   A discussion of compound and word order.   In: Li 1975, 149-162.

_____ 1976.   From topic to subject in Indo-European.   In: Li ed. 1976, 445-456.

_____ ed. 1978.   Syntactic typology (Studies in the phenomenology of language).   Sussex: The Harvester Press.

_____ 1978a.   The great underlying ground-plans.   In: Lehmann ed. 1978, 3-55.

_____ 1978b.   English: A characteristic SVO language.   In: Lehmann ed. 1978, 169-222.

_____ 1978c.   Conclusion: Toward an understanding of the profound unity underlying languages.   In: Lehmann ed. 1978, 395-432.

Levinsohn, S.H. 1976.   The Inga language.   The Hague: Mouton.

Li, C.N. ed. 1975.   Word order and word order change.   Austin: University of Texas Press.

_____ ed. 1976.   Subject and topic.   New York: Academic Press.

_____ ed. 1977.   Mechanisms of syntactic change.   Austin: University of Texas Press.

_____ and R. Lang. 1979.   The syntactic irrelevance of an ergative case in Enga and other Papuan languages.   In: Plank ed. 1979, 307-324.

Li, C.N. & S.A. Thompson. 1974a.   Historical change of word order: A case study in Chinese and its implications.   In: Anderson & Jones eds. 1974, 199-217.

_____ and S.A. Thompson. 1974b.   An explanation of word-order change SVO → SOV.   FL 12, 201-214.

_____ and S.A. Thompson. 1975.   The semantic function of word order: A case study in Mandarin.   In: Li ed. 1975, 163-195.

_____ and S.A. Thompson. 1976a.   Subject and topic: A new typology of language.   In: Li ed. 1976, 457-490.

_____ and S.A. Thompson. 1976b.   Strategies for signalling grammatical relations in Wappo.   CLS 12, 450-458.

_____ and S.A. Thompson. 1978.   An exploration of Mandarin Chinese. In: Lehmann ed. 1978, 223-266.

Li, P.J-K.   1973.   Rukai structure.   University of Hawaii doctoral dissertation.

Li, Y.C. & M. Yip. 1979.   The $b\check{a}$ construction and ergativity in Chinese.   In: Plank ed. 1979, 103-114.

Lichtenberk, F. 1978.   A sketch of Houailou grammar.   Working Papers in Linguistics (Hawaii) 10, 76-116.

Lieb, H. 1978.   Universals and linguistic explanation.   In: Greenberg et al. eds. 1978, vol. 1, 157-202.

Lightfoot, D.W. 1979.   Principles of diachronic syntax.   Cambridge: Cambridge University Press.

Lindenfeld, J. 1973.   Yaqui syntax.   Berkeley: University of California Press.

Loetscher, A. 1972.   Some problems concerning standard German relative clauses.   In: Peranteau et al. eds. 1972, 47-58.

Lowenstamm, J. 1977.   Relative clauses in Yiddish: A case for movement.   Linguistic Analysis 3, 197-216.

Lukas, J. 1967.   A study of the Kanuri language.   Oxford: University Press (facsimile reprint by Dawsons of Pall Mall, London).

Mallinson, G. 1977.   On recognising rule-bending and rule-breaking in English co-ordination.   Folia Linguistica 11, 109-144.

_____ 1978.   Crystallized syntactic structures in Romanian. Miorița 5, 8-28.

_____ 1979.   On the over-pruning of trees.   Glossa 13, 158-180.

_____ 1981a.   Constraints on gapping in modern standard Romanian. International Journal of Romanian Studies.

_____ 1981b.   On what an adequate syntax textbook should do. Review article of Baker 1978.   Lingua 53, 227-254.

_____ in prep.,a.   Complex structures in Romanian syntax.

_____ in prep.,b.   Concord and the Romanian neuter.

Malone, J.L. 1980.   Irish $n\acute{a}$, a disambiguator of perceptually equivocal surface structures.   Studies in Language 4, 25-63.

Mao, T-w. & T-y Chou. 1972.   A brief description of the Yao language.   In: Miao and Yao linguistic studies, ed. by H.C. Purnell, 1972, 239-255.

Maratsos, M. 1978.   New models in linguistics and language
      acquisition.   In: Halle, Bresnan & Miller eds. 1978, 247-263.

Martin, S.E. 1964.   Review of Greenberg ed. 1963.   Harvard Educa-
      tional Review 34, 353-5.

Masica, C. 1972.   Relative clauses in south Asia.   In: Peranteau
      et al. eds. 1972, 198-204.

_____ 1976.   Defining a linguistic area: South Asia.   Chicago:
      University of Chicago Press.

Matteson, E. 1965.   The Piro (Arawakan) language.   Berkeley:
      University of California Press.

Matthews, G.H. 1965.   Hidatsa syntax.   The Hague: Mouton.

McCarus, E.N. 1958.   A Kurdish grammar.   American Council of
      Learned Societies.

McCawley, J. 1972.   Japanese relative clauses.   In: Peranteau et
      al. eds. 1972, 205-214.

_____ 1974.   English as a VSO language.   In: Seuren ed. 1974, 75-
      95.

McKay, G.R. 1975.   Rembarnga, a language of central Arnhem Land.
      Australian National University doctoral dissertation.

_____ 1976.   Rembarnga.   In: Dixon ed. 1976, 494-505.

McLendon, S. 1978.   Ergativity, case, and transitivity in eastern
      Pomo.   IJAL 44, 1-9.

Meščaninov, I.I.   1936.   Novoe učenie o jazyke.   Leningrad:
      Nauka.

Milner, G.B. 1973.   It is aspect (not voice) which is marked in
      Samoan.   Oceanic Linguistics 12, 621-639.

Mirikitani, L.T. 1972.   Kapampangan syntax.   Oceanic Linguistics
      special publication no. 10.   Hawaii: University Press.

Mithun, M. & W.L. Chafe. 1979.   Recapturing the Mohawk language.
      In: Shopen ed. 1979, 3-34.

Miyake, S. in prep.   Questions of Japanese syntax.

_____ and G. Mallinson. in prep.   Extraposition and afterthoughts
      in Japanese.

Moravcsik, J.M.E. 1967.   Linguistic theory and the philosophy of
      language.   FL 3, 209-233.

Moravcsik, E.A. 1978a.   Universals of language contact.   In:
      Greenberg et al. eds. 1978, vol. 1, 93-122.

_____ 1978b.   On the case marking of objects.   In: Greenberg et al.
      eds. 1978, vol. 4, 249-290.

_____ 1978c.   Agreement.   In: Greenberg et al. eds. 1978, vol. 4,
      331-374.

_____ 1978d.   On the distribution of ergative and accusative
      patterns.   Lingua 45, 233-279.

Morgan, J.L. 1972.   Some aspects of relative clauses in English
      and Albanian.   In: Peranteau et al. eds. 1972, 63-72.

Müller, F.M. 1880.   Lectures on the science of language.   Vols. 1
      and 2.   6th edition.   London: Longmans, Green.

Munro, P. 1977.   From existential to copula: The history of Yuman
    BE.   In: Li ed. 1977, 445-490.

Nadkarni, M.V. 1975.   Bilingualism and syntactic change in
    Konkarni.   Lg 51, 672-683.

Nass, R.B. 1964.   Thai reference grammar.   Washington, D.C.:
    Foreign Service Institute.

Nedjalkov, V.P. 1979.   Degrees of ergativity in Chukchee.   In:
    Plank ed. 1979, 241-262.

Needham, J.F. 1894.   Outline grammar of the Tai (Khamti) language.
    Rangoon: Government Printer.

Neijt, A. 1979.   Gapping.   A contribution to sentence grammar.
    Dordrecht: Foris.

Newmeyer, F.J. 1980.   Linguistic theory in America.   The first
    quarter-century of transformational generative grammar.   New
    York: Academic Press.

Nida, E.A. 1948.   The identification of morphemes.   Lg 24, 414-441.

Oates, L.F. 1964.   A tentative description of the Gunwinggu
    language (of western Arnhem Land).   Sydney: Oceania Linguistic
    Monographs.

O'Grady, G.N., C.F. Voegelin & F.M. Voegelin. 1966.   Languages of
    the world: Indo-Pacific, fascicle 6.   Anthropological
    Linguistics 8.

Ohman, W.A. & H. Fulass. 1976.   Welamo.   In: Bender et al. 1976,
    155-163.

Osborne, C.R. 1974.   The Tiwi language.   Canberra: Australian
    Institute of Aboriginal Studies.

Palmer, F.R. 1961.   Relative clauses in Tigre.   Word 17, 23-33.

Panupong, V. 1970.   Inter-sentence relations in modern conversa-
    tional Thai.   Bangkok: The Siam Society.

Peranteau, P.M., J.N. Levi & G.C. Phares eds. 1972.   The Chicago
    which hunt.   Papers from the relative clause festival.
    Chicago: Chicago Linguistic Society.

Perlmutter, D.M. 1972.   Evidence for shadow pronouns in French
    relativization.   In: Peranteau et al. eds. 1972, 73-105.

_____ 1978.   Impersonal passives and the unaccusative hypothesis.
    BLS 4, 157-189.

_____ and P.M. Postal.   Toward a universal characterization of
    passivization.   BLS 3, 394-417.

Peterson, T.H. 1969.   A case for the declarative performative verb:
    Dependent and independent conjunction in Moore and English.
    CLS 5, 421-428.

Pickering, W.N. 1973a.   Command in Apurinã.   MS.

_____ 1973b.   Gapping and constituent order in Apurinã.   MS.

_____ 1977.   Relativização em Apurinã.   Série Lingüística 7,
    127-140.   Brazil: Summer Institute of Linguistics.

Pirejko, L.A. 1979.   On the genesis of the ergative construction
    in Indo-Iranian.   In: Plank ed. 1979, 481-488.

Plank, F. ed. 1979.   Ergativity.   London: Academic Press.

Platero, P.R. 1974.   The Navajo relative clause.   IJAL 40,
    202-246.

Poppe, N. 1970.   Mongolian language handbook.   Washington, D.C.:
    Center for Applied Linguistics.

Postal, P.M. 1974.   On raising: One rule of English grammar and
    its theoretical implications.   Cambridge, Mass.: M.I.T. Press.

_____1977.   Antipassive in French.   Proceedings of the seventh
    annual meeting of the North Eastern Linguistic Society,
    273-313.

Poutsma, H. 1928.   A grammar of late modern English, volumes 1-4.
    Groningen: Noordhoff.

Pullum, G.K. 1974.   A note on coordination reduction and word
    order in Hindi.   WPLU 14, 95-101.

_____1977.   Word order universals and grammatical relations.   In:
    Cole & Sadock eds. 1977, 249-277.

_____1980.   Syntactic relations and linguistic universals.   TPS
    1980, 1-39.

Pulte, W. 1971.   Gapping and word order in Quechua.   CLS 7,
    193-197.

Rabel, L. 1961.   Khasi, a language of Assam.   Baton Rouge:
    Louisiana State University Press.

Reed, I., O. Miyaoka, S. Jacobson, P. Afcan & M. Krauss. 1977.
    Yupik Eskimo grammar.   University of Alaska (no place of
    publication available).

Regamey, C. 1954.   A propos de la 'construction ergative' en
    indo-aryen moderne.   In: Sprachgeschichte und Wortbedeutung.
    Festschrift Albert Debrunner, 363-384.   Bern: Francke Verlag.

Reibel, D.A. & S.A. Schane eds. 1969.   Modern studies in English.
    Englewood Cliffs: Prentice-Hall.

Reiner, E. 1966.   A linguistic analysis of Akkadian.   The Hague:
    Mouton.

Ridley, W. 1875.   Kamilaroi and other Australian languages.
    Sydney: New South Wales Government Printer.

Rigsby, B. 1974.   Sahaptin grammar.   Manuscript prepared for
    languages volume of new Handbook of North American Indians, to
    be published by the Smithsonian Institution.

_____1975.   Nass-Gitksan: An analytic ergative language.   IJAL 41,
    346-354.

Robins, R.H. 1967.   A short history of linguistics.   London:
    Longman.

_____1971.   General linguistics: An introductory survey.   London:
    Longman.

_____1973.   The history of language classification.   In: Sebeok
    ed. 1973, 3-41.

Rodman, R. 1977.   Constraints on coordination in Thai, Korean and
    Mandarin Chinese.   Linguistica Antverpiensia xi, 143-154.

Rood, D. 1971.   Agent and object in Wichita.   Lingua 28, 100-107.

Rose, J.H. 1969.   Relational variation and limited productivity in
    some Indonesian and English verbal derivations.   University
    of Michigan doctoral dissertation.

Rosenbaum, H. 1977.   Zapotec gapping as counterevidence to some universal proposals.   LI 8, 379-395.

Rosenthal, J.M. 1972.   On the relative clauses of Classical Nahuatl.   In: Peranteau et al. eds. 1972, 246-255.

Ross, J.R. 1967.   Constraints on variables in syntax.   M.I.T. doctoral dissertation (reproduced by IULC).

_____ 1969a.   On the cyclic nature of English pronominalization. In: Reibel & Schane eds. 1969, 187-200.

_____ 1969b.   Adjectives as noun phrases.   In: Reibel & Schane eds. 1969, 352-360.

_____ 1970.   Gapping and the order of constituents.   In: Progress in linguistics, ed. by M. Bierwisch & K.E. Heidolph, 249-259. The Hague: Mouton.   Revised version of paper read at the Tenth International Congress of Linguists, Bucharest 1967.

Roth, W.E. 1897.   Ethnological studies among the north-west-central Queensland Aborigines.   Brisbane: Government Printer.

Ruhlen, M. 1975.   A guide to the languages of the world.   Stanford University, Language Universals Project.

Sanders, G. 1975.   On the explanation of constituent order univer- sals.   In: Li ed. 1975, 389-436.

_____ 1976.   A functional typology of elliptical coordinations. IULC.

_____ and J. Tai. 1969.   Immediate dominance and identity deletion in Mandarin Chinese.   Paper read at 1969 winter meeting of the LSA.

Sandfeld, Kr. 1930.   Linguistique balkanique.   Problèmes et résultats.   Paris: Klincksiek.

Sapir, E. 1921.   Language.   New York: Harcourt, Brace and World (copyright renewed 1949).

_____ 1922.   The Takelma language of southwestern Oregon.   In: Handbook of American Indian languages, ed. by F. Boas, part 2, 1-296.   Reprinted 1969, Anthropological Publications. Oosterhout.

_____ and H. Hoijer. 1967.   The phonology and morphology of the Navaho language.   Berkeley: University of California Press.

Schachter, P. 1973a.   On syntactic categories.   IULC.

_____ 1973b.   Focus and relativization.   Lg 49, 19-46.

_____ 1974.   Constraints on coordination.   IULC.

_____ 1976.   The subject in Philippine languages: Topic, actor, actor-topic, or none of the above.   In: Li ed. 1976, 491-518.

_____ 1977.   Reference-related and role-related properties of sub- jects.   In: Cole & Sadock eds. 1977, 279-306.

_____ and F. Otanes. 1972.   Tagalog reference grammar.   Berkeley: University of California Press.

Schwartz, A. 1971.   General aspects of relative clause formation. WPLU 6, 139-171.

_____ 1974.   The VP-constituent of SVO languages.   In: Heilmann ed. 1974, vol. II, 619-637.

Scott, G. 1978.   The Fore language of Papua New Guinea.
    Canberra: Pacific Linguistics.

Sebeok, T.A. 1973.   Current trends in linguistics.   Volume 11,
    Diachronic, areal and typological linguistics.   The Hague:
    Mouton.

Sedlak, P.A.S. 1975.   Direct/indirect object word order: A cross-
    linguistic analysis.   WPLU 18, 117-164.

Seiler, H. ed. 1978.   Language universals.   Tübingen: Gunter Narr
    Verlag.

Seuren, P.A.M. 1974.   Autonomous versus semantic syntax.   In:
    Seuren ed. 1974, 96-122.

_____ ed. 1974.   Semantic syntax.   London: Oxford University Press.

Sharpe, M.C. 1972.   Alawa phonology and grammar.   Canberra:
    Australian Institute of Aboriginal Studies.

Sheldon, A. 1977.   Speakers' intuitions about the complexity of
    relative clauses in Japanese and English.   CLS 12, 558-567.

Sherzer, J. 1976.   An areal-typological study of American Indian
    languages north of Mexico.   Amsterdam: North Holland.

Shibatani, M. ed. 1976.   Syntax and semantics, volume 6.   The
    grammar of causative constructions.   New York: Academic Press.

_____ 1977.   Grammatical relations and surface cases.   Lg 53,
    789-809.

Shopen, T. ed. 1979.   Languages and their status.   Cambridge,
    Mass.: Winthrop.

Siewierska, A. 1980.   The passive: A comparative study.   Monash
    University Master's thesis.

Silverstein, M. 1976.   Hierarchy of features and ergativity.   In:
    Dixon ed. 1976, 112-171.

Smith, C.S. 1964.   Determiners and relative clauses in a generative
    grammar of English.   Lg 40, 37-52.

Smith, I. 1978.   Realignment and other convergence phenomena.
    University of Melbourne Working Papers in Linguistics 4, 67-76.

_____ 1979.   Convergence in South Asia: A creole example.   Lingua
    48, 193-222.

Smith, N.V. 1969.   Relations between languages: Typological and
    areal classifications.   In: Encyclopaedia of linguistics, in-
    formation and control, ed. by A.R. Meetham, 486-489.

_____ 1980.   Review of Lehmann ed. 1978.   JL 16, 150-164.

_____ and D. Wilson. 1979.   Modern linguistics.   The result of
    Chomsky's revolution.   London: Penguin.

Sohn, H. & B.W. Bender. 1973.   A Ulithian grammar.   Canberra:
    Pacific Linguistics.

Sommer, B.A. 1972.   Kunjen syntax.   Canberra: Australian Institute
    of Aboriginal Studies.

Starosta, S. 1978.   The one per sent solution.   In: Abraham ed.
    1978, 459-576.

Steele, S. 1975.   On some factors that affect and effect word
    order.   In: Li ed. 1975, 197-268.

Steele, S. 1977.   Clisis and diachrony.   In: Li ed. 1977, 539-579.

_____ 1978.   Word order variation: A typological study.   In: Greenberg et al. eds. 1978, vol. 4, 585-624.

Steever, S.B., C.A. Walker & S.S. Mufwene eds. 1976.   Papers from the parasession on diachronic syntax.   Chicago: Chicago Linguistic Society.

Stockwell, R.P. 1977.   Motivations for exbraciation in Old English. In: Li ed. 1977, 291-314.

_____ and R.K.S. Macaulay eds. 1972.   Linguistic change and generative theory.   Bloomington: Indiana University Press.

Sugita, H. 1973.   Semitransitive verbs and object incorporation in Micronesian languages.   Oceanic Linguistics 12, 393-406.

Tagashira, Y. 1972.   Relative clauses in Korean.   In: Peranteau et al. eds. 1972, 215-229.

Tai, J. 1969.   Coordinate reduction.   IULC.

_____ 1973.   Chinese as a SOV language.   CLS 9, 659-671.

Tchekhoff, C. 1979.   La construction ergative en Avar et en Tongan. Paris: Klincksiek.

Thompson, S.A. 1971.   The deep structure of relative clauses.   In: Fillmore & Langendoen eds. 1971, 79-94.

Thurman, R. 1978.   Clause chains in Chuave.   U.C.L.A. Master's thesis.

Topping, D.M. 1973.   Chamorro reference grammar.   Honolulu: University Press of Hawaii.

Trubetzkoy, N.S. 1939.   Grundzüge der Phonologie.   Travaux du Cercle Linguistique de Prague VII.

Tryon, D.T. 1968.   Iai grammar.   Canberra: Pacific Linguistics.

_____ 1971a.   Dehu grammar.   Canberra: Pacific Linguistics.

_____ 1971b.   Nengone grammar.   Canberra: Pacific Linguistics.

Tsunoda, T. 1978.   The Djaru language of Kimberley, Western Australia.   Monash University doctoral thesis.

_____ 1980.   A semantic condition and case marking in ergativity. MS, Nagoya University.

Tucker, A.N. 1940.   The eastern Sudanic languages.   London: International African Institute.

_____ and M.A. Bryan. 1966.   Linguistic analyses: The non-Bantu languages of north-eastern Africa.   Handbook of African Language.   London: Oxford University Press.

Ultan, R. 1969.   Some general characteristics of interrogative systems.   WPLU 1.

_____ 1978.   Some general characteristics of interrogative systems. In: Greenberg et al. eds. 1978, vol. 4, 211-248.

Underhill, R. 1972.   Turkish participles.   LI 3, 87-99.

Vaxtin, N.B. 1979.   Nominal and verbal ergativity in asiatic Eskimo: Splits in the person and mood paradigms.   In: Plank ed. 1979, 279-289.

Vennemann, T. 1973.   Explanation in syntax.   In: Syntax and semantics, vol. 2, ed. by J.P. Kimball, 1-50.   New York: Seminar Press.

Vennemann, T. 1974a.   Topics, subjects and word order: From SXV to
    SVX via TVX.   In: Anderson & Jones eds. 1974, 339-376.

_____ 1974b.   Theoretical word order studies: Results and problems.
    Papiere zur Linguistik 7, 5-25.

_____ 1974c.   Analogy in generative grammar: The origin of word
    order.   In: Heilmann ed. 1974, vol. II, 79-83.

_____ 1975.   An explanation of drift.   In: Li ed. 1975, 269-305.

Voeltz, E. 1971.   Surface constraints and agreement resolution:
    Some evidence from Xhosa.   Studies in African Linguistics 2,
    37-60.

Vogt, H. 1971.   Grammaire de la langue georgienne.   Oslo:
    Universitetsforlaget.

Walsh, M.J. 1976.   The Murinypata language of north-west Australia.
    Australian National University doctoral thesis.

Walusimbi, L. 1976.   Relativization and focusing in Luganda and
    Bantu.   U.C.L.A. doctoral dissertation.

Watters, J. 1980.   Review of Dik 1978.   Lingua 50, 155-71.

Wells, M.A. 1979.   Siroi grammar.   Canberra: Pacific Linguistics.

Westermann, D. & M.A. Bryan. 1952.   Languages of West Africa.
    Handbook of African languages, part 2.   London: Oxford
    University Press.

Whitman, R.L. & K.L. Jackson. 1972.   The unpredictability of con-
    trastive analysis.   Language Learning 22, 29-42.

Wierzbicka, A. 1980.   The case for surface case.   Ann Arbor:
    Karoma.

_____ 1981.   Case marking and 'human nature'.   Australian Journal
    of Linguistics 1, 43-80.

Wolfart, H.C. 1973.   Plains Cree: A grammatical study.   Trans-
    actions of the American Philosophical Society 63,5.

Woodbury, A.C. 1977.   Greenlandic Eskimo, ergativity, and relatio-
    nal grammar.   In: Cole & Sadock eds. 1977, 307-336.

Wurm, S. 1976.   Accusative marking in Duungidjawu.   In: Dixon ed.
    1976, 106-111.

_____ ed. 1979.   Australian linguistic studies.   Canberra: Pacific
    Linguistics.

Yang, I-S. 1972.   Korean syntax: Case markers, delimiters, comple-
    mentation and relativization.   Seoul: Paek Hap Sa.

Yates, A. 1975.   Catalan.   London: Hodder and Stoughton.

Zimmermann, R. 1972.   Themenfrontierung, Wortstellung und Intona-
    tion im Deutschen und Englischen.   Neueren Sprachen 71,
    15-28.

Ziv, Y. & P. Cole. 1974.   Relative extraposition and the scope of
    definite descriptions in Hebrew and English.   CLS 10, 772-786.

Zwicky, A.M. 1977.   Hierarchies of person.   CLS 13, 714-733.

INDEX OF LANGUAGES

INDEX OF NAMES

INDEX OF SUBJECTS